uncovered editions

THE WORLD WAR I COLLECTION

GALLIPOLI AND THE EARLY BATTLES, 1914–15

∞◦◦∞

THE DARDANELLES COMMISSION, 1914–16

BRITISH BATTLES OF WORLD WAR I, 1914–15

London: The Stationery Office

Applications for reproduction should be made in writing to
The Stationery Office Limited, St Crispins, Duke Street, Norwich NR3 1PD.

ISBN 0 11 702466 X

The Dardanelles Commission, 1914–16 was first published as Cd 8490 (1917) and Cmd 371 (1918).
© Crown copyright
Also available as two separate books, ISBN 0117024236 and 0117024554,
© The Stationery Office 2000

British Battles of World War I was first published by HMSO as *Naval and Military Despatches,* 1914, 1915, 1916.
© Crown copyright
Also available separately, ISBN 0117024473, © The Stationery Office 2000

A CIP catalogue record for this book is available from the British Library.

Cover photograph of troops landing at Anzac Cove, Gallipoli, 1915 © Corbis.
All maps, with the exception of the map on p. 278, were produced by Sandra Lockwood of Artworks Design, Norwich.

Typeset by J&L Composition Ltd, Filey, North Yorkshire.
Printed in the United Kingdom by The Stationery Office, London.
TJ4700 C30 08/01 652946 19585

CONTENTS

About the series

Uncovered editions are historic official papers which have not previously been available in a popular form. The series has been created directly from the archive of The Stationery Office in London, and the books have been chosen for the quality of their story-telling. Some subjects are familiar, but others are less well known. Each is a moment in history.

About the series editor, Tim Coates

Tim Coates studied at University College, Oxford and at the University of Stirling. After working in the theatre for a number of years, he took up bookselling and became managing director, firstly of Sherratt and Hughes bookshops, and then of Waterstone's. He is known for his support for foreign literature, particularly from the Czech Republic. The idea for *uncovered editions* came while searching through the bookshelves of his late father-in-law, Air Commodore Patrick Cave OBE. He is married to Bridget Cave, has two sons, and lives in London.

Tim Coates welcomes views and ideas on the *uncovered editions* series. He can be e-mailed at tim.coates@theso.co.uk

THE DARDANELLES
COMMISSION, 1914–16

CONTENTS

MAPS

At the outbreak of World War I in 1914, political tensions had divided Europe into two camps, with Germany and Austria ranged against Russia and France. When Germany invaded Belgium in August of the same year, Britain was brought into the war on the side of France. In November 1914, Turkey formed an alliance with Germany.

The Dardanelles is a narrow strait of water which forms the main shipping route to the ports of southern Russia, and consequently its control was thought to be of vital military and economic significance. The Gallipoli Peninsula lies on the European side of this waterway, and was part of Turkey at this time.

In 1915, in response to a request from the tsar of Russia to open a war front in the eastern Mediterranean, the British and their allies decided to mount an attack on the Gallipoli Peninsula in western Turkey, even though their forces were already heavily engaged in France. At first it was thought that the Allies could capture the peninsula merely by naval bombardment, but it soon became apparent that ground forces would also have to be deployed. Having openly committed themselves to taking the peninsula, the British military commanders did not feel they could accept the loss of face which would have resulted had they simply withdrawn. But in the months of delay leading up to the main attack, the enemy had had ample time to fortify and prepare their defences.

Thousands of men were to perish at Gallipoli within a few months of the initial landings. As a result of this disastrous military campaign, ten commissioners were appointed by the British government in 1916 "for the purpose of inquiring into the origin, inception, and conduct of operations of war in the Dardanelles and Gallipoli, including the supply of drafts, reinforcements, ammunition and equipment to the troops and Fleet, the provision for the sick and wounded, and the responsibility of those departments of government whose duty it has been to minister to the wants of the forces employed in that theatre of war". The story which unfolds in the following pages is the text of the first and final reports of that commission.

Name	Functions in the autumn of 1914 and the spring of 1915
Sir George Arthur, Bart.	Private Secretary to Lord Kitchener
The Rt. Hon. H. Asquith, PC	Prime Minister
Brigadier-General Sir George Aston, KCB	Employed at the Admiralty up to the end of August, 1914
Vice-Admiral Sir Reginald Bacon, KCB, DSO	Now in command of the Dover Patrol
The Rt. Hon. A.J. Balfour, PC	Generally summoned to the War Council
Commodore de Bartolomé, CB	Naval Secretary to the First Lord of the Admiralty
Sir Reginald Brade, KCB	Permanent Under-Secretary at the War Office
Major-General Charles Callwell, CB	Director of Military Operations
Vice-Admiral Sir Sackville Carden, KCMG	In command of the Mediterranean Fleet up to March 17th
The Rt. Hon. W. S. Churchill	First Lord of the Admiralty
H. J. Creedy, Esq., CB	Private Secretary to Lord Kitchener
The Marquis of Crewe, KG, PC	Secretary of State for India
Admiral of the Fleet Lord Fisher of Kilverstone, GCB, OM, GCVO	First Sea Lord of the Admiralty
Field-Marshal Viscount French, OM, KCMG	Commanding the Expeditionary Force in France
Sir Graham Greene, KCB	Secretary to the Admiralty
Viscount Grey of Fallodon, KG	Secretary of State for Foreign Affairs
Viscount Haldane of Cloan, KT	Lord Chancellor
Captain Hall, RN	Director of the Intelligence Division of the Admiralty
Admiral Sir F. Hamilton, KCB, CVO	Second Sea Lord of the Admiralty
General Sir Ian Hamilton, KCB, DSO	In command at the Dardanelles from March 13th (date of leaving London)
Lieut.-Col. Sir Maurice Hankey, KCB	Secretary to the War Council
Major-General H. Hickman	Commanding the Plymouth Garrison
Commander Hubbard	Retired Royal Naval Reserve, formerly in the Turkish Service
Admiral Sir Henry Jackson, KCB, KCVO, FRS	Admiralty Staff
Rear-Admiral Thomas Jackson, CB, MVO	Director of the Operations Division of the Admiralty War Staff
Commodore Cecil Lambert	Fourth Sea Lord of the Admiralty
The Rt. Hon. D. Lloyd George, PC	Chancellor of the Exchequer
The Rt. Hon. R. McKenna, PC	Secretary of State for the Home Department

Name	Functions in the autumn of 1914 and the spring of 1915
Vice-Admiral Sir Henry Oliver, KCB, MVO	Chief of the War Staff
Vice-Admiral Sir John de Robeck, KCB	In command of the Mediterranean Fleet from March 17th
Rear-Admiral Morgan Singer, CB	Director of Naval Ordnance at the Admiralty
Rear-Admiral F. Tudor, CB	Third Sea Lord of the Admiralty
Major-General Sir Stanley Von Donop, KCB	Master-General of the Ordnance
Admiral of the Fleet Sir Arthur Wilson, GCB, OM, VC, GCVO	Member of the War Staff Group at the Admiralty
Lieut.-General Sir James Wolfe Murray, K.C.B.	Chief of the Imperial General Staff

Eastern Mediterranean, 1915

PART I

⚜

LORD KITCHENER AND WINSTON CHURCHILL

(DEALING WITH THE ORIGIN AND INCEPTION OF THE ATTACK ON THE DARDANELLES, FROM AUGUST 4TH 1914 TO MARCH 23RD 1915)

PRELIMINARY OBSERVATIONS BY THE COMMITTEE

In the first place, it has to be remembered that the events which we shall have to narrate happened in the last five months of 1914 or the first three months of 1915; that at that time a very heavy strain of work was thrown on all the Departments of the Government which were concerned; that in respect to many points of considerable importance the various witnesses called have had, in the absence of complete written records, to speak from memory of what actually occurred, and that the constant strain of work resulting from subsequent events of equal, or perhaps even of greater, importance may possibly, in view of the period which has elapsed, have, to some extent, obscured their recollection of all the circumstances. It can, therefore, be no matter for surprise that the evidence given as to the views expressed at the time by some of the leading officials should be, in certain cases, somewhat conflicting.

We have, of course, attached special importance to opinions which were unquestionably expressed during the period when the desirability or otherwise of making an attack on the Dardanelles was under consideration. Without casting any sort of imputation on the good faith of the witnesses themselves, it is conceivable that, in giving to the Commission an account of the past they may have been to some extent unconsciously influenced by their knowledge of subsequent events.

In the second place, we have to remark that the premature and deeply regretted death of Lord Kitchener naturally renders it impossible for us to state, with the same confidence as that which obtains in the case of living witnesses, whether we have faithfully represented the opinions he entertained and the aims which he had in view at different periods of the proceedings. The difficulty is enhanced owing to the strong opinion which

Lord Kitchener entertained as to the absolute necessity of maintaining the strictest secrecy in respect to all matters connected with military operations. Sir Maurice Hankey, indeed, stated that some difficulties at times arose owing to Lord Kitchener's unwillingness to impart full information even to the members of the War Council. We have, however, done all that is possible to ascertain both his views and intentions by closely examining such contemporaneous records as exist and by enquiry from those who were associated with him during his life-time. It is, in this connection, singularly unfortunate that that gallant officer, Colonel Fitzgerald, who was Lord Kitchener's personal military secretary, and who was probably better acquainted with his opinions than any other individual, shared the fate of his distinguished chief.

We have not thought that we should be justified, in deference to the consideration which is rightly shown to the memory of the illustrious dead, in abstaining from a complete revelation of the action which Lord Kitchener took during the various phases of the events under consideration, nor have we hesitated to express our views on that action. It is necessary to do justice to the living as well as to the dead.

Moreover, it must be steadfastly borne in mind that, at the time when the attack on the Dardanelles was under consideration, Lord Kitchener occupied a position such as has probably never been held by any previous Secretary of State for War. The circumstances of the case cannot be understood unless the nature of his position is fully realised. In this connection, we may quote the following passage from Mr Winston Churchill:

> Lord Kitchener's personal qualities and position played at this time a very great part in the decision of events. His prestige and authority were immense. He was the sole mouthpiece of War Office opinion in the War Council. Everyone had the greatest admiration for his character, and everyone felt fortified, amid the terrible and incalculable events of the opening months of the war, by his commanding presence. When he gave a decision it was invariably accepted as final. He was never, to my belief, overruled by the War Council or the Cabinet in any military matter, great or small. No single unit was ever sent or withheld contrary, not merely to his agreement, but to his advice. Scarcely anyone ever ventured to argue with him in Council. Respect for the man, sympathy for him in his immense labours, confidence in his professional judgment, and the belief that he had plans deeper and wider than any we could see, silenced misgivings and disputes, whether in the Council or at the War Office. All-powerful, imperturbable, reserved, he dominated absolutely our counsels at this time. If the course of my observations and the documents it is my duty to lay before you appear to constitute any reflection upon his military policy, I wish here to testify to the overwhelming weight of the burdens laid upon him, to his extraordinary courage and patience in all the difficulties and perplexities through which we were passing and to his unvarying kindness to me.

Although, however, we have thought that we should be failing in our duty if we did not deal fully with the part Lord Kitchener played in these transactions, we would ask those who may read this report to remember, in justice to his memory, in the first place, that it has not been possible to check his recorded opinions by the light of subsequent explanation, and, secondly, that if, in the eyes of any critics, he may, under circumstances of very great difficulty, be held to have committed some errors of judgment, the fact cannot in any way obscure the very distinguished services which he rendered to his country in other directions.

HIGHER ORGANISATION PRIOR TO THE OUTBREAK OF WAR

Before proceeding to deal with the facts connected with the origin and inception of the Dardanelles Expedition, we think it will be desirable to explain, in the first place, the higher organisation for the conduct of war which prevailed at the time of its outbreak, and, secondly, the changes which were subsequently made in that organisation. Further, we trust that we are not interpreting erroneously the wishes either of His Majesty's Government or of the Legislature when we say that, if our inquiry is to be of any real practical use for future guidance, we should not confine ourselves to a bald statement of facts, or even to the mere assignment of a proper share of responsibility to individuals or departments in connection with past events, but that we should go somewhat further and indicate briefly and in general terms the conclusions at which we have arrived in respect to the merits and demerits of the original, as also of the revised organisations which have been instrumental in conducting the war. It would, however, be exceeding the scope of our functions if we were to discuss in detail the measures which should be taken to remedy any administrative defects which the light of recent experience has revealed.

Before the war, and after its outbreak until nearly the end of November, 1914, the higher direction of military and naval operations was vested in the Cabinet, who were assisted by the Committee of Imperial Defence. This Committee was tentatively initiated in 1901 and reconstructed in 1904. The main functions of the Secretariat, as set forth in a Treasury Minute dated May 4th of that year, were "to collect and co-ordinate for the use of the Committee information bearing on the wide problem of Imperial Defence," and "to make possible a continuity of method in the treatment of the questions which may from time to time come before the Committee." It was laid down that the Committee was to be "merely a consultative or advisory body." This view was frequently confirmed in statements made by responsible Ministers in Parliament. It is quite correct in this sense that the Committee exercised no executive functions, that it was not a body which supervised the proceedings of the War Office or the Admiralty, that it was not a Court of Appeal against the decisions of either of those two Departments, and that it did not interfere in any War Office or Admiralty details. Nevertheless, the view that the Committee was purely advisory requires some qualification.

In practice, it did more than advise. It decided. On being asked whether the Committee "decided on certain courses," the Secretary, Sir Maurice Hankey, replied in the affirmative, and, on being further asked whether "action was taken on their decisions," he replied: "Yes, what would happen would be that after the meeting the conclusion would be notified by me officially to the Department responsible for taking action."

It might, at first sight, perhaps be thought that, under such circumstances, the Committee might possibly encroach on the constitutional prerogatives of the Cabinet. Fears that this would happen have, indeed, from time to time been expressed. In dealing with this subject, however, the composition of the Committee has to be borne in mind. It varied slightly as occasion might demand, but the Prime Minister was always the President, and he usually invited the attendance of the Chancellor of the Exchequer, the Secretaries of State for War, Foreign Affairs and India, and also the First Lord of the Admiralty.

Mr Arthur Balfour, although not at the time of which we are now treating a member of the Cabinet, was also usually invited to attend the meetings both of the Committee of Imperial Defence and of the War Council which subsequently took its place. On the one hand, when any question came before the Cabinet, several of its most important members were, it is true, already pledged to views expressed in their capacities of Members of the Committee of Imperial Defence. On the other hand, the united Cabinet had the great advantage of learning the opinions which their colleagues had formed on any particular subject after it had been discussed in the presence of qualified experts. The Committee of Imperial Defence was, in fact, for all practical purposes, a Committee of the Cabinet with some experts added. It does not appear that the creation of such a body in any way fails to harmonise with sound constitutional practice.

Before leaving this branch of the subject, it may be remarked that, in explaining the functions of the Committee of Imperial Defence, Sir Maurice Hankey said that they had been "laid down in time of peace, and with a view to peace requirements." The natural result ensued. Very shortly after the outbreak of war, the Committee, although never formally abolished, fell into abeyance. Another institution was substituted in its place. It appears to us that a body such as the Committee of Imperial Defence, whose sole duty it is to prepare for war, should be organised to meet the requirements not of peace, but of war. We should add that the reason which dictated the transformation of the Committee of Imperial Defence was based, not so much on any defect inherent in that institution itself, but rather on the proved necessity of curtailing the number of members of the Cabinet who actually participated in the conduct of the war.

HIGHER ORGANISATION AFTER THE OUTBREAK OF WAR

THE WAR COUNCIL

From the commencement of the war until November 25th, 1914—that is to say, for a period of nearly four months—no change was made in the machinery for the superior conduct of naval and military operations. That machinery consisted, as we have already mentioned, of the Cabinet, assisted by the Committee of Imperial Defence, with the War Office and the Admiralty acting as its executive agents. The Cabinet at that time consisted of twenty-two members. It must have been obvious from the first that it was far too numerous to control effectively the conduct of the war, more especially by reason of the fact that many of the Ministers presided over Departments which, in some cases, were very slightly and, in others, were in no degree concerned with warlike operations.

It is to be regretted that this rudimentary fact was not recognised immediately after the outbreak of war. Thus, for four months, during which time events of the utmost importance were occurring, the machinery employed for designing and controlling the higher operations of the war was both clumsy and inefficient. Eventually some improvement was effected. The War Council took the place of the Committee of Imperial Defence.

The composition and functions of the War Council did not materially differ from those of the Committee of Imperial Defence. A change of some importance was, however, made in the procedure. It had been the practice to pass round the notes of the proceedings at the meetings of the Committee of Imperial Defence to all the members who had been present, and who were thus able to correct any inaccuracies that might occur in the representation of their views. Owing to the great press of business, this practice was abandoned by the War Council. Longhand notes were, indeed, kept by the Secretary, but these, of course, cannot carry the same authority as corrected minutes.

A very full and, we believe, accurate account of what occurred in connection with the Dardanelles Expedition at the various meetings of the Council was, however, furnished to us by the Secretary, and the full text of the notes, which record the proceedings in many matters wholly unconnected with the Dardanelles Expedition, was placed at the disposal of our Chairman, who was able to assure us of the general adequacy and correctness of the summary communicated to us by Sir Maurice Hankey.

The main change which was effected was, however, in connection with the powers of the Council as compared to those of the Committee of Imperial Defence. Whilst the latter body was in existence, the responsibility for all important decisions remained, theoretically in all, and practically in most cases, with the united Cabinet. The War Council remained, like the Committee of Imperial Defence, a Committee of the Cabinet with some experts added. Theoretically, the powers of the united Cabinet remained the same as before. Practically, they underwent a radical change.

It was the Council, and not the united Cabinet, which finally decided the most important matters, and gave effect to its decisions without necessarily waiting for any expression of assent or dissent from the Cabinet. The Cabinet appear to have been generally informed of any important decisions which may have been taken by the Council, but not until after the necessary executive steps had been taken to give whole or partial effect to those decisions. This is what actually happened in the case both of the naval and military operations undertaken at the Dardanelles.

Further, we have been given to understand that some members of the Cabinet did not wish to be informed of what was going on. Mr Winston Churchill, in the course of his examination, said: "I have often heard the Cabinet say: 'We do not wish to be told about this—this is a secret matter, and the fewer who know about it the better.'"

It would be an exaggeration to say that, in consequence of this method of conducting business, those members of the Cabinet who did not attend the meetings of the War Council were relieved of all responsibility in connection with the conduct of the war. But their responsibility was slight. It was limited to the fact that they, very rightly in our opinion, were content to delegate the full powers of the united Cabinet to their colleagues who were members of the War Council.

For all practical purposes it may be held that, during the period under review, the powers and prerogatives of the united Cabinet were, in so far as the conduct of the war was concerned, held almost entirely in abeyance. The correctness of this view is confirmed by the testimony of Mr McKenna, who, although a member of the Cabinet, did not, during the early stages of the war, attend the meetings of the War Council. Mr McKenna was asked the following question by the Chairman:

Should I be correct in stating broadly that the responsibility of the united Cabinet amounted to this, that they had delegated their powers more or less to the War Council?

His reply was:

If I may say so, I think you have expressed it absolutely. There was a general acceptance by the Cabinet of the constitution and action of the War Council. But if the question is put to me that the Cabinet had in any real sense any responsibility for the individual decisions of the War Council, whether communicated to them or not, I can only say that, for my own part, it would be asking the Cabinet to accept the responsibility without any means of judging.

Further, a distinction has to be made between the real responsibility which devolved on the several Cabinet Ministers who were members of the War Council. The Chancellor of the Exchequer (Mr Lloyd George), the Secretary of State for Foreign Affairs (Sir Edward, now Viscount Grey of Fallodon) and the Secretary of State for India (the Marquis of Crewe) exercised undoubted and very legitimate influence, and occasionally stated their opinions, but the main responsibility rested on three members of the Council—namely, the Prime Minister (Mr Asquith), the Secretary of State for War (Lord Kitchener) and the First Lord of the Admiralty (Mr Winston Churchill).

The latter, in the course of his evidence, said:

In the early stages the war was carried on by the Prime Minister, and Lord Kitchener and me, I think, in the next place, but I was on a rather different plane. I had not the same weight or authority as those two Ministers, nor the same power, and if they said, this is to be done or not to be done, that settled it.

We believe this description of the actual working of the machine to be substantially correct, save that Mr Winston Churchill probably assigned to himself a more unobtrusive part than that which he actually played.

It is obvious that the main questions which came under the consideration of the War Council in connection with the Dardanelles operations were of a highly technical nature on which the opinions only of those who were possessed of naval or military knowledge or experience would be of any real value. It is, therefore, essential to ascertain, with as great a degree of accuracy as possible, what was the precise position assigned to the expert members of the Council. We have devoted much attention to this subject. We think that the best plan which can be adopted in order to explain the situation will be to quote passages from the evidence both of the experts themselves and of the Ministers who were members of the Council.

It is clear that, in dealing with this question, a distinction has to be drawn between the War Office and the Admiralty.

The Secretary of State for War (Lord Kitchener) was himself a distinguished expert. The only other officer possessing military experience who regularly attended the meetings of the Council was Lieutenant-General Sir James Wolfe

Murray, who, on October 25th, 1914, succeeded the late Sir Charles Douglas as Chief of the Imperial General Staff. Sir James Murray told us that "Lord Kitchener acted very much as his own Chief of the Staff." When asked whether he "considered himself the Staff Officer of Lord Kitchener and that he was not called upon to express any independent opinion unless he was especially asked to do so," he replied, "Certainly." He added that he was "never asked" to express any opinion.

The case of the Admiralty was different. The First Lord (Mr Winston Churchill) was not himself an expert. Expert naval advice was represented by Lord Fisher, the First Sea Lord, and by Sir Arthur Wilson, who, although he did not occupy any official position at the Admiralty, was, from the commencement of the war, habitually consulted both by the First Lord and the First Sea Lord. On one important occasion (January 28th) Sir Henry Oliver was also present.

The view taken by Lord Fisher of his own position at the War Council may be gathered from the following extract from his evidence:

Q.　I should like you to explain why you thought that at the War Council there were only two alternatives before you, one to yield your opinion absolutely and the other to resign. You were a consultative body. Is it possible to carry on business with a consultative body on such a basis as that?

A.　I can make it clear to you. The War Council only consisted of the Cabinet Ministers. We were not members of the War Council. I was not a member of the War Council, nor was Sir Arthur Wilson, nor Sir James Wolfe Murray. It is a mistake to call us members of the War Council—it was no such thing. We were the experts there who were to open our mouths when told to.

Q.　Nothing else?

A.　Nothing else.

Q.　And you did not consider yourselves members of the War Council?

A.　Absolutely not. The members of the Cabinet were members of the Council, and the others were simply there ready to answer questions if asked.

Q.　And they never were asked?

A.　They were sometimes, because I was asked how many battleships would be lost, and I said twelve.

Q.　But they were never asked anything about the Dardanelles?

A.　No.

The following extract from Sir Arthur Wilson's evidence shows that the view which he took of his position was generally identical with that entertained by Lord Fisher.

Q.　I want to understand what exactly your position, and that of the other members of the Council, was, because when the First Lord expounded the naval view if you did not agree would it not have been your duty to say so?

A.　Probably not, unless I was asked. I was there to help the First Lord.

Q.   And you were never asked?

A.   No.

Q.   And you were there to help the First Lord?

A.   Yes.

Q.   But not necessarily to agree with him?

A.   Not to express agreement if I did not agree, but not to oppose him when
it was not a matter which specially concerned me.

It is now necessary to explain the light in which the Ministerial
Members of the Council regarded the position occupied by the experts.
Mr Winston Churchill stated:

> Whenever I went to the War Council I always insisted on being accompanied by the
> First Sea Lord and Sir Arthur Wilson, and when, at the War Council, I spoke in the name
> of the Admiralty, I was not expressing simply my own views, but I was expressing to the
> best of my ability the opinions we had agreed upon at our daily group meetings; and I
> was expressing these opinions in the presence of two naval colleagues and friends who
> had the right, the knowledge, and the power at any moment to correct me or dissent
> from what I said, and who were fully cognisant of their rights.

Viscount Grey of Fallodon said that the War Council "went entirely in
these naval and military matters by the opinions expressed by the two
Ministers." Further, he was asked the following question by Sir William
Pickford:

> I think we were told that of course the First Lord of the Admiralty would put
> the view of the Admiralty, and if the First Sea Lord were present and said
> nothing he would be taken to assent to the plan?

To this he replied:

> I think the natural assumption would be that either he actively assented, or that he
> did not think it of sufficient importance to record a separate opinion, or did not
> desire to record a separate opinion, whatever the reason might be.

Mr Arthur Balfour's views may be gathered from the following extracts
from his evidence:

Q.   We want to arrive particularly at what was your view and the views of
others similarly placed to yourself on the position of the expert advisers
towards the War Council?

A.   I think they were there to offer technical professional advice upon
questions on which they could speak with authority, but on which a
layman could not speak with authority.

Q.   Do you think they were under any obligation to initiate opinions or
merely to wait until they were asked?

A.   That would depend on the view the Chairman took of their duties. My
own view is that if professional advisers are present at such a Council as
that, it is the business of the Chairman, and perhaps of other members, to

see that nothing is passed over their heads on which they have an opinion until the opinion has been extracted.

Q.   With regard to any decision taken when the expert advisers did not express dissent, would you from that infer that they assented?

A.   I should certainly assume that.

Q.   And if they dissented they must express dissent at the meeting?

A.   I should certainly have assumed that.

Q.   Will you refer to Lord Fisher's evidence?

A.   Having read that, I do not assent to it as a broad question of principle. I think it is true that a technical adviser brought into a meeting of Cabinet Ministers might not care to start or initiate a discussion, but if the question before the Committee was, do the Admiralty or do the War Office concur with such and such a view, with such and such a question, I certainly do not think they ought to be silent if they do not agree.

Q.   Supposing the Chief of a Department, taking particularly the Admiralty, presents certain views and gives the Council generally to understand that his expert advisers are behind him and agree to those views, do you think it would be the duty of the expert advisers present to say, 'That does not represent our views'?

A.   I think the expert advisers—I do not refer particularly to Lord Fisher or Sir Arthur Wilson, but generally—if they feel their expert advice is not before the Council, that the Council are not aware of what their views are, ought to take means for letting their views be known. It need not necessarily be an interruption of the proceedings, thrusting themselves in, as it were, in the discussion, though that would be the natural method of doing it.

Q.   You look to them to state their opinions in the event of any expert advice being given in which they do not agree. Would you make a distinction between expert advice and matters of policy for the Cabinet?

A.   Certainly.

Q.   We have had evidence given on this point, and Sir Arthur Wilson distinctly says he did not think he was called upon to give any opinion whatever, unless he was asked to do so, and there is a very similar statement by Lord Fisher, who, in fact, goes very far in that direction. I think I am not incorrectly stating both their views when I say they stated that they were there to be what they called loyal to their Chief, and in fact they were not to contradict him, and Lord Fisher goes so far as to say, when I pointed out to him that it was very difficult to carry on any consultation on that basis, that the only alternative left for him was to hold his tongue, though he dissented, or to resign. Does that suggest itself to you?

A.   I dissent personally from that method of conducting business. I do not believe it is any use having in experts unless you try and get at their inner thoughts on the technical questions before the Council.

Q.   The military experts stood on rather a different footing, because during the period we are discussing Lord Kitchener was himself a military expert. We have had Sir James Wolfe Murray here, and he said that both in respect to his position at the War Office and in respect to his position on the Council he considered himself in the light of Lord Kitchener's Staff Officer and nothing else?

A.   That may be so, and I think you are right in saying that Lord Kitchener's position was exceptional: though even there personally I think it is very little use having an expert present except to remind his Chief of particular facts and give him particular statistics, unless you are to find out what his opinion is.

Q.   But, of course, there was a great difference in Lord Kitchener's position and Mr Churchill's position, because Lord Kitchener was himself an expert and a distinguished soldier, whereas Mr Churchill had to rely on others. You think, then, it was the duty of the naval experts there to dissent if anything was said which did not represent their views?

A.   Yes, with this qualification. I think their task ought to be facilitated by the Cabinet Ministers present, the Heads of their Departments or the Cabinet Minister who was in the chair.

Q.   By asking them?

A.   By asking them.

Viscount Haldane of Cloan, who was at the time Lord Chancellor, gave the following evidence:

Q.   Did you generally hold the view that if they (the expert members) did not dissent they assented?

A.   I thought so, because they were there for the purpose of giving us information . . .

Q.   You expected Lord Fisher, if he had any great objection, to state it at the Council?

A.   I certainly did . . . If they (Lord Fisher and Sir Arthur Wilson) were what they were at the Defence Committee; it was their business to give the counsel which they were called there to give, and if they misunderstood their position they ought to have found out what it was. I am perfectly certain that if Lord Fisher had said to the Prime Minister, 'Do you wish me to speak?' he would have said, 'I most certainly do,' and we all did. We all looked upon him as there to take counsel with us.

Q.   In fact, you do not concur in the view of the War Council as expressed by Lord Fisher?

A.   I do not. I think it is an excusable thing from the fact that the body sat in the Cabinet room in Downing Street instead of 2, Whitehall Gardens, and that there were a good many Cabinet Ministers present. For the rest, I think it was just the old Defence Committee, and certainly they had every opportunity of uttering as much as they liked. Not one of us was asked to speak. Questions were not put round. It was a general question.

Q.   And you also relied wholly on what the experts said at the Council, and nothing else? You did not go outside that at all? If they did not express dissent at the Council you considered they more or less assented?

A.   Yes. When I heard it said, for instance, 'We have considered it and we think the forts can be reduced within a certain time, and with a certain expenditure of ammunition,' and the details were given to us, and Lord Fisher and Sir Arthur Wilson sat silent, I thought he (the First Lord of the Admiralty) was giving the view of the Admiralty War Staff, of which Lord Fisher was the head.

Lord Crewe, who was at the time Secretary of State for India, expressed the opinion "that the political members of the Committee did too much of the talking and the expert members as a rule too little"—a view in which Lord Haldane also concurred.

Lord Crewe further said that the fact that the expert members did not express dissent at the meetings involved in his opinion, either "assent or at any rate acquiescence." On being asked whether he "expected that they (the experts) would express dissent on technical matters unless their chief represented their views," he replied, "Unquestionably."

Mr Lloyd George did not concur in the description given by Lord Fisher of the position he occupied on the War Council. On being asked the question, "If the experts present did not express dissent, did you assume that they assented to what was done?" he replied "Certainly."

The views entertained by the Prime Minister on the point now under discussion are, of course, of special importance. Mr Asquith stated that he did not concur in the view that it was the duty of the experts on the Council only to give their opinions if they were asked. When asked whether he held that if the experts did not dissent from the views expressed by the Heads of their Departments, it would be held that they assented, he replied: "Normally and regularly, yes." Speaking of an important meeting which took place on January 13th, Mr Asquith said: "I should have expected any of the experts there, if they entertained a strong personal view on their own expert authority, to express it."

Sir Maurice Hankey gave the following evidence:

Q.   You were asked about the procedure of the Committee of Imperial Defence. Is it not the custom, when a naval or military member does not say anything after the First Lord or the Secretary of State speaks, to admit that he concurs, otherwise there would be such a lot of talk?

A.   Yes, that is certainly very strongly my view.

Q.   And to avoid conversation as much as possible, if you do not object, either the First Lord speaks or the Secretary of State speaks?

A.   Yes.

Q.   If one or the other remains silent it is understood that he concurs?

A.   Yes.

There is one further feature in connection with the methods adopted in conducting the business of the War Council to which it is necessary to draw attention. The evidence as to whether, at the close of each meeting, the decisions were read out and understood by all present is contradictory. Thus, as regards a very important meeting held on January 13th, 1915, to which we shall presently revert, Sir Arthur Wilson, in reply to a question addressed to him, said: "I was under the impression that no decision had been taken at all." The following dialogue then ensued:

Q. If you thought there had been a decision taken would you have said you did not agree to it?
A. No.
Q. Why not?
A. Because it was not my business. I was not in any way connected with the question, and it had never in any way officially been put before me.

Sir James Murray, in answer to a question addressed to him by Mr Clyde, said: "I sometimes left the War Council with a very indistinct idea of any decision having been arrived at at all."

Speaking of the meeting of January 13th, Lord Fisher said:

A. I have not the least doubt a decision was come to, because very likely the Prime Minister went and wrote it down when the meeting was over, but it was never read out to us that that was the decision.
Q. You were not aware that any decision was come to?
A. No; I do not remember it; no more does Wilson.

On the other hand, Mr Asquith states very positively that the decision taken on January 13th was read out before the Council broke up, although possibly some of the members may have left before this was done. Mr Asquith's description of what occurred is confirmed by Sir Maurice Hankey.

The following are the conclusions to be drawn from the evidence which we have received as to the proceedings of the War Council:

1. It was not the practice to ask the experts attending the Council to express their opinions.
2. The experts themselves did not consider it their duty either to express any opinions unless they were asked to do so, or to intimate dissent, at the Council board, if they disagreed with the views set forth by the Ministers in charge of their respective Departments.
3. The Chairman and the Ministerial members of the War Council looked to the naval and military experts to express their opinions if they dissented from the views put forward by the heads of their respective departments. As the experts did not express their opinions the Council was in technical matters guided wholly by the views laid before them by the Secretary of State for War and the First Lord of the Admiralty.
4. The functions of the experts were, to a great extent, differently understood by the experts themselves and the Ministerial members of the Council.

We have dwelt at some length on this subject, as it has a very important bearing on the events which we are about to narrate.

THE ADMIRALTY

The Committee of Imperial Defence was not the only body which underwent considerable changes after the outbreak of the war. Important alterations were also made in the methods of conducting business both at the Admiralty and the War Office.

The authority of the Board of Admiralty is based on Letters Patent issued under the Great Seal in pursuance of certain Acts of Parliament, and on various Orders in Council, the latest and most important of which bear the dates of August 10th, 1904, January 7th, 1912, and July 19th, 1912.

The Board consisted at the commencement of the war, and still consists, of:

A First Lord
Four Sea Lords
Two Civil Lords
The Parliamentary Secretary
The Permanent Secretary

The First Lord is "solely responsible to the Crown and Parliament for all the business of the Admiralty."

The functions of the First Sea Lord are defined, *inter alia*, in the following terms:

Preparation for war. All large questions of Naval policy and Maritime warfare—to advise.

The other members of the Board are charged with various Departmental duties.

Neither the First Lord, nor the First Sea Lord, are under any legal obligation to consult either the Board collectively or any individual members of the Board, but the "Official Procedure and Rules", p. 51, contains the following note:

It is to be understood that in any matter of great importance the First Sea Lord is always to be consulted by the other Sea Lords, the Civil Lord, the Additional Civil Lord, and the Parliamentary and Permanent Secretaries; but each Member of the Board and the Parliamentary and Permanent Secretaries will communicate direct with the First Lord.

Immediately after the outbreak of war, and whilst Prince Louis of Battenberg was still First Sea Lord, a War Staff Group was formed at the Admiralty. At Lord Fisher's instance this Staff Group was "greatly strengthened" in November, 1914, and "became still more the supreme and isolated centre of Naval war direction." From that time onwards it consisted of the First Lord, the First Sea Lord, the Chief of the Staff (Vice-Admiral Sir Henry

Oliver), Admiral of the Fleet Sir Arthur Wilson, the Secretary to the Board (Sir Graham Greene) and the Naval Secretary (Commodore de Bartolomé). The Second Sea Lord (Admiral Sir Frederick Hamilton), who was previously included in the War Staff Group, ceased to be a member of that body.

The creation of a War Staff Group inevitably tended to diminish the authority and to minimise the collective activity of the Board of Admiralty. The meetings of the Board were less frequent than before the war. In 1913, Mr Churchill being then First Lord, twenty-four meetings were held. From August 4th, 1914, to May 17th, 1915, when a change in the constitution of the Board took place, only twelve meetings were held. The frequency or infrequency of the official meetings of the Board afford, however, little or no real indication of the influence and authority exercised by its members, either collectively or individually. The functions of the Board, in its collective capacity, have never formed the subject of any very precise definition. The Second Sea Lord (Sir Frederick Hamilton) said:

> There was considerable misapprehension always as to what the precise powers of the Board were. The popular notion, I fancy, is that the Board are severally and collectively responsible for anything that takes place, or any measures that are decided upon. In theory that may be very well, but in practice I doubt if it has ever been the case. Although undoubtedly the Board is collectively responsible for any large questions of policy ... it is very difficult to say where a thing ceases to be a matter of detail and becomes a large question of policy.

In point of fact, the position occupied by the Junior Lords of the Admiralty depends almost wholly on the attitude assumed towards them by the First Lord, and, in a minor degree, by the First Sea Lord. The former especially can, at his will, utilise their services in matters lying outside their purely departmental duties, or he can decline to do so. Mr McKenna informed us that, during the time he was First Lord of the Admiralty, the Board was habitually consulted on all important matters. He stated that in practice he never found any difficulty in harmonising the sole responsibility of the First Lord with the collective responsibility of the Board. "If," he added, "I were First Lord of the Admiralty and I did not consult my Board but consulted expert advisers, I should suggest to the Prime Minister that the Board ought to be changed. The expert advisers to whom the First Lord would naturally look would be his Board."

Sir Graham Greene informed us that from time to time a good deal of discontent had existed at the Admiralty owing to the dubious positions occupied by the Junior Sea Lords. On being asked whether this discontent was especially acute at the period with which we are dealing, he replied: "It may have been felt rather more keenly at that time, because there were two very active and strong personalities in the position of First Lord and First Sea Lord."

There can, indeed, be no doubt that, at the commencement of the war, the Junior Sea Lords resented the position in which they were placed. None of them were consulted about the Dardanelles Expedition.

The Second Sea Lord, Sir Frederick Hamilton, though generally of opinion that the Board of Admiralty had "a right to give their views on large matters of policy," did not complain of the treatment the Board received in the special case of the Dardanelles. He considered that that was "a matter for the Cabinet to decide." The Third Sea Lord (Rear-Admiral Tudor) said that the only opportunity he had of expressing an opinion on the subject was in the course of an informal conversation with Mr Churchill. He added that his action "was not welcomed and it had no effect."

The Fourth Sea Lord (Commodore Lambert) testified to the fact that the Board had not been consulted about the Dardanelles Expedition, and expressed an opinion that "it would have been a wise and proper subject for the Board's discussion."

On November 22nd, 1915, the Junior Sea Lords addressed collectively a Minute to the present First Lord (Mr Arthur Balfour), in which they said:

> The principle on which the Order in Council is based that the supremacy of the First Lord is complete and unassailable has been pushed too far, and has tended to imperil and at some future time may again tend to imperil national safety ... The present time may not be the proper one for effecting drastic changes, but of this we are certain, it is the proper and opportune moment to again call the attention of the First Lord to these matters and to express our conviction that had the naval members of the Board been regularly and collectively consulted on large questions of war policy during the progress of the present naval campaign, some at least of the events which the Empire does at this moment deplore so bitterly would not have happened, and that until the authority and responsibility of the Sea Lords is enlarged and defined, there will be no adequate assurance that similar disasters will not recur in the future.

It should be added that in answer to a minute addressed to him by the Junior Lords on May 18th Mr Churchill wrote:

> I agree that the four Sea Lords should be more fully consulted on large questions of War policy as apart from the day to day conduct of the War, where action must proceed easily and rapidly. But neither Prince Louis of Battenberg nor Lord Fisher were in favour of this practice, considering that War plans and War policy lay wholly in the domain of the First Sea Lord, with the First Lord directly over him exercising supreme executive power. It would appear desirable in future that the War situation should be reviewed each week by the naval members of the Board under the Presidency of the First Lord.

Lord Fisher does not, however, appear to have concurred in this view. In the course of the evidence which he gave before us, he said:

> With regard to the other Sea Lords, they were tremendously occupied with their business in providing the personnel and stores and other things for the Fleet. I think it would have been a very great pity to have taken them away from their proper duties to have sat round that table.

It is thus abundantly clear that, although no formal and official change was made, the spirit in which the business of the Admiralty was conducted underwent a great transformation immediately after the outbreak of the war. The Board of Admiralty sank into insignificance, its place being taken by the War Staff Group. The Board was, even to a less extent than previously, able to assume any "collective responsibility" for the general conduct of affairs. The individual members of the Board were not kept well-informed of passing events. They were not consulted before the naval attack on the Dardanelles was made.

It is clear that Mr Asquith was ill-informed as regards the methods under which Admiralty business was conducted when he stated to the Commission that the Members of the War Council "were entitled to assume" that any view laid before them by the First Lord of the Admiralty "was the considered opinion of the Board of Admiralty as a whole."

THE WAR OFFICE

The superior administration of the War Office is regulated by Letters Patent, dated February 6th, 1904, and by various Orders in Council issued in 1904, 1909 and 1910. Of these, the most important is the Order dated August 10th, 1904.

As in the case of the Admiralty, the Secretary of State is solely responsible to the Crown and to Parliament for "all the business of the Army Council."

The Council consists of:

A first military member, the Chief of the General Staff
A second military member, the Adjutant-General
A third military member, the Quartermaster-General
A fourth military member, the Master-General of the Ordnance
A finance member
A civil member

The Secretary of the War Office is also Secretary to the Army Council.

All the members of the Council are responsible to the Secretary of State for the performance of such duties as he may from time to time assign to them, the duties assigned to each member being specified in King's Regulations, 1914, Appendix IV.

In consequence of the illness and subsequent death, in October, 1914, of Sir Charles Douglas, Sir James Wolfe Murray became Chief of the Imperial General Staff almost immediately after the war commenced. Otherwise, no changes took place in so far as the military members of the Army Council were concerned. Sir Henry Sclater remained Adjutant-General, Sir John Cowans Quartermaster-General, and Sir Stanley Von Donop Master-General of the Ordnance.

Neither did any formal change take place in the duties and responsibilities of the Council. Viscount Haldane has informed us that, during the time he was Secretary of State for War, formal meetings of the Council were not of frequent occurrence, that they were usually held merely to register decisions which had already been taken, and that the informal were of far greater importance than the formal meetings. So far as outward form was concerned, the practice adopted by Lord Kitchener constituted no innovation on the practice which prevailed under his predecessors.

On the other hand, on Lord Kitchener's becoming Secretary of State for War considerable changes had taken place in the military personnel at the War Office, and more important changes were introduced by him in the methods of administration. As regards personnel, according to an arrangement which Sir Reginald Brade informed us had been made previous to the outbreak of war, several of the most important members of the General Staff left the War Office and assumed commands or Staff appointments in the field. Numerous changes were also made amongst the junior members of the Staff.

Mr Winston Churchill, in speaking of the relations between the War Office and the Admiralty, said: "All the principal officers we were accustomed to work with went off to the war, and a new staff came in."

As regards administrative methods, we think it is much to be regretted that the principles of the devolution of authority and responsibility upon which the War Office system was based were ignored by Lord Kitchener. All the evidence laid before us points to the conclusion that Lord Kitchener was not in the habit of consulting his subordinates, that he frequently gave orders over the heads of the Chiefs of Departments and sometimes without the knowledge of the Chief of the General Staff, and, in fact, that he centralised the whole administration of the War Office in his own hands.

Sir James Murray stated that that portion of the Field Service Regulations which deals with the duties of the Chief of the General Staff were "practically non-existent." On being asked whether he considered that Lord Kitchener centralised too much authority in his own person, he replied, "Yes, I do undoubtedly," and he added that the excessive centralisation of which he complained "was due not to the system, but to the personality of the individual who was Secretary of State."

General Callwell, the Director of Military Operations, stated that "the real reason why the General Staff practically ceased to exist was because it was not consulted." He added that, so far as he was aware, Lord Kitchener never "conferred with anyone very much." General Callwell considered that the extreme centralisation practised "did not tend to the smooth working of the machine."

At a later period of the war, an Order in Council was issued restoring the power of the Chief of the Imperial General Staff which had been allowed to lapse. Sir Reginald Brade, on being asked why this Order was issued, replied:

I think the idea was that Lord Kitchener was in the habit of sending on his own orders in regard to operations, and that he did not ask, or disregarded, the advice of the officers of the General Staff. I think that was the object of it. I do not say that was the fact, but that was understood to be what happened—why that Order in Council was passed.

There can, in fact, be no doubt that the principle of centralisation was pushed to an extreme point by Lord Kitchener. It proved eminently successful during the minor operations in the Sudan, which he conducted with conspicuous skill. But it was unsuitable to a stronger force than that which Lord Kitchener commanded in the Sudan or to operations on so large a scale as those in which this country has recently been engaged. Its result was to throw on the hands of one man an amount of work with which no individual, however capable, could hope to cope successfully.

CONCLUSIONS

It will thus be seen that, almost immediately after the outbreak of war, the following important changes took place:

(1) The ordinary functions of the Cabinet practically lapsed in so far as the conduct of the war was concerned.
(2) A War Council, with supreme powers, was instituted to take the place of the Committee of Imperial Defence.
(3) The consultative functions which would ordinarily have been performed by the Board of Admiralty were transferred to a new body termed the "War Staff Group".
(4) Some important changes were made in the personnel of the War Office. The staff and administrative functions of the office were practically centralised in the hands of one man.

NARRATIVE OF EVENTS

From the outbreak of war until January 13th, 1915

It had for long been recognised by the naval and military authorities of this country that any attack on the Dardanelles would be an operation which presented very great difficulties. In 1878, Admiral Hornby, on the occasion of a naval demonstration made, with the consent of the Ottoman Government, before Constantinople, wrote a report on the subject.

In 1906–07, at a time when the relations between the British Government and the Porte, the Turkish Parliament, were somewhat strained, the matter came under consideration. Both the General Staff of the War Office and the Director of Naval Intelligence at the Admiralty were alive to the great risks which would be involved even in a joint naval and military enterprise against the Gallipoli Peninsula. In a memorandum, dated December 19th, 1906, prepared by the General Staff, the following passage occurs:

> Military opinion, looking at the question from the point of view of coast defence, will be in entire agreement with the naval view that unaided action by the Fleet, bearing in mind the risks involved, is much to be deprecated.

Further, the works of Mr Julian Corbett and other authorities had familiarised the general public with the view that it had become almost a fundamental principle of naval strategy that the attack of ships on forts, without military aid, was rarely productive of satisfactory results. The experience gained at Port Arthur, Santiago, Wei-Hai-Wei and elsewhere was held to confirm this view.

It was contended that the improvements made in modern artillery, the experience recently gained in Belgium, in connection especially with the

The Gallipoli Peninsula, 1915

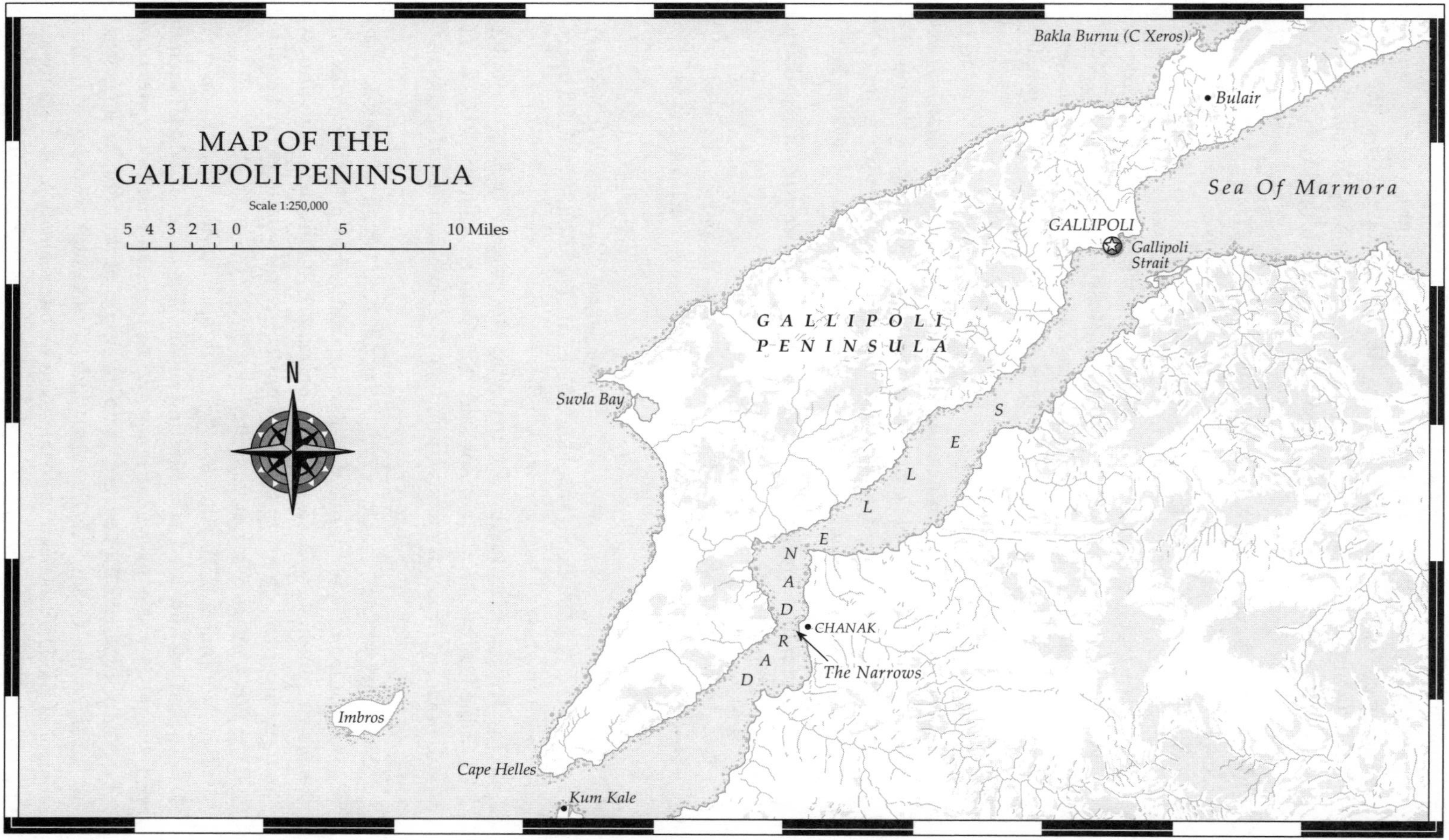

bombardment of Liège, Namur and Antwerp, and the use of aircraft, had rendered any analogy between the present and the past of little value. *A fortiori*, the experience gained by Admiral Duckworth in 1807 was valueless. We shall revert presently to this subject, with a view to discussing how far these precedents were applicable to the case of the recent attack on the Dardanelles.

Towards the end of August 1914 Mr Churchill formed the opinion that Turkey would join Germany and the other Central Powers. On the 1st September he wrote privately to General Douglas, who was then Chief of the Imperial General Staff, in the following terms:

> I arranged with Lord Kitchener yesterday that two officers from the Admiralty should meet two officers from the DMO's Department of the War Office to-day to examine and work out a plan for the seizure, by means of a Greek Army of adequate strength, of the Gallipoli Peninsula, with a view to admitting a British Fleet to the Sea of Marmora.
>
> In his absence I would ask you to give the necessary directions, as the matter is urgent, and Turkey may make war on us at any moment.
>
> The meeting can take place either here or at the War Office as soon as you can arrange with our Chief of the Staff. I will myself explain verbally to the Committee the points on which His Majesty's Government desire information.

On September 3rd General Callwell, the Director of Military Operations, wrote a Memorandum on the subject, in which he said that:

> it ought to be clearly understood that an attack upon the Gallipoli Peninsula from the sea side (outside the Straits) is likely to prove an extremely difficult operation of war.

He referred to the discussions which had taken place in 1906–07, and expressed the opinion that it would not be justifiable to undertake the operation with an army of less than 60,000 men.

On October 31st, Turkey declared war. On November 3rd, the outer forts of the Dardanelles were bombarded for about ten minutes. The object of this bombardment was merely to find out, by a practical test, the effective range of the guns of the Turkish forts.

Sir Henry Jackson has expressed the opinion, in which we concur, that this bombardment was a mistake, as it was calculated to place the Turks on the alert. Commodore de Bartolomé characterised this demonstration as "unfortunate". The orders to bombard emanated solely from the Admiralty and the War Council was not consulted.

On November 25th, the idea of making a serious attack on the Dardanelles was discussed at a meeting of the War Council. Mr Churchill said that the best way to defend Egypt was to make an attack on some part of the coast of Asiatic Turkey, and, as an extension of this idea, he suggested an attack on the Gallipoli Peninsula, which, if successful, would give us the control of the Dardanelles and enable us to dictate terms at Constantinople. He added that this would be a very difficult operation and would require a large force. Lord Kitchener agreed that it might become necessary to make a diversion by an attack on the Turkish communications, but considered that the moment had not yet arrived for doing so.

A proposal to collect transport, horse-boats, etc., at some British port in the Mediterranean was also discussed. The idea at the time was that a feint attack might be made on the Gallipoli Peninsula, in order to convey the impression that a landing was intended there, whereas the real point of attack would be made at some other point on the Turkish coast. This proposal was rejected owing to the shortage of tonnage for mercantile purposes, due partly to military demands. It was thought undesirable to aggravate this evil.

Nevertheless, on November 30th, Vice-Admiral Sir Henry Oliver, the Chief of the Staff at the Admiralty, again proposed that transport should be collected in Egypt sufficient to convey one division. Mr Churchill passed this suggestion on to the War Office, adding that he thought transport should be collected, or kept in readiness at short notice sufficient to convey 40,000 men. Lord Kitchener at once replied: "I will give the Admiralty full notice. I do not think transports need be detained in Egypt yet."

On receipt of this reply, Mr Churchill "put the project on one side and thought no more of it for the time." Nevertheless, horse-boats continued to be despatched to Alexandria whenever the occasion was offered, "in case the War Office should, at a future stage wish to undertake joint naval and military operation in the Eastern Mediterranean."

Thus matters stood until January 2nd, 1915, when a very important telegram, which materially affected the situation, was received from His Majesty's Ambassador at Petrograd. In this telegram it was represented that the Russians were being somewhat hardly pressed in the Caucasus, and a hope was expressed, on behalf of the Russian Government, that, in order to relieve this pressure, a demonstration against the Turks would be made in some other quarter.

On the following day (January 3rd) a reply was sent to the Ambassador, authorising him to assure the Russian Government that a demonstration would be made against the Turks, but stating it was feared that any such action would be unlikely seriously to affect the withdrawal of enemy troops in the Caucasus. This telegram was sent from the Foreign Office, but it was drafted at the War Office. Lord Grey explained to us that the Foreign Office merely acted as a medium of communication. But it is not on this account to be inferred that Lord Grey in any way disapproved of the telegram. On the contrary, he held that "When an Ally appealed for assistance we were bound to do what we could," and that it would have had a bad effect if that assistance had been refused.

Mr Asquith thinks that he did not see this telegram before it was sent, but it must not be by any means inferred on that account that he would not have approved of its despatch if he had seen it.

Mr Churchill did not see the telegram before it was sent, but he had a long conversation with Lord Kitchener on January 2nd, after the receipt of the Petrograd message, and he thinks that Lord Kitchener's reply was the outcome of that conversation.

This, therefore, was the first phase in the whole transaction. By January 3rd His Majesty's Government was pledged to make a demonstration against the Turks. The time and method of making that demonstration were, as yet, wholly undecided.

On January 2nd, Mr Churchill received the following private letter from Lord Kitchener:

> I do not see that we can do anything that will seriously help the Russians in the Caucasus. The Turks are evidently withdrawing most of their troops from Adrianople and using them to reinforce their army against Russia, probably sending them by the Black Sea ... We have no troops to land anywhere ... The only place that a demonstration might have some effect in stopping reinforcements going East would be the Dardanelles ... We shall not be ready for anything big for some months.

It will be convenient to interrupt the thread of the narrative at this point in order to deal briefly with the question, which has formed the subject of much discussion, of who was primarily responsible for originating the proposal to make a purely naval attack on the Dardanelles.

In considering this question, it has to be remembered that Mr Churchill himself, in common with all the experts who were consulted at the time, as well as those who gave their opinions subsequently, was greatly in favour of a joint naval and military attack rather than one conducted by ships alone.

Lord Fisher, in giving his evidence, spoke of the "purely naval operation at the Dardanelles" as "Lord Kitchener's proposal", and condemned it in strong terms. He based this opinion on Lord Kitchener's letter to Mr Churchill of January 2nd, quoted in the preceding paragraph. We are unable to concur in Lord Fisher's view. Lord Kitchener suggested and pressed for a demonstration, but that did not necessarily involve a deliberate attempt to force a passage. The proper conclusion seems to be that when a demonstration appeared to be necessary the First Lord thought it was possible to convert and extend that demonstration into an attempt to force a passage, and took the steps which are detailed in the immediately succeeding paragraph.

On a review of the whole of the evidence on this point, a fairly safe conjecture may be made of what was passing through Lord Kitchener's mind early in January. It has to be borne in mind that the question which both Lord Kitchener and the Government generally had to decide was not whether the attack on the Dardanelles should be amphibious or purely naval, but whether, owing to the impossibility of supplying an adequate military force, any attack at all should be undertaken, or whether, on the other hand, the operation should be limited to a mere demonstration. Lord Kitchener was, without doubt, strongly impressed with both the military and political necessity of acting on the appeal made by the Russian Government. The new army he was creating was not yet ready. He had to provide for home defence, to which he attached the utmost importance. He was most unwilling to withdraw a single man from France. The views entertained by Mr Churchill at the time as to the prospects of success of a purely naval operation, were, as we shall presently show, somewhat more optimistic than was warranted by the opinions of the experts.

Under these circumstances, Lord Kitchener grasped, perhaps rather too eagerly, at the proposal to act through the agency of the Fleet alone, though he recognised the objections to any such undertaking, but it cannot with justice or accuracy be said that the responsibility for proposing the adoption of this course rested with him. It rested rather on the First Lord.

We should here mention that at a somewhat late stage of our Inquiry, Sir George Arthur intimated to us that he was in a position to give evidence bearing upon the question of the extent to which Lord Kitchener was primarily responsible for the initiation of the Dardanelles expedition. He subsequently handed in a statement descriptive of a conversation which he had held with Lord Kitchener, and which was to the following effect:

Lord Kitchener stated that "at a conference to which he was invited by the First Lord of the Admiralty, when the passage of the Dardanelles was the subject of discussion, he protested vigorously against any such an undertaking by the Navy without very strong and very carefully prepared support from and co-operation with the Army"; that the First Lord had stated that the experience of the past was no longer admissible by reason of the "marvellous potentialities of the *Queen Elizabeth*," which ship was about to be sent to the Dardanelles; that Lord Kitchener admitted that "he had no expert knowledge of the *Queen Elizabeth*, and was therefore not in a position to contradict or depreciate the opinion as to her astounding effectiveness, which the First Lord had alleged would revolutionise all previous estimates of naval warfare"; and that he "contented himself with renewing his protest in which he was sure that he voiced all military opinion; but he said also that his inevitable uneasiness would have been considerably diminished had he been able to satisfy himself that the First Lord's confidence both in the *Queen Elizabeth* and in the success of his plan was wholly and whole-heartedly shared by his chief naval advisers."

Much depends upon the date upon which this conversation occurred. Sir George Arthur was unable to give a precise date, but it resulted from his examination that without any doubt it was held about the same time as the War Council which took place on May 14th. At that Council, indeed, Lord Kitchener expressed himself in terms somewhat similar to those used by Sir George Arthur. He read the following statement:

> When the Admiralty proposed to force the passage of the Dardanelles by means
> of the Fleet alone, I doubted whether the attempt would succeed, but was led to
> believe it possible by the First Lord's statements of the power of the *Queen
> Elizabeth* and the Admiralty Staff paper showing how the operation was to be
> conducted . . . I regret that I was led to agree in the enterprise by the statements

made, particularly as to the power of the *Queen Elizabeth*, of which I had no means of judging.

It will be seen, therefore, that Sir George Arthur's evidence has no direct bearing upon the immediate subject of our Inquiry, namely, the opinions Lord Kitchener expressed during the period of origin and inception, which we consider to have closed on March 23rd, 1915.

We also called Major-General Sir Stanley Von Donop and Mr H. J. Creedy, one of Lord Kitchener's private secretaries, to give evidence on the same point, but neither added any material information to the facts which were already in our possession.

To resume the narrative of events. On January 3rd, 1915, the following telegram was despatched from the Admiralty to Vice-Admiral Carden:

Do you think that it is a practicable operation to force the Dardanelles by the use of ships alone?

It is assumed that older battleships would be employed, that they would be furnished with mine sweepers and that they would be preceded by colliers or other merchant vessels as sweepers and bumpers.

The importance of the results would justify severe loss. Let me know what your views are.

On January 5th, Vice-Admiral Carden replied to the Admiralty telegram of the 3rd, in the following terms:

I do not think that the Dardanelles can be rushed, but they might be forced by extended operations with a large number of ships.

In the course of the evidence given before us, Vice-Admiral Carden was asked to explain more fully what he meant by saying that the Dardanelles "might be forced." In reply, he stated:

I did not mean distinctly that they could be forced. I had it in my mind that it was impossible to form a real opinion on the subject until one had destroyed the outer forts at the entrance, and was able to get inside and actually find out the extent of the gun defences, of the mine field and the extent of the movable armament on both sides of the Straits.

It is to be observed, however, that no reservation of this sort was made in the telegram sent to the Admiralty on January 5th. On January 6th, this telegram was sent from the First Lord to Vice-Admiral Carden:

High authorities here concur in your opinion. Forward detailed particulars showing what force would be required for extended operations. How do you think it should be employed, and what results could be gained?

The wording of this telegram is certainly open to criticism. We shall deal presently with the views entertained by the various authorities at the Admiralty. Here we need only remark that at the time Lord Fisher was by far the highest naval authority at the Admiralty, and that, in the absence of any explicit statement to the contrary, Vice-Admiral Carden would naturally suppose that he was included amongst those who concurred in the view set forth in his telegram of January 5th.

This, in fact, is what actually happened. Vice-Admiral Carden, on being asked "What high authorities did you think were meant?" replied: "Well, I knew that Lord Fisher was there and Sir Henry Jackson. I thought it was either or both of them." Now, Lord Fisher agreed with the telegram to Vice-Admiral Carden of January 3rd, but he does not think he was shown the telegram of the 6th before it was sent. "I think," he said in his evidence, "that I should have objected to that, and asked him (Mr Churchill) to word it in some other way. Naturally, Carden would think I was in it, would he not?" Mr Churchill, on the other hand, did not wish it to be inferred that Lord Fisher was included amongst the "high authorities". "I do not," he said, "think it would have been fair to include Lord Fisher then." As regards Sir Henry Jackson, to whose supposed concurrence Vice-Admiral Carden alluded in his evidence, he stated to the Commission that he could not remember whether he was or was not consulted before the telegram of January 6th was despatched. But Mr Churchill, in reply to a question put to him by Mr Clyde, stated that when he spoke of "high authorities" he meant only Sir Henry Jackson and Admiral Oliver, both of whom had expressed their opinions to him verbally.

On January 3rd, simultaneously with the despatch of the telegram to Vice-Admiral Carden, Mr Churchill requested Sir Henry Jackson to prepare a memorandum on the project, which Sir Henry Jackson described as a "Note on forcing the Passages of the Dardanelles and Bosphorus by the Allied Fleets in order to destroy the Turko-German squadron and threaten Constantinople without military co-operation." On January 5th, Sir Henry Jackson wrote a memorandum, which was not, however, received by Mr Churchill till some time after the despatch of the telegram of the 6th to Vice-Admiral Carden. In this memorandum, Sir Henry Jackson did not pronounce any definite opinion either for or against the attack on the Dardanelles. He only dwelt on the minimum force required to undertake the operation, on the losses which would probably be involved in any attempt to "reach the Straits," to which he was strongly opposed, and on the necessity of providing a large supply of ammunition.

He added:

> Assuming the enemy squadron destroyed and the batteries rushed, they would
> be open to the fire of field artillery and infantry, and to torpedo attack at night,
> with no store ships with ammunition, and no retreat without re-engaging the
> shore batteries, unless these had been destroyed when forcing the passage.
> Though they might dominate the city and inflict enormous damage, their
> position would not be an enviable one, unless there were a large military force
> to occupy the town. Strategically, such a diversion would only be carried out

when the object to be gained was commensurate with the loss the Fleet would sustain in forcing the passage. The actual capture of Constantinople would be worth a considerable loss; but its bombardment alone would not greatly affect the distant military operations; and even if it surrendered, it could not be occupied and held without troops, and would probably result in indiscriminate massacres.

On January 11th, Vice-Admiral Carden replied to the telegram sent to him from the Admiralty on the 6th. Four operations, he said, were possible. These were:

(*a*) The destruction of defences at the entrance to the Dardanelles.
(*b*) Action inside the Straits, so as to clear the defences up to and including Cephez Point battery N.8.
(*c*) Destruction of defences of the Narrows.
(*d*) Sweeping of a clear channel through the mine field and advance through the Narrows, followed by a reduction of the forts further up, and advance into the Sea of Marmora.

He estimated that it would take a month to carry out all these operations.

This telegram, Mr Churchill informed us, "made a great impression on every one who saw it. It was in its details an entirely novel proposition." We understand that the novelty of the proposition consisted in the abandonment of any attempt to rush the Dardanelles, and in the substitution in its place of a scheme by which the forts would be methodically attacked and destroyed one by one. "That, of course," Mr Churchill said, "squared with the impression produced in many people's minds by the destruction of the strong forts on land by the German heavy artillery."

On January 15th, Sir Henry Jackson recorded his opinion on Admiral Carden's proposal. His memorandum began with the following remark: "Concur generally in his plans." After dealing at some length with the detailed proposals, Sir Henry Jackson concluded by saying:

I would suggest (a) might be approved at once, as the experience gained would be useful.

He did not recommend the undertaking of (*c*) and (*d*) unless the experience gained from (*a*) and (*b*) justified it. It will be observed that this memorandum is dated January 15th, that is to say, two days after the meeting of the War Council on January 13th, to which we shall presently allude.

Sir Henry Jackson insisted strongly in the evidence which he gave before us that, in writing his Memorandum of January 15th, he agreed to an attack on the outer forts and nothing more. He did not consider that an attempt made by the Fleet alone to get through the Dardanelles was "a feasible operation". He thought that "it would be a mad thing to do". He denied the accuracy of the statement made by Mr Churchill that he, Sir Henry Oliver, and Vice-Admiral Carden "were all agreed". He thought that Mr Churchill was "very much more sanguine" than they were. But nothing of this sort was put on record at the time.

The concurrence expressed by Sir Henry Jackson in his Memorandum of January 15th with the whole of Vice-Admiral Carden's plans is unqualified save by the expression of an opinion that only the first item of the programme, viz., that which involved the destruction of the outer forts, should be approved at once, with a view to gaining experience. The explanation of Sir Henry Jackson's reticent attitude is probably to be found in the answer which he gave to a question addressed to him by Mr Fisher to the effect that it was not part of his duty to "unduly interfere with the naval policy except if he were invited to do so by some superior." He also said in the course of his evidence: "It was not for me to decide. I had no responsibilities whatever as to the decision. I had no responsibilities except just for the staff work which I did." He was consulted before the initial telegram of January 3rd was sent to Vice-Admiral Carden and expressed his concurrence with its contents.

Sir Henry Oliver would greatly have preferred to wait until the army was ready, when a joint naval and military attack might have been made. But he, nevertheless, acquiesced in the naval attack. He thought "we should push on slowly till either we overcame the enemy's defence, or till the enemy's defence brought us to a standstill." Further, he stated, "I think the view was that we would go on, and by the time that we had got over the initial difficulties the military force would have been provided."

Commodore de Bartolomé's opinion was expressed before the Commission in the following terms:

> My impression was always that the naval members would much sooner have had a combined operation, and that they only agreed to a purely naval operation on the understanding that we could always draw back—that there should be no question of what is known as forcing the Dardanelles.

We shall refer presently more particularly to the views entertained by Lord Fisher and Sir Arthur Wilson. Here it will be sufficient to state that as regards the other members of the Admiralty staff who were consulted, all would have preferred a joint naval and military attack, but none dissented from the bombardment of the outer forts. Their concurrence was not apparently very cordial; at the same time there can be no doubt that it was given. They were apparently much influenced by the consideration that the matter could be reconsidered after the results of bombarding the outer forts had been ascertained.

The meeting of the War Council on January 13th

Before proceeding any further, it may be desirable to describe briefly the military and political situation which existed at the moment when the very important meeting of the War Council took place on January 13th.

At that time the rival armies in the Western theatre of war had reached a state of deadlock. The desperate attacks made by the Germans on the British position at Ypres had been repulsed with great losses to the enemy. It seemed tolerably clear that no attempts to break through the French and British lines could prove successful. On the other hand, the Allies were not in sufficiently superior strength to justify any hope that they would speedily break through the German lines.

In the Eastern theatre of war, the Austrians had sustained some serious defeats. But the Russian position, though for the moment satisfactory, was in reality somewhat precarious, owing to a lack of munitions and inadequate railway communications, both being defects which could not be speedily corrected.

In Serbia the position was very menacing. The attitude likely to be assumed by Bulgaria was the dominating factor in the Balkan Peninsula. All attempts to secure the military co-operation of the Balkan States had failed. "Diplomacy," as Lord Grey explained to us, "was perfectly useless without military success." Bulgaria was still neutral, but the proclivities of its ruler were well known. It was thought that a decisive military success on the part of the Allies would prove the most effective method for securing the continued maintenance of his neutrality. Italy was still neutral.

It was under such circumstances that the British Government had to consider in what direction a blow could most effectively be delivered, in order at one and the same time to relieve the pressure on Russia and to deter Bulgaria from active adherence to the cause of the Central Powers.

We do not think it necessary, neither, so long as the war lasts, would it be at all advisable, to deal in a report intended for publication with the alternative projects which at the time came under the consideration of the Government. It will suffice to say that for various reasons, some political and others either naval or military, all, save the proposal to make an attempt on the Dardanelles, were rejected. The entrance of the Allied Fleets into the Sea of Marmora, followed, as would probably have been the case, by the occupation of Constantinople, would, it cannot be doubted, have exercised a profound effect on the future course of the war. The advantages capable of being secured by success in this enterprise were, indeed, so obvious that it is unnecessary to dwell on them at any length. But they may be briefly mentioned.

It would, without doubt, have finally deterred Bulgaria from joining the cause of the Central Powers. It would have enabled the Russian Government to import the war material of which they stood greatly in need. It would, to the great advantage of Russia herself and of the rest of the world, have enabled Russian agricultural products to be exported. Finally, it would have gone far to settle a question which has been a constant source of trouble to Europe for centuries past. These advantages were so great that they may possibly have produced a tendency on the part of the members of the War Council to be governed by them to an excessive degree, and to neglect unduly the sole question which was really open to discussion, namely, the advisability of undertaking at that time a purely naval enterprise. That question was obviously one on which only the opinions expressed by naval and military experts would be of any value. It becomes, therefore, essential to consider what were the views entertained and expressed on January 13th by the naval and military advisers of the Government.

The principal and, indeed, the sole adviser of the Government on military questions was Lord Kitchener. The actual proposal on which Lord Kitchener had to give an opinion at the meeting held on January 13th was thus summarised in Sir Maurice Hankey's notes of the proceedings:

> Mr Churchill said he had interchanged telegrams with Vice-Admiral Carden, the Commander-in-Chief in the Mediterranean, in regard to the possibilities of a naval attack on the Dardanelles. The sense of Admiral Carden's reply was that it was impossible to rush the Dardanelles, but that, in his opinion, it might be possible to demolish the forts one by one. To this end Admiral Carden had submitted a plan.
>
> His proposal was first to concentrate his fire on the entrance forts. When they were demolished he would proceed to deal with the inner forts, attacking them from the Straits and from the seaward side of the Gallipoli Peninsula. This plan was based on the fact that the Dardanelles forts are armed mainly with old guns of only thirty-five calibre. These would be outranged by the guns of the ships, which would effect their object without coming into range. Three modern ships, carrying the heaviest guns, would be required for reducing some of the more modern works, and about twelve old battleships would deal with the remainder. These could now be spared for the task without reducing our strength in the main theatre of war. Among others, he mentioned the *Triumph*, *Swiftsure*, *Goliath*, *Glory*, and *Canopus*, all of which had been employed hitherto for trade protection. Four of the Majestic class, which were to have been "scrapped", their 12-inch guns being utilised for monitors, could also be made available, though this would entail a delay in the completion of the monitors. Two battle-cruisers were, he said, already in the Mediterranean. The new battle-cruiser *Queen Elizabeth* was already to be sent to Gibraltar for gun trials, and it would be feasible to allow her to conduct her trials against the Dardanelles forts, instead of against a target.
>
> The Admiralty were studying the question, and believed that a plan could be made for systematically reducing all the forts within a few weeks. Once the forts were reduced the minefields would be cleared, and the Fleet would proceed up to Constantinople and destroy the *Goeben* [Turkish battleship]. They would have nothing to fear from field guns or rifles, which would be merely an inconvenience.

Sir Maurice Hankey then records:

> Lord Kitchener thought the plan was worth trying. We could leave off the bombardment if it did not prove effective.

Lord Fisher said nothing, but it is essential to inquire fully as to what views he really entertained at this moment. He occupied a position of great responsibility. It is highly probable that if either Lord Kitchener or Lord Fisher had, from the first, expressed, on technical grounds, strong objections to the attack on the Dardanelles, the project would have been abandoned, and it may be regarded as quite certain that, under this hypothesis, the plan would have been much more carefully examined than appears to have been the case.

Lord Crewe, in the course of his evidence, stated:

> I should be very sorry indeed to state what the effect would have been on our minds if Lord Fisher had made a full statement of his actual objections from the naval point of view, speaking as First Sea Lord. Of course then the Government would have had to consider whether the political advantages were worth the risk. I cannot say what the ultimate decision would have been, but I have not the least doubt that it would have altered the form and manner of our consideration of the whole subject to a great extent.

Lord Grey also said:

> Of course if we had thought that we were forcing upon naval officers an operation which they were reluctant to undertake, I think we should not have contemplated it for a moment; but we understood that the naval officers who were on the spot who were to carry it out, and who had advised about it, were in favour of it, and we were attracted by what we were told about big guns and forts, and so forth, and we were prepared to authorise the operation being proceeded with.

Lord Fisher made a very full statement to us of the views which he entertained. Mr Churchill also dwelt at length on this subject, and allusion has been made to it by many other witnesses. We think that we can now confidently describe the attitude he assumed both on January 13th and at later periods. It is certain that Lord Fisher did not underrate the importance of the Dardanelles enterprise. On January 3rd, in a "private and personal" letter to Mr Churchill, Lord Fisher said: "I consider the attack on Turkey holds the field." He then sketched out the broad outlines of a general plan of operations in the Eastern theatre of war. This plan involved, *inter alia*, the withdrawal of a considerable force from France, and was, therefore, at all events for the time being, incapable of execution. Lord Fisher, in fact, like all other experts, both naval and military, was in favour of a combined attack, but not of action by the Fleet alone. It is certain that, from the very first, he disliked the purely naval operation, but it is especially to be observed that his main objection was not based upon the impracticability of the scheme, considered on its own merits, but on the strong opinion which he entertained that the British Fleet could be better employed elsewhere. All the evidence we have received, including that of Lord Fisher himself, tends to confirm the perfect accuracy of the following statement made to us by Mr Asquith:

> As I understand, because I had frequent conversations with him, Lord Fisher's objection to the Dardanelles operations was not so much a technical objection upon

naval grounds. It is quite true that, I think throughout, he thought the best chance of success for such an operation would have been a combined operation in which both the land and sea forces were engaged; but Lord Fisher's main objection, at least the one he always impressed on me, was not based in any degree upon the technical or naval merits or demerits of the Dardanelles operations, but upon the fact that he preferred another objective . . . So far as I understood, from all the conversations I had with him, it was much more upon that ground than upon any specific objection on what you may call technical naval grounds that he was opposed to it.

We have already mentioned that in our present Report we propose only to deal with events which occurred up to March 23rd, but it may be advisable so far to forestall the contents of our future Report as to say that throughout the whole of the proceedings Lord Fisher consistently maintained the attitude described in the above extract from Mr Asquith's evidence. He reluctantly acquiesced in the Dardanelles operations so long as he thought they would not seriously interfere with the plans which he wished to carry into execution elsewhere. But when in the month of May he became convinced that the demands made on the Fleet for action in the Dardanelles would prejudice his alternative schemes, he resigned his post at the Admiralty. It should be clearly understood that his resignation was due solely to this cause and not to objections he entertained to the original scheme for attacking the Dardanelles considered exclusively on its own merits. Lord Fisher did, indeed, state in the course of his evidence that he "was dead against the naval operation alone because he knew it must be a failure." He also said, "I must reiterate that as a purely naval operation I think it was doomed to failure." But he did not at the time record any such strongly adverse opinions as these, neither does he appear to have impressed others with the strength of his objections. Lord Grey stated:

We (the Members of the War Council) understood that the naval authorities, who were to be charged with the carrying out of the operation, considered it a practicable operation by naval means alone.

Lord Grey "got to know that Lord Fisher did hold views of his own," but he thinks that this fact did not come to his knowledge until after the decision of January 13th had been taken. Mr Asquith, on being asked in what light he interpreted the views of the experts, replied: "Very favourable. Mr Churchill told me so, and I thought they were." Further, on being asked whether Lord Fisher had ever given him to understand that from the first he considered that the Dardanelles expedition was "doomed to failure", Mr Asquith replied: "No, he never said that to me. He would always have preferred a conjoint military and naval operation, but he never said it was doomed to failure; and I do not think he thought it was."

Mr Churchill said to us: "I think I am entitled to state that it was my impression, and it was the impression of every one present at this meeting of the 13th, that in what I said I carried with me the full agreement of those who were there." It is perhaps somewhat overstating the case to say that Lord Fisher was in "full agreement", but it is undeniable that, by not dissenting, Lord Fisher may reasonably have been held to agree, and that, so far as we have been able to ascertain, he did not, before the meeting, express anything approaching strong disapproval save on the ground to which we have already alluded, namely, that he feared that the Dardanelles operations would interfere with the execution of other schemes which he favoured. Indeed, on January 12th, Lord Fisher initialled and passed on to the Chief of the Staff the following Minute, which had been written by the First Lord:

> Secret. Minute by the First Lord to Secretary, First Sea Lord, Chief of Staff. The forcing of the Dardanelles as proposed and the arrival of a squadron strong enough to defeat the Turkish Fleet in the Sea of Marmora would be victory of first importance and change to our advantage the whole situation of the war in the East. It would appear possible to provide the force required by Admiral Carden without weakening the margin necessary in Home waters, as follows.

The details connected with the proposed movements of ships were then given.

Moreover, on January 14th, Lord Fisher concurred with a memorandum which was sent from the First Lord to the Prime Minister in which the following passage occurs:

> The attack on the Dardanelles will require practically our whole available margin. If that attack opens prosperously it will very soon attract to itself the whole attention of the Eastern theatre, and if it succeeds it will produce results which will undoubtedly influence every Mediterranean Power. In these circumstances we strongly advise ... that we should devote ourselves to action in accordance with the third conclusion of the War Council, viz., the methodical forcing of the Dardanelles.

We shall have presently to revert to the views entertained both by Lord Fisher and Sir Arthur Wilson when we come to deal with a further meeting of the War Council, which took place on January 28th.

The actual decision arrived at by the War Council on January 13th, after hearing the views expressed by Lord Kitchener and Mr Churchill—Lord Fisher, Sir Arthur Wilson and Sir James Murray remaining silent—was couched in the following terms:

> The Admiralty should prepare for a naval expedition in February to bombard and take the Gallipoli Peninsula, with Constantinople as its objective.

It is impossible to read all the evidence, or to study the voluminous papers which have been submitted to us, without being struck with the atmosphere of vagueness and want of precision which seems to have characterised the proceedings of the War Council. We have already mentioned that some of those present at the meetings of the Council left without having any very clear idea of what had or had not been decided. The decision of the Council, taken on January 13th, is another case in point. The Admiralty was to "pre-pare" for a naval expedition, and nothing more. It would naturally be inferred from the wording of the decision that the matter was to be recon-sidered by the Council when the preparations were complete, and after the Admiralty plan was matured. Actual approval of the bombardment was with-held. The following extract from the evidence given by Mr Asquith will show that this is the way in which he understood the decision:

Q. Did you understand that it (the decision) was merely provisional, to prepare, but nothing more? It did not pledge you to anything more?

A. No.

Q. You did not think it approved it?

A. No. I think all of us thought this was a very promising operation, and the Admiralty ought to get ready for it.

Q. But nothing more?

A. No, no more than that.

Mr Churchill apparently considered that the decision of January 13th went further than the approval of mere preparation. Employing Parliamentary metaphor, he likened the meetings of January 13th and 28th respectively to the Second and Third readings of a Bill. "I do not think," he said, "that the meeting of the 13th would be the introduction; it was more than that—it was the approval of a principle, with the general knowledge of how it was to be given effect to."

The statement made by Lord Crewe probably represents with accuracy the manner in which the decision was generally understood by the mem-bers of the Council. "I think," he said, in answer to a question which was addressed to him, "I should say that it was approved subject to the occur-rence of any unforeseen event which might have made it from one point of view unnecessary."

The following extract from General Callwell's evidence shows how he regarded the decision taken on January 13th. It may, with some confidence, be presumed that General Callwell's views were shared by other officials both at the War Office and the Admiralty.

Q. When the naval operation was undertaken, did you understand it to be an undertaking to force the Dardanelles with ships only?

A. Yes, certainly, to force it gradually.

Q. As undertaken, did you understand it to be anything of the limited character of a demonstration?

A. No, certainly not …

Q. In short, you regarded it from the beginning as a definite serious project definitely to force the passage of the Dardanelles?

A. Certainly.

Q. From the early stage in January?

A. Yes, from the very beginning, the 13th January.

The decision taken at this meeting of the Council calls for one further observation. When Mr Churchill spoke of the "general knowledge" imparted to the Council of how the "principle" which he advocated should be carried into effect, he, without doubt, meant that the force to be employed was to be purely naval. On this point all the witnesses whom we have examined were unanimous.

Thus, Lord Grey said:

> My recollection is that it was distinctly said to us that the troops would not be asked
> for; that if the Navy could not carry out the operation by itself, the operation would
> not be proceeded with; and that our first consent was given on that understanding;
> and I gave my consent on that understanding because I was informed—I believed
> Lord Kitchener's opinion to be—that no troops were available.

The determination to employ ships alone must be considered in connection with the phrase used in the recorded decision taken on January 13th, that the Admiralty, in preparing for the bombardment, was to consider "Constantinople as its objective".

It was from the first recognised by all the naval experts that small bodies of troops would have to be landed on the Gallipoli Peninsula, partly for finally demolishing the forts which had been bombarded by the Fleet, and partly also, in all probability, to attack those batteries which could not effectively be reached by the ships' guns. It is almost inconceivable that any one, whether military, naval or civilian, could have imagined for one moment that Constantinople would be captured without military help on a somewhat large scale. It is clear that by the decision of January 13th, although the War Council only pledged itself for the moment to naval action, they were, in reality, committed to military action on a large scale in the event of the attempt to force the Dardanelles by the Fleet alone proving successful.

We have mentioned that the first phase of these transactions was reached on January 3rd, when the Russian Government was informed that a "demonstration" of some sort would be made against the Turks.

A demonstration may, as Lord Grey pointed out, "of course, not mean active operations at all." The second phase was reached on January 13th. The idea of a mere demonstration, which would not involve active operations, was then definitely abandoned. A decision, which was somewhat variously interpreted, was taken that the Admiralty should "prepare" for an attack on the Gallipoli Peninsula, with the ulterior object of pushing on to Constantinople. The attack was intended to be purely naval, but if successful, in our opinion, necessarily involved, at a somewhat later period, the active co-operation of considerable military forces with the Fleet.

Co-operation with the French and the advantages of a purely naval attack

The first step very wisely taken by the First Lord of the Admiralty after he had received from the War Council a mandate to "prepare" for a bombardment of the Gallipoli Peninsula was to communicate with the French Government with a view to securing the co-operation of the French fleet. M. Augagneur, the French Minister of Marine, visited London. In the course of the discussions which took place with him an arrangement was speedily made as to the sphere of maritime action in the Mediterranean to be assigned respectively to the naval forces of the two countries. The French squadron at the Dardanelles was to be placed under the command of Admiral Carden. The detailed plan of action proposed by the Admiralty was then communicated to the French Government and examined by the Ministry of Marine at Paris [by whom it was accepted].

The allusion made in M. Augagneur's letter to the possibility of desisting from the naval attack if "insurmountable difficulties" were encountered renders this a convenient opportunity for dwelling at somewhat greater length on this argument, which played an important part in the decision taken at the meeting of the War Council of January 28th, which we are about to describe, and which assumed even greater importance at a later stage of the proceedings.

It may confidently be asserted that anyone conversant with Eastern affairs would have predicted, in January, 1915, that if a serious attack on the Dardanelles was made and if it failed, the result would be to give a shattering blow to British prestige and influence throughout the East. As a matter of fact, the attack failed, but, so far as can at present be judged, the political consequences, although a serious check to British arms was shortly afterwards experienced in Mesopotamia, have been so slight as to be almost inappreciable.

An additional proof is thus furnished of the extreme difficulty experienced by any Western when he endeavours to forecast the ratiocinative processes of the Eastern mind. But this result could not be, and was not, foreseen at the time when the decision had to be taken. Lord Kitchener, as might naturally be expected from his long Eastern experience, was more especially impressed with the harm which would ensue from failure, but although he and others realised the inevitable risk which would have to be run, they thought, in the first instance, that any serious loss of prestige could, in any case, be avoided by desisting from the attack if, after some experience had been gained, the prospect of success was greatly diminished. A great distinction was made between the withdrawal of the fleet and evacuation by a military force when it had once been landed.

Lord Grey said:

> Once you got fairly in and made it apparent to the whole world that you were making a serious effort to force the Straits, of course there was loss of prestige if you failed; but I do not think there would have been much lost if we had failed to take the outer forts and then gone away again.

Mr Asquith stated:

> One of the great reasons put forward in the first instance which appealed to
> Lord Kitchener and everybody was that if it was merely a naval attack, it could
> have been abandoned at any moment without any serious loss of prestige.

Mr Arthur Balfour said:

> I think it was always in the view of the Admiralty and of the responsible people
> that if the outer forts attack failed, you could always divert all your naval efforts
> to some other theatre of operations.

Sir Arthur Wilson, also, looking at the matter from the naval rather than
from the political point of view, was asked the following question by Sir
William Pickford: "So long as you were not so far committed that you could
not stop, you did not see much objection to it?" His reply was: "I did not
think there was any harm."

It will be seen in the sequel to this report that, when the time came for
applying the principles enunciated above, the argument based upon the loss
of prestige, which would result from the acknowledgment of a partial failure, exercised so predominant an influence as practically both to nullify the
intentions which had been originally formed and to obliterate the recollection of the considerations which were advanced prior to any definite action
having been taken.

The effect of modern artillery

It may be as well here also to allude to another consideration which
appears to have carried great weight at the War Council on the occasion of their meeting on January 28th. Sir Maurice Hankey gives the
following amongst other reasons for differentiating the position in
1914-15 from that discussed by the Committee of Imperial Defence in
1907.

> The fall of the Liège and Namur forts had led to the belief that permanent
> works were easily dealt with by modern long-range artillery, and this was
> confirmed by the fall of the outer forts.
>
> The utilisation of aircraft had led to the hope that, in a comparatively
> confined space like the Gallipoli Peninsula, the value of naval bombardment,
> particularly by indirect laying, would be enormously increased.

We have received abundant evidence to show that these arguments weighed
strongly both in the minds of Ministers and experts. Lord Grey said:

> The experience of this war was supposed to have changed the prospect of
> successful attack upon forts and made successful attack upon forts a practicable
> operation where it had not been a practicable operation before.

Mr Churchill said:

This war had brought many surprises. We had seen fortresses reputed
throughout Europe to be impregnable collapsing after a few days' attack by field
armies without a regular siege.

The arguments involved in the consideration of this subject are of so
highly technical a character that none but specialists can express any very
confident opinion upon them. At the same time, the presumed analogy
between the Belgian forts and the position in the Dardanelles weighed so
strongly in the minds of the Government that we think it incumbent on us
to deal briefly with the subject, and to state such conclusions as we have
been able to form from the evidence laid before us.

It is, we think, correct to say that the rapid destruction of the Belgian
fortresses by heavy howitzers came as a surprise in land warfare. It may be
accounted for:

(1) By the foresight and reticence displayed by the German military author-
    ities in ascertaining the results obtainable from the high-angle fire of
    howitzers of large calibre, and in providing the requisite ordnance and
    ammunition.
(2) By the increased facilities now available for transporting and mounting
    such heavy ordnance.
(3) By the advantage derivable from the use of aircraft for observing and reporting
    the fall of the projectiles.

It must also be remembered that, when the heavy armament of the
fortresses had been dismounted or silenced, an ample military force was
immediately forthcoming to seize and hold the works.

Comparing heavy howitzers as used in the destruction of the Antwerp,
Namur and Liège forts with heavy guns, as mounted in the ships that made
the attack on the Dardanelles, the advantages of the howitzer over the gun
are:

(1) The projectile descends at such an obtuse angle that it clears the parapet
    or vertical defence of the guns in the forts and explodes more nearly in
    the centre and does more damage.
(2) The penetration of any overhead protection of the forts is assured.
(3) The steep angle of descent enables the projectiles to clear any hills in
    front of the forts and also to reach batteries in concealed positions, such
    as those mounted in a hollow of the land.

The disadvantages are:

(1) To ensure any degree of accuracy the howitzers must be fixed in rela-
    tion to the object.

(2) The wind, especially at very long ranges, is detrimental to the accuracy of fire.

(3) The range is comparatively short.

The advantages of the gun over the howitzer are:

(1) Higher velocity and consequently greater penetration.

(2) Greater accuracy.

The disadvantages are:

(1) Although penetration is greater, the protection that can be given to shore guns would probably resist all direct hits. There is no limit to the protection that may be given to guns in forts, and therefore to ensure each gun being silenced the gun itself would have to be hit.

Guns as mounted on board ships cannot be given sufficient elevation to obtain high-angle fire similar to howitzers, but at long ranges or at short ranges by reducing the muzzle velocity an angle of descent of about 21 degrees can be obtained. The *Queen Elizabeth's* mountings can give about 20 degrees of elevation, but this is not sufficient for really high-angle fire. Thus, in the case of the *Queen Elizabeth*, lying 15,000 yards from Gabe Tepe and firing with reduced three-quarter charge at Kilid Bahr, the angle of descent would be 17° 18'; firing at Chanak the angle of descent would be 20° 20'.

(2) Guns, owing to the small angles of descent, are not able to attack concealed forts and batteries.

(3) Guns mounted in ships cannot fire from concealed positions, but provided their gun power is greater than that of the forts, the ships could keep out of range.

Thus it will be seen that for the destruction of forts, and especially those in concealed positions, the howitzer is a superior weapon to the gun. With reference to Mr Churchill's statement regarding the destruction of the Belgian fortresses, the new and surprising fact was mainly due to the causes we have mentioned, only the third of which is applicable to guns mounted on board ships. On the other hand, the improvement in the power of the latest naval guns in comparison with the defensive capabilities of forts is certainly appreciable, especially in the case of the heavy guns in the new ships—*Queen Elizabeth* and *Inflexible*—that were used in the Dardanelles operations.

In the case of the Dardanelles, the reduction of the forts was a very much more difficult and hazardous operation than the naval attacks which had failed in the cases of Port Arthur, Santiago or Wei-Hai-Wei, because after the outer forts were silenced, the forts on each side of a long, narrow strait had to be dealt with.

The waters readily lent themselves to be defended by mines, and the mine-fields could be easily protected by gun fire.

The facilities for firing Whitehead torpedoes from fixed tubes on each side of the Straits were very good, and many of these positions might be concealed. A certain number of them were known to exist.

The topography of the land on each side of the Straits was most favourable for concealed batteries of guns and howitzers, and the breadth of the Peninsula opposite Kilid Bahr was about 6 to 7 miles, and at Chanak was about 8 to 9 miles. Thus, ships bombarding those forts by indirect fire from off Gaba Tepe might find concealed batteries that would compel them to go some distance from the land, and might force them out of range. Ships bombarding from inside the Straits would also be fairly certain to be attacked by concealed batteries. Lastly, it was not certain when submarines might appear on the scene.

In the evidence of Mr Churchill and certain naval officers of high position, stress was laid on the result of the bombardment of the outer forts as indicating what might be expected from similar action inside the Straits. In our opinion there was little analogy between the two operations, as in the former case the ships bombarding could keep out of range; the concealed batteries could not attack them; they were free from mines and Whitehead torpedoes.

The Fleet bombarding the Dardanelles had the important advantage over fleets previously engaged in the bombardment of forts that seaplanes were available for observation; but apparently they did not fulfil expectations, as the engine power was deficient, and there was much difficulty experienced in rising from the water when there was any sea.

In the bombardment of the outer forts ships were placed to observe the fall of the projectiles, and succeeded in doing so; but when the forts inside the Straits were attacked, ships were not very effective for this purpose, and it would seem that on the 18th March, when the determined attack was made, there was hardly any attempt to observe the fall of the shots.

Looking to all the facts of the case, we are disposed to think that undue importance was attached to the ease with which the Belgian forts were destroyed, and that the extent to which there was any analogy between those forts and the forts at the Dardanelles was over-rated.

The meeting of the War Council on January 28th

Mr Churchill stated to us that, in the early days of January, Lord Fisher "assented" to the purely naval attack on the Dardanelles. It was, of course, known that, in common with all other experts, he would have preferred a joint naval and military attack had troops been available. It was also known that he would have preferred operations in another theatre of war. But, so far as we have been able to ascertain, there is no contemporary record to show that he expressed any opinion adverse to the proposed attack on the Dardanelles considered exclusively on its own merits.

Shortly after the meeting of January 13th, Lord Fisher's attitude underwent some change. The real divergence between his views and those of Mr

Churchill became more apparent than heretofore. The latter thus describes what occurred:

> During the weeks that followed I could see that Lord Fisher was increasingly worried about the Dardanelles situation. He reproached himself for having agreed to begin the operation. Now it was going to broaden out into a far larger and far longer undertaking than he had contemplated, his great wish became to put a stop to the whole thing. Although our relations continued to be friendly and pleasant, it was clear to me that there was a change. Although we agreed on every definite practical step that had to be taken, there was a deep difference in our underlying view. He knew that I wanted the fleet to carry out its plan in its integrity. I knew that he wanted to break off the whole operation and come away.

Mr Asquith has borne testimony to the fact that there were at this time constant differences of opinion between the First Lord and the First Sea Lord, but he added: "They got on well together, all the same." The evidence given to us by both Mr Churchill and Lord Fisher amply confirms this latter statement.

These differences eventually culminated in the submission by Lord Fisher direct to the Prime Minister on January 25th of a memorandum setting forth his views. It is an interesting and, in many respects, important paper. But it has no very direct bearing on the immediate subject of our inquiry. Moreover, inasmuch as it dwells exclusively on the general naval policy which should be adopted by this country, and does not discuss the practicability or otherwise of the attack on the Dardanelles, it would be most inadvisable that it should be reproduced in this report. It may, however, without detriment to the public interest, be said that Lord Fisher generally deprecated the use of the fleet for coastal bombardments or attacks on fortified positions. His memorandum was immediately answered by another prepared by Mr Churchill on January 27th, in which, whilst expressing full concurrence in the general principles of naval policy advocated by Lord Fisher, he contended that the proposal to bombard the Gallipoli Peninsula did not conflict with those principles. Mr Churchill further informed us that it was not until he had seen Lord Fisher's memorandum of January 26th, that he "perceived ... that the First Sea Lord had, since the first meeting of the War Council, developed serious misgivings about it" (i.e. about the decision taken on January 13th).

It appears that subsequent to the submission of this memorandum, Lord Fisher intimated that he did not wish to attend any more meetings of the War Council. The Prime Minister was extremely desirous that Lord Fisher should not absent himself from the meeting which was about to take place. It was arranged, therefore, that, prior to the official meeting on January 28th, Lord Fisher and Mr Churchill should meet in the Prime Minister's room and discuss the matter with him. Save in respect to some points of slight importance as regards the precise language used, the accounts given to us by Mr

Asquith and Lord Fisher, as regards what occurred at this private meeting, tally.

Mr Churchill advocated the attack on the Dardanelles. Lord Fisher spoke in favour of those alternative schemes, which we have not thought it advisable to describe, but to which we have already alluded. He did not criticise the attack on the Gallipoli Peninsula on its own merits. Neither did he mention to the Prime Minister that he had any thought of resigning if his opinions were overruled. The Prime Minister, after hearing both sides, expressed his concurrence in Mr Churchill's views. Immediately afterwards, the War Council met at 11.30 a.m.

Sir Maurice Hankey's record of this meeting, in so far as it concerns the subject of our inquiry, is as follows:

> Mr Churchill said that he had communicated to the Grand Duke Nicholas and to the French Admiralty the project for a naval attack on the Dardanelles. The Grand Duke had replied with enthusiasm, and believed that this might assist him. The French Admiralty had also sent a favourable reply, and had promised co-operation. Preparations were in hand for commencing about the middle of February. He asked if the War Council attached importance to this operation, which undoubtedly involved some risks.
>
> Lord Fisher said that he had understood that this question would not be raised to-day. The Prime Minister was well aware of his own views in regard to it.
>
> The Prime Minister said that, in view of the steps which had already been taken, the question could not well be left in abeyance.
>
> Lord Kitchener considered the naval attack to be vitally important. If successful, its effect would be equivalent to that of a successful campaign fought with the new armies. One merit of the scheme was that, if satisfactory progress was not made, the attack could be broken off.
>
> Mr Balfour then dwelt on the advantages which would accrue from a successful attack on the Dardanelles, and concluded by saying that it was difficult to imagine a more helpful operation.
>
> Sir Edward Grey said it would also finally settle the attitude of Bulgaria and the whole of the Balkans.
>
> Mr Churchill said that the naval Commander-in-Chief of the Mediterranean had expressed his belief that it could be done. He required from three weeks to a month to accomplish it. The necessary ships were already on their way to the Dardanelles.

It is to be observed that the memorandum addressed by Lord Fisher to the Prime Minister on January 25th was not in the hands of the War Council when this meeting took place, neither were they informed of the conversation between the Prime Minister, Lord Fisher and Mr Churchill which immediately preceded the meeting. The result, coupled with Lord Fisher's silence, was that the Members of the War Council, although they may have had some rather vague idea that Lord Fisher was not in agreement with the First Lord, were by no means well-informed of his views.

Lord Fisher has explained to us the reasons of his silence. He "did not want to have an altercation with his Chief at the Council." Mr Churchill, he said, "was my Chief, and it was silence or resignation." When asked what he meant by stating to the Council that "he had understood that the (Dardanelles) question would not be raised to-day," he replied: "I thought we would have time to think over it. I did not think that it would be gone on with at the meeting."

When Lord Fisher found that he was mistaken in this opinion and that a final decision was at once to be taken, he was greatly dissatisfied. He rose from his seat with the intention of going to the room of Mr Bonham Carter, the Prime Minister's Private Secretary, and intimating his intention to resign. Lord Kitchener at the same time rose from his seat and, before Lord Fisher could leave the room, had some private conversation with him at the window. He strongly urged Lord Fisher not to resign, and pointed out that he was the only one present who disagreed with the Dardanelles operation. Eventually, according to a note Lord Fisher made at the time, the latter "reluctantly gave in to Lord Kitchener's entreaty and resumed his seat".

During all these proceedings, Sir Arthur Wilson, for reasons very analogous to those which inspired Lord Fisher's attitude, remained silent. In the course of his evidence he said to us that he was "moderately adverse" to the plan of bombarding the Dardanelles. He added:

> I thought other things might be better, but both the First Lord and I recognised that it was not my business to interfere, and if they decided on a plan all I was to do was to help them to the best of my ability. In fact, the main object in my declining to have any official appointment was that I might be put into a position in which I should have to oppose the First Lord or the First Sea Lord, or to support one against the other.

The following extracts from Sir Arthur Wilson's evidence are also worthy of attention:

Q.　In the discussions prior to the 13th January, leaving the First Lord out, was there any general consensus of opinion favourable to an exclusively naval attack?

A.　I do not think there was.

Q.　In representing the opinion of the Admiralty to the War Council on the 13th January or on the 28th January, did the First Lord reflect these unfavourable opinions?

A.　No. I think he rather passed them over. He was very keen on his own views.

Q.　In what way did you think the First Lord on the 28th failed to represent the difficulties to the War Council?

A.　In the first place, he kept on saying he could do it without the army; he only wanted the army to come in and reap the fruits, I think, was his expression; and I think he generally minimised the risks from mobile guns, and treated it as if the armoured ships were immune altogether from injury. I do not mean to say he actually said they were immune, but he minimised the risk a great deal.

Mr Churchill, in answer to a question addressed to him by the Chairman, said:

A.   The effect produced upon my mind was that Sir Arthur Wilson's state of mind on the subject, which I watched very carefully, was favourable to the bombardment, and encouraged me in thinking the bombardment would be successful. All the same, if Sir Arthur Wilson had been asked to give a vote, he would have voted in the negative.

Q.   He would have voted in the negative because he wanted to do some other operation?

A.   Yes.

Q.   He never said to you, on the ground of the merits of the thing itself and the practicability of the thing itself, independently of operations elsewhere, that he thought you had better not undertake that operation?

A.   No one of those who were consulted—there were very few, but they were very important people—ever argued against the practicability. No one ever said: 'This is a thing which you cannot do' and showed by practical simple reasons that it could not be done; the only arguments which were ever used were these general arguments which you have heard and I thought myself to some extent a judge of those.

A further meeting took place on January 28th at 6 p.m., but in the interval between the two meetings an incident occurred which is thus related by Mr Churchill:

Although the War Council had come to a decision in which I heartily agreed, and no voice had been raised against the naval plan, I felt I must come to a clear understanding with the First Sea Lord. I had noticed the incident of his leaving the table, and Lord Kitchener following him to the window and arguing with him, and I did not know what was the upshot in his mind. After lunch I asked him to come to see me in my room, and we had a talk. I strongly urged him to undertake the operation, and he definitely consented to do so. I state this positively. We then repaired to the afternoon War Council meeting, Admiral Oliver, the Chief of the Staff, coming with us, and I announced finally on behalf of the Admiralty and with the agreement of Lord Fisher that we had decided to undertake the task with which the War Council had charged us so urgently.

This I take as the point of final decision. After it, I never looked back. We had left the region of discussion and consultation, of balancings and misgivings. The matter had passed into the domain of action.

Thus the third phase of these transactions was reached. There was no longer, as on January 13th, any question of "preparing" for an attack on the Dardanelles. It was finally decided that an attack should be made, by the fleet alone, with Constantinople as its ultimate objective.

We wish to add some comments on these proceedings. Both Lord Fisher and Sir Arthur Wilson are distinguished officers who, in the course of their honourable careers, have rendered eminent services to their country. We have not the least doubt that the attitude which they adopted at the War Council was dictated by a strong sense of duty. But we have no hesitation in recording our opinion that it was a mistaken sense of duty. Lord Fisher, indeed, himself recognised that he "stretched loyalty to an extreme pitch".

It has probably happened to most officials who occupy or have occupied high places that they have at times disagreed with the heads of their departments. There may perhaps be occasions when such disagreement justifies resignation. But those occasions are extremely rare. More generally, it is the duty of the official not to resign but to state fully to the head of his department and, should any proper occasion arise, to other members of the Ministry, what are the nature of his views. Then, if after due consideration those views are over-ruled, he should do his best to carry out the policy of the Government, even although he may not be in personal agreement with it. This duty was in a very special degree incumbent upon an officer placed in Lord Fisher's position, though it perhaps applies to a somewhat less extent to Sir Arthur Wilson. Both of these officers were distinguished experts. They must have been aware that the questions which the Council had to decide were of so technical a nature that none but expert opinion could be of any value, and they must also have been aware that none of the Ministerial members of the Council had any expert naval knowledge.

We hold, therefore, that although they were not asked definitely to express their opinions, they should have done so. We dwell on this point because we consider that if the principles on which Lord Fisher and Sir Arthur Wilson acted were to be generally accepted by officials in other departments, they would exercise an extremely bad effect upon the general efficiency of the public services. They would tend to cripple independence of thought and their application would leave the Parliamentary heads of the various departments without that healthy assistance which they have a right to expect, and which is, at times, much more likely to be rendered by reasonable and deferential opposition than by mere agreement resting wholly on the ties of discipline.

There can be no doubt that at the two meetings on January 28th, Mr Churchill strongly advocated the adoption of the Dardanelles enterprise. When Sir Arthur Wilson was asked "Did the First Lord express an opinion in favour of it?" he replied: "Yes; very much. He pressed it very strongly." We think that, considering what Mr Churchill knew of the opinions entertained by Lord Fisher and Sir Arthur Wilson, and considering also the fact that the other experts at the Admiralty who had been consulted, although they assented to an attack on the outer forts of the Dardanelles and to progressive operations thereafter up the Straits as far as might be found practicable, had not done so with any great cordiality or enthusiasm, he ought, instead of urging Lord Fisher, as he seems to have done at the private meeting after luncheon on January 28th, to give a silent, but manifestly very reluctant, assent to the undertaking, not merely to have invited Lord Fisher and Sir Arthur Wilson to express their views freely to the Council, but further to have insisted on their doing so, in order that the Ministerial members might be placed in full possession of all the arguments for and against the enterprise. We have not the least doubt that, in speaking at the Council, Mr Churchill thought that he was correctly representing the collective views of the Admiralty experts. But, without in any way wishing to impugn his good faith, it seems clear that he was carried away by his sanguine temperament and his firm belief in the success of the undertaking which he advocated. Although none of his expert advisers absolutely expressed dissent, all the evidence laid before us leads us to the conclusion that Mr Churchill had obtained their support to a less extent than he himself imagined.

Further, we are very clearly of opinion that the other members of the Council, and more especially the Chairman, should have encouraged the experts present to give their opinion, and, indeed, should have insisted upon their doing so; and, moreover, that if the latter had expressed any doubts a short adjournment should have taken place, in order to allow the matter to be further considered, possibly by the light of what other experts, not having seats on the Council, might have to say. It was common knowledge that naval opinion generally condemned the attack on forts by ships unaided by any military force. The Prime Minister was himself aware of this fact. Such being the case, it would appear that special care should have been taken to elicit a full expression of the opinions entertained by the experts, and that they should have been urged to state them in their own way. What actually happened was that the stress laid upon the unquestionable advantages which would accrue from success was so great that the disadvantages which would arise in the not improbable case of failure were insufficiently considered.

January 28th to February 16th, 1915

At the end of January the methods by which the Government hoped that the Fleet would reach Constantinople, if open to some objections on the ground of their practicability, were perfectly clear and comprehensible. They had resolved that an attempt should be made by the Fleet alone in order to force the passage of the Dardanelles. There was no intention of calling for military aid on any large scale. Admiral Carden thought that the operation was "worth trying", though at a later period, when he found that the defences "were much more extensive and powerful than had been anticipated", he changed his mind. In the first instance, he considered that only some small landing parties, consisting principally of Marines, would be required to complete the demolition of the forts. None of the responsible authorities appear to have paid much attention to the course of action which it would be necessary to adopt after the passage of the Dardanelles had been forced. Admiral Carden thought that "as the operations progressed he would receive further orders from the Admiralty as to the precise lines they wished him to act upon."

The fact that, even after the passage had been forced, communications with the Fleet in the Sea of Marmora might, to some extent, be impeded by such batteries as had not been destroyed, was recognised. But in London, where, according to General Callwell's evidence, the resistance likely to be offered by the Turks had, from the first, been greatly under-estimated, no great importance appears to have been attached to this argument.

Lord Kitchener was of opinion that directly the passage had been forced the Gallipoli garrison would evacuate the Peninsula, inasmuch as their communications with Constantinople would be cut off. In a memorandum dated March 23rd he wrote: "Once the ships are through, the position of the Gallipoli Peninsula ceases to be of any military importance." Moreover, he and others, including Lord Grey, confidently looked forward to a revolution taking place in Constantinople once the British Fleet appeared in the Sea of Marmora.

An officer from the Admiralty was asked the following question: "Did the intelligence in your possession favour the idea that the arrival of the British Fleet would have produced a revolution in Constantinople?" He replied: "Oh, yes; certainly it would. I feel no hesitation in saying that."

After the meeting of January 28th, the objective of the British Government remained the same, but the views entertained as to the means of realising it underwent a gradual but profound change. The necessity for employing a large military force became daily more apparent. The idea of a purely naval operation was gradually dropped. The prestige argument grew in importance. It does not appear that either the Cabinet or the War Council ever definitely discussed and deliberately changed the policy. General Callwell says that it would be very difficult to assign any date at which the change took place. "We drifted," he said, "into the big military attack."

At the evening meeting on January 28th, Lord Kitchener had stated very plainly, in connection with the question which was then under discussion of affording assistance to Serbia, that "we had at present no troops to spare." Mr Churchill was of a different opinion. He said: "I assert that in February there was nothing in the situation in France, or on the Russian front, or in this island, which would have prevented the War Office from concentrating within striking distance either of Salonika or the Dardanelles eight or nine, or even ten, infantry divisions." But, of course, on a matter of this sort Lord Kitchener's opinion carried the greatest weight. He would not go further than stating at a meeting on February 9th that "if the Navy required the assistance of the land forces at a later stage, that assistance would be forthcoming."

There appears, indeed, to be some reason for supposing that Lord Kitchener realised from the first that the aid of the Army would eventually be necessary at the Dardanelles. At a meeting on May 14th, he said: "I realised that if the Fleet failed to achieve their object, the Army would have to be employed to help the Navy through."

On February 15th, Sir Henry Jackson wrote a long memorandum, which was sent to Admiral Carden not as orders, but as "suggestions, to be adopted by him or not at his discretion." This memorandum concludes:

> The provision of the necessary military forces to enable the fruits of this heavy naval undertaking to be gathered must never be lost sight of; the transports carrying them should be in readiness to enter the Straits as soon as it is seen the forts at the Narrows will be silenced.
>
> To complete their destruction, strong military landing parties with strong covering forces will be necessary. It is considered, however, that the full advantage of the undertaking would only be obtained by the occupation of the Peninsula by a military force acting in conjunction with the naval operations, as the pressure of a strong field army of the enemy on the Peninsula would not only greatly harass the operations, but would render the passage of the Straits impracticable by any but powerfully armed vessels, even though all the permanent defences had been silenced.
>
> The naval bombardment is not recommended as a sound military operation, unless a strong military force is ready to assist in the operation, or, at least, follow it up immediately the forts are silenced.

A very important informal meeting of some of the Ministers took place on February 16th. It must be borne in mind that at that time no bombardment of the Gallipoli Peninsula had as yet taken place. The idea, therefore, of a purely naval operation was by no means abandoned. At the same time, owing to the repulse of the Turkish attack on Egypt, which had recently taken place, and to further changes in connection with plans in the Western theatre of war, to which we need not allude more particularly, it was decided to mass a considerable force in the Mediterranean to be used as occasion might require. Sir Maurice Hankey was, unfortunately, not present at this informal meeting, but the decisions which were arrived at were eventually incorporated into those of the War Council. They were as follows:

(1) The 29th Division, hitherto intended to form part of Sir John French's Army, to be despatched to Lemnos at the earliest possible date. It is hoped that it may be able to sail within nine or ten days.

(2) Arrangements to be made for a force to be despatched from Egypt, if required.

(3) The whole of the above forces, in conjunction with the battalions of Royal Marines already despatched, to be available in case of necessity to support the naval attack on the Dardanelles.

(4) Horse-boats to be taken out with the 29th Division, and the Admiralty to make arrangements to collect small craft, tugs, and lighters in the Levant.

(5) The Admiralty to build special transports and lighters suitable for the conveyance and landing of a force of 50,000 men at any point where they may be required.

Sir Maurice Hankey states that this was "the all-important decision from which sprang the joint naval and military enterprise against the Gallipoli Peninsula."This decision may,in fact,be regarded as the fourth phase of the trans-actions.It had not been definitely decided to use troops on a large scale, but they were to be massed so as to be in readiness should their assistance be required.

The bombardment of February 19th, 1915

The first bombardment of the outer forts took place on February 19th. In his report on the operation, dated March 17th, Admiral Carden said:

> The result of the day's action on the 19th February showed apparently that the effect of long-range bombardment by direct fire on modern earthwork forts is slight. Forts 1–4 appeared to be hit on many occasions by 12-inch common shell well placed; but when the ships closed in all four guns opened fire. And on the second day, although a heavy and prolonged fire at short range was poured into the forts, 70 per cent of the heavy guns were found to be in a serviceable condition when the demolition parties landed.

In his evidence before us he qualified this by saying:

> About 70 per cent of the guns appeared to the officers in command of the landing parties to be efficient; but I do not think it actually follows that they were. Their magazines were all blown up; their electrical communications to their firing point or whatever their communications were, were probably all destroyed, so that though the gun itself was intact, it does not at all follow that it could be made effective under a considerable time ... The forts were in such a state when the bombardment was finished that it would have taken a considerable time to make use of even the guns that were not actually disabled by having the muzzles blown off or having a charge put in the breach or something of that sort; it would have taken a considerable time, I think, to make use of that 70 per cent of guns. The personnel would have had to have been undisturbed for a considerable time to have come back to the forts and made use of that 70 per cent of guns. But 70 per cent of the guns were apparently intact on their mountings.

Vice-Admiral Sir Reginald Bacon, also, who can speak with authority on this subject, inasmuch as he has had, during the present war, a wide experience of bombardments in the North Sea, generally confirmed Admiral Carden's view."If," he said,"they actually destroyed 30 per cent in the short time they did very well."

It may here be mentioned that the decisions taken by the War Council on January 13th and 28th were not communicated to the whole of the Cabinet until a day or two before the bombardment took place. Mr Asquith informed us that the approval of the Cabinet was "unanimous".

Mr McKenna was the only Cabinet Minister who appeared before us and who was not present at the early meetings of the War Council. He was asked whether he concurred in the view that the Cabinet approved. His reply was as follows:

From Mr Asquith's point of view I readily understand how he came to that conclusion. The statement was made to us that the War Council had come to a unanimous decision that the bombardment of the Dardanelles should be undertaken, and we were told that all the necessary orders had been given, and that the bombardment would open within either twenty-four or forty-eight hours of the time at which he was speaking. So far as my recollection goes, there was no comment and certainly no criticism of Mr Asquith's statement, and consequently I do not think it was open to him to come to any other conclusion in the circumstances than that the Cabinet approved. But from my point of view and from the point of view of many of my colleagues with whom I have spoken on the subject, our view of the matter would be somewhat different. I should say for myself that I had not at the time the means of forming an opinion, much less of expressing one. We accepted without comment or criticism ... I fully recognise the justification for the Prime Minister in assuming our approval. Assent I distinguish from approval. He, having all the facts in his mind and not knowing how ignorant we were of the reasons which led up to it, assumed that assent was approval.

February 16th to February 26th, 1915

Sir Maurice Hankey states in his memorandum that a series of "acute discussions" took place at the War Council on February 19th, 24th and 26th. Subsequent events proved that the decisions taken during this period marked a very important epoch in the first stage of the Dardanelles operations. It was in the course of these ten days that the views of Lord Kitchener, who was in reality the leading spirit of the triumvirate which was conducting the war, underwent a considerable change. It is not necessary to quote at length the proceedings which took place during this period, but it is essential to gain a clear insight into the nature and importance of the decisions which were actually taken.

The first point which must strike any one who has carefully studied the documents and listened to the evidence submitted to us is that the original idea of possibly breaking off the attack on the Dardanelles, which had manifestly been waning ever since its first conception early in January, altogether disappeared from the purview of the responsible authorities by the middle of February. At the meeting on the 24th, Lord Kitchener said that he:

> felt that if the Fleet would not get through the Straits unaided, the Army ought to see the business through. The effect of a defeat in the Orient would be very serious. There could be no going back. The publicity of the announcement had committed us.

Lord Grey said that "failure would be morally equivalent to a great defeat on land." Whilst, however, the expression of these views is conclusive as showing that the original idea of limiting the operations wholly to the Fleet had been greatly modified, even if it had not been wholly abandoned, and that military operations on a large scale were contemplated, it is not easy to define with precision the nature of the programme which took its place. The scope of the intended military operations was left in doubt.

Lord Kitchener and others still clung to the idea that success was attainable by naval action alone. In the course of the discussion on February 24th he asked Mr Churchill whether he "contemplated a land attack." The latter said, in reply, that "he did not, but it was quite conceivable that the naval attack might be temporarily held up by mines, and some local military operation required."

The telegrams sent from the War Office give some indication of what was passing in Lord Kitchener's mind at this time.

On February 23rd, he sent through Sir John Maxwell, who was in Egypt, instructions to General Birdwood, who was about to proceed to the Dardanelles, to report

> whether it is considered by the Admiral that it will be necessary for troops to be employed to take the forts, and, if so, what force will be necessary; whether a landing force will be required of the troops to take the forts in reverse, and generally in what manner it is proposed to employ the troops.

On February 24th, he telegraphed to Sir John Maxwell:

> It is proposed that the Navy should silence the guns and destroy the forts with gun fire. It is not intended that parties should be landed on the Gallipoli Peninsula, except under cover of the naval guns, to help in total demolition when the ships get to close quarters.

On February 26th, Sir John Maxwell telegraphed that the French officer, who had formerly been military attaché at Constantinople, thought that "a military expedition is essential for opening the Dardanelles passage to the Allied Fleet, and it would be extremely hazardous to land on the Gallipoli Peninsula, as the peninsula is very strongly organised for defence."

On the evening of the same day, Lord Kitchener telegraphed to General Birdwood through Sir John Maxwell:

> The forcing of the Dardanelles is being undertaken by the Navy, and as far as can be foreseen at present the task of your troops, until such time as the passage has actually been secured, will be limited to minor operations, such as final destruction of batteries, after they have been silenced, under the covering fire of the battleships. It is possible, however, that howitzer batteries may be concealed inland with which the ships cannot deal effectively, and, if called upon by Admiral Carden, you might have to undertake special minor operations from within the Straits for dealing with these. Remember, however, that there are large enemy military forces stationed on both sides of the Straits, and you should not commit yourself to any enterprise of this class without aerial reconnaissance and assurance of ample covering fire by the Fleet. At any time during the bombardment of the Dardanelles you can, of course, apply for and obtain any additional forces from your corps in Egypt that you may require up to the total of its strength.

In the meanwhile, the Admiralty, in accordance with the decision arrived at on February 16th, had been preparing transports to convey the 29th Division to the Mediterranean. It was calculated that their departure would commence on the 22nd. On the 20th, however, Colonel Fitzgerald, Lord Kitchener's Personal Military Secretary, called at the Admiralty and stated that it had been decided that the 29th Division were not to go.

This decision led to an acute difference of opinion between Lord Kitchener and Mr Churchill. The discussions on the subject at the meetings of the War Council on February 24th and 26th were animated. Mr Churchill made "the strongest possible appeal" for the immediate despatch of the 29th Division. He formally recorded his dissent at the Division being retained in this country, and added that he "must disclaim all responsibility if disaster occurred in Turkey owing to the insufficiency of troops." Lord Kitchener, on the other hand, held that the Naval Division and Marines, together with the Australians and New Zealanders, whom it was proposed to bring from Egypt, constituted an adequate force and that the 33,000 men available from the 29th Division and a Territorial Division which it was proposed to send from home would not be likely to make the difference between success and failure. He was also uneasy about the position both in the Western and Russian theatres of war. He therefore declined to yield, and the Council, although Mr Churchill's views appear to have received some support, finally decided in accordance with Lord Kitchener's advice.

It is clear that, at the time of the discussion, Lord Kitchener still thought that the Fleet, unaided, would be able to obtain entrance into the Sea of Marmora. "He felt convinced, from his knowledge of Constantinople and the East, that the whole situation in Constantinople would change the moment the Fleet had secured a passage through the Dardanelles. We should be in a better position to judge the situation when the defences at the Narrows began to collapse."

With the decision finally taken on February 26th, the fifth phase in these transactions may be said to have closed. On February 16th, it had been decided to employ troops on a large scale. This decision still held good, but its execution was to be delayed. At the same time, the idea of forcing the Dardanelles by the action of the Fleet alone had not been abandoned.

February 26th to March 10th, 1915

Another meeting of the War Council was held on March 3rd. By this time Lord Kitchener's opposition to the despatch of the 29th Division had apparently weakened. On the question being raised by Mr Churchill, he said that "he proposed to leave the question open until March 10th, when he hoped to have heard from General Birdwood."

General Birdwood, however, arrived at the Dardanelles before the 10th. On the 5th, he telegraphed to Lord Kitchener:

> I am very doubtful if the Navy can force the passage unassisted. In any event the forcing of the passage must take a considerable time; the forts that have been taken up to the present have been visible and very easy, as the ships could stand off and shoot from anywhere, but inside the Straits the ships are bothered by unknown fire.

This was followed on the 6th by a telegram to the following effect:

> I have already informed you that I consider the Admiral's forecast is too sanguine, and though we may have a better estimate by March 12th, I doubt his ability to force the passage unaided.

On March 10th, Lord Kitchener, being then somewhat reassured as regards the position in other theatres of war, and being also possibly impressed by General Birdwood's reports, announced to the War Council that "he felt that the situation was now sufficiently secure to justify the despatch of the 29th Division."

The sixth phase in these transactions was thus reached. The decision of February 16th, the execution of which had been suspended on the 20th, again became operative on March 10th. In the meanwhile, three weeks of valuable time had been lost. The transports, which might have left on February 22nd, did not get away till March 16th.

It is with great reluctance and hesitation that we comment on these proceedings, for it is obvious that Lord Kitchener was mainly responsible for the decisions taken during the critical period between February 16th and March 10th, and it is quite possible that, were he alive, he might be able to throw a new light upon them. Nevertheless, we think it is incumbent on us to state the conclusions at which, with the evidence before us, we have arrived.

Lord Kitchener's position at this time was one of great difficulty. With the forces at his disposal he had to provide for home defence and also for maintaining an adequate force both in Flanders and Egypt. Was he to add to the demands which he had to meet the further liability of undertaking an additional military operation on a large scale in another and distant theatre of war? It can be no matter for surprise that he hesitated to do so. Subsequent events showed that the fears he entertained for the immediate future were groundless, but to impute any shadow of blame on that account would involve judging by the light of the wisdom which is the product of after-knowledge. Dealing, however, solely with the evidence which was available at the time, it certainly seems strange that the actualities of the situation should not have been more fully realised both by Lord Kitchener and his colleagues.

From the moment when large bodies of troops were massed in the immediate neighbourhood of the Dardanelles, even although they were not landed, the situation underwent a material change. Whatever may have been the intentions of the Government, the public opinion of the world must have been led to believe that an intention existed of making a serious attack both by land and sea. The loss-of-prestige argument, therefore, naturally acquired greater force than had been formerly the case. From the time the decision of February 16th was taken there were really only two alternatives which were thoroughly defensible.

One was to accept the view that by reason of our existing commitments elsewhere an adequate force could not be made available for expeditionary action in the Eastern Mediterranean; to face the possible loss of prestige which would have been involved in an acknowledgment of partial failure, and to have fallen back on the original plan of abandoning the naval attack on the Dardanelles, when once it became apparent that military operations on a large scale would be necessary.

The other was to have boldly faced the risks which would have been involved elsewhere and at once to have made a determined effort to force the passage of the Dardanelles by a rapid and well-organised combined attack in great strength. Unfortunately, the Government adopted neither of these courses. Time, as Mr Asquith very truly said to us, was all-important. Yet for at least three weeks the Government vacillated and came to no definite decision in one sense or the other.

The natural result ensued. The favourable moment for action was allowed to lapse. Time was given to the Turks, with the help of German officers, to strengthen their position, so that eventually the opposition to be encountered became of a far more formidable character than was originally to have been anticipated. Moreover, even when the decision was taken, it was by no means thorough.

As we shall presently show, the hope of dispensing altogether with military assistance, save in respect to what were called "minor operations", was not abandoned. We think that Mr Churchill was quite justified in attaching the utmost importance to the delays which occurred in despatching the 29th Division and the Territorial Division from this country.

Appointment of General Sir Ian Hamilton

Early in March it was decided to send out General Sir Ian Hamilton to command the troops which were being assembled in the neighbourhood of the Dardanelles. His instructions are dated March 13th. These and the conversation he had with Lord Kitchener immediately before his departure from London render it abundantly clear that the scope of the intended military operations was at that time not fully decided. Sir Ian Hamilton's instructions contain the following passages:

(1)   The Fleet have undertaken to force the passage of the Dardanelles. The employment of military forces on any large scale for land operations at

this juncture is only contemplated in the event of the Fleet failing to get through after every effort has been exhausted.

(2) Before any serious undertaking is carried out in the Gallipoli Peninsula, all the British military forces detailed for the expedition should be assembled, so that their full weight can be thrown in.

(3) Having entered on the project of forcing the Straits, there can be no idea of abandoning the scheme. It will require time, patience and methodical plans of co-operation between the naval and military commanders. The essential point is to avoid a check which will jeopardise our chances of strategical and political success.

(4) This does not preclude the probability of minor operations being engaged upon to clear areas occupied by the Turks with guns annoying the Fleet or for the demolition of forts already silenced by the Fleet. But such minor operations should be as much as possible restricted to the forces necessary to achieve the object in view, and should as far as practicable not entail permanent occupation of positions on the Gallipoli Peninsula.

Sir Ian Hamilton, in the evidence which he gave before us, dwelt strongly on the total absence of information furnished to him by the War Office Staff. No preliminary scheme of operations had been drawn up. "The Army Council had disappeared." No arrangements had been made about water supply. There was "a great want of staff preparation".

As regards the verbal instructions given to him by Lord Kitchener before he left London, he spoke as follows:

Q. Did you gather from that conversation with Lord Kitchener that he contemplated military operations then?

A. No; he repeatedly said—he broke in talking about landing by saying: 'I do not expect you to do it at all. I hope to get through without it.' He contemplated certainly landing on the Bosphorus.

Q. As far as I gather he contemplated that the Navy would do the forcing of the Straits?

A. Certainly.

Q. And you went out under that impression?

A. Yes, I did entirely.

Q. Until you got the telegram from Lord Kitchener of the 19th March those were the first instructions you received from him that you were to undertake landing operations to take the Peninsula?

A. No doubt in conversation with me Lord Kitchener did contemplate such a thing, except that he insisted I must not do so piecemeal.

Q. You recollect the telegram: 'You know my views that the passage of the Dardanelles must be forced,' and so on—'those operations must be undertaken after careful consideration.' I read those as rather peremptory instructions that you were to take the Peninsula?

A. Undoubtedly.

Q. That is how I read it, and that is the way you read it?

A.   Yes. I do not mean to say I had altogether parted with my discretion, and if I had chosen to say, 'This is altogether an impossibility', I might have said so, but I did not think so.

March 10th to March 16th, 1915

Between March 10th and March 16th some important telegrams were exchanged between the First Lord and Admiral Carden. On March 11th, the First Lord sent the following telegram to the Admiral:

[101] Personal and Secret. Caution and deliberate methods were emphasised in your original instructions, and the skill and patience which have enabled your progress to be carried thus far without loss are highly appreciated.

If, however, success cannot be obtained without loss of ships and men, results to be gained are important enough to justify such a loss. The whole operation may be decided and consequences of a decisive character upon the war may be produced by the turning of the corner Chanak; and we suggest for your consideration that a point has now been reached when it is necessary to choose favourable weather conditions to overwhelm forts of the Narrows at decisive range by bringing to bear upon them the fire of the largest possible number of guns, great and small. Under cover of this fire landing parties might destroy the guns of the forts, and sweeping operations to clear as much as possible of the mine-field might also be carried out.

It might be necessary to repeat the operation until the destruction of all the forts at the Narrows and the clearing of the approaches of mines had been accomplished.

We have no wish to hurry you or urge you beyond your judgment, but we recognise clearly that at a certain period in your operations you will have to press hard for a decision; and we desire to know whether, in your opinion, that period has now arrived. Every well-conceived action for forcing a decision, even should regrettable losses be entailed, will receive our support.

Before you take any decisive departure from the present policy we wish to hear your views.

At midnight on March 13th, Admiral Carden replied:

Your 101 is fully concurred in by me.

I consider the stage when vigorous sustained action is necessary for success has now been reached. I am of opinion that, in order to ensure my communication line immediately Fleet enters the Sea of Marmora, military operations on a large scale should be opened at once.

On March 15th, the First Lord sent the following further telegram to Admiral Carden:

[109] When General Hamilton arrives on Tuesday night concert with him in any military operations on large scale which you consider necessary ... The

29th Division (18,000 additional men) cannot arrive till the 2nd April.

We understand that a good clear passage is intended to be swept through the minefields, and the forts at the Narrows eventually attacked at close range. Further, that the battle fleet will support by its fire as necessary the operations against the forts or the light and movable armament, and that several days will be required to complete this task. We understand that you propose then to put the forts at the Narrows effectually out of action by engaging them at a decisive range, and that when this is done forts beyond will be attacked at convenience, and further sweeping carried out as necessary. Assuming this to be your intention, we cordially approve it and desire the scheme to be pressed forward. No time is to be lost, but there should be no undue haste. We gather that an attempt to rush the passage without having previously cleared a channel through the mines and destroyed the primary armament of the forts is not contemplated at this stage. No operation of this nature should be decided upon before consulting us. Before undertaking it careful study will be required of the parts to be played by the Army and Navy in close co-operation, and it might then be found that a naval rush will be costly, without decisive military action to take the Kilid Bahr plateau.

On March 16th, Admiral Carden replied:

Your 109. I will consult with General Hamilton as soon as he arrives. My intentions are exactly expressed by your second paragraph. Plans of operations are practically complete, and I hope to commence on the 17th March; but as it is essential to have good visibility and a wind which will prevent smoke interference, a later date may be chosen. Meanwhile, careful search is being made for mines in the area in which ships will have to manoeuvre ...

It is not intended to rush the passage before a channel is cleared.

On March 16th, Admiral Carden was obliged to resign his command for reasons wholly based on the state of his health.

The appointment of Admiral de Robeck

On March 17th, the First Lord sent the following telegram to Vice-Admiral de Robeck:

Secret and Personal. I am conferring upon you the command of the Mediterranean Detached Fleet, with fullest confidence in your ability. In doing so I presume that you fully agree with Admiralty telegrams 101 and 109 and your predecessor's replies thereto, and that in your independent and separate judgment the immediate operations proposed are practicable. Do not hesitate to say if you think otherwise. If you agree, the operations should be carried out without delay and without further reference at the first favourable opportunity. You should work in closest harmony with General Hamilton.

On the same day (March 17th) Admiral de Robeck replied:

[105] Personal and Secret. I am very grateful for your telegram. Telegrams mentioned by you meet with my full concurrence.

Weather permitting, I will proceed with operations to-morrow.

I am convinced that success depends on our ability to clear the mine-fields for forcing Narrows. To do this successfully the forts must be silenced while sweeping operations are in progress.

I have had to-day an entirely satisfactory interview with Generals Hamilton and D'Amade and Admiral Wemyss on my flagship.

The following extracts from Admiral de Robeck's evidence give some indication of the manner in which at the time he approached the subject:

Q.   Did you agree that that operation (i.e., the destruction of the forts without military aid) was practicable?

A.   I think everyone thought it was better to have a combined operation, but one was not consulted as to whether it was the right way to do it or not—we were told to bombard these forts, so we did it.

Q.   You were told from the Admiralty?

A.   Yes.

Q.   Was that your view of what Admiral Carden thought—that he was told to do it—that he had no discretion?

A.   I think he was directly told to get on and do it.

Q.   Therefore, you were in agreement with Admiral Carden as to the possibility of a successful issue to the operations which were then being proposed?

A.   Yes.

Q.   That is to say, that you thought the forts could be demolished one by one without the help of an army?

A.   Well, you see, I say that depended on clearing the mine-field. You see I add: "It depends on our ability to clear the mine-field in forcing the Narrows." That is telegram 105.

Q.   When you got the telegram from the Admiralty did you consider that there was any sort of moral pressure being put on you to agree, or that you were free to give an independent judgment?

A.   I think I would always give my opinion. Of course, one thing one must remember—at that time we had already started the operation. We had already bombarded the outer forts once, so that the operation had begun. In my opinion it would never have done then to have stopped at that moment, having once commenced the attack.

Q.   It would never have done on what ground?

A.   I think as regards the Turks.

Q.   On purely naval or on political grounds?

A.   On political grounds, I think; not on naval grounds.

Q.   You thought there would be very great loss of prestige if we had stopped then?

A.   Yes ...

Q.   ....

A. What was in our minds was that we would have got straight through to Constantinople, and it was generally anticipated that the arrival of the Fleet there would be the end of the ruling powers in Turkey. That was what we were always given to understand—that there would have been a revolution in Constantinople if we had arrived there with the Fleet ...

Q. As a matter of fact, you entirely relied upon the political situation—that there would be a revolution in Turkey and that the whole situation would be altered, so that you would not need supplies, and you would not need a force to make good your position?

A. We fully realised that we could only stay in the Marmora, if they did not alter their attitude, for a given length of time, say a fortnight, or at the most three weeks.

Q. If you had got through, transports could not have followed you up?

A. Then, I think not—not with the guns we could not get at.

Q. And if this political situation had not so changed to our advantage, and there had not been a revolution, our Fleet would have been bottled up there?

A. We should have had to come down again. Yes, like Admiral Duckworth ...

Q. What ground had you then on the 17th of March for concurrence?

A. The necessity for going on. We were sent there to carry out a certain object, and the thing was to try and do it.

Q. I think from the first when you went there you rather looked at the matter from the point of view of an Admiralty order to force the Dardanelles, and your job was to do it if you could?

A. Yes; that was our first object. Therefore, the order was to carry out a certain operation or try and do it, and we had to do the best we could.

From these explanations it may be gathered that Admiral de Robeck at the time considered the exclusively naval operation practicable if only the mine-field could be cleared, that his opinion was greatly influenced by political considerations, and particularly by the loss of prestige which would be involved if the attack were abandoned, and that the main reason which dictated the answer sent to the Admiralty questions on March 17th was "the necessity of going on." In fact, Admiral de Robeck thought he had orders to force the passage of the Dardanelles, and that it was his duty to do his best to carry out those orders.

The bombardment of March 18th

The facts connected with the bombardment on March 18th are already so well known that we need not dwell on them at any length. The results may be summarised as follows:

The *Irresistible*, the *Ocean* and the *Bouvet* were sunk, and the crew of the latter were nearly all lost.

Admiral de Robeck reported: "Squadron is ready for immediate action except as regards ships lost and damaged, but it is necessary to reconsider the plan of attack. A method of dealing with floating mines must be found."

Events from March 19th to March 23rd, 1915

On March 19th, Sir Ian Hamilton telegraphed to Lord Kitchener:

> I have not yet received any report on the naval action, but from what I actually saw of the extraordinarily gallant attempt made yesterday I am being most reluctantly driven towards the conclusion that the Dardanelles are less likely to be forced by battleships than at one time seemed probable, and that if the Army is to participate its operations will not assume the subsidiary form anticipated.
>
> The Army's share will not be a case of landing parties for the destruction of forts, etc., but rather a case of a deliberate and progressive military operation carried out in force in order to make good the passage of the Navy.

Lord Kitchener at once replied in the following terms:

> You know my views that the passage of the Dardanelles must be forced, and that if large military operations on the Gallipoli Peninsula by the Army are necessary to clear the way, those operations must be undertaken after careful consideration of the local defences, and must be carried through.

We have already mentioned that Sir Ian Hamilton regarded this telegram in the light of a "peremptory instruction that he was to take the Peninsula." We think that he was justified in doing so.

On March 22nd, Sir Ian Hamilton again telegraphed to Lord Kitchener stating that he proposed to go to Alexandria. On March 23rd, Lord Kitchener telegraphed to Sir Ian Hamilton:

> I hear that April 14th is considered by you as about the date for commencement of military operations if the Dardanelles have not been forced by the Fleet before that date. I think that you had better know at once that I regard any such postponement as far too long. I should like to know how soon you could act on shore.

These telegrams are conclusive proof that Lord Kitchener had by that time wholly abandoned the idea of a purely naval operation, and realised the fact that military operations on a large scale were necessary. The telegrams also prove that Lord Kitchener, in contemplating military action, had no clear idea as to when a landing could be made. As a matter of fact the landing did not take place until April 25th.

On March 23rd, Sir Ian Hamilton telegraphed to Lord Kitchener:

I have now conferred with Admiral and we are equally convinced that to enable the Fleet effectively to force the passage of the Dardanelles the co-operation of the whole military force will be necessary.

The first impression produced by the receipt of the news of the bombardment was that the naval operations should continue in spite of the losses which had been incurred. The following statement in Mr Churchill's narrative shows what happened.

I regarded it as only the first of several days' fighting, though the loss in ships sunk or disabled was unpleasant. It never occurred to me for a moment that we should not go on, within the limits of what we had decided to risk, till we reached a decision one way or the other. I found Lord Fisher and Sir Arthur Wilson in the same mood. Both met me that morning (the 19th) with expressions of firm determination to fight it out. The First Sea Lord immediately ordered two battleships, *London* and *Prince of Wales*, to reinforce Admiral de Robeck's fleet to replace casualties, in addition to the *Queen* and *Implacable*, which were on the way.

It should also be added that the French Ministry of Marine ordered another old battleship, the *Henri IV*, to replace the *Bouvet* which had been lost. The first telegrams received from Admiral de Robeck dated March 19th and 20th clearly indicate that he shared the view entertained at the Admiralty. On the latter date, especially, he said:

Dardanelles will not be entered by any ships unless everything is ready for sustained attack. Meantime, in order to draw off some of enemy's field guns, feints at landing in various places will be made.

A meeting of the War Council was held on the morning of the 19th, at which it was decided "to inform Vice-Admiral de Robeck that he could continue the naval operation against the Dardanelles if he thought fit."

On March 23rd, however, Admiral de Robeck changed his views. He spoke of the "mine menace" being "much greater than we expected." He said that time would be required for "careful and thorough treatment, both in respect of mines and floating mines." He added: "Time will be required for this, but arrangements can be made by the time the army will be ready. A decisive operation about the middle of next month appears to me better than to take great risks for what may well be only half measures." He further said: "It does not appear to me practicable to land a sufficient force inside the Dardanelles to carry out this service. This view is shared by General Hamilton."

On the 26th, Admiral de Robeck further telegraphed:

The check on the 18th March is not, in my opinion, decisive, but on the 22nd March I met General Hamilton and heard his views, and I now think that, to obtain important results and to achieve the object of the campaign, a combined operation will be essential.

This telegram, Mr Churchill says, "involved a complete change of plan and was a vital decision. I regretted it very much. I believed then, as I believe now, that we were separated by very little from complete success."

The whole question was then discussed at great length at the Admiralty. Mr Churchill records:

> I proposed that we should direct the Admiral to renew the naval attack, according to his previous intention. The First Sea Lord, however, did not agree; nor did Sir Arthur Wilson; nor did Sir Henry Jackson. Lord Fisher took the line that hitherto he had been willing to carry the enterprise forward, because it was supported and recommended by the Commander on the spot. But now that Admiral de Robeck and Sir Ian Hamilton had decided upon a joint operation, we were bound to accept their view.
>
> I do not at all blame Lord Fisher for this decision. The arguments for it were very strong indeed. But so were the arguments against it. Both the Prime Minister and Mr Balfour, with whom I discussed the matter, were inclined to my view, but as our professional advisers and the Admiral on the spot were against it, it was impossible to go further, and I bowed to their decision. But with regret and anxiety.

This was the last phase of the "origin and inception" period. From this time onward two points became perfectly clear. One was that the Government had no intention of abandoning the attack on the Dardanelles; the second was that the attack would be made both by the Navy and by military forces who would be employed on a large scale.

Summary

The various stages through which these transactions passed may be summarised as follows:

(1) As early as November, 1914, the idea of attacking the Dardanelles had been mooted, but there does not appear at that time to have been any sort of intention of making a purely naval attack.

(2) On January 3rd, 1915, the Russian Government were informed that a "demonstration" would be made against the Turks in some quarter.

(3) On January 13th, the Admiralty were instructed to "prepare" for an attack on the Dardanelles. It was understood at the time by the First Lord, and apparently by others, that this involved approval of the attack. The intention at the time was that the operations should be purely naval and that no troops, save small parties for such purposes as the demolition of forts, should be used. It was thought that if the experience gained by attacking the outer forts was unsatisfactory, the attack might be broken off without any loss of prestige.

(4) On January 28th, the decision to attack the Dardanelles by ships alone was definitely confirmed. There was still no intention of using troops, save for minor operations.

(5) On February 16th, it was decided to mass large bodies of troops in the neighbourhood of the Dardanelles with a view to assisting further operations when once the Fleet had forced a passage.

(6) On February 19th, the first bombardment took place. The results were not decisive, but at the same time were fairly satisfactory.

(7) On February 20th, principally owing to the anxiety felt by Lord Kitchener in respect to the state of affairs in other theatres of war, the decision to send troops from England to the Dardanelles was suspended.

(8) On March 10th, Lord Kitchener resolved to sanction the departure of troops from England.

(9) On March 18th, the second bombardment took place. The losses incurred were heavy, but, in the first instance, both Admiral de Robeck and the officials at the Admiralty wished to continue the purely naval attack.

(10) On March 23rd, owing to representations made by Admiral de Robeck and Sir Ian Hamilton, it was decided to postpone further operations until adequate military forces could be assembled. The idea of making a purely naval attack was definitely abandoned.

THE RESULTS OF THE OPERATIONS

There can be no doubt that, as a result of these and subsequent operations the main objective, as defined in the decision of the War Council on January 13th, was not attained. The attempt to force the Dardanelles and to reach Constantinople failed.

It would, however, be an exaggeration to say that the expedition, considered as a whole, was a complete failure. Such was by no means the case. The enterprise was originally undertaken in order to create a diversion in favour of the Russians. In this respect it may be said to have been very fairly successful.

Another point to which great importance was attached was to influence the attitude of all the Balkan States, and especially to secure the neutrality of Bulgaria. That neutrality was not secured, but it can scarcely be doubted that, had it not been for the Dardanelles expedition, Bulgaria would have joined the Central Powers at a far earlier date than was actually the case. Further, a large force of Turks, which might have been employed in other theatres of war, was for some long while immobilised.

The Prime Minister spoke very decisively on these points. We give the following extracts from his evidence:

Q.   In spite of the fact that it was a failure in one sense, do you think it was a success in another, and that if you had not carried out that expedition to the Dardanelles, the position of the Allies would have been very much worse than it is now?

A.   Yes, I am unhesitatingly of that opinion. I say so now, after all the experience we have gained, and after what one must admit to have been the ultimate failure of the expedition. I say deliberately that there is no operation in the whole of this war which promised better results than the Dardanelles operation. If it had succeeded, and it would have succeeded but for things which in the course of your inquiry you will come across and no doubt pronounce upon, in my judgment it would have produced a far greater effect upon the whole conduct of the war than anything that has been done in any other sphere of the war.

Q.   I think nobody can doubt that for a moment, but it does not go very far. If successful it would have had an enormous effect; but the question I wanted to ask you was this; even as it was, you think the effect was very beneficial?

A.   I do, even though it failed. If you like I will tell you why.

Q.   Yes, please.

A.   I will give you two reasons. There are a great many I might give, but I will give two. In the first place, it undoubtedly staved off and postponed for months the adhesion of Bulgaria to the Central Powers. There is no doubt whatever about that. In the second place—and this was the point Lord Kitchener always insisted upon up to the end—he said to me a hundred times it contained and immobilised very nearly 300,000 Turkish soldiers for the best part of nine months, who otherwise would have been a most formidable accretion to the enemy forces. Even though it failed, I consider it had very effective and powerful results.

Q.   You feel very confident that the Bulgarians would have gone in on the German side sooner if it had not been for that?

A.   Yes, I am certain of it.

Lord Grey also said:

A.   I have no doubt whatever that some untoward consequence would have happened if it had not been for the Dardanelles operations. Whether the staving off of those untoward consequences was worth the cost of life and the expenditure of energy, ending of course in failure to get through, is a matter really on which everyone must form their own opinion. I can only state that there were certain consequences which would have happened sooner if the Dardanelles Expedition had not been going on. I should strongly controvert any statement that the expedition was of no use at all.

Q.   You think it was decidedly of use?

A.   Yes, I think it was decidedly of use; but if you put the question whether it was worth such a tremendous expenditure of effort, that must remain a matter of opinion.

Q.   But it did gain valuable time?

A.   It did gain valuable time.

Q.   And heartened the Russians?

A.   Oh, yes, it did.

We are generally in agreement with these views expressed by Mr Asquith and Lord Grey, but we regard Lord Kitchener's estimate of the number of Turkish troops immobilised for nearly nine months as conjectural.

Whether the advantages obtained were in any degree commensurate with the loss of valuable lives and treasure which was incurred, must, of course, as Lord Grey very truly said, remain a matter of opinion, but there can be no doubt that those advantages were important.

We repeat that it would be an exaggeration to regard the Dardanelles Expedition as a complete failure. We have already mentioned that the loss of prestige in abandoning the expedition, which at one time caused great anxiety, was in reality inappreciable.

It is interesting, but perhaps not very profitable, to speculate on what might have occurred if, subsequent to the bombardment of March 18th, the naval attack had been at once pressed on aided by such troops as were then on the spot. We have already stated that Mr Churchill was strongly in favour of adopting this course, and that he received some support both from Mr Asquith and Mr Balfour. The idea, however, had to be abandoned because the weight of both naval and military authority was much opposed to it. But there were exceptions. Commodore de Bartolomé agreed with Mr Churchill. Sir Ian Hamilton also stated that General Birdwood wished to "land at once," and he added "I think there was a good deal to be said for it." Sir Ian, however, held that "Lord Kitchener's original orders not to land if he could avoid it" held good.

Enver Pasha, at a much later date, is reported to have said:

> If the English had only the courage to rush more ships through the Dardanelles they could have got to Constantinople, but their delay enabled us thoroughly to fortify the Peninsula, and in six weeks' time we had taken down there over 200 Austrian Skoda guns.

At the time of the bombardment it was suspected by the Admiralty that the forts of the Dardanelles were getting short of ammunition. Evidence was subsequently obtained which showed that the suspicion was well-grounded.

Mr Asquith, in dealing with this branch of the question, said:

> I have always thought myself—but it is an opinion of no value, because it is the opinion of a layman—that if they had pushed then they would have got through, in which case the results would have been incalculable.

Whatever weight may be attached to these opinions and reports it must be remembered that out of the sixteen ships which attacked the Straits on March 18th, three were sunk and four were rendered unfit for further immediate action. Had the attack been renewed within a day or two there is no reason to suppose that the proportion of casualties would have been less, and, if so, even had the second attack succeeded, a very weak force would have been left for subsequent naval operations.

CONCLUSIONS

We trust that we have given so full a summary of the somewhat involved events, which have formed the subject of our inquiry, that any member of the public who reads this report will be able to draw his own conclusions. Those conclusions, it may be anticipated with some confidence, will vary.

The facts, indeed, are such that no one, who approaches the subject in a thoroughly judicial spirit, will be inclined to dogmatise about them. Notably, there is wide room for difference of opinion as to the relative degree of responsibility, as also to the amount of praise or blame which may reasonably be assigned to the principal authorities and departments concerned. All we can say is that we have endeavoured to the best of our ability to assess this responsibility, judging wholly by the evidence which has been laid before us to the complete exclusion of all other considerations of whatsoever character. It is for others to judge how far we have succeeded in this attempt.

The general conclusions at which we have arrived are as follows:

(a) The question of attacking the Dardanelles was, on the initiation of Mr Churchill, brought under the consideration of the War Council, on November 25th, 1914, as "the ideal method" for defending Egypt.

(b) It may reasonably be assumed that, inasmuch as all the authorities concerned were, *prima facie*, in favour of a joint naval and military rather than a purely naval attack, such attack, if undertaken at all, would have been of the former rather than of the latter character had not other circumstances led to a modification of the programme.

(c) The communication from the Russian Government on January 2nd introduced a fresh element into the case. The British Government considered that something must be done in response to it, and in this connection the question of attacking the Dardanelles was again raised. The Secretary of State for War declared that there were no troops immediately available for operations in the East. This statement was accepted by the War Council, who took no steps to satisfy themselves by reports or estimates as to what troops were available then or in the near future. Had this been done we think that it would have been ascertained that sufficient troops would have been available for a joint naval and military operation at an earlier date than was supposed. But this matter was not adequately investigated by the War Council. Thus the question before the War Council on January 13th was whether no action of any kind should, for the time being, be undertaken, or whether action should be taken by the Fleet alone, the navy being held to be the only force available.

(*d*) The political arguments which were adduced to the War Council in favour of prompt and effective action, if such were practicable, were valid and of the highest importance, but the practicability of whatever action was proposed was of equal importance.

(*e*) Mr Churchill appears to have advocated the attack by ships alone before the War Council on a certain amount of half-hearted and hesitating expert opinion, which favoured a tentative or progressive scheme, beginning with an attack upon the outer forts. This attack, if successful, was to be followed by further operations against the main defences of the Narrows. There does not appear to have been direct support or direct opposition from the responsible naval and military advisers, Lord Fisher and Sir James Wolfe Murray, as to the practicability of carrying on the operation as approved by the War Council, viz., "To bombard and take the Gallipoli Peninsula, with Constantinople as its objective."

(*f*) The First Sea Lord and Sir Arthur Wilson, who was the only other naval adviser present at the War Council, expressed no dissent. Lord Kitchener, who occupied a commanding position at the time the decision was taken, was in favour of the project. Both Lord Fisher and Sir Arthur Wilson would have preferred a joint naval and military attack, but they did not express to the War Council and were not asked to express any opinion on the subject, and offered no objection to the naval operations as they considered them experimental and such as could be discontinued if the first results obtained were not satisfactory. Moreover, such objections as they entertained were mainly based on their preference for the adoption of other plans in other theatres of war.

(*g*) We think that there was an obligation first on the First Lord, secondly on the Prime Minister and thirdly on the other Members of the War Council to see that the views of the naval advisers were clearly put before the Council; we also think that the naval advisers should have expressed their views to the Council, whether asked or not, if they considered that the project which the Council was about to adopt was impracticable from a naval point of view.

(*h*) Looking at the position which existed on January 13th, we do not think the War Council were justified in coming to a decision without much fuller investigation of the proposition which had been suggested to them that "the Admiralty should prepare for a naval expedition in February to bombard and take the Gallipoli Peninsula with Constantinople as its objective." We do not consider that the urgency was such as to preclude a short adjournment to enable the naval and military advisers of the Government to make a thorough examination of the question. We hold that the possibility of making a surprise amphibious attack on the Gallipoli Peninsula offered such great military and political advantages that it was mistaken and ill-advised to sacrifice this possibility by hastily deciding to undertake a purely naval attack which from its nature could not attain completely the objects set out in the terms of the decision.

(*i*) We are led to the conclusion that the decision taken on February 16th to mass troops in the neighbourhood of the Dardanelles marked a very critical stage of the whole operation. It ought to have been clear at the time that, when this was once done, although the troops might not have been actually landed, it would become apparent to all the world that a really serious attack was intended, and that withdrawal could no longer be effected without running a serious risk of loss of prestige. We consider that at that moment, inasmuch as time was all-important, no compromise was possible between making an immediate and vigorous effort to ensure success at the Dardanelles by a joint naval and military occupation, or falling back on the original intention of desisting from the naval attack if the experiences gained during the bombardment were not satisfactory.

(*j*) On the 20th February Lord Kitchener decided that the 29th Division, part of the troops which by the decision of February 16th were to have been sent to the East, should not be sent at that time, and Colonel Fitzgerald by his order instructed the Director of Naval Transports that the transports for that division and the rest of the Expeditionary Force would not be required. This was done without informing the First Lord, and the despatch of the troops was thus delayed for three weeks. This delay gravely compromised the probability of success of the original attack made by the land forces, and materially increased the difficulties encountered in the final attack some months later.

(*k*) We consider that, in view of the opinions expressed by the naval and military authorities on the spot, the decision to abandon the naval attack after the bombardment of March 18th with the loss of three ships was inevitable.

(*l*) There was no meeting of the War Council between March 19th and May 14th. Meanwhile important land operations were undertaken. We think that before such operations were commenced the War Council should have carefully reconsidered the whole position. In our opinion the Prime Minister ought to have summoned a meeting of the War Council for that purpose, and if not summoned, the other Members of the War Council should have pressed for such a meeting. We think this was a serious omission.

(*m*) We consider that the responsibility of those members of the Cabinet who did not attend the meetings of the War Council was limited to the fact that they delegated their authority to their colleagues who attended those meetings.

(*n*) We are of opinion that Lord Kitchener did not sufficiently avail himself of the services of his General Staff, with the result that more work was undertaken by him than was possible for one man to do, and confusion and want of efficiency resulted.

(*o*) We are unable to concur in the view set forth by Lord Fisher that it was his duty, if he differed from the Chief of his Department, to maintain silence at the Council or to resign. We think that the adoption of any such principle generally would impair the efficiency of the public service.

(*p*) We think that, although the main object was not attained, certain important political advantages, upon the nature of which we have already dwelt, were secured by the Dardanelles expedition. Whether those advantages were worth the loss of life and treasure involved is, and must always remain, a matter of opinion.

We cannot close this report without expressing our high appreciation of the services rendered to us both by Sir Maurice Hankey, whose memoranda, which we have frequently quoted, have been of the utmost service to us, and by our able secretary, Mr Grimwood Mears.

All which we humbly report for your Majesty's gracious consideration.

CROMER
ANDREW FISHER
THOMAS MACKENZIE
FREDK. CAWLEY
J. A. CLYDE
STEPHEN L. GWYNN
W. H. MAY
NICHOLSON
W. PICKFORD

E. GRIMWOOD MEARS,
Secretary
February 12th, 1917

MINUTE OF THE RIGHT HONOURABLE ANDREW FISHER

I am not in agreement with the majority as regards the form their Report takes, though I readily recognise they have drawn it up as it is with the sole aim of helping others who may read it to arrive at the conclusions they believe to be justified by what they have seen and heard as Commissioners.

Though I have no rooted objections to the recitation of introductory events and of established facts which are necessary for an intelligent understanding of the points at issue before the Commission, I am of opinion it is unwise for Commissioners (in this case a jury of the nation) to traverse particular portions of the evidence which have led them to arrive at their verdict. I am in a greater difficulty to understand the point of view which, whilst arriving at certain conclusions upon the evidence, cheerfully admits that the perusal of the same evidence may lead other people—not members of the Commission—to other conclusions; the net result suggesting an absence of decision which will go far to destroy the whole value of the findings.

The particular conclusions of the Majority Report from which I dissent are as follows:

(g)   ... we also think that the naval advisers should have expressed their views to the Council, whether asked or not, if they considered that the project which the Council was about to adopt was impracticable from a naval point of view.

(o)   We are unable to concur in the view set forth by Lord Fisher that it was his duty, if he differed from the Chief of his Department, to maintain silence at the Council or to resign. We think that the adoption of any such principle generally would impair the efficiency of the public service.

I dissent in the strongest terms from any suggestion that the departmental advisers of a Minister in his company at a Council Meeting should express any views at all other than to the Minister and through him, unless specifically invited to do so. I am of the opinion it would seal the fate of responsible government if servants of the State were to share the responsibility of Ministers to Parliament and to the people on matters of public policy.

The Minister has command of the opinions and views of all officers of the Department he administers on matters of public policy. Good stewardship demands from Ministers of the Crown frank, fair, full statements of all opinions of trusted experienced officials to colleagues, when they have direct reference to matters of high policy.

ANDREW FISHER

DISSENT AND SUGGESTION BY THE HONOURABLE SIR THOMAS MACKENZIE, KCMG

Whilst agreeing that if conclusions are introduced at this stage it is necessary to support them by the descriptive narrative (although, in my opinion, such narrative should not embody the findings arrived at), I take exception to certain conclusions, which should, I think, be struck out of the Report.

We are only at the "Origin and Inception" stage of the inquiry, and it seems to me premature to express any opinion on general results at this point of the proceedings. Sufficient evidence has not been taken to enable us to arrive at a decision on the objects attained by the operations. Connecting this section with paragraph (*p*) of the "Conclusions", I do not think the Commission is as yet justified in reaching the conclusions mentioned. It will be necessary for us to investigate such questions as the conduct of the offensive on the Peninsula, and the carrying out of the various subsidiary operations, etc., before we can estimate with any degree of accuracy the costs involved and form an opinion as to the results of the enterprise, for only then will events assume their true perspective.

Indeed, it may well be that our further investigations will shed a different light on the results attained, and reveal facts which may have the effect of materially altering the judgment expressed in the two paragraphs under notice. They may even demand inquiries being instituted outside the scope of those entrusted to the Commission; and, in any case, it is only after we have brought under review all the available evidence on the Dardanelles campaign as a whole that we shall be able to estimate cost and assess results and also apportion blame or credit where called for or merited.

I also dissent from paragraphs (*g*) and (*o*) of the "Conclusions". I hold that if the departmental adviser of a Minister states his opinion to his

Minister, he has discharged what may be reasonably considered to be his official duty. And in such a case as we have under notice, where the Minister and his adviser were both present at a meeting of the War Council, I feel that the adviser had fulfilled all that was required of him, seeing that he was not asked to express his views to the meeting. The Minister, and not the adviser, must be regarded as responsible for representing the departmental view, but in such circumstances the Minister should have stated his adviser's opinion fully to the assembly.

The report shows that this view does not commend itself to the majority of the Commission, and as it is of importance that the opinions of such expert advisers should at all times be readily available and given in connection with the deliberations of the War Committee, and to assist members in arriving at right conclusions, I am of opinion that the Chief of Staff and the First Sea Lord should be appointed members of the War Committee.

THOMAS MACKENZIE

MINUTE AND MEMORANDUM BY MR ROCH

MINUTE BY MR ROCH

While I concur in some of the conclusions contained in this report, I regret that I am unable to sign it.

The conclusions which I have come to, and the review of the evidence which, I think, justifies those conclusions are contained in a separate memorandum.

22nd *December*, 1916   WALTER ROCH

MEMORANDUM BY MR ROCH

Consideration of the scope of the inquiry showed that the story of these operations fell naturally into three chapters. First, the circumstances leading up to the campaign, second, the conception, execution and failure of the plan for forcing the Dardanelles by ships alone, and third, the attempt and failure to take the Gallipoli Peninsula by military operations aided by the Fleet.

This memorandum is presented dealing with the first two chapters.

The policy and higher direction of the war, during the period under review, were in the hands of a body known as the War Council. This body— a development of the Committee of Imperial Defence—consisted of the following Cabinet Ministers:

Mr Asquith (Prime Minister)
Lord Haldane (Lord Chancellor)

Lord Kitchener (Secretary of State for War)
Mr Lloyd George (Chancellor of the Exchequer)
Sir E. Grey (Secretary of State for Foreign Affairs)
Mr Churchill (First Lord of the Admiralty), and
Lord Crewe (Secretary of State for India)

Its Councils were attended regularly by Mr A. J. Balfour, Lord Fisher, Sir Arthur Wilson, Sir Jas. Wolfe Murray and Lt.-Col. Hankey, who acted as Secretary.

Particular meetings were attended by other Cabinet Ministers and various officers, including Sir John French, the Commander-in-Chief of the British Forces in France.

During the same period the naval strategy of the war was controlled by a body known as "The War Group" presided over by Mr Churchill as First Lord and consisting of:

Lord Fisher (First Sea Lord)
Admiral Oliver (Chief of the Staff)
Admiral of the Fleet, Sir A. Wilson, and
Commander de Bartolomé (Naval Secretary to Mr Churchill)

The consultations of this body were on occasions attended by Sir Henry Jackson, who was serving on Admiral Oliver's staff.

The Board of Admiralty occupied a subordinate position. Its members (other than Mr Churchill and Lord Fisher) were not consulted on naval policy or even kept well-informed on naval events. They were merely managers of the different departments assigned to them.

At the War Councils Mr Churchill was the spokesman of the Admiralty, attended by Lord Fisher and Sir Arthur Wilson.

Lord Fisher and Sir Arthur Wilson both insisted that they were not members of this Council in the same sense as the Cabinet Ministers who were present. They considered themselves to be merely naval advisers, and only entitled to express their opinions when asked for them.

Neither Mr Churchill nor the Cabinet Ministers who were members of the Council accepted this view, and were equally insistent that they assumed the assent of both Lord Fisher and Sir Arthur Wilson to be implied unless they expressed their dissent.

The military strategy and conduct of the war were under the complete and sole control of Lord Kitchener. He, in effect, combined in himself the functions and duties of Secretary of State and Commander-in-Chief. Under his régime the General Staff was not consulted and really ceased to exist.

Lord Kitchener was attended at the War Council by Sir James Wolfe Murray, the Chief of the Imperial General Staff.

At these Councils Sir Jas. Wolfe Murray stated that he neither gave nor was asked for any opinion.

The problem of forcing the Dardanelles had been considered in recent years on different occasions and under varying circumstances:

(a) By Lord Fisher when the Mediterranean Fleet under his command lay at Lemnos during the South African War.
(b) By Lord Fisher in 1904 when as First Sea Lord he satisfied himself that "even with military co-operation the operation was mightily hazardous."
(c) By the Committee of Imperial Defence in 1906. The General Staff was then opposed to any naval or military action at the Dardanelles.

This view was substantially concurred in by the Director of Naval Intelligence, the sole difference of opinion recorded between the General Staff and the Director of Naval Intelligence being that:

> While the former appear to regard the enterprise in question as too hazardous, the latter, while recognising the great risk involved, is of opinion that it is within the bounds of possibility that an operation of this nature might be forced upon us ... and that in such an event there is no reason to despair of success, though at the expense, in all likelihood, of heavy sacrifices.

The possibility of an attack on the Dardanelles was discussed, for the first time, at a War Council on 25th November, 1914.★

Mr Churchill then expressed the view that the best way of defending Egypt was an attack on some part of the coast of Asiatic Turkey, and suggested an attack on the Gallipoli Peninsula, which, if successful, would give us the control of the Dardanelles, and enable us to dictate terms at Constantinople.

A feint attack on the Gallipoli Peninsula—the real objective being some other point on the Turkish Coast—was discussed.

Owing to the shortage of merchant shipping, occasioned largely by military demands, the project was put on one side.

By the end of November, 1914, the great German effort to reach the Channel Ports had been defeated at the first battle of Ypres, and a winter lull set in during the succeeding weeks.

The end of 1914, and the beginning of 1915, was spent by the War Council in attempts to arrive at their future military policy, and to make plans for the employment of the new armies in the spring.

On the 28th December, 1914, a memorandum was circulated to the members of the War Council by Sir Maurice Hankey.

This memorandum called attention to the "remarkable deadlock" which had occurred in the Western theatre of war. It invited consideration of the possibility of seeking some other outlet for the effective employment of the new armies. It further suggested that Germany could perhaps "be struck

★ Turkey had declared war against Britain on 31st October 1914.

most effectively, and with the most lasting results on the peace of the world, through her Allies, and particularly Turkey." And asked the question whether it was not possible "now to weave a web around Turkey, which will end her career as a European power?"

This was followed on the 1st January by a memorandum from Mr Lloyd George also pointing to the East as the true objective and outlining a far-reaching policy directed against Austria in co-operation with the Greeks, Romanians and Serbians, and also against Turkey.

Other plans and policies were discussed, producing three schools of thought at the War Council.

(a) One school holding that all efforts should be concentrated in the Western theatre of war, since there and there alone could decisive success be achieved.

(b) A second school maintaining that a complete deadlock had already set in the West and advising operations designed to obtain the support of Italy and Romania against Austria, secure Greek co-operation, and achieve the destruction of Turkey as a European power.

(c) A third school advocating the intermediate view that the theory of a complete deadlock in the West was not yet proved or disproved, and that our main military efforts should be concentrated on the Western line until failure showed the necessity of seeking other theatres.

It is remarkable that none of these various policies and plans were ever discussed by the War Council in the light of written detailed staff estimates of men and munitions.

While the minds of the members of the War Council were engaged on these general discussions, on the 2nd January, 1915, a telegram was received at the Foreign Office from the British Ambassador at Petrograd conveying a request from the [Russian Military Authorities] to Lord Kitchener, that a naval or military demonstration against the Turks should be arranged in order to relieve the pressure felt by the Russian troops at the Caucasus.

To this telegram, Lord Kitchener on his own initiative replied through the Foreign Office on the following day, promising to make a demonstration, but expressing a doubt as to whether any such steps would cause any serious withdrawal by Turkish troops.

On the 2nd January, the position was discussed by Lord Kitchener and Mr Churchill and Lord Kitchener then asked Mr Churchill if the Navy could make a demonstration at the Dardanelles.

Lord Kitchener on the same day in a letter to Mr Churchill expressed the view that he did not see "that we can do anything that will seriously help the Russians in the Caucasus ... We have no troops to land anywhere. The only place that a demonstration might have any effect in stopping reinforcements going East would be the Dardanelles ... We shall not be ready for anything big for some months." Simultaneously Lord Fisher expressed his view of the position in a private letter to Mr Churchill. "I consider the attack on Turkey holds the field, but only if it is immediate; however, it won't be. We shall decide on a futile bombardment of the Dardanelles, which wears out the invaluable guns of the *Indefatigable*, which probably will require replacement. What good resulted from the last bombardment? Did it move a single Turk from the Caucasus?"

And he concluded by sketching out an ambitious policy requiring the co-operation of Romania, Bulgaria, Greece and Serbia, and necessitating the withdrawal of substantial forces from France.

On the 4th January, Lord Fisher further embodied his views in a formal Minute to Mr Churchill.

It seems necessary to lay down in the first place what the British Naval policy is:

(a)   In the first place that policy is to conserve our naval superiority over the Germans, and in no wise jeopardise by minor operations, whose cumulative effect is to wear out our vessels, and incur losses in ships and men. We cannot afford any more losses or any further deterioration, except for absolutely imperative operations.

(b)   The naval advantages of the possession of Constantinople, and the getting of wheat from the Black Sea, are so overwhelming that I consider Colonel Hankey's plans for Turkish operations vital and imperative, and very pressing.

During the next few days, the following telegrams were exchanged between Mr Churchill and Admiral Carden, who was then in command of the Mediterranean Fleet.

(1) 3rd January: From Mr Churchill to Admiral Carden:

Are you of opinion that it is practicable to force the Dardanelles by the use of ships alone? It is assumed that older battleships would be employed, that they would be furnished with mine sweepers, and that they would be preceded by colliers or other merchant vessels as sweepers, and the importance of the results would justify severe losses. Let me know what your views are.

(2) January 5th: From Admiral Carden to Mr Churchill:

I do not think that the Dardanelles can be rushed, but they might be forced by extended operations with a large number of ships.

(3) January 6th: From Mr Churchill to Admiral Carden:

High authorities here concur in your opinion. Forward detailed particulars showing what force would be required for extended operations. How do you think it should be employed, and what results can be gained?

Admiral Oliver, though doubtful, if he saw this last telegram, did concur with it.

Lord Fisher did not see it.

Sir Henry Jackson did not remember whether he was consulted with regard to it or not.

Mr Churchill explained that by "high authorities" he did not include Lord Fisher, and that he meant Sir Henry Jackson and Admiral Oliver.

Admiral Carden understood Mr Churchill to include either Lord Fisher or Sir Henry Jackson or both.

By the 5th of January Sir Henry Jackson had completed a memorandum in accordance with instructions given to him by Mr Churchill on the 3rd.

It was not seen by Mr Churchill until some days later.

This memorandum was in the main directed to the possibility of rushing the Dardanelles, and entered into minute details of the force required, and the losses which would be involved in "reaching the Straits".

It contained also the following observations under the heading of "General Remarks".

> Assuming the enemy squadron destroyed and the batteries rushed, they would be open to the fire of field artillery and infantry, and to torpedo attack at night, with no store ships with ammunition, and no retreat without re-engaging the shore batteries, unless those had been destroyed when forcing the passage.
>
> Though they might dominate the city and inflict enormous damage, their position would not be an enviable one unless there was a large military force to occupy the town.
>
> Strategically such a diversion would only be carried out when the object to be gained was commensurate with the loss the fleet would sustain in forcing the passage.
>
> The actual capture of Constantinople would be worth a considerable loss, but the bombardment alone would not greatly affect the distant military operations, and even if it surrendered, it could not be occupied and held without troops, and would probably result in indiscriminate massacres.

This memorandum was not circulated to the members of the War Council.

Sir Henry Jackson insisted in his evidence that he had "always stuck" to this memorandum: "that it would be a very mad thing to try and get into the Sea of Marmora without having the Gallipoli Peninsula held by our own troops or every gun on both sides of the Straits destroyed. He had never changed that opinion and he had never given any one any reason to think he had."

Admiral Carden's reply to Mr Churchill's telegram of 6th January was received on the 11th January. This telegram suggested four successive operations as being possible:

(a) The destruction of defences at the entrance to the Dardanelles.

(b) Action inside the Straits, so as to clear the defences up to and including Cephez Point, Battery No. 8.

(c) The destruction of defences of the Narrows.

(d) Sweeping of a clear channel through the minefield, and advance through the Narrows followed by a reduction of forts farther up, and advance into the Sea of Marmora.

And estimated that a month would be necessary to carry out these operations. This telegram was immediately circulated to members of the War Council.

Admiral Carden stated in his evidence that he "had it in his mind that it was impossible to form a real opinion on the subject until one had destroyed the outer forts at the entrance and was able to get inside and actually find out the extent of the gun defences, of the minefield, and the extent of the movable armament on both sides of the Straits." But there is no indication of this view in any of his telegrams to the Admiralty.

Admiral Carden's plan was then discussed by the members of the War Group at the Admiralty at their daily consultations.

Their views were not expressed in any written memoranda, and it is, therefore, difficult to state precisely what those views were.

I think there was no real consensus of favourable opinion.

Lord Fisher told us that he "was instinctively against it," and that to a large extent "having expressed his indisposition to have much to do with it, he more or less left it alone. Sir Henry Jackson was a very able man and so was Admiral Oliver, and he (Lord Fisher) more or less stood aside. He backed it up in every possible way so far as executive work was concerned."

Sir Arthur Wilson stated that "he never recommended it. He never strongly resisted it because it was not his business to do so, but so far as he did remark on it he was against it," and that "the question of the Dardanelles had never been put to him definitely at all. Sir Henry Jackson was working at the details of the scheme and he (Sir A. Wilson) was looking at the details of others."

Admiral Oliver stated that "his opinion always was that we might go a certain length by naval attack but it would depend on the resistance that the enemy made and the state of their defences how far we could go," and that he would have preferred not "stirring the place up until it had been decided to make a proper attempt, that is to say to make a big attempt with Army and Navy."

Commodore Bartolomé stated that "his view had always been that it should be a combined operation, but he thought that if the Dardanelles were attacked by a purely naval force a certain proportion, probably not more than half, could get through ... but having got through he did not see what they could do."

All were agreed in thinking that the proposed operations could not lead to disaster as they could be broken off at any moment. All assumed that the War Council looked upon immediate action as a political necessity, and that no troops for a joint operation could be obtained.

Sir Henry Jackson was not a member of the War Group, though he was present at some of the meetings at which the proposed operations were discussed. He alone expressed his views in writing.

Those views are contained in the memorandum of the 5th January, which has been referred to, and in a further memorandum of the 15th January, in which he deals specifically with Admiral Carden's plan.

On the 12th January Lord Fisher suggested the possible employment of the *Queen Elizabeth* in the proposed operations, in the following minute to Admiral Oliver:

> I have told Crease to find out from Percy Scott and the gunnery experts of anything to prevent *Queen Elizabeth* firing all her ammunition at the Dardanelles forts instead of uselessly into the sea at Gibraltar and to let you know. If this is practicable she could go straight there, hoist Carden's flag, and go on with her exercises and free the *Indefatigable* to Malta for refit and allow *Inflexible* to go straight from Gibraltar to join the second Battle Cruiser Squadron.

On the same day Admiral Oliver also received a minute from Mr Churchill, which was formally concurred in by Lord Fisher, and was in the following terms:

> The forcing of the Dardanelles as proposed and the arrival of a squadron strong enough to defeat the Turkish fleet in the Sea of Marmora would be a victory of first importance and change to our advantage the whole situation of the war in the East. It would appear possible to provide the force required by Admiral Carden without weakening the margin necessary in home waters.

The minute then gave full details of the ships to be employed and concluded by saying:

> All arrangements should be secretly concerted for carrying the plan through, the sea-planes and auxiliary craft being provided, Admiral Carden to command ... definite plans should be worked out accordingly.

On the 13th January, 1915, Admiral Carden's plan was unfolded in detail by Mr Churchill to the War Council. He concluded, in the words of Sir M. Hankey's note, by stating that

> the Admiralty were studying the question and believed that a plan could be made for systematically reducing all the forts within a few weeks. Once the forts were reduced the minefields would be cleared, and the Fleet would proceed up to Constantinople and destroy the *Goeben*. They would have nothing to fear from field guns or rifles, which would be merely an inconvenience.

At this Council, Lord Fisher and Sir Arthur Wilson expressed no opinion. The actual decision come to was that:

> The Admiralty should prepare for a naval expedition in February to bombard and take the Gallipoli Peninsula, with Constantinople as its objective.

At this Council it was assumed that no troops were available, and this was accentuated by the fact that the Council on the same day sanctioned a plan of Sir John French's for offensive military operations in France. This decision by the War Council set the mechanism of the Admiralty in motion.

The plan of attack was communicated to the French, the co-operation of a French squadron was sought, and arrangements were made for the command by a British Admiral. A Fleet concentration scheme was prepared by the Chief of the Admiralty War Staff.

All these preparations were made through the ordinary routine of the Admiralty. They were concurred in by Lord Fisher, who himself added the *Lord Nelson* and *Agamemnon* to the Fleet allocated to the operations.

On the 14th January the abandonment of a subsidiary naval bombardment in the East was recommended by Mr Churchill in a formal minute to the Prime Minister. This minute, which was concurred in by Lord Fisher, was in the following terms:

> The attack on the Dardanelles will require practically our whole available margin. If that attack opens prosperously, it will very soon attract to itself the whole attention of the Eastern theatre, and if it succeeds, it will produce results which will undoubtedly influence every Mediterranean power.
>
> In these circumstances we strongly advise ... that we should devote ourselves to ... the methodical forcing of the Dardanelles.

On the 15th January, Sir Henry Jackson completed a memorandum on Admiral Carden's plan.

This memo began with the words—"Concur generally in his (i.e. Admiral Carden's) plans. Our previous appreciations of the situation differed only in small details."

It then dealt in detail with the two first operations (*a*) and (*b*) outlined by Admiral Carden's plan. Suggesting that when these had been attempted "the experience thus gained would show the practicability of continuing this direct attack on other forts in the Narrows," and ended by suggesting that "(*a*) might be approved at once as the experience gained would be useful."

Sir Henry Jackson insisted that in this memorandum he recommended only an attack on the outer forts.

He also insisted that when he prepared his memorandum he accepted the policy of a purely naval attack. To use his own words: "It was not for me to decide. I had no responsibilities whatever as to the decision. I had no responsibilities except just for the staff work which I did." And he stated further that he gave his expert advice on Admiral Carden's plan "if it was approved to do it. Whether the game was worth the candle is another thing."

This memorandum, though it was read by Mr Churchill at the War Council of the 28th January, was not circulated to the members.

The plans for the purely naval attack were thus maturing.

As the time for final decision by the War Council drew near, Lord Fisher's attitude of passive dislike developed into one of active hostility.

On the 25th January, he took the very unusual step of submitting a memorandum on naval policy direct to the Prime Minister.

This memorandum, Mr Churchill stated, gave him the first indication "that the First Sea Lord had, since the first meeting of the War Council, developed serious misgivings about it."

Lord Fisher's memorandum was in two parts.

The second part contained the outline of a large naval scheme which was directed to what seemed to Lord Fisher a more decisive theatre of the war, and which had been his main pre-occupation.

The first part set forth Lord Fisher's objections to the proposed operations in the Dardanelles as being opposed to what he conceived to be the British naval policy.

The following extracts sufficiently illustrate those views:

> They (i.e. the Germans) have already endeavoured without success to scatter our naval strength by attacks on our trade and not much more successfully to reduce our main strength by submarines and mines.
>
> Pressure of sea power . . . is still a slow process and requires great patience. In time it will almost certainly compel the enemy to seek a decision at sea, particularly when he begins to realise that his offensive on land is broken. This is one reason for husbanding our resources.
>
> Another reason is that the prolongation of war at sea tends to raise up fresh enemies for the dominant naval power in a much higher degree than it does on land owing to the exasperation of neutrals. The tendency will only be checked by the conviction of an overwhelming naval supremacy behind the nation exercising sea power.
>
> The sole justification of coastal bombardments and attacks by the fleet on fortified places, such as the contemplated prolonged bombardment of the Dardanelles forts by our fleet, is to force a decision at sea, and so far and no further can they be justified.
>
> So long as the German High Sea Fleet possesses its present great strength and splendid gunnery efficiency, so long is it imperative, and indeed vital, that no operation whatever should be undertaken by the British Fleet calculated to impair its present superiority, which is none too great in view of the heavy losses already experienced in valuable ships and invaluable officers and men whose places cannot be filled in the period of the war (in which respect the Navy differs so materially from the Army).
>
> Even the older ships should not be risked, for they cannot be lost without losing men, and they form the only reserve behind the Grand Fleet.

Mr Churchill at once himself drafted a reply to Lord Fisher which was also submitted to the Prime Minister.

This memorandum contained an elaborate analysis of the comparative strength of the British and German navies, showing that for all existing purposes the margin of the British fleet for all requirements was, in Mr Churchill's opinion, ample and even overwhelming.

It concluded with the following general reply to Lord Fisher's argument.

> It is believed that, with care and skill, losses may be reduced to a minimum, and certainly kept within limits fully justified by the importance and necessity of the operations. It cannot be said that this employment of ships which are (except the *Duncans*) not needed and not suited to fight in the line of battle, conflicts

with any of the sound principles of naval policy set forth by the First Sea Lord. Not to use them where necessary because of some fear that there will be an outcry if a ship is lost would be wrong, and, if a certain proportion of loss of life among officers and men of the Royal Navy on these ships can achieve important objects of the war and save a very much greater loss of life among our comrades and allies on shore, we ought certainly not to shrink from it.

Lord Fisher had also intimated to Mr Churchill that he was not going to the War Council, as he did not like "this Dardanelles affair".

On the night of the 27th January, Lord Fisher was informed that the Prime Minister considered it imperative that Lord Fisher should be in his private room with Mr Churchill half an hour before the War Council began. They met as arranged on the morning of the 28th. It is impossible to expect, after so long a lapse of time, an actual reproduction of what took place at this interview.

My view of the evidence is that Lord Fisher left the room under the impression that the Prime Minister was in favour of the proposed operations at the Dardanelles and that the Prime Minister had formed the conclusion that Lord Fisher's objections were due to his preference for his own alternative scheme as a matter of high policy, and were not directed against the practicability of the operations.

The Prime Minister, Mr Churchill and Lord Fisher then went at once to the meeting of the War Council.

The following is the note of what occurred supplied to us by Sir Maurice Hankey:

> Mr Churchill informed the War Council that he had communicated to the Grand Duke Nicholas and to the French Admiralty the project for a naval attack on the Dardanelles. The Grand Duke had replied with enthusiasm, and believed that this might assist him. The French Admiralty had also sent a favourable reply, and had promised co-operation. Preparations were in hand for commencing about the middle of February.
>
> Mr Churchill asked if the War Council attached importance to this operation, which undoubtedly involved some risks.
>
> There was no hostile criticism, though Lord Fisher said that he had understood that this question would not be raised today, and that the Prime Minister was well aware of his own views with regard to it.
>
> To this the Prime Minister replied in the sense that, in view of the steps which had been taken, the question could not well be left in abeyance.
>
> Apart from this the opinions expressed were entirely favourable to the enterprise. Among the advantages claimed for it were that:
>
> (a) It would cut the Turkish Army in two.
> (b) It would put Constantinople under our control.
> (c) It would finally settle the attitude of Bulgaria and the whole of the Balkans.
> (d) It would give us the advantage of having the Russian wheat, and enable Russia to resume exports. (This would restore the Russian exchanges

which were falling, owing to her inability to export, and causing great embarrassment.)

(e) It would open a passage to the Danube.

(f) If successful, its effect would be equivalent to that of a successful campaign fought with the new armies.

One merit of the scheme was that, if satisfactory progress was not made, the attack could be broken off.

The War Council were informed by Mr Churchill that the naval Commander-in-Chief in the Mediterranean had expressed his belief that it could be done. He required from three weeks to a month to accomplish it. The necessary ships were already on their way to the Dardanelles. He also said that, in response to his inquiries, the French had expressed their confidence that Austrian Submarines would not get as far as the Dardanelles, and that, so far as could be ascertained, the Turks had no submarines. He did not anticipate that we should sustain much loss in the actual bombardment, but in sweeping the mines some losses must be expected. The real difficulties would begin after the outer forts had been silenced, and it became necessary to attack the Narrows.

Mr Churchill fully explained the plan of attack on a map.

To this account one incident—not without dramatic intensity—must be added. Lord Fisher learnt in the course of the discussion that a final decision was being come to.

Thereupon [to quote from a note made by Lord Fisher at the time] Lord Fisher left the Council table, followed by Lord Kitchener, who asked Lord Fisher what he intended to do. Lord Fisher replied to Lord Kitchener that he would not return to the Council table and would resign his office as First Sea Lord. Lord Kitchener then urged on Lord Fisher that he (Lord Fisher) was the only dissentient, that the Dardanelles operations had been decided upon by the Prime Minister, and he put it to Lord Fisher that his duty to his Country was to carry on the duties of First Sea Lord. Lord Fisher, after further conversation, reluctantly gave in to Lord Kitchener's entreaty and resumed his seat.

This incident had not escaped the attention of Mr Churchill, who felt, to use his own words, that he "must come to a clear understanding with the First Sea Lord." They met after the adjournment of the War Council in Mr Churchill's room. Mr Churchill strongly urged Lord Fisher to undertake the operations. Lord Fisher definitely consented.

Accompanied by Admiral Oliver, in place of Sir A. Wilson, they then repaired to the afternoon meeting of the War Council. At the close of this meeting Mr Churchill stated that the Admiralty had decided to push on with the project to make a naval attack on the Dardanelles.

It is remarkable to have to record:

(*a*) That Lord Fisher's memorandum and Mr Churchill's reply were not placed before the War Council at these meetings.

(*b*) That no members of the Council—other than the Prime Minister, Mr Churchill and Lord Fisher—knew until a later date of the discussion which had preceded their deliberations.

Lord Fisher insisted in his evidence that he had taken every step—short of resignation—to show his dislike of the proposed operations. He told us:

> that in his judgment it is not the business of the chief technical advisers of the Government to resign because their advice is not accepted unless they are of opinion that the operations proposed must lead to disastrous results. The attempt to force the Dardanelles as a purely naval operation would not have been disastrous so long as the ships employed could be withdrawn at any moment, and only such vessels were engaged, as in the beginning of the operations was in fact the case, as could be spared without detriment to the general service of the fleet.

In answer to the question why he made no protest at the meetings of the War Council, Lord Fisher further stated:

> Mr Churchill knew my opinion. I did not think it would tend towards good relations between the First Lord and myself nor to the smooth working of the Board of Admiralty to raise objections in the War Council's discussions. My opinion being known to Mr Churchill in what I regarded as the proper constitutional way, I preferred thereafter to remain silent.

When on the 14th May the War Council decided to continue the operations at the Dardanelles and to divert further ships for the purpose Lord Fisher thought that his great alternative scheme, which had been his main pre-occupation during this period, and to which his mind and energies had been almost exclusively devoted, was doomed. To use his own words again: "It seemed to me that I was faced at last by a progressive frustration of my main schemes of naval strategy." On the following day he resigned his post as First Sea Lord.

The decision of the War Council was then translated into action.

The plan of operations was finally approved by M. Augagneur (the French Minister of Marine), who pronounced them to be "prudent et prévoyant".

The final arrangements for the naval attack were completed and a detailed staff paper on the proposed operations were sent by the Admiralty to Admiral Carden on the 5th February.

On the 17th or 18th of February the Prime Minister conveyed to the Cabinet the unanimous decision of the War Council. It was accepted by them without question, criticism, or discussion of any kind. The bombardment opened on the 19th February.

Attention has been called to the varying schools of thought which existed in the War Council at the beginning of 1915.

During the ensuing weeks what may be called the Eastern school of thought gained strength under the shadow of the threatened Austro-German attack on Serbia, the coming offensive against Russia, the failure of our diplomacy in the Balkans due to the want of military success, and the grow-ing appreciation of the fact that the naval attack on the Dardanelles might after all be fruitless without considerable military support.

In the course of the discussions which then took place rival plans and policies were constantly before the Council. But I am unable to find that the War Council ever really faced or ever really decided whether it was within their power to undertake military operations on a large scale in another the-atre of war, or that the great and obvious political advantages to be gained by operations in the East were ever considered in the light of military pos-sibility. This was due to the complete absence during their discussions of detailed staff estimates in terms of munitions and men, and to the too con-fident belief in the success of the purely naval attack on the Dardanelles, in the chance of an ineffective Turkish resistance and in the decisive effect of the appearance of the Fleet off Constantinople.

Early in February a proposal was made that a British and French divi-sion should be sent to Salonica to support Serbia in conjunction with the Greeks. Lord Kitchener was ready to send the 29th Division and expressed the opinion that it would be very useful to the Navy in their attack on the Dardanelles to have some good troops at Salonica.

On the 15th February this scheme ultimately broke down owing to the lack of Greek co-operation. Meanwhile the necessity for troops to support the naval attack grew more apparent. It was emphasized by a memorandum which Sir Henry Jackson had completed on the 15th February and sent, by way of suggestion, to Admiral Carden. This memo, while giving detailed notes on the proposed operations, concluded with the following general remarks:

> The provision of the necessary military forces to enable the fruits of this heavy naval undertaking to be gathered must never be lost sight of; the transports carrying them should be in readiness to enter the Straits as soon as it is seen the forts at the Narrows will be silenced.
>
> To complete this destruction strong military landing parties with strong covering forces will be necessary.
>
> It is considered, however, that the full advantage of the undertaking would only be obtained by the occupation of the Peninsula by a military force acting in conjunction with the naval operations, as the pressure of a strong field army of the enemy on the Peninsula would not only greatly harass the operations, but would render the passage of the Straits impracticable by any but powerfully-armed vessels, even though all the permanent defences had been silenced.
>
> The naval bombardment is not recommended as a sound military operation unless a strong military force is ready to assist in the operation, or at least, follow it up immediately the forts are silenced.

On the 16th February the War Council came to the following decision:

(1)   The 29th Division, hitherto intended to form part of Sir John French's Army, to be dispatched to Lemnos at the earliest possible date. It is hoped

that it may be able to sail within nine or ten days.

(2)   Arrangements to be made for a force to be dispatched from Egypt, if required.

(3)   The whole of the above forces, in conjunction with the battalions of the Royal Marines already dispatched, to be available in case of necessity to support the naval attack on the Dardanelles.

(4)   Horse boats to be taken out with the 29th Division, and the Admiralty to make arrangements to collect small craft, tugs and lighters in the Levant.

(5)   The Admiralty to build special transports and lighters suitable for the conveyance and landing of 50,000 men at any point when they may be required.

This decision marks a great development of the plan which had been sanctioned by the War Council of the 28th January.

Confidence still existed that the Fleet would force the Dardanelles and that local military operations would only be necessary to complete the demolition of the forts and deal with concealed howitzers. But the idea grew steadily that the character of these operations was extending, and that considerable forces (estimated by Lord Kitchener on the 19th February at three divisions) would be necessary to secure the passage of the Dardanelles after the fall of the forts.

Side by side with the development of the original plan, referred to in the last paragraph, there grew up also the idea that it would be impossible for reasons of prestige and policy to break off operations in the event of the failure of the Fleet.

The notes of the War Council show that on the 24th of February, Lord Kitchener felt:

that if the Fleet would not get through the Straits unaided, the Army ought to see the business through. The effect of a defeat in the Orient would be very serious. There could be no going back. The publicity of the announcement had committed us.

And that Sir E. Grey expressed the view that "Failure would be equivalent to a great defeat on land."

But that a different opinion was given by Mr Lloyd George who:

strongly urged that the Army should not be required or expected to pull the chestnuts out of the fire for the Navy and that if the Navy failed, we should try somewhere else, in the Balkans, and not necessarily at the Dardanelles.

The necessary steps to concentrate troops in the Mediterranean went forward.

On the 20th of February, the two Australian and New Zealand divisions in Egypt were prepared for service at the Dardanelles, and placed under the command of General Birdwood. Transports were arranged for them and for the 29th Division and the naval division at home. By the end of February, a French division was ready to embark.

The naval division sailed on the 3rd of March.

On the 20th of February, Lord Kitchener, on his own initiative, without communicating with Mr Churchill, cancelled the transports for the 29th Division. And, owing to his anxiety as to the position in France, would not consent to its release until the 10th of March.

This action by Lord Kitchener led to a strong protest on the part of Mr Churchill, who at a War Council on the 26th of February asked "that it might be placed on record that he dissented altogether from the retention of the 29th Division in this country. If a disaster occurred in Turkey owing to the insufficiency of troops, he said he must disclaim all responsibility."

On the 23rd February, General Birdwood was ordered to proceed to the Dardanelles to confer with Admiral Carden.

General Birdwood then made a reconnaissance of the position, and from the telegrams which passed between him and Lord Kitchener it is clear:

(a) That Lord Kitchener still intended that troops should be used for minor operations only.

(b) That General Birdwood did not expect that the Navy would be able to force the passage of the Straits unaided.

(c) But that General Birdwood fully appreciated the formidable character of the defences of the Peninsula and anticipated that major military operations would be necessary.

These telegrams, however, were not circulated to the members of the War Council.

On the 10th of March, Lord Kitchener announced to the War Council the approximate strength of the forces available against Constantinople [supplied in table].

At this Council, Mr Churchill informed the members that the Admiralty still believed that they could effect the passage of the Straits by naval means alone, but they were glad to know that military support was available if required.

On the 12th March, Sir Ian Hamilton was nominated to command these forces, and left for the Dardanelles on the 13th. He was assisted by no staff preparation, and no preliminary scheme of operations of any kind. And it was still assumed that the Navy would force the passage of the Straits.

While the concentration of troops was being made in the Mediterranean, and the events which have been described were taking place in the Councils at home, the naval attack at the Dardanelles was proceeding.

The details of this attack, and the gallantry displayed by the naval forces are well known.

The attack on the outer forts began on the 19th February and was completed on the 25th, though when the demolition parties landed they found 70 per cent of the heavy guns in a serviceable condition, and had to blow them up with guncotton.

Mine-sweepers were then able to enter and sweep the lower reaches of the Straits. The ships of the fleet entered on the 27th, and attacked Fort

Forces available to take Constantinople

	All ranks	Guns	Horses
Naval Division	11,000	6	1,266
Australian Infantry	30,600	64	9,370
Australian Mounted Troops	3,500	12	4,000
XXIXth Division	18,000	56	5,400
French Division	18,000	40	5,000
Russian Army Corps	47,600	120	10,750
	128,700	298	35,786

Dardanus, which was sufficiently damaged on the 1st and 2nd of March to make sweeping possible up to within 3,000 yards of Cephez Point.

The success of this first attack at once produced important diplomatic results. The eyes of the Balkan nations were fixed on the Dardanelles.

On March 1st the British Minister in Athens telegraphed that M. Venizelos proposed to offer the co-operation of a Greek army corps of three divisions in the Gallipoli Peninsula. He telegraphed again on 2nd that this proposal had been made after the King had already been "sounded", and that he heard from another source that the King "wanted war".

Within a fortnight Intelligence reports showed that the Turks were moving back to Adrianople and developing their front against Bulgaria. On March 17th General Paget, who was engaged on a special mission in the Balkans, telegraphed to Lord Kitchener that:

> The operations in the Dardanelles have made a deep impression; that all
> possibilities of Bulgaria attacking any Balkan State that might side with the
> Entente is now over, and there is some reason to think that shortly the Bulgarian
> Army will move against Turkey to co-operate in the Dardanelles operations.

Meanwhile the progress of the Fleet in the early days of March was slow.

On the 7th the forts at the Narrows were engaged, but with only partial success, and sweeping made no progress. Trawlers and destroyers were then sent by night above the mine-fields so that they might sweep down with the current. They came under the enemy's searchlights and were exposed to a terrible fire. The Turkish mobile armament began to develop with harassing effect on the sweepers. The results were small, few mines being exposed or destroyed.

This slow progress was watched by the Admiralty with anxious eyes. The following telegrams were then exchanged between the Admiralty and Admiral Carden:

101. 11 March
Personal and Secret. From First Lord to Vice-Admiral, Eastern Mediterranean.

Caution and deliberate methods were emphasised in your original instructions (and the skill and patience which has enabled your progress to be carried thus far without loss are highly appreciated.)

If, however, success cannot be obtained without loss of ships and men, results to be gained are important enough to justify such a loss. The whole operation may be decided and consequences of a decisive character upon the war may be produced by the turning of the corner Chanak; and we suggest for your consideration, that a point has now been reached when it is necessary to choose favourable weather conditions to overwhelm forts of the Narrows at decisive range by bringing to bear upon them the fire of the largest possible number of guns, great and small. Under cover of this fire landing parties might destroy the guns of the forts, and sweeping operations to clear as much as possible of the minefield might also be carried out.

It might be necessary to repeat the operation until the destruction of all the forts at the Narrows and the clearing of the approaches of mines had been accomplished.

We have no wish to hurry you or urge you beyond your judgment, but we recognise clearly that at a certain period in your operations you will have to press hard for a decision and we desire to know whether, in your opinion, that period has now arrived. Every well-conceived action for forcing a decision, even should regrettable losses be entailed, will receive our support.

Before you take any decisive departure from the present policy we wish to hear your views.

13 March
105. From First Lord to Vice-Admiral, Mediterranean.
From the above it is evident that methodical and resolute conduct of the operations by night and day should be pursued, the inevitable losses being accepted. The enemy is harassed and anxious now. Interference with submarines will be a very serious complication. Time is of the essence.

13 March
From Vice-Admiral, Eastern Mediterranean, to Admiralty:
Your 101 is fully concurred in by me. I consider stage when vigorous sustained action is necessary for success has now been reached. I am of opinion that in order to ensure my communication line immediately fleet enters Sea of Marmora military operations on a large scale should be opened at once.

On the 16th March Admiral Carden was compelled by the advice of the Medical Officer to go on the Sick List.

On the 17th March Admiral de Robeck was appointed in his place. He was asked by the First Lord to give the operations suggested in the telegrams to Admiral Carden his "separate and independent judgment"; to which he expressed his full concurrence. The great naval attack began on the 18th. This attack, although carried out with much skill and gallantry, met with little or no success and resulted in the following damage being done to the Fleet:

The *Irresistible*, the *Ocean* and the *Bouvet* lost. The *Inflexible* had various compartments flooded, and at one time was in danger of sinking.

The *Suffren* was also hit below water, and had to be docked. The *Gaulois* was badly damaged and had to be beached on Drepana Island.

The *Charlemagne* had her stoke-hold flooded; the *Agamemnon* had one 12-inch gun damaged. The *Lord Nelson* had one 9.2-inch gun put out of action; the *Albion's* foreturret was put out of action for some days.

Thus, out of the 16 attacking ships, three were sunk, and four others so severely damaged that they had to be docked. In spite of these losses Admiral de Robeck telegraphed to the Admiralty on the following day that the squadron "was ready for immediate action except as regards ships lost and damaged but it was necessary to reconsider the plan of attack."

News of these events reached the Admiralty on the following day. Lord Fisher and Sir A. Wilson, when consulted by Mr Churchill, were determined to continue the attack. Lord Fisher immediately ordered two battleships, the *London* and the *Prince of Wales*, to reinforce the fleet in addition to the *Queen* and *Implacable*. On the same day the War Council authorised "the First Lord of the Admiralty to inform Vice-Admiral de Robeck that he could continue the naval operations against the Dardanelles if he thought fit."

The War Council did not meet again until the 14th May.

Meanwhile on the 23rd March Admiral de Robeck had met in Council with Generals Hamilton and Birdwood. Admiral de Robeck told us that at this conference it was apparent to him that an army was necessary to keep his lines of communication and that to effect this it was "necessary to hold the Peninsula." While ready to continue the action he therefore telegraphed that day to the Admiralty his opinion that "a decisive operation about the middle of next month appears to me better than to take great risks for what may well be only half measures."

The final decision to abandon the naval attack was told by Mr Churchill in his statement to us in the following words:

> We discussed the whole question at length on the morning of the 23rd at our daily meeting (i.e., of the War Group at the Admiralty), Sir Henry Jackson being present. I proposed that we should direct the Admiral to renew the naval attack according to his previous intention. The First Sea Lord, however, did not agree; nor did Sir A. Wilson. Nor did Sir Henry Jackson. Lord Fisher took the line that hitherto he had been willing to carry the enterprise forward, because it was supported and recommended by the Commander on the spot. But now that Admiral de Robeck and Sir Ian Hamilton had decided upon a joint operation, we were bound to accept their view. I do not at all blame Lord Fisher for this decision. The arguments for it were very strong indeed.
>
> Both the Prime Minister and Mr Balfour, with whom I discussed the matter, were inclined to my view, but as our professional advisers and the Admiral on the spot were against it, it was impossible to go further, and I bowed to their decision, but with regret and anxiety.

The naval attack on the Narrows was never resumed. The story of the landing on the 25th April, the preparations which preceded it, the delay in concentrating troops for the subsequent operations, do not come within the scope of this memorandum.

I wish to record the following conclusions:

(1) The facts disclosed in the course of the inquiry show that the War Council concentrated their attention too much on the political ends to be gained by an offensive policy in the East and gave too little attention to the means by which that policy could be translated into terms of naval and military action. The War Council never had before them detailed staff estimates of men, munitions, and material, or definite plans showing them what military operations were possible.

The War Council also underestimated without any real investigation the strength of the Turkish opposition.

(2) The War Council rejected without sufficient consideration all previous opinions against a purely naval attack on forts. The problem of forcing the Dardanelles, even by a purely naval attack, required the consideration of the expert engineer and artilleryman as much as that of the expert naval officer, and should therefore have been submitted to a joint naval and military staff for investigation.

(3) Mr Churchill failed to present fully to the War Council the opinions of his naval advisers, and this failure was due to his own strong personal opinion in favour of a naval attack. Mr Churchill should also have consulted the Board of Admiralty before such a large and novel departure in naval policy was undertaken.

(4) It is difficult to understand why the War Council did not meet between the 19th March and the 14th May. The failure of the naval attack on the 18th March showed the necessity of abandoning the plan of forcing the passage of the Dardanelles by purely naval operations. The War Council should then have met and considered fully the future policy to be pursued.

(5) Important political advantages were gained by the first success of the naval attack and the possibility of further success. But these advantages would not have continued unless further operations had been undertaken at the Dardanelles or elsewhere in the East after the failure of the naval attack on the 18th March.

(6) Finally, I strongly recommend that operations of a similar character should in future be thoroughly considered by a joint naval and military staff before they are undertaken. It is essential for the success of such operations that both the Navy and the Army should be recognized as integral factors consulting and co-operating in the common policy to be pursued.

WALTER ROCH

PART II

❦

DEFEAT AT GALLIPOLI

(DEALING WITH THE JOINT NAVAL AND MILITARY OPERATIONS ON AND AROUND THE GALLIPOLI PENINSULA DURING 1915)

THE ORIGIN AND INCEPTION OF THE JOINT
NAVAL AND MILITARY ATTACK

When the naval attack [on the Dardanelles] was sanctioned by the War
Council on January 28th, 1915, there was no question of supporting it
with large military forces. Such forces were not then available, and Lord
Kitchener represented that they would not be available for some considerable time.

During January, 1915, the War Council were occupied in discussing their
future military policy, based on the possibility of a stalemate in the Western theatre of war, and on the necessity of operations elsewhere.

In the course of these discussions, Lord Kitchener, on January 8th,
expressed an opinion in favour of an attack on the Dardanelles. He then
informed the Council that the Dardanelles appeared to be the most suitable
military objective, as an attack there could be made in co-operation with the
Fleet. He estimated that 150,000 men would be sufficient for the capture of
the Dardanelles, but reserved his final opinion until a close study had been
made.

These discussions resulted in two general conclusions.

The first conclusion was expressed in a despatch from Lord Kitchener
to Sir John French on January 9th, in which Lord Kitchener wrote with
regard to the possibility of the employment of British forces in a different
theatre of war.

> The Council considered carefully your remarks on this subject in reply to Lord
> Kitchener's letter, and came to the conclusion that, certainly for the present, the
> main theatre of operations for British forces should be alongside the French
> Army, and that this should continue as long as France was liable to successful
> invasion and required armed support. It was also realised that should the
> offensive operations subsequently drive the Germans out of France and back to

Germany, British troops should assist in such operations. It was thought that after another failure by Germany to force the lines of defence held by the French Army and yours, the military situation in France and Flanders might conceivably develop into one of stalemate, in which it would be impossible for German forces to break through into France, while at the same time the German defences would be impassable for offensive movements of the Allies without great loss of life and expenditure of more ammunition than could be provided. In these circumstances it was considered desirable to find some other theatre where such obstructions to advance would be less pronounced, and from where operations against the enemy might lead to more decisive results.

For these reasons the War Council decided that certain of the possible projects for pressing the war in other theatres should be carefully studied during the next few weeks, so that as soon as the new forces are fit for action plans may be ready to meet any eventuality that may be then deemed expedient, either from a political point of view or to enable our forces to act with the best advantage in concert with the troops of other nations throwing in their lot with the Allies.

And the second conclusion was embodied in the decision recorded by the War Council on January 13th:

That if the position in the Western theatre of war becomes, in the spring, one of stalemate, British troops should be despatched to another theatre and objective, and that adequate investigation and preparation should be undertaken with that purpose and that a sub-committee of the Committee of Imperial Defence be appointed to deal with this aspect of the question.

Lieutenant-Colonel Sir Maurice Hankey in his statement comments on the second conclusion as follows:

Although this conclusion does not mention the Dardanelles as an objective, and probably had little influence over the decision to use troops against the Dardanelles, which was forced on the Allies by pressure of circumstances, it is of some importance as an indication that, in the opinion of the War Council, troops might have to be employed in some theatre of war other than the Western Front. Even the early investigations which preceded this decision had shown—what those held subsequently were to confirm—that there were only two alternative theatres of war to the Western Front at that time in the region of feasibility, namely, the Dardanelles and Serbia.

On January 13th and 28th, 1915, the War Council decided to attempt to force the Dardanelles by means of the Navy alone. A joint naval and military operation was not considered in consequence of Lord Kitchener's statement, accepted by the War Council, that there were not, and would not for some months be, any troops available for such an operation. At a meeting of the War Council on May 14th, Mr Churchill stated that if he had known three months before that an army of from 80,000 to 100,000 men would be available in May for an attack on the Dardanelles, the attack by the Navy alone would never have been undertaken.

Towards the end of January, diplomatic efforts were made to secure the co-operation of Greece with Serbia, which met with no success. As by February 15th the negotiations to secure Greek co-operation with Serbia had failed, attention began once more to be directed to the Dardanelles, and on February 16th the War Council decided to send the 29th Division, and a force from Egypt, to Lemnos to support the naval attack. It was also decided that the Admiralty should build special transports and lighters [large open boats used for loading and unloading ships], suitable for the conveyance of a force of 50,000 men and their landing at any point where they might be required. The despatch of the 29th Division was afterwards postponed till March 10th. The transports collected for this Division were countermanded by a message, delivered to the Director of Transports by Colonel Fitzgerald on behalf of Lord Kitchener. It is right, however, to say that the Director of Transports did not act on these instructions until he had orders to do so given to him by Lord Fisher, who was then First Sea Lord.

Future military plans were discussed in a series of meetings of the War Council on February 19th, 24th and 26th. At these meetings there arose an acute difference of opinion as to whether the 29th Division should be sent at once to the Eastern Mediterranean, and Lord Kitchener's anxiety about a possible German offensive on the Western Front caused him to withhold his consent to the despatch of that Division until March 10th.

From the record of these discussions it appears that the policy contemplated was:

(a) To support the naval attack with three divisions which Lord Kitchener thought might be required to secure the passage of the Straits after the fall of the forts.

(b) To concentrate as large a military force as possible in the Eastern Mediterranean ready to secure control of the Sea of Marmora, the Bosphorus, and Constantinople, after the Straits had been forced by the Fleet.

(c) As an alternative, to hold these forces ready for any action which might determine the attitude of the Balkan States, and thus bring into the struggle at least Romania and Greece, possibly Bulgaria, and unite the whole of the south-east of Europe with Britain and France in a combined action against the Central Powers.

In the course of these discussions, Lord Kitchener informed the Council "that if the Fleet could not get through the Straits unaided, the Army ought to see the business through. The effect of a defeat in the Orient would be very serious. There could be no going back." The naval attack on the Dardanelles had committed us to offensive action in the Near East. The same view was expressed by Sir E. Grey, who stated that failure would be equivalent to a great defeat on land. Mr Asquith also told us that from this time onward Lord Kitchener was determined that the Army should see the naval attack through.

At the War Council on February 19th, Mr Asquith read out extracts from a memorandum of the General Staff prepared on December 19th, 1906, for the Committee of Imperial Defence, which was afterwards circulated to the members of the Council, and in which the possibility of a combined attack, naval and military, upon the Dardanelles had been considered.

This memorandum pointed out that:

When the question of despatching a military expeditionary force to the Gallipoli Peninsula comes to be passed in review, the first point to be considered is the general one of whether a landing is possible at all, in face of active opposition under modern conditions.

In regard to this, history affords no guide. The whole conditions of war have been revolutionised since such an operation was last attempted. Military opinion, however, will certainly lean strongly to the view that no landing could nowadays be effected in the presence of an enemy, unless the co-operating naval squadron was in a position to guarantee, with its guns, that the men, horses, and vehicles of the landing force should reach the shore unmolested, and that they should find, after disembarkation, a sufficiently extended area, free from hostile fire, to enable them to form up for battle on suitable ground.

In the opinion of the General Staff, a doubt exists as to whether the co-operating fleet would be able to give this absolute guarantee.

The successful conclusion of a military operation against the Gallipoli Peninsula must hinge, as already stated, upon the ability of the fleet, not only to dominate the Turkish defences with gunfire, and to crush their field troops during that period of helplessness which exists while an army is in actual process of disembarkation, but also to cover the advance of troops once ashore, until they could gain a firm foothold, and establish themselves upon the high ground in rear of the coast defences of the Dardanelles.

However brilliant as a combination of war, and however fruitful in its consequences such an operation would be, were it crowned with success, the General Staff, in view of the risks involved, are not prepared to recommend its being attempted.

The Director of Naval Intelligence, while generally in agreement with the General Staff, and fully concurring as to the great risks involved in a joint naval and military enterprise against the Gallipoli Peninsula, expressed the view that:

The memorandum somewhat underrates the value of the assistance which might be rendered by a co-operating fleet by means of a heavy covering fire at the actual point of disembarkation and during the stages of the advance, immediately succeeding the landing, as well as by feints [distraction tactics] and diversions along the 45 nautical miles of littoral between the Bulair line and Cape Helles.

The effectiveness of covering fire from men of war, as an adjunct to land forces, was well illustrated by the Japanese attack on Kinchow, where the fire of the Japanese gun-boats turned the scale at the critical moment, and enabled the attackers to force the left of the Russian position, while the torpedo boats, in rear of the Russian lines, interrupted, by their fire, the passage of trains in either direction.

In that enterprise, the co-operating vessels were very small, and the fire they were able to develop was insignificant, compared with what might be brought to bear in the Gallipoli Peninsula, where the hydrographical conditions are such that any number of vessels of the largest size and power could be employed to support the land forces.

Sir Maurice Hankey informed us that it was generally held by the War Council that the General Staff memorandum of 1906 was not wholly applicable to the conditions obtaining in 1915. There is no record of the precise reasons for this opinion, but speaking from memory he thinks that they were somewhat as follows:

(a) Turkey in the Balkan wars had shown herself to be much less formidable as a military power than had been previously assumed.
(b) There had been a considerable development of naval ordnance since 1906.
(c) The fall of the Liège and Namur forts led to the conclusion that permanent works could easily be dealt with by modern long-range guns.
(d) By the use of aircraft the value of naval bombardment, especially by indirect laying, would be enormously increased.
(e) The development of submarines led to the hope that the Turkish communications to the Gallipoli Peninsula through the Sea of Marmora would be very vulnerable.

On February 24th, the question of the appointment of a military commander was mentioned at the War Council, and the first to be considered was Lieutenant-General Sir William Birdwood. The scope of the military operations, however, gradually became enlarged, and it was thought advisable to select an officer of greater experience and higher rank. General Sir Ian Hamilton was appointed on March 12th, and sailed on the next day.

Following the decisions of the War Council, Lord Kitchener gave orders on February 20th for two Australasian divisions in Egypt to prepare for service at the Dardanelles; and by the end of February a French Division and the Royal Naval Division were ready to embark for the same destination. All these were placed under the command of Sir William Birdwood.

On February 23rd, Sir William Birdwood was ordered to proceed to the

Dardanelles to confer with Admiral Carden. He then made a reconnaissance of the position and the telegrams which subsequently passed between him and Lord Kitchener show:

(a) That Lord Kitchener still intended troops to be used for minor operations only;

(b) That Sir William Birdwood, on the other hand, did not expect the Navy to force the Straits unaided; and

(c) That Sir William Birdwood fully appreciated the formidable character of the defences of the Peninsula, and anticipated that large military operations would be necessary.

In the course of these preparations Lieutenant-General Sir John Maxwell, Commander-in-Chief in Egypt, telegraphed to Lord Kitchener on February 24th that he understood that the Gallipoli Peninsula was everywhere heavily fortified and prepared for defence, and was practically a fort, advance against which from any quarter without heavy guns would seem to be hazardous. Sir John Maxwell was also impressed by the views of Colonel Maucorps, who was a member of the French military mission in Egypt, and who had been for five years the military attaché at Constantinople. On February 26th he telegraphed to Lord Kitchener an appreciation by Colonel Maucorps, which recommended an attack on the Asiatic side of the Peninsula as presenting the least difficulties, and expressed the opinion that it would be extremely hazardous to land on the Gallipoli Peninsula, as the peninsula was very strongly fortified for defence. It was also pointed out that the garrison of the peninsula was 30,000 strong, composed of the 9th Division of the IIIrd Army Corps, with reserve formations, under the command of Djevad Pasha, who was an excellent and very energetic officer; and that the Bulair lines had been re-made and re-armed.

The object of the operations at the Dardanelles was to gain an entrance to the Sea of Marmora and dominate Constantinople. At a meeting on March 10th Lord Kitchener announced to the War Council that the "approximate strength of the forces available against Constantinople" would be 128,700 [see table on p. 104].

It should be noted that the despatch of the Russian Corps referred to in the table was to follow and be contingent upon our obtaining access to Constantinople through the Dardanelles and the Sea of Marmora.

The facts which have been mentioned show that from an early date in February a military landing on some scale on the Gallipoli Peninsula was contemplated, and that, as time went on, a landing in considerable force became increasingly probable. There was therefore sufficient time for a preliminary plan of operations and plan of landing to be put forward by the General Staff. Such would be the usual course. In fact, among the duties assigned to the department of the Chief of the Imperial General Staff in the King's Regulations is the preparation of plans of offensive operations and of plans of concentration and reinforcement in connection therewith. When asked by the Prime Minister at the War Council meeting of March 19th whether any general plan and scheme of disembarkation had been worked out, Lord Kitchener said that, though the question had been examined in the War Office, sufficient information was not forthcoming for the preparation of a detailed scheme of landing, which would be undertaken by Sir Ian Hamilton in concert with the Naval Commander-in-Chief. No general plan of operations had been prepared by the War Office. We can see no reason why a general plan or alternative general plans should not have been worked out, and we think that the elaboration of such a plan or plans by competent officers of the General Staff would have put the military problem in a clearer light before the War Council.

While the concentration of troops in the Eastern Mediterranean was proceeding, Admiral Sir Henry Jackson, who was writing frequent appreciations of the position in regard to naval action, presented a minute to Mr Winston Churchill on March 11th, in which he stated:

> The position has considerably changed recently; there are now ample military forces ready at short notice for co-operation with him [i.e. the Admiral], and I suggest the time has arrived to make use of them.
>
> To advance further with a rush over unswept mine-fields, and in waters commanded at short range by heavy guns, howitzers,* and torpedo-tubes, must involve serious losses in ships and men, and will not achieve the object of making the Straits a safe water-way for the transports. The Gallipoli Peninsula must be cleared of the enemy's artillery before this is achieved, and its occupation is a practical necessity before the Straits are safe for the passage of troops as far as the Sea of Marmora.
>
> I suggest the Vice-Admiral be asked if he considers the time has now arrived to make use of military forces to occupy the Gallipoli Peninsula, and clear away the enemy artillery on that side—an operation he would support with his squadrons.
>
> With the peninsula in our possession, the concealed batteries on the Asiatic side, which are less formidable, could be dealt with more easily from the heights on shore than by ships' guns afloat, and the troops should be of great assistance in the demolition of the fortress's guns.

Mr Churchill communicated this minute to Lord Kitchener, and asked him for a "formal statement of the War Office view as to land operations." To which Lord Kitchener replied on March 13th:

> Most Secret.
>
> In answer to your questions, unless it is found that our estimate of the Ottoman strength on the Gallipoli Peninsula is exaggerated, and the position on the Kilid

---

* A short gun used for shelling at a steep angle; used in trench warfare.

Bahr Plateau less strong than anticipated, no operations on a large scale should be attempted until the 29th Division has arrived and is ready to take part in what is likely to prove a difficult undertaking, in which severe fighting must be anticipated.

On March 12th, Sir Ian Hamilton was appointed to command the Mediterranean Expeditionary Force, and was summoned to the War Office to receive his instructions from Lord Kitchener. In his evidence Sir Ian Hamilton told us that he made full notes of this interview shortly afterwards, and that Lord Kitchener informed him:

That I knew his feelings as to the value of the Near East. He said, rifle for rifle, at that moment he had made up his mind we could nowhere make as good use of the 29th Division as by sending them to the Dardanelles. With good luck each of its 12,000 rifles might attract 100 more to our side of the war.

But the diversion of this Division had been opposed.

I must clearly understand (1) that the 29th Division was only a loan, to be returned the moment they could be spared. (2) That every man, gun, rifle, or cartridge sent out to me is looked upon as sheer waste by powerful interests, both those at home and in France, who have strategical ideas.

He said we soldiers were clearly to understand that we were string number 2. The sailors said they could force the Dardanelles on their own, and we were not to chip in unless the Admiral definitely chucked up the sponge.

Once we started fighting we had to see the enterprise right through at all costs. No Asiatic adventure was to be countenanced.

Lord Kitchener then explained, at some length, that owing to our command of the sea, military operations on the peninsula itself would be a limited liability ... meaning thereby that the area was restricted, and as the numbers of the enemy would be restricted, so the numbers which would have to be drawn from home would be restricted. His idea was once we began to march about Asia Minor the liability would become unlimited, and I would very likely have to make demands on him for reinforcements of all descriptions, which in the present state of affairs would be very difficult to give.

The only information which Sir Ian Hamilton was able to obtain before leaving consisted of the official handbooks; the outline of a plan which had been worked out by the Greek General Staff for an attack on the Dardanelles; and a statement by Lord Kitchener that the Kilid Bahr Plateau had been entrenched and would be sufficiently held by the Turks, and that south of Achi Baba the point of the peninsula would be so swept by the guns of the fleet that no enemy positions would be encountered in that quarter. This last statement was made on the authority of a map which afterwards proved inaccurate, and of little use. From Sir Ian Hamilton's evidence it would seem that no really good maps were available until some were taken from Turkish prisoners.

He was not supplied with the memorandum, prepared by the General Staff in 1906, for the consideration of the Committee of Imperial Defence, together with the remarks of the Director of Naval Intelligence thereon, in which the possibility of a joint naval and military attack upon the Dardanelles was fully discussed; nor were the views of Colonel Maucorps, late French Military Attaché at Constantinople, reported by Sir J. Maxwell to Lord Kitchener on February 26th, communicated to him.

Sir Ian Hamilton was also informed that Major-General Braithwaite was to be his Chief of the General Staff. General Braithwaite himself had been informed of his appointment on the afternoon of March 11th, and told to get a staff together. This he proceeded to do, and he also obtained such information as was available at the War Office, which was of a very meagre description.

On March 13th Sir Ian Hamilton again saw Lord Kitchener, and was given formal written instructions for his guidance.

These instructions were as follows:

(1) The Fleet has undertaken to force the passage of the Dardanelles. The employment of military forces on any large scale for land operations, at this juncture, is only contemplated in the event of the Fleet failing to get through after every effort has been exhausted.

(2) Before any serious undertaking is carried out in the Gallipoli Peninsula, all the British military forces detailed for the expedition should be assembled so that their full weight can be thrown in.

(3) Having entered on the project of forcing the Straits, there can be no idea of abandoning the scheme. It will require time, patience, and methodical plans of co-operation between the naval and military commanders. The essential point is to avoid a check [repulse], which will jeopardise our chances of strategical and political success.

(4) This does not preclude the probability of minor operations being engaged upon, to clear areas occupied by the Turks with guns annoying the Fleet, or for the demolition of forts already silenced by the Fleet. But such minor operations should be as much as possible restricted to the forces necessary to achieve the object in view, and should as far as practicable not entail permanent occupation of positions on the Gallipoli Peninsula.

(5) Owing to the lack of any definite information we presume that the Gallipoli Peninsula is held in strength, and that the Kilid Bahr Plateau has been fortified and armed for a determined resistance. In fact we must pre-suppose that the Turks have taken every measure for the defence of the Plateau, which is the key to the Western Front at the Narrows, until such time as reconnaissance has proved otherwise.

(6) Under present conditions it seems undesirable to land any permanent garrison, or hold any lines on the Gallipoli Peninsula. Probably an entrenched force will be required to retain the Turkish forces on the peninsula and

prevent reinforcements arriving at Bulair, and this force would naturally be supported on both flanks by gun-fire from the Fleet. Troops employed on the minor operations mentioned above (paragraph 4), should be withdrawn as soon as their mission is fulfilled.

(7) In order not to reduce forces advancing on Constantinople, the security of the Dardanelles passage, once it has been forced, is a matter for the Fleet, except as in paragraph 6 with regard to Bulair. The occupation of the Asiatic side, by military forces, is to be strongly deprecated [argued against].

(8) When the advance through the Sea of Marmora is undertaken, and the Turkish fleet has been destroyed, the opening of the Bosphorus, for the passage of Russian forces, will be proceeded with. During this period, the employment of the British and French troops, which will probably have been brought up to the neighbourhood of Constantinople, should be conducted with caution. As soon as the Russian Corps has joined up with our troops, combined plans of operations against the Turkish army (if it still remains in European Turkey) will be undertaken, with a view to obtaining its defeat or surrender. Until this is achieved, landing in the town of Constantinople, which may entail street fighting, should be avoided.

(9) As it is impossible now to foretell what action the Turkish military authorities may decide upon, as regards holding their European territories, the plan of operations for the landing of the troops and their employment must be left for subsequent decision. It is, however, important that as soon as possible after the arrival of the Fleet at Constantinople, all communications from the West to the East across the Bosphorus, including the telegraph cables, should be stopped. Assuming that the main portion of the Turkish army is prepared to defend European Turkish territory, it may be necessary to land parties to hold entrenched positions on the East side of the Bosphorus, and thus assist the Fleet in preventing all communication across the Bosphorus.

(10) Should the Turkish army have retired to the East side of the Bosphorus, the occupation of Constantinople and the Western territories of Turkey may be proceeded with.

(11) As in certain contingencies, it may be important to be able to withdraw our troops from this theatre at an early date, the Allied troops working in conjunction with us should be placed in those positions which need to be garrisoned, and our troops might, with advantage, be employed principally in holding the railway line, until a definite decision is come to as to future operations.

(12) You will send all communications to the Secretary of State for War, and keep him fully informed of the operations and your anticipations as to future developments.

March 13th, 1915   KITCHENER

Sir Ian Hamilton, General Braithwaite, and the General Staff left on March 13th, arriving at Mudros [in Lemnos] on the 17th.

The administrative branches of the Staff did not start until a later date, arriving at Alexandria on April 1st.

Immediately on his arrival Sir Ian Hamilton attended a conference with Vice-Admiral Sir John de Robeck on board the *Queen Elizabeth*. This conference was attended by Admiral de Robeck, Sir Ian Hamilton, Général d'Amade, Admiral Guepratté, Admiral Wemyss, General Braithwaite, Commodore Keyes and Captain Pollen.

Sir Ian Hamilton told us that in the course of this conference he was informed by Sir John de Robeck that:

> The peninsula is rapidly being fortified, and thousands of Turks work like beavers all night on trenches, redoubts, and entanglements.
>
> Not one living soul has yet been seen, but each morning brings evidence of nocturnal activity. All landing places are now commanded by lines of trenches, and are effectively ranged by field guns and howitzers, which so far cannot be located, even approximately, as our naval seaplanes are too heavy to rise out of rifle range.
>
> He said the Turkish searchlights were fixed and mobile, they were of the latest pattern, and were run by skilled observers. The Germans evidently got hold of the Turks, and all that sort of work was being done in shipshape style by the Turks . . .
>
> The War Office had taken too sanguine a view in thinking that the ships' guns would be able to prevent the Turkish troops lodging themselves on the peninsula, because de Robeck said he knew they were there from seeing the trench work increased every morning.
>
> Many more troops have come down. The German officers have grappled with the situation, and have got their troops scientifically disposed, and heavily entrenched. So much so that they have not much to fear from the flat-trajectory guns of the Navy. The number of field guns on the peninsula is now many times greater than it was.

On March 18th the substance of this conference, except as regards the small effect likely to be produced by the flat-trajectory gun-fire of the Navy, was telegraphed by Sir Ian Hamilton to Lord Kitchener.

And in a private letter, Sir Ian Hamilton, on the same day, wrote to Lord Kitchener:

> Here, at present, Gallipoli looks a much tougher nut to crack than it did over the map in your office.
>
> The increases to the garrison, the new lines of trenches, nightly being excavated, the number of concealed field guns, the rapidity of the current, are all brought forward when discussing military operations.
>
> My present impression is that, if it eventually becomes necessary to take the Gallipoli Peninsula by a military force, we shall have to proceed bit by bit.

It may here be noted that on May 9th Sir John de Robeck telegraphed to the Admiralty:

> The Navy has not been able to give the Army as great assistance as was anticipated. The Navy is of small assistance when it is a matter of trenches and machine guns, and the check of the Army is due to these factors.

On March 19th the failure of the naval attack on the previous day was discussed at a meeting of the War Council, and Mr Churchill was authorised to inform Sir John de Robeck that he could continue the naval operations if he thought fit. In the course of the discussion which followed, Sir Maurice Hankey's notes show that Lord Kitchener said he had given Sir Ian Hamilton as many men as he could use on the ground.

On March 18th Sir Ian Hamilton made a reconnaissance down the coast, arriving at Cape Helles to find the naval engagement in "full blast".

On the 19th the result of this reconnaissance was communicated by him to Lord Kitchener in the following telegram, which was received after the War Council mentioned in the last paragraph:

> Yesterday we steamed close along the western shore of the Gallipoli Peninsula. Here and there landing places were, of course, observed.
>
> So near were we that we could see quite clearly the barbed wire defences covering the trenches ...
>
> I have not yet received any report of the naval action, but from what I actually saw of the extraordinary gallant attempt made yesterday, I am being most reluctantly driven towards the conclusion that the Dardanelles are less likely to be forced by battleships than at one time seemed probable, and that if the Army is to participate, its operations will not assume the subsidiary form anticipated.
>
> The Army's share will not be a case of landing parties, for the destruction of forts, etc., but rather a case of a deliberate and progressive military operation, carried out in order to make good the passage of the Navy.

This telegram had been despatched at 2 pm. At 5.45 pm on the same day the following reply was sent by Lord Kitchener:

> With reference to the last paragraph of your telegram of today. You know my views that the passage of the Dardanelles must be forced, and that if large military operations on the Gallipoli Peninsula by the Army are necessary to clear the way, they must be undertaken, after careful consideration of the local defences, and must be carried through.

On March 20th Sir Ian Hamilton intimated to Lord Kitchener that "he understood his views completely."

On March 22nd Sir Ian Hamilton had another conference with Sir John de Robeck on board the *Queen Elizabeth*. This conference was attended by Admiral de Robeck, Sir Ian Hamilton, Admiral Wemyss, General Braithwaite, General Birdwood, and Captain Pollen.

Sir Ian Hamilton's note of this conference is to the following effect:

He [i.e. Vice-Admiral de Robeck] is now quite clear and strong that he cannot get through without the help of all my troops.

Wemyss agreed with de Robeck.

No voice was raised to question the momentous decision.

The result of this important conference was then communicated by Sir Ian Hamilton to Lord Kitchener, and by Sir John de Robeck to Mr Churchill, in the following telegrams:

(1) Sir Ian Hamilton to Lord Kitchener, March 23rd:

I have now conferred with the Admiral, and we are equally convinced that to enable the Fleet effectively to force the passage of the Dardanelles, the co-operation of the whole military force will be necessary.

The strength of the enemy on the Gallipoli Peninsula is estimated at about 40,000, with a reserve of 30,000 somewhere west of Rodosto.

The unsettled weather prevailing in March introduces a dangerous, incalculable factor into the operation of landing a large force in face of certain opposition, but the weather next month should be more settled, and I am sanguine of the success then of a simple, straightforward scheme, based on your broad principles.

I have already worked out the main features of my scheme, and I can communicate them, if you think it safe to do so.

Practically the whole of my force will be required to effect what I have planned, and on the thoroughness with which I can make the preliminary arrangements, of which the proper allocation of troops, etc., is not the least important, the success of my plans will largely depend.

This is one of the principal reasons why I attach importance to the thorough organisation of the expedition at a convenient base like Alexandria.

(2) Sir John de Robeck to First Lord [Mr Churchill], March 23rd:

At a meeting today with Generals Birdwood and Hamilton, was informed by the latter that the Army will not be ready to commence military operations until the 14th April.

All guns of position guarding the Straits must be destroyed, in order to keep up our communications when the Fleet gets through the Sea of Marmora. These guns are numerous, and not more than a small proportion of them can be put out of action by gun-fire.

The enemy were obviously surprised by the landing of a demolition party on the 26th February.

Judging by the events of the 4th March, future operations of this nature will probably meet strenuous and well-considered opposition.

It does not appear to me practicable to land a sufficient force inside the Dardanelles to carry out this service. This view is shared by General Hamilton.

On the other hand failure to destroy the guns may well nullify any success of the Fleet, by enabling the Straits to be closed up, after the ships have gone through, and there may not then be ships available to keep the Straits open, as losses may be heavy.

Until the Sea of Marmora is reached, the mine menace, which is much greater than we expected, will remain. This requires careful and thorough treatment, both in respect of mines and floating mines.

Time will be required for this, but arrangements can be made by the time the Army will be ready.

A decisive operation about the middle of next month appears to me better than to take great risks for what may well be only half measures.

It now appears to me that there may, possibly, be above the Narrows, mine-fields of which we have very little information.

Obstacles may be sunk in the Channel by the Germans, and submerged hulks and pontoons placed there. I have in mind particularly the very large pontoons in the Golden Horn, on which the old Road Bridge from Stambul to Pera was laid.

The howitzers, which it is so difficult to spot from the sea, will, of course, remain.

I think it will be necessary to take and occupy the Gallipoli Peninsula by land forces before it will be possible for first-rate ships, capable of dealing with the *Goeben* [German battlecruiser] to be certain of getting through, and for colliers [coal-bearing boats] and other vessels, upon which the usefulness of the big ships largely depends, to get through.

(3) Sir John de Robeck to First Lord [Mr Churchill], March 26th:

The check on the 18th March is not, in my opinion, decisive, but on the 22nd March I met General Hamilton, and heard his views, and I now think that to obtain important results, and to achieve the object of the campaign, a combined operation will be essential ...

For the Fleet to attack the Narrows now would jeopardise the success of a better and bigger scheme and would, therefore, be a mistake.

(4) Sir John de Robeck to First Lord [Mr Churchill], March 27th:

On the 22nd after conference with the General and acquaintance with his views, I gathered that he considered co-operation of the Army and Navy to be a sound operation of war, and that he was quite prepared to co-operate with the Navy in forcing the Straits, although he could not take action until the 14th April.

In my opinion, decisive and overwhelming results will be effected by the plan discussed with General Hamilton, and now being prepared ...

The assumption underlying the plan originally approved for forcing the Dardanelles, by ships, was that forts could be destroyed by gun-fire alone. As applied to the attacking of open forts, by high velocity fire, this assumption has been conclusively disproved.

For example, the damage caused to Fort 8 is, possibly, the disablement of one gun, though this fort has frequently been bombarded at long and close range.

The destructive power of shells which hit, was either uselessly expended on the parapet, or only effected the demolition of some unimportant outwork in the background of the fort.

It has been impracticable, even at ranges of 700 or 800 yards, to obtain direct hits on each gun. This was attempted in the case of Forts 3 and 6. In Fort 4, on the 26th February, although the fort had been heavily shelled for 2 days, at both long and short range, one gun was found loaded and ready to fire. At the most it is possible for ships to dominate the forts to such an extent that the guns cannot be fought by their crews. To effect more permanent disablement would require an excessive expenditure of ammunition at point blank range.

This opinion is strengthened by recently received information on the operations against Tsin Tau. The analogy of the attack on the cupola forts at Antwerp by heavy howitzer fire is quite misleading, when applied to the case I have described.

It is necessary for ships to come under fire at the Narrows, in order to engage Forts 7 and 8 at close range. It is necessary, therefore, to silence these, and this entails expenditure of valuable ammunition. I am also in some anxiety as to the wear of the old guns. Several premature bursts of common shell occurred on the 18th and put guns out of action from time to time. A bombardment, which could not be carried to a decisive result, would be the worst policy. It is, therefore, necessary to land demolition parties to destroy forts.

General Hamilton is not prepared to undertake the task of covering these parties at the Narrows and I quite agree. It is impracticable to carry out the demolition by surprise. The difficulties of clearing a passage for the Fleet (and the forts have to be kept silenced by gun-fire, while it is carried out) are materially increased by the dangers from mines, which are greater than we anticipated, and the number of torpedo tubes, which are reported to have increased, and which cannot be destroyed.

I consider the result of naval action might be either a brilliant success or quite indecisive. A great factor towards success is the effect that would be produced on the Turkish Army by the appearance of the Fleet off Constantinople. The situation in Turkey, at present, appears to be controlled by the Army, but this in itself is dominated by the Germans.

If the advent of the Fleet into the Sea of Marmora fails to dismay the Turkish Army, and they close the Straits behind us, ships would only be able to operate and maintain themselves in the Marmora for a length of time that is governed almost entirely by the number of ammunition ships and colliers which can accompany them, and the percentage of unprotected ships which we can expect to get through is small, as the passage will be contested.

While the forts are still intact I can see no practical solution to the problem of passing supply ships for the Fleet through the Dardanelles. It would be vital, in this event, for the peninsula to be occupied by the Army, as the guns on the Asiatic side can be commanded from the European shore, sufficiently to permit ships to pass through. This would open the Strait.

The assistance of all naval forces available will, in my judgment, be needed to land the Army of the size contemplated, in the teeth of strenuous opposition. The Turks would not, necessarily, be induced to abandon the peninsula by a landing at Bulair, and there is no doubt that this can better be done by a fleet intact outside the Straits than by the remnants of a fleet, short of ammunition, inside the Straits.

Our success would be assured when the Army holds the peninsula and the squadron is through the Dardanelles.

Co-operation, which would really prove the deciding factor in reducing the length of time necessary for the completion of the campaign in the Sea of Marmora, and for the occupation of Constantinople, will be ensured by this delay of perhaps a fortnight.

These telegrams mark the close of the period of consultation between Sir Ian Hamilton and Sir John de Robeck as to the policy to be pursued. Thereafter these officers were occupied with detailed plans for the landing. It is only necessary to observe:

(a) That Sir John de Robeck's views, as expressed in his telegram of March 27th, were endorsed by Mr Churchill's telegram, in reply, of the same date:

That the result might have been achieved without involving the Army, according to the original plan, had been my hope, but I see clearly that a combined operation is now essential for the reasons you mention.

The date is not distant, for time has passed and the troops are available. The Admiralty telegram, approving all your proposals, will, therefore, be sent.

(b) That Sir Ian Hamilton's plan of operations was to some extent antici- pated by Lord Kitchener in a telegram to him on April 2nd:

Limpus's report, which I have been reading, and of which the Admiral has a copy, seems to point to the advisability of effecting the main landing in the neighbourhood of Cape Helles and Morto Bay, while making a feint [diversion tactic] in considerable force south of Kaba Tepe, with the possibility of landing and of commanding the ground of Sari Bahr, so that the enemy, on its southern slopes, may be prevented from supporting those on the Kilid Bahr Plateau.

I presume that, preparatory to destroying the forts at the Narrows, you will attack in force to occupy this plateau. The most necessary points for consideration seem to me, at a distance, to be night attacks, and crossing barbed wire entanglements.

As to entanglements, which artillery fire has not completely cleared, it is worth remembering how thorn zaribas [barriers] were successfully crossed in the Sudan by means of the native angerib bed. Men carrying angeribs are placed immediately behind the hand grenade and attacking lines and directly the fire of the defence is dominated, they rush forward and place the angerib on the entanglement. A recrudescence [fresh break out] of fire from the trench may ensue, which is again dominated, and the process continued until men can jump over the last entanglement. If each attacking company does this, many roads over obstructions can be made.

I do not in the least wish to influence your judgment, formed locally, on the situation to be dealt with in the Gallipoli Peninsula, but only give you all this for what it is worth.

I hope that arrangements will be made for adequate bombardments by the Navy of the positions to be attacked, and for the advance of your troops to be covered by its shell fire. When you have decided on your plans, I shall be glad to have a general idea of them. Secrecy will be observed here.

To which Sir Ian Hamilton replied on April 4th:

Reference concluding sentence, there is no need to send you my general idea as you have already got it in one, even down to the details.

I have not got enough gun ammunition to destroy barbed wire by field guns, howitzers, or machine guns, and the entanglements are mostly defiladed [protected end-to-end] from naval guns. I therefore must rely on other methods, including that suggested by you.

After March 19th there was no further meeting of the War Council until May 14th, and we are unable to ascertain any precise date on which, after the failure of the naval attack, military operations on the Gallipoli Peninsula were definitely decided on. Mr Asquith informed us that between these dates there were thirteen meetings of the Cabinet, at eleven of which the operations at the Dardanelles were brought up for report; and that they were on several occasions the subject, not merely of report, but of long and careful discussion.

It would appear therefore that these operations and the policy they involved were undertaken with the knowledge of the Cabinet, but we think, as was stated in our previous report, that they should have been fully discussed by the War Council.

During this period negotiations took place for the intervention of Italy on the side of the Allies; and the course of these negotiations made it undesirable to discontinue operations after the failure of the naval attack. Lord Kitchener had, as we have previously stated, told the War Council on February 24th that, if the Fleet could not get through the Straits unaided, the Army ought to see the business through. The same opinion was expressed in his written instructions to Sir Ian Hamilton on March 13th.

In addition, the failure to penetrate the German lines at the battle of Neuve Chapelle and in the Champagne (Perthes) had strengthened the view that a stalemate had set in in the West. The need for relieving the pressure in the Caucasus still existed. The urgency of opening up a line of communications, first to supply Russia with munitions and military stores, and secondly, to enable the Russian harvest of 1914 to be exported and thus re-establish the Russian exchanges, had not diminished. And undoubtedly the fear existed that to abandon the enterprise might have a bad effect in Russia.

These considerations, together with the fact that the military difficulties had not been sufficiently realised, seem to have led to the decision to initiate the joint naval and military attack on the Gallipoli Peninsula.

THE PREPARATIONS FOR THE LANDING

Sir Ian Hamilton's Administrative Staff did not arrive at Alexandria [in Egypt] until April 7th. The preparations for the landing were, therefore, carried out by his General Staff. With regard to these preparations it is necessary to consider:

(a) The change of the main base from Lemnos to Alexandria.
(b) The necessity for re-loading and re-arranging the transports of the 29th and the Royal Naval divisions, and
(c) The estimates of the strength of the Turkish forces to be encountered.

Change of base from Lemnos to Alexandria

Lemnos had been originally selected as a base for the naval attack in February and March. Lemnos was also contemplated as the base when, on February 16th, the War Council decided to send out the 29th Division. On February 20th, 30,000 Australian troops under Sir William Birdwood were ordered by Lord Kitchener to get ready to lend further support to the naval attack, and a brigade of these troops was sent from Egypt to Lemnos, arriving there early in March. On February 23rd Vice-Admiral Sir Sackville Carden telegraphed to Sir John Maxwell that, before the landing on the Gallipoli Peninsula, the troops sent from Egypt would have to live on board their transports; and on February 26th he sent a similar message, adding that the troops could land for exercise.

On March 2nd, the War Office telegraphed to Sir William Birdwood:

> Reports from Athens indicate that there is no water at Mudros Bay. Special arrangements for distilling and for tank vessels are being made by the Admiralty, but there may be some delay.
>
> After consulting the naval authorities on the spot, please report on the subject.

On March 9th the Royal Naval and the French Divisions began to arrive at Lemnos, and on that date Sir John Maxwell transmitted to the War Office a telegram from Admiral Carden to the effect that, since the water supply was not assured, no more troops should be sent from Egypt for the present. This was followed, on March 12th, by a further telegram transmitted from Admiral Wemyss, reporting that a water supply for 10,000 men and their horses was available, but that disembarkation was difficult and tedious with the appliances at their disposal, that embarkation would be still more difficult, and suggesting that troops coming from Egypt should be held in readiness there. On March 16th, Sir John Maxwell informed the War Office that "he gathered from Admiral Wemyss and the officers on the spot that Lemnos could not be a base for a large force." In addition to this, it was found necessary to repack the transports, and it was impossible to do this at Mudros. On March 18th Lord Kitchener sanctioned Alexandria as the main base, subject to the final decision of Sir Ian Hamilton and Sir John de Robeck.

Thereafter Alexandria was used as the main, and Lemnos as the advanced base.

The re-loading and re-arrangement of transports

The allocation of the transports for the 29th and Royal Naval Divisions was made by the War Office and by the Royal Marine Office of the Admiralty respectively. When the transports for the 29th Division arrived at Avonmouth, it was found that some of them had already been partially loaded at another port with fodder for horses, and it was accordingly impossible to stow on them all the vehicles forming the first line transport for the units on board. This part of the first line transport was sent on three freight ships which had been told off [detailed] to take the Mechanical Transport belonging to the Division, and these ships arrived ten days later than the transports.

In addition to this, some of the ships were not well or conveniently stowed.

The units of the Royal Naval Division, also, were not embarked complete, the personnel having been placed in one ship, the transport in another, and the horses in another. The stores were not packed as they should have been owing to their not having arrived until a few hours before the ships sailed.

Proposals were made to restow at Malta the transports which were bringing out the 29th Division, but the accommodation in the harbour did not permit this. The transports were, therefore, sent to Alexandria, and some delay was caused by the fact that they had to await the arrival of the slower ships (presumably the freight ships), which had essential things on board.

No special instructions were given in the first instance as to how the transports should be packed. The reason for this was that the exact use to be made of the troops was not decided, and no plan of operations had been prepared. The ordinary principles which govern embarkation in the absence of special instructions therefore applied. We were informed by the Director of Movements that these principles are:

(1) To split up units as little as possible.
(2) To ensure that, when units are split up, the ships on which they are embarked should sail on the same day, or on dates as near each other as possible.
(3) To embark troops in such a way that they should be able to take to the field at once on disembarkation.

He explained, however, that these principles cannot always be adhered to, especially in the matter of sending men and their transport together. Many transports, especially the larger ships, some of which were used in this instance, are not fitted to carry animals or vehicles. Transports are not collected at a port and then loaded simultaneously, but dealt with as they arrive. It is possible to carry units and their first line transport together if instructions are given to do so, but it takes a longer time and requires a larger number of transports, because in that case the transports would have to sail only partly loaded.

In this case no such special instructions were issued. It would have been hardly possible to do so, as the plan of operations was not determined. General Braithwaite, Sir Ian Hamilton's Chief of the General Staff, says that no one could have given the order satisfactorily unless he had worked it backwards from the shore on which he wished to disembark the men, and nothing of that kind was possible here. Indeed the plan was so little known that a great deal of transport which was quite useless for the actual expedition was taken, e.g. a much larger number of horses than was necessary, and all the mechanical transport required according to the ordinary war establishments [military forces]. The Quartermaster-General's department at the War Office pointed out that the mechanical transport would not be needed, but it was sent by the direct order of the Secretary of State. When the objects of the expedition became more clearly defined, this was discontinued.

We think therefore that, in the absence of a scheme of operations, a considerable amount of re-stowage would in any case have been necessary. The chief complaint made against the packing was the separation of the men from their first line transport and animals, and this has been explained above. There was some bad stevedoring [loading and unloading], but it must be remembered that at Liverpool, where part of the force embarked, there were considerable troubles as to dock labour; that this was the first long sea embarkation that had been undertaken by the officers in charge; and that the orders were suddenly given and had to be carried out at once.

On the whole we think that, though there may have been instances of bad stowage, the real reason for the extensive repacking was the absence of knowledge of the operations for which the embarkation was required, and that the embarkation officers at the ports of loading were not to blame.

At first sight the delay caused by this repacking and the change of base from Lemnos to Egypt appears serious, but on examination we think that the effect was very slight. When the transports were ordered to Alexandria and Port Said to repack, no plan of operations had been settled, the whole of the Staff had not yet arrived, and there were many arrangements to be made. The first mention of repacking is on March 18th, 1915, and the last repacked transport left Alexandria on April 16th, 1915. The landing was on April 25th, 1915. We think that plans and arrangements could not have been completed until the greater part of this interval had elapsed, and that the effective delay did not amount to more than a few days, which was not important.

The Administrative Staff did not arrive in Alexandria until April 1st.

The Commander-in-Chief and General Staff left for Mudros shortly after, leaving the Administrative Staff behind. Major-General Woodward, the Deputy Adjutant-General, protested against this decision to the Commander-in-Chief and the Chief of the General Staff, but did not succeed in getting it reversed. We think that the Chiefs of the Administrative Staff should have accompanied General Headquarters, it being of high importance that these officials should be in touch with the Commander-in-Chief and work in close concert with the Chief of the General Staff.

Estimate of Turkish forces

Before the landing Sir Ian Hamilton estimated the strength of the Turkish forces on the Gallipoli Peninsula as 40,000 with a reserve of 30,000 west of Rodosto. This estimate was increased, later, by the addition of the 2nd Army Corps Nizam, which had been moved in April from the Caucasus to Constantinople, and made available to reinforce the forces on the peninsula.

A more detailed and comprehensive estimate was conveyed by the War Office in a telegram to the General Staff in India on March 1st:

We appreciate the situation as follows:

It is believed that divisions now consist of Nizam brought up to establishment by Redif.

In European Turkey, including Gallipoli, are nine divisions, totalling 120,000 men.

In Smyrna, Asiatic Dardanelles, and Panderma there are two strong divisions, and depot battalions, totalling 40,000 men.

In Caucasus there are 17 divisions, many of which are weak, totalling 190,000 men.

In Syria and Palestine there are five divisions, totalling 70,000 men.

In Mesopotamia is a 4th Division (new formation) of 1st Corps of 12 battalions, lately arrived Baghdad, also 35th and 38th divisions.

It is possible that the 6th Reserve Corps is also in the Caucasus, though its reported existence is not yet confirmed.

After the landing had been effected, Sir Ian Hamilton presented a revised estimate in his telegram to Lord Kitchener of April 30th:

The Turkish troops are as follows:

(1) 2nd, 7th, 8th and 9th divisions, all of 3rd Army Corps; Pamir Division of 3rd Reserve Corps; part of 5th division, 2nd Army Corps. Total, say, 44,000.

(2) Probably on peninsula, but not definitely ascertained, 11th Division and part of 10th, both of 4th Army Corps, and perhaps 44th and 58th Regiments unallotted. Total, say, 26,000. This information has mainly been ascertained from statements by prisoners. Documents obtained locally and found on dead Turks show that two regiments have just come from Plagak.

(3) Not on peninsula, but available at short notice, part of 6th Army Corps. Say, 20,000.

Bulair is watched by the Fleet, and already three demonstrations have been made, but it is impossible to stop reinforcements crossing the Isthmus during the night.

Generally reinforcements arrive by the sea to Gallipoli, but as the fleet have now two submarines off that town, I hope this will be rendered very dangerous in future.

Area of military operations on the Gallipoli Peninsula, 1915

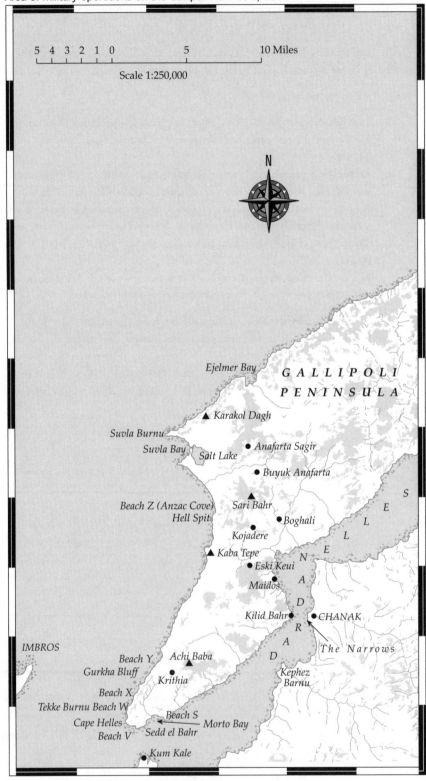

5 4 3 2 1 0   5   10 Miles

Scale 1:250,000

N

Ejelmer Bay

GALLIPOLI PENINSULA

▲ Karakol Dagh

Suvla Burnu
Suvla Bay   Salt Lake

● Anafarta Sagir

● Buyuk Anafarta

Beach Z (Anzac Cove)
Hell Spit

▲ Sari Bahr

● Boghali

● Kojadere

▲ Kaba Tepe

● Eski Keui

● Maidos

Kilid Bahr ●   ● CHANAK

The Narrows

DARDANELLES

IMBROS

Beach Y   Achi Baba ▲
Gurkha Bluff
Krithia ●

Beach X

Tekke Burnu Beach W

Cape Helles
Beach V   Sedd el Bahr

Beach S ← → Morto Bay

Kephez
Barnu

● Kum Kale

THE LANDING ON APRIL 25TH, 1915

Two important questions to be considered concurrently in drawing up a plan of operations were the place or places of landing on the peninsula, and the objective or objectives of the troops when landed.

As regards the first of these questions, Sir Ian Hamilton had, when at Mudros, made such reconnaissance as could be made from the sea, and states that the dominating features in the southern part of the peninsula were:

(1) Sari Bahr mountain, 970 feet high.
(2) Kilid Bahr Plateau, 700 feet high, a natural fortification artificially fortified, covering the Narrows from an attack from the Aegean.
(3) Achi Baba, 600 feet high, commanding the extreme south of the peninsula near Cape Helles.

After considering the other plans open to him he decided to make two main landings: one, which was divided into several subordinate landings, in the extreme south of the peninsula; and the other north of Kaba Tepe and near the south-western foothills of Sari Bahr.

In his despatch he mentions two other main alternatives which he considered:

(1) A landing on the north coast of the Gulf of Xeros, and
(2) A landing on the Asiatic shore of the Dardanelles.

He rejected the first on the ground that Bulair would lie between him and the Narrows, and that in attacking Bulair he would be open to attack from the Turkish forces in Thrace.

He had made a reconnaissance of Bulair, and had come to the conclusion that it was not possible to effect a landing there.

He did not think that he had a sufficient force for operations on the Asiatic shore, and his instructions from Lord Kitchener were opposed to a landing there.

These are the only alternatives discussed in the despatch, but others were considered, and Suvla is mentioned in an appreciation signed by Colonel Aspinall and submitted to Sir Ian Hamilton's Chief of the General Staff. A landing there is dismissed in a few words, and it does not seem to have been thought to be a place which merited the same attention as Bulair and the Asiatic coast. Probably the reason for this was that when it was decided to land on the European side, but not to attempt a landing at or near Bulair, it was considered that the best way to help the Fleet was to attack at the southern end of the peninsula. This is the opinion expressed by Sir Ian Hamilton and by General Braithwaite.

The question also must have arisen whether the available force was sufficient for more than two main landings. In order to make Suvla Bay secure as a base it was necessary to occupy the northern ridge by the sea, the Karakol Dagh, up to Ejelmer Bay, and thence the heights running south from Ejelmer Bay to Anafarta Sagir. Sir Ian Hamilton did not consider that he had sufficient force to do this as well as land at Anzac and Helles, and Lieutenant-General Sir Aylmer Hunter-Weston also said that the force would not have been strong enough for such an operation.

Sir William Birdwood expressed the opinion that, looking at the matter in the light of after-events and assuming that there was no greater force defending Suvla at that time than at the later landing, Sir Ian Hamilton's force was sufficient to have landed at Suvla with safety, and that it would have been well to do so; but he added: "I also think I should have done what Sir Ian Hamilton had done, only in the light of what has happened since and the inability to force Achi Baba."

Sir Aylmer Hunter-Weston informed us that, once a landing had been decided upon, he thought Sir Ian Hamilton's choice of landing places was a perfectly justifiable one.

On the other hand, several witnesses criticised the selection of the landing places, and expressed themselves in favour of other schemes of disembarkation. Whatever weight may attach to these divergent opinions, we consider that the choice of landing places was a matter lying within the discretion of the General Officer Commanding-in-Chief, and Sir Ian Hamilton appears to us to have exercised his discretion with reasonable care and circumspection.

As regards the objective or objectives of the troops when landed, we gather from the instructions issued by General Braithwaite to the General Officers commanding the Australian and New Zealand Army Corps and the 29th Division respectively, and the latter's Operation Orders based on these instructions, that the following movements were contemplated.

At Anzac the force which landed first, called the covering force, after it had overcome any resistance at or near the shore which the Turks might offer, was to occupy the Sari Bahr heights and thus cover the left flank of the force, called the main body, which was to land shortly afterwards. This body was to advance four miles east of the landing-place and assault Mal Tepe, a hill overlooking the Straits and three-quarters of a mile south of Boghali.

At Helles the troops were similarly divided into a covering force and main body, and after overcoming any resistance at or near the shore which the Turks might offer, they were to occupy Krithia and Achi Baba.

When the Anzac and Helles forces had established themselves at Mal Tepe and Achi Baba, the intention was that a converging attack should be made from those points upon the Turkish position at Kilid Bahr.

As the Turkish resistance near the shore proved too strong at Anzac and Helles, the proposed advance inland to Sari Bahr, Mal Tepe, Krithia, and Achi Baba did not take place.

It has been already stated that there were several distinct landings at the extreme southern end of the peninsula, and this was the subject of considerable comment by several witnesses. Speaking generally, it is not wise to divide a force, as it is thereby exposed to the danger of being attacked and beaten in detail. Sir Ian Hamilton's reasons for doing so in this case are given in his despatch of May 20th, 1915, published in the *London Gazette* of July 6th, 1915, where he says:

> Nothing but a thorough and systematic scheme for flinging the whole of the troops under my command very rapidly ashore could be expected to meet with success, whereas on the other hand, a tentative or piecemeal programme was bound to lead to disaster . . . The beaches were either too well defended by works and guns or else so restricted by nature that it did not seem possible, even by two or three simultaneous landings, to pass the troops ashore quickly enough to enable them to maintain themselves against the rapid concentration and counter-attack which the enemy was bound in such case to attempt. It became necessary, therefore, not only to land simultaneously at as many places as possible, but to threaten to land at other points as well. The first of these necessities involved another unavoidable if awkward contingency—the separation by considerable intervals of the force.

In view of the restricted space on the beaches and the importance of preventing a concentration of the Turkish forces against the small numbers which could be landed at any one place, we are not prepared to question the propriety of Sir Ian Hamilton's dispositions [arrangements].

The landing places selected were S at the north-east corner of Morto Bay, V and W (called Lancashire landing) on each side of Cape Helles, X (called Implacable landing) just above Tekke Burnu, and Y, just above Gurkha Bluff, and due west of Krithia. There was another beach called Y2, which was considered, but no landing was made there. What afterwards was known as Anzac was Beach Z, a little to the north of Kaba Tepe. The nature of the beaches is fully described in Sir Ian Hamilton's despatch, to which reference has already been made, and the description need not be repeated. A landing was also made by the French at Kum Kale, on the Asiatic side, but this was only intended to be temporary, and these troops were soon withdrawn to a position on the right of the British forces at Helles.

The landings at V, W and X were intended to be the main landings, those at S and Y being intended mainly "to protect the flanks, to disseminate the forces of the enemy, and to interrupt the arrival of his reinforcements."

A feint was also made in the neighbourhood of Enos in order to prevent Turkish troops from being sent from the north of the peninsula to resist the landings.

We propose to discuss the arrangements for the provision of water and the care of the sick and wounded in a separate part of this report, and it is not necessary therefore to refer to them here except to say that the landing operations at Helles and Anzac were not checked by a lack of water.

The landings, as described in Sir Ian Hamilton's despatch, appear to have been well planned, and were carried out in the face of exceptional difficulties and at the cost of heavier casualties than had been expected. The conduct of the forces engaged was exemplary.

An unfortunate sense of unfairness was created by the fact that when Sir John de Robeck's despatch dealing with these operations was published, the troops employed at certain landings were praised by name, whereas those who landed at Beach V, which was regarded as the most difficult of all to capture, were praised without identifying them. The explanation is that Sir John de Robeck's despatch, as written, contained a detail of the troops assigned to the several landings, and reference to this showed at once that the battalions whose successful accomplishment of their task at Beach V "bordered almost on the miraculous" were the 1st Royal Dublin Fusiliers, 1st Royal Munster Fusiliers, and 2nd Hampshire Regiment. But this detailed list was withheld from publication as likely to give useful information to the enemy, and the troops in question were inadvertently denied the public tribute of Sir John de Robeck's praise.

It is not necessary to discuss the landings except in the case of that on Beach Y, as to which there seems to have been some misunderstanding. The landing on this beach was made by the 1st King's Own Scottish Borderers, under Colonel Koe, and the Plymouth Battalion of the Royal Marine Light Infantry, under Colonel Matthews. Colonel Matthews, as the senior officer, was in command.

The object was to move inland and try to capture a gun which was stated to be in position there, and make a demonstration so as to draw the enemy in that direction, and relieve the pressure at the foot of the peninsula. The force was then to withdraw and work up towards Beach X to join the rest of the 87th Brigade, to which the Royal Marine Light Infantry were attached. The united force would then move on Krithia.

The landing was made without opposition, and 2,000 men were on the ridge in a very short time. They advanced in the direction ordered, but were not met by the force coming from Beach X, which was unable to make its advance as proposed. Colonel Matthews then withdrew to the head of the gully up which he had advanced, and entrenched there.

The force was undisturbed by the enemy until between 4 and 5 pm, when it was attacked by a large number of Turks coming from the direction of Krithia. After hard fighting extending over many hours, the force under Colonel Matthews, having suffered many casualties and exhausted practically all its ammunition, was obliged to retire to the beach and re-embark.

The decision to withdraw was made by Colonel Matthews.

Immediately after landing, he had reported that there was no opposition, and afterwards, when attacked by superior forces and in want of ammunition, had sent a message to say that unless he had more ammunition he must withdraw: but he did not receive an answer to either message.

If a larger force had been landed at this beach in the first instance, or if it had been possible, either by diverting some part of the troops from Beach X or otherwise, to send reinforcements before the Turkish troops came up in the evening, a further advance might have been made, but it is difficult to say whether, without the expected co-operation from Beach X, it would have been successful.

At Anzac the landing was effected after severe fighting at a place rather further north than was intended, and in the confusion of landing the tows crossed one another, and the battalions got mixed, which checked the advance and made delay for reorganisation necessary.

The fighting was so severe throughout April 25th and the ground gained so small that by the evening, Sir William Birdwood feared that it might be necessary to withdraw the troops and informed Sir Ian Hamilton accordingly.

In reply the latter directed him to maintain his position at all costs.

Both at Anzac and at the south of the peninsula the troops by the evening of the first day after the disembarkation were occupying positions on and near the shore. At the south, contact had been established across the extreme end of the peninsula. In neither case, however, was it found possible to carry the advance beyond a short distance from the shore.

At Anzac it had been intended to occupy Sari Bahr and Mal Tepe, and at Helles to occupy Krithia and Achi Baba, within a very short time of the first landing, and ultimately to have effected a junction of the Anzac–Helles forces. In both cases the difficulties proved too great to permit these intentions being carried out, and in fact none of these objectives was ever attained.

The nature of the ground was a formidable obstacle, but the main difficulty lay in the fact that the Turks had been warned of the probability of an attack by the bombardment of the forts, followed by the assembling of troops, and consequently had made preparations by trenches, wire entanglements, etc., protected by artillery, machine-guns and rifle fire, to resist the attack; that they were in considerable force and well led (partly by German officers); and that they fought extremely well both in defence and counter-attack.

An opinion had prevailed, in consequence of the events of the Balkan wars and some recent fighting in Mesopotamia, that the Turkish soldiers had deteriorated as fighting men, but the fighting at Helles and Anzac during the landing and in the following months proved this to be a mistaken view.

Heavy and continuous fighting, described in Sir Ian Hamilton's despatch, followed for several days, with the result that a little more ground was gained and the positions improved, but very little real progress was made. The force at Helles was reinforced during May by the arrival of the 29th Indian Brigade, the 42nd (Territorial) Division, and three Battalions of the Royal Naval Division. If the Indian Brigade and the 42nd Division had been assembled at Mudros and ready to support the attack of the 29th Division, Brigadier-General Street, senior General Staff Officer with Sir Aylmer Hunter-Weston, was of the opinion that the attack would have been successful.

Sir Aylmer Hunter-Weston was not so confident on this point.

The evidence does not make it clear why these troops were not sent at once, but if it were possible, looking to all the circumstances, to send them, we think it would have been well to do so. On the evidence before us we see no reason why they should not have been sent. Sir Ian Hamilton expressed a wish for the services of a brigade of Gurkhas, but we cannot find that he definitely applied for the troops mentioned above.

Throughout these attacks there was a shortage of artillery and gun ammunition.

We must again refer to Sir Ian Hamilton's despatch for the particulars of this fighting, but it may be useful to quote some of his telegrams. They express an optimistic opinion of the chances of ultimate success, but they do not disguise the difficulties.

On April 30th, 1915, he gave as an estimate of the Turkish forces in or about the peninsula:

(1) On the peninsula, 44,000.
(2) Probably on the peninsula, 26,000.
(3) Not on the peninsula, but available at short notice, 20,000.

On May 4th he reported that the supply of ammunition was becoming a serious matter owing to the continuous fighting, to which Lord Kitchener replied that the supply was not calculated on the basis of a prolonged occupation of the Gallipoli Peninsula, and said: "It is important to push on." On May 7th he reported that some progress, but not so much as he had hoped, had been made, and that progress was slow and opposition stubborn. On May 9th, after describing the third consecutive day's attack on Achi Baba, he said:

> I might represent the battle as a victory, but actually the result has been failure, as the main object remains unachieved. Our troops have done all that flesh and

blood can do against semi-permanent works, and they are not able to carry them. More and more munitions will be needed to do it. I fear this is a very unpalatable conclusion, but I see no way out of it.

He then estimated the forces engaged in the following manner:

I estimate that the Turks had about 40,000 opposed to our 25,000 rifles. There are 20,000 more in front of the Australian–New Zealand Army Corps, 12,000 rifles at Kaba Tepe. By bringing men over from the Asiatic side the Turks seem able to keep up their strength. I have only one more Brigade of the Lancashire Territorial Division to come, and that will not suffice to make any appreciable difference in the situation as regards pushing through.

To this Lord Kitchener replied that the whole situation naturally gave him some anxiety, particularly as the transport service was much hampered by the want of ships.

On May 10th, Sir Ian Hamilton reported that the guns of the Navy had not been able to give him so much help as he had hoped, because of the spoon-shaped nature of the ground from Achi Baba to Cape Helles, which exposed only the outer edges to direct fire, while the inner slopes consisted of broken ground facilitating concealed works.

He explained that the 25,000 rifles which he had mentioned the day before had been a reference to the number of British rifles actually in the fighting line. The telegram continues:

With regard to future operations, the Admiral agrees with me in thinking that the only sound procedure is to hammer away until the enemy gets demoralised. Meanwhile grand attacks are impracticable and we must make short advances during the night and dig in for the day until we get Achi Baba. I then hope to be able to make progress without this trench method, but Achi Baba is really a fortress. If two fresh divisions organised as a corps could be spared me I could push on from this end and from Kaba Tepe with good prospects of success, otherwise I am afraid it will degenerate into trench warfare with its resultant slowness.

On May 11th, Lord Kitchener cabled that he was sending out the Lowland Division and some artillery, and this message was acknowledged on May 12th.

On May 13th, Sir Ian Hamilton telegraphed, expressing a hope that the 29th Division would be made up to strength by drafts.

It was the rule to send out 10 per cent of an expeditionary force to replace casualties in the first instance. At the time of this expedition the rule had fallen into abeyance in the case of units going to France, the distance being short and communication rapid. Although the troops for the Dardanelles were to operate at a distance from England, Lord Kitchener would not allow the additional 10 per cent to be sent with them. The matter was mentioned to him by Lieutenant-General Sir Henry Sclater, the Adjutant-General, to whom it had been represented by Brigadier-General Woodward, who was Director of Mobilization at the War Office at the time of his appointment as Deputy Adjutant-General of the Expeditionary Force. Sir Henry Sclater said the reason given to him by Lord Kitchener for his decision was that the operations in Gallipoli would so soon be over that to form a base in Egypt would be practically locking up men who were much more urgently required in France. In Sir Henry Sclater's opinion, the men could not have been sent without denuding France of reinforcements, but General Woodward dissented from this view.

THE DECISION TO CONTINUE THE OPERATIONS

In these circumstances an important meeting of the War Council was held on May 14th to discuss the situation.

It was clear that the conditions had materially changed. The landings had been successfully effected, but the expectation that it would be possible to carry the important positions of Achi Baba and Sari Bahr in the first rush had definitely failed, the task having proved far more difficult than was anticipated. The casualties had been very heavy; they amounted to about 14,000, exclusive of the French. This made the question of drafts and reinforcements very serious. It was now apparent that the operations would not follow the course which had been expected. Instead of the troops on landing being able rapidly to drive the Turks out of their positions and to occupy the heights dominating the defences of the Narrows, they found themselves confronted by lines of entrenchments and entanglements, possession of which could only be gained by the deliberate methods of trench warfare.

Probably at this time the very large expenditure of ammunition required to reduce hostile trenches had not been thoroughly realised, but, as already pointed out, Sir Ian Hamilton had informed Lord Kitchener on May 9th, 1915, that more and more munitions would be needed, and it was known that, as afterwards stated on May 17th, 1915, the advance could probably be made with half the loss of life then reckoned upon if there were a liberal supply of gun ammunition, especially of high explosive. The positions held by the force were unfavourable: they consisted of hardly more than a fringe. They were, including the beaches, commanded by shell-fire, and there were no opportunities for withdrawing the troops for rest behind the line. At Helles the positions were exposed also to shell-fire from the Asiatic shore, though this was afterwards kept down to a great extent by the fire of monitors.

The problem of transport was serious. There was a scarcity of ships and, owing to the necessity of using Mudros as a subsidiary base for troops, munitions, and stores, this scarcity was aggravated. Mudros had practically none of the usual facilities of a port. Stores not immediately wanted had to be kept on board the transports. Communication with different ships and different parts of the harbour was much impeded by want of light craft. Besides, there was always the probability of danger from submarines. In consequence the transports were detained at Mudros, and great delay and congestion resulted.

This condition of Mudros as a port was probably not of much importance so long as the operations were expected to be of short duration, but it was a serious matter which had to be faced if the operations were materially prolonged in time and enlarged in extent.

The Dardanelles Expedition could not be considered by itself; though great results were expected from it if successful, it was subsidiary, in the view of the military authorities in England, to the main operations in France.

The demands from France for both men and munitions were very great, and there was much difficulty in supplying them. An offensive at Festubert, disappointing in its result, took place in May, and it was obvious that the demands of France were likely to increase rather than decrease. Moreover, there were requirements in Egypt, Mesopotamia, and elsewhere, which had to be met.

There was another matter which had to be considered. As stated in our interim report, the occurrence which led to action being taken with a view to forcing the passage of the Dardanelles was an enquiry from the Russian Government on January 2nd, 1915, as to whether the British Government could do anything to relieve the Turkish pressure upon their troops in the Caucasus. A reply was sent that a demonstration would be made in the direction of the Dardanelles; and when this demonstration took shape, it was arranged that in the event of our gaining access to the Sea of Marmora the Russians should co-operate with us, if possible, by sea and land in the vicinity of Constantinople.

A Russian Army Corps was designated for the purpose of military co-operation; but before the scheme, so far as Constantinople was concerned, had any chance of becoming operative, the Russian reverse in Galicia had begun, and it seemed possible that this occurrence, apart from its influence on the Balkan states, might lead to a diversion of the force which was to be available near Constantinople, should we succeed in forcing the passage of the Dardanelles.

On May 12th the Admiralty ordered the withdrawal of the *Queen Elizabeth* from the Dardanelles Expedition, this decision being strongly opposed by Lord Kitchener. It is difficult to say why Lord Kitchener should have attached so much importance to the retention of the *Queen Elizabeth*. Naval gun-fire in support of the military operations had not hitherto proved to be as valuable as had been anticipated, and the reduction in naval gun power entailed by the withdrawal of the warship in question was stated by the Admiralty to be more than made good by the addition of monitors and other vessels to the Fleet.

The War Council had to determine whether, in the changed circumstances, the requirements of all the different areas of war could be supplied, and whether it was wise to continue the operations on the peninsula. Diplomatic efforts had been made ever since the beginning of the Dardanelles Expedition to secure the co-operation of the Balkan states, the most prominent and powerful being Bulgaria, and these states were much influenced not only by the course of current events, but by their appreciation of the consequences likely to result from the action in the Near East which was being taken or contemplated by the Central Powers on the one hand and the Entente Allies on the other. It was important, therefore, not to do anything which would show weakness. The expedition had been begun in consequence of a communication from Russia, and the Russians considered that the effect so far had been to hold up Turkish troops and relieve the pressure on their forces. It was hoped that, if successful, the expedition would open the way to Constantinople.

Finally, it was anticipated that an abandonment of the expedition would have a very bad effect upon British prestige in the East.

All these matters were taken into consideration, as well as the purely military question of the prospects of success of the operations in which we were engaged.

The tendency was towards sending out sufficient reinforcements for a further effort, but no final decision was reached, except that Lord Kitchener should ask Sir Ian Hamilton what force he would require to ensure success at the Dardanelles.

As a result of this decision, Lord Kitchener telegraphed to Sir Ian Hamilton on May 14th:

> The War Council would like to know what force you consider would be necessary to carry through the operations on which you are engaged. You should base this estimate on the supposition that I have adequate forces to place at your disposal.

On May 17th, Sir Ian Hamilton answered, pointing out the difficulties of the position, and concluded:

> If the present condition of affairs were changed by the entry into the struggle of Bulgaria or Greece or by the landing of the Russians, my present force kept up to strength by the necessary drafts, plus the Army Corps asked for on May 10th, would probably suffice to finish my task. If, however, the present situation continues unchanged, and the Turks are still able to devote so much exclusive attention to us, I shall want an additional Army Corps, i.e. two Army Corps additional in all. I could not land these reinforcements on the peninsula until I can advance another 1,000 yards, and so free the beaches from the shelling to which they are subjected on the western side, and gain more space, but I could land them on the adjacent islands of Tenedos, Imbros and Lemnos, and take

them over later to the peninsula for battle. This plan would surmount the difficulties of water and space on the peninsula, and would perhaps enable me to effect a surprise with the fresh divisions. I believe I could advance with half the loss of life that is now reckoned upon if I had a liberal supply of gun ammunition, especially of high explosive.

Lord Kitchener, on May 18th, replied, expressing his disappointment that his preconceived views as to the conquest of positions necessary to support the troops on land were miscalculated, and his opinion that the question of whether we could long support two fields of operations draining on our resources, required grave consideration. He concluded:

> I know that I can rely on you to bring the present unfortunate state of affairs in the Dardanelles to as early a conclusion as possible, so that any consideration of a withdrawal, with all its dangers in the East, may be prevented from entering the field of possible solutions.

Sir Ian Hamilton's telegram of May 17th afforded the information called for by the War Council on May 14th, and would, no doubt, have been considered at once, but, unfortunately, just at this time the political crisis which resulted in the formation of the Coalition Government took place, and no authoritative conclusion was arrived at until June 7th.

Between these two dates the War Council had been increased in numbers by the addition of some members of the Unionist Party, and its name had been changed to that of the Dardanelles Committee. Its members were Mr Asquith, Lord Lansdowne, Lord Curzon, Lord Grey, Lord Crewe, Lord Kitchener, Lord Selborne, Mr Lloyd George, Mr Bonar Law, Mr McKenna, Mr Balfour and Mr Winston Churchill. Sir Edward Carson became a member in August, after the Suvla operations.

In Mr Churchill's opinion this political crisis produced an unfortunate delay by preventing an "unbroken and uninterrupted stream of reinforcements." According to his evidence Lord Kitchener, before May 14th, had informed him that it was intended to send two divisions. Therefore Mr Churchill had provided the transport for them, and informed Sir Ian Hamilton of the fact, but after May 14th Lord Kitchener changed his mind and sent one division only. At the same time Sir Ian Hamilton's telegram of May 17th was held over till after the formation of the new Government, and no action was taken on it. Mr Asquith agrees that the political situation was the main cause of the delay in sending reinforcements, but thinks that there was a shortage of available troops. Lieutenant-General Sir John Cowans also says that there was a difficulty in getting and equipping the men. We think that the political crisis was the main cause of delay. The Government had to decide whether operations other and larger than were originally contemplated should be undertaken. This was a question of policy, and some of the new members

of the Government had to be satisfied that the expedition was a justifiable enterprise.

On May 28th, Lord Kitchener prepared a memorandum for the
Dardanelles Committee, describing the objects and progress of the operations up to that date, and setting out what he considered to be the different
courses then open. This appreciation shows that the difficulties which had
been experienced by Sir Ian Hamilton had been communicated to Lord
Kitchener, and that they were brought by him to the distinct notice of the
members of the Committee. In this document he pointed out that

> the difficulties of the enterprise had proved more formidable than was at first
> anticipated, and that a much greater effort than was originally budgeted for was now
> required.

After describing the course of events, he repeated:

> The main advantage of withdrawing from the Dardanelles is to put an end to an
> operation the difficulties of which have been underestimated, which has already
> made a considerable inroad on our resources, and which will make a very
> considerable drain on both our naval and military resources before it is brought to a
> successful conclusion.

He then discussed the advantages of withdrawal, and summarised his conclusions as follows:

> Three solutions offer themselves:
>
> (1) Withdrawal
> (2) To seek, if possible, an immediate decision
> (3) To continue to push on and make such progress as is possible.
>
> The disadvantages of withdrawal have been shown above to be so great that
> this course could, in my opinion, only be justified in order to avoid a great
> disaster.
>
> On the other hand, it has been shown that the military forces and, what is
> even more important, the necessary supplies of ammunition asked for by the
> General Officer Commanding on the spot cannot be spared to bring the affair
> to a rapid conclusion, though I am somewhat in doubt, from the experience of
> trench warfare in Flanders, whether such increased forces would enable him to
> carry the position as he anticipates. Sir John French's forces have been increased
> very greatly, but no such advance as he had anticipated has occurred.
>
> The third course, however, has much to commend it. It avoids any immediate
> blow to our prestige; it keeps the door open to Balkan intervention; it ensures
> our hold on a strategical position of great importance, which rivets the attention
> of the Turks and in all probability limits active operations on their part against
> Egypt, or in Mesopotamia, or the Caucasus.
>
> The only thing to be said against it is that it involves certain dangers, viz., the
> risk arising from German submarines and of gas, assisted by the prevailing north

winds. There are furthermore, in my opinion, possibilities of the Turks not being able to maintain resistance on the present scale. This would enable our troops to advance, as well as to take advantage of any movement that Bulgaria or Greece may take in our favour.

On June 2nd, Sir Ian Hamilton had telegraphed to the effect that, in his opinion, the change in the Russian military position owing to reverses in Galicia had set free 100,000 Turks; that there were 80,000 in the peninsula; and that he might have, in all, a quarter of a million men brought against him. He concluded:

> Taking all these facts into consideration, it would seem that for an early success some equivalent to the suspended Russian co-operation is vitally necessary. It is, broadly, my view that we must obtain the support of a fresh ally in this theatre, or else that there should be got ready British reinforcements to the full extent mentioned in my telegram of May 17th, though, as stated above, the disappearance of Russian co-operation was not contemplated in my estimate.

In a further message, five days later, Sir Ian Hamilton stated that direct progress would be slow, and that he had been considering another line of operations starting from Enos, which he had rejected because of the objections of Sir John de Robeck.

Lord Kitchener's memorandum and the whole situation were considered by the Dardanelles Committee on June 7th, 1915, and the following conclusions were reached:

(1) To reinforce Sir Ian Hamilton with the three remaining divisions of the New Army, with a view to an assault in the second week of July.
(2) To send out certain naval units, which would be much less vulnerable to submarine attack than those under Admiral de Robeck's command.

There are no minutes of this meeting, but it is stated by Mr Churchill that the intention of the Committee was to authorise a more energetic prosecution of the operations than that mentioned in Lord Kitchener's third proposition of May 28th, and that Lord Kitchener himself said: "Do not let Sir Ian Hamilton throw away his strength in the interval, but let us send out ample reinforcements to carry the thing through." Lord Selborne agrees that the decision of the Dardanelles Committee contemplated a more vigorous continuation of the joint military and naval operations than the course proposed by Lord Kitchener.

Just after midnight on June 7th Sir Ian Hamilton sent a telegram reviewing the situation and emphasising the need for reinforcements.

> Without additional troops sufficient to provide for reliefs, as well as reinforcements, the men are undoubtedly getting worn out, and this will end in reducing our forces at Cape Helles to position of defenders in state of close siege, as is practically the case at Australian and New Zealand Army Corps already . . .

In the action of June 4th the troops succeeded in breaking through the centre of the enemy's line, but were so weakened by the effort that they could not take advantage of success, nor even retain all the ground gained. The whole position might have been captured and a great step made in advance, had there been plenty of fresh reserves available to push through and confirm success.

Lord Kitchener had in fact a few hours earlier cabled to Sir Ian Hamilton assuring him that the Government intended to make due provision for reinforcements. The full text of the telegram is as follows:

> Your difficulties are fully recognised by the Cabinet, who are determined to support you. We are sending you three divisions of the New Army. The first of these will leave about the end of this week, and the other two will be sent as transport is available. The last of the three divisions ought to reach you not later than the first fortnight in July. While steadily pressing the enemy, there seems no reason for running any premature risks in the meantime.

As a matter of fact the embarkation of the 13th Division took place from June 16th to June 23rd; of the 11th Division from July 1st to July 7th; and of the 10th Division from July 7th to July 14th.

Another cause contributed at this time to weaken the British troops and make the requests for reinforcements urgent. The weather had become very hot and with the heat there came swarms of flies. On the whole the sanitation of the British camps and trenches was satisfactorily carried out so far as was possible with the appliances which could be procured, but the Turkish trenches were very near, and the state of them was very bad; there were many unburied bodies, both of men and animals, at no great distance, and it was found impossible to keep down the plague of flies. These conveyed a great amount of infection, and this was also disseminated by the dust constantly carried about by the wind. The most common illness which resulted was a kind of dysentery, though para-typhoid and other complaints prevailed. Apart from reduction in numbers caused by death, the force was seriously weakened by the number of men always ill and the lowering of vitality produced in those who were still on duty.

On June 9th the Cabinet confirmed the decision of the Dardanelles Committee. This conclusion was an acknowledgment that the attempt to seize the peninsula by a rapid advance had failed; and that a larger force, more continued operations, and greater supplies of ammunition would be necessary to obtain success.

Another meeting of the Dardanelles Committee was held on June 12th, 1915, at which the Prime Minister submitted for consideration a memorandum by Mr Ashmead Bartlett, who had been on the peninsula as a war correspondent. In this memorandum Mr Ashmead Bartlett expressed an unfavourable view of the positions then occupied at Anzac and Helles and of the prospects of success in an advance from those positions, and advised an attack at or near the isthmus of Bulair. The Committee decided to ask Sir

Ian Hamilton for information on the matter, and a telegram was sent accordingly on June 12th. Sir Ian Hamilton answered on June 13th, giving his reasons against an attack in the neighbourhood of Bulair. He had sent substantially the same information the day before in answer to an enquiry from the War Office. These reasons seem to have satisfied the Committee, and an attack at Bulair was not further considered at that time.

It should be mentioned here that on June 21st Lord Kitchener had asked if Sir Ian Hamilton required a fourth division, and he had answered that he did not feel justified in refusing it, and that on June 25th Lord Kitchener had said that the Cabinet would like to know whether he considered it necessary or desirable that a fifth division should be sent. On June 29th Sir Ian Hamilton answered that, as the fourth and fifth divisions could not arrive with the first three, he adhered to his original plan of trying to turn the enemy's right at Anzac with the first three divisions and to gain a position from Kaba Tepe to Maidos. He would use the fourth and fifth, in case of non-success at first, to reinforce this wing; and in case of success, possibly to push through from Helles, but more probably to effect a landing on the southern shore of the Dardanelles. He concluded:

> To summarise, I think I have reasonable prospects of success with three divisions, with four the risk of miscalculation would be minimised, and with five, even if the fifth division had little or no gun ammunition, I think it would be a much simpler matter to clear the Asiatic shore subsequently of big guns, i.e., Kilid Bahr would be captured at an earlier date, and success would be generally assured.

In accordance with the views expressed by Sir Ian Hamilton, it was decided to send him a fifth as well as a fourth division.

During July, Sir Ian Hamilton further considered the scheme outlined in his telegram to Lord Kitchener of June 29th and a definite plan of action was elaborated under his orders.

This plan is described in Sir Ian Hamilton's despatch of December 11th, 1915. In June he had asked for and been promised a reinforcement consisting of three divisions of the New Army, to which the infantry of two Territorial Divisions had been subsequently added. He expected all these troops to arrive between July 10th and August 10th, and this anticipation was realised. After considering several other courses, he decided to employ a part of them to strengthen the Australian and New Zealand Army Corps at Anzac, and the remainder to effect a surprise landing in Suvla Bay. In his despatch Sir Ian Hamilton's objectives are defined as follows:

(1) To break out with a rush from Anzac and cut off the bulk of the Turkish Army from land communication with Constantinople.

(2) To gain such a command for my artillery as to cut off the bulk of the Turkish Army from sea traffic whether with Constantinople or with Asia.

(3)   Incidentally, to secure Suvla Bay as a winter base for Anzac and all the troops operating in the northern theatre.

Sir Ian Hamilton determined that the operations should begin on August 6th, as the moon would then rise at an hour favourable for night landings, and the last of his reinforcements were due to arrive a day or two before that date. The plan is described in greater detail in the instructions issued by the Chief of the General Staff, Mediterranean Expeditionary Force, to the General Officer Commanding VIIIth Corps at Helles, and the General Officer Commanding IXth Corps at Imbros, dated July 29th, and to the General Officer Commanding Australian and New Zealand Army Corps at Anzac, dated July 30th.

At Helles the troops of the VIIIth Corps were to attack the Turks on August 4th and following days, not so much with a view to gaining ground in the direction of Krithia or Achi Baba as for the purpose of distracting the enemy's attention from the contemplated operations at Anzac and Suvla, and of preventing him from reinforcing the positions which it was intended to seize and occupy.

The operations at Anzac were held by Sir Ian Hamilton to be of primary importance, those at Helles and Suvla being described as complementary.

THE OPERATIONS IN MAY, JUNE AND JULY, 1915

In the meantime, fighting had continued on both the Anzac and Helles fronts. At Anzac severe fighting took place by reason of very heavy attacks made by the Turks. These attacks were defeated and some slight ground was gained, but it did not amount to more than straightening out short lengths of trench here and there and, broadly speaking, the force remained in the position which it had occupied on the day of landing.

At Helles, up to June 4th, only minor operations were undertaken, and small advances were made in parts of the lines, but on that day a great attack was made along the whole front from the Straits to the sea.

The attack was partially successful, and the Manchester Brigade and some companies of the 5th Lancashire Fusiliers and part of the 42nd Division, which arrived early in May, got nearly to Krithia, reaching a position favourable to an attack on Achi Baba.

Unfortunately, the Turks, by a counter-attack, were able to carry a redoubt called the Haricot, which had been taken from them at the first attack, and this redoubt enfiladed [sent a volley of gun-fire the length of] the positions won by the Naval Division on the right of the Manchester Brigade. It [the Naval Division] was obliged to fall back, uncovering the Manchester Brigade, which also had to retire. Sir Ian Hamilton speaks of the day as having promised great things, but ended disappointingly, and describes the result in the following terms:

> To sum up, a good advance of at least 500 yards, including two lines of Turkish trenches, has been made along a front of nearly three miles in the centre of our southern section, but we are back to our original right and left. Making fresh effort now to advance the left to bring it into line with the centre, though the Turkish position here is extraordinarily strong naturally, with a deep ravine on one side and the sea on the other.

On June 21st the French stormed the Haricot redoubt and repulsed the Turkish counter-attacks, and on June 28th another great attack was made by the British force, which had considerable success.

As described by Major-General de Lisle, commanding the 29th Division, an advance was made of about a mile, and five lines of trenches were taken. Sir Ian Hamilton speaks of this advance as running up level to Krithia. He says that, if he had had reinforcements and ammunition on the spot, the success could have been made decisive: "We had the Turks beaten then." But, naturally, the result of this continuous fighting had much exhausted and depleted the British troops, the stocks of ammunition were low, the drafts were coming forward very slowly, so that all units were much under strength, and no large reinforcements would arrive for some time. He was, therefore, unable to follow up the success, and during July only small operations took place. In the meantime the continuance of Russian reverses in Galicia encouraged the Turks, lessened their apprehension of a Russian landing near Constantinople, and enabled them to send up reinforcements.

On June 29th and 30th a heavy attack was made on the Anzac position and was repulsed.

Details of these operations will be found in Sir Ian Hamilton's despatch of August 26th, 1915, published in the *London Gazette Supplement* of September 20th, 1915.

On June 22nd Lord Kitchener sent the following description of the Divisions of the New Army to Sir Ian Hamilton:

> The three divisions being sent to you are well trained with fine personnel. From the training point of view, there is not much to choose between them, but they might be placed in the following order—11th, 13th, 10th. The infantry is excellent, and their shooting good. The artillery have fired well. The RE, RAMC, and ASC are above the average. You will understand that the new officers' knowledge is not yet instinctive, and allowance should be made for this by the staff; if so, in a short time there will be no finer troops in Europe. Upon the personality of the commander, of course, will depend the choice of divisions for any particular operation.

It will be seen that for new troops a high character was given to them, and possibly this was the main reason why the landing at Suvla was entrusted to a portion of them without the help of more experienced troops. A night attack in an unknown country was a difficult task for inexperienced soldiers, and they would have been much strengthened by an admixture of more seasoned units. The fourth and fifth divisions (the 53rd Welsh and 54th East Anglian) consisted of Territorial troops.

Selection of officers

At this point it will be convenient to refer to the selection of a commander for the IXth Corps, which consisted of the 10th, 11th and 13th Divisions, and of commanders for those divisions and the two Territorial divisions.

On June 15th Sir Ian Hamilton had submitted to Lord Kitchener his opinion of the qualities necessary for a Corps Commander on the Gallipoli Peninsula in these words:"In that position only men of good, stiff constitution and nerve will be able to do any good."To secure such qualities it would have been advantageous to select some officer who had proved the possession of them in the fighting of the previous ten months. Most of these officers, however, were employed on the Western Front, and could not easily be replaced. The difficulty was increased by the fact that Sir Bryan Mahon, who commanded the 10th Division, was a Lieutenant-General.

Sir Ian Hamilton asked for one of two Lieutenant-Generals then in France, Sir Julian Byng or Sir Henry Rawlinson, but neither could be spared. The former was sent to take over the command of the IXth Corps after the failure at Suvla. There may have been reasons for allowing him to leave France then which did not exist in June, but had it been possible it might, perhaps, have been better to appoint him in the first instance. In the result the choice practically lay between Sir Frederick Stopford and another Lieutenant-General whom Sir Ian Hamilton considered for physical reasons to be unsuited for trench warfare, and Sir Frederick Stopford was appointed. It is only to this extent that Sir Ian Hamilton can be said to have asked for Sir Frederick Stopford.

Sir Frederick Stopford was an officer with a good record, but he had not been actively employed for some time.

The qualifications mentioned by Sir Ian Hamilton would apply equally to the Divisional Commanders. As regards these we find little or nothing in the evidence that reflects on the capacity for command in the field of Sir Bryan Mahon, who had trained and commanded the 10th Division in Ireland. Major-General Hammersley had similarly trained and commanded the 11th Division, upon which the heaviest of the fighting at Suvla fell, and in ordinary course he took out his division to the Gallipoli Peninsula. We think this was unfortunate, as he had suffered from a breakdown some two years before; and although he had apparently recovered, his previous illness may account for the want of promptitude and decision which, we regret to say, he appears to have shown when faced by what were, no doubt, exceptional difficulties.

The 13th Division was commanded by Major-General F. C. Shaw, who proved himself to be well qualified for the appointment. Sir Ian Hamilton detached this division from the IXth Corps and placed it at Sir William Birdwood's disposal. Major-General the Hon. J. E. Lindley commanded the 53rd Territorial Division. The division was much split up and disintegrated as soon as it landed at Suvla, and on August 17th he resigned the command, his reason being that he understood Sir Ian Hamilton to be dissatisfied with him and thought that his division might have a better chance under another commander. Major-General F. S. Inglefield, commanding the 54th Territorial Division, was 60 years old when he took out the division to the Gallipoli Peninsula, and at this age was, perhaps, hardly equal to the strain of field service under specially arduous conditions.

THE OPERATIONS IN AUGUST 1915 AT HELLES
AND ANZAC

The operations in August were, as we have already said, divided into three attacks: one at Helles, one at Anzac, and one at Suvla. These attacks were made by three distinct forces not in direct communication with one another. The control of operations so divided was difficult, and Sir Ian Hamilton decided that the best position from which he could exercise such control was Imbros, where he had his headquarters. He was then in cable communication with the three Corps Headquarters, and could reach any one of them in less than an hour. This choice of Imbros has been criticised, but we think that the reasons given for it are satisfactory.

HELLES

The attack at Helles was made on the same day as the other attacks—August 6th, 1915. Its scope and form were, as has been said, to be determined solely with reference to its effects on the main operations, and it was directed against certain Turkish trenches mentioned in the Instructions to General Officer Commanding, VIIIth Corps. Unfortunately, when it was made these trenches were found to be occupied by a very strong force of Turks collected there for the purpose of an attack on the British position. The British attack on that day failed, but fighting continued for about a week, the severest taking place round what was called the Vineyard, a plot of ground 200 yards long by 100 yards wide. No substantial success was obtained by this fighting so far as an advance was concerned, but the result was to keep the Turkish troops in that part engaged and to draw some reinforcements from other parts of the peninsula which could otherwise have been employed at Anzac or Suvla. In view of the fact that the Turks were in sufficient force to resist the attacks at Anzac and Suvla, we think the value to be attached to the subsidiary operations at Helles must remain problematical.

ANZAC

The operations at Anzac and Suvla were more closely connected with one another than with those at Helles. Certain times were specified at which important points were to be occupied. We are of the opinion that, considering the nature of the country, it was impossible to rely upon this time-table being carried out, but we do not think that the accurate carrying out of the time-table was vital to the general success of the operations. The principal assistance to be given to the Anzac Force by the troops landing at Suvla was the seizure of Yilghin Burnu and Ismail Oglu Tepe, on account of the presence there of artillery likely to interfere with the Anzac Force, and any other help by moving troops up the slopes of Sari Bahr was only to be given, if possible, after the fulfilment of the primary mission of the General Officer Commanding IXth Corps, i.e., securing Suvla Bay as a base. In fact, Ismail Oglu Tepe was never occupied, but we have not any evidence to show that the presence of artillery on that hill had any material effect on the Anzac attack.

For the purpose of the attack from Anzac, General Birdwood's force had been reinforced by the 13th Division, the 29th Brigade of the 10th Division, and the 29th (Indian) Brigade. These had been taken over to the peninsula at night and concealed in dug-outs near the shore so that they might escape the notice of the Turks. This operation seems to have been carried out with credit to those engaged in it, and to the Dominion troops who prepared the dug-outs.

Sir William Birdwood had under his command 37,000 rifles and 72 guns, and he could count on naval support from two cruisers, four monitors, and two destroyers. The force was divided into two main portions—one (consisting of the Australian Division together with the 1st and 3rd Light Horse Brigades and two battalions of the 40th Brigade) which was to hold the existing position and make frontal attacks from it; the other (consisting of the New Zealand and Australian Division, less the 1st and 3rd Light Horse Brigades, the 13th Division less five battalions, the 29th Indian Infantry Brigade, and the Indian Mountain Artillery Brigade) which was to attack the Chunuk Bahr ridge. The 29th Brigade of the 10th Division less one battalion and the 38th Brigade were in reserve.

About 5 pm on August 6th, the operations began by an attack on the position known as Lone Pine, its main object being to divert the enemy's attention and reserves from the principal attack on the Sari Bahr heights. The position is described by Sir Ian Hamilton as having been strongly entrenched and obstinately held. According to his despatch it was carried with great gallantry by the Australian troops, and held against counter-attacks which were continued until August 12th. The assault on Lone Pine was presumably effective in keeping a considerable Turkish force from opposing the main attack on the Sari Bahr heights.

It may be mentioned here that two minor attacks were also made with the same object as the attack on Lone Pine, namely, to distract the enemy's attention from the main attack on the Sari Bahr heights. The first of these minor attacks took place at midnight on the 6th, and was directed on a Turkish trench opposite the extreme right of the Anzac front; the second took place at 4.30 am on the 7th, and was directed on a point called Baby 700, just north of Hill 180, opposite the centre of the Anzac front. Both these attacks were repulsed with heavy loss.

Beginning at 9.30 pm on the 6th, the flanking or encircling movement on the Chunuk Bahr ridge and Sari Bahr was made in two covering and two attacking columns. The constitution of these columns and the tasks assigned to them are thus described in the despatch:

> It was our object to effect a lodgment along the crest of the high main ridge with two columns of troops, but, seeing the nature of the ground and the dispositions of the enemy, the effort had to be made by stages. We were bound, in fact, to undertake a double subsidiary operation before we could hope to launch these attacks with any real prospect of success.
>
> (1) The right covering force was to seize Table Top, as well as all other enemy positions commanding the foothills between the Chailak Dere and the Sazli Beit Dere ravines. If this enterprise succeeded it would open up the ravines for the assaulting columns, whilst at the same time interposing between the right flank of the left covering force and the enemy holding the Sari Bahr main ridge.
>
> (2) The left covering force was to march northwards along the beach to seize a hill called Damakjelik Bahr, some 1,400 yards north of Table Top. If successful it would be able to hold out a hand to the IXth Corps as it landed south of Nebrunesi Point, whilst at the same time protecting the left flank of the left assaulting column against enemy troops from the Anafarta valley during its climb up the Aghyl Dere ravine.
>
> (3) The right assaulting column was to move up the Chailak Dere and Sazli Beit Dere ravines to the storm of the ridge of Chunuk Bahr.
>
> (4) The left assaulting column was to work up the Aghyl Dere and prolong the line of the right assaulting column by storming Hill 305 (Koja Chemen Tepe), the summit of the whole range of hills.
>
> To recapitulate, the two assaulting columns, which were to work up three ravines to the storm of the high ridge, were to be preceded by two covering columns. One of these was to capture the enemy's positions commanding the foothills, first to open the mouths of the ravines, secondly to cover the right flank of another covering force whilst it marched along the beach. The other covering column was to strike far out to the north until, from a hill called Damakjelik Bahr, it could at the same time facilitate the landing of the IXth Corps at

Nebrunesi Point, and guard the left flank of the column assaulting Sari Bahr from any forces of the enemy which might be assembled in the Anafarta valley.

The whole of this big attack was placed under the command of Major-General Sir Alexander J. Godley, General Officer Commanding New Zealand and Australian Division. The two covering and the two assaulting columns were organized as follows:

Right Covering Column, under Brigadier-General A. H. Russell—New Zealand Mounted Rifles Brigade, the Otago Mounted Rifles Regiment, the Maori Contingent and New Zealand Field Troop.

Right Assaulting Column, under Brigadier-General F. E. Johnston—New Zealand Infantry Brigade, Indian Mountain Battery (less one section), one Company New Zealand Engineers.

Left Covering Column, under Brigadier-General J. H. Travers—Headquarters 40th Brigade, half the 72nd Field Company, 4th Battalion South Wales Borderers, and 5th Battalion Wiltshire Regiment.

Left Assaulting Column, under Brigadier-General (now Major-General) H. V. Cox—29th Indian Infantry Brigade, 4th Australian Infantry Brigade, Indian Mountain Battery (less one section), one Company New Zealand Engineers.

Divisional Reserve—6th Battalion South Lancashire Regiment and 8th Battalion Welsh Regiment (Pioneers) at Chailak Dere, and the 39th Infantry Brigade and half 72nd Field Company at Aghyl Dere.

The right covering column took Old No. 3 Post and Table Top, both of them stated to be positions of great strength, and so opened up the Sazli Beit Dere and also cleared the Chailak Dere; in doing so it had to pass a barbed wire obstacle of a formidable nature. It also occupied Bauchop's Hill, described as a "maze of ridge and ravine everywhere entrenched".

The left covering column advanced up the Aghyl Dere, rushing the Turkish trenches on the way, and occupied Damakjelik Bahr, thus protecting the left rear of the whole Anzac attack.

The right assaulting column advancing over difficult country reached Rhododendron Spur, a point 500 yards west of Chunuk Bahr.

The left assaulting column advanced up the Aghyl Dere, which divides into a northern and southern branch, and one half of the column followed the northern half and got across into the northern end of the Azmak Dere ravine. The other half followed the southern branch and reached the lower slopes of Hill Q, a point on the Sari Bahr ridge a little lower than the highest point—Koja Chemen Tepe—and separated from it by a deep ravine.

This was the position on the afternoon of August 7th, and that evening the force was re-organized for a fresh advance to take place on the early morning of the 8th. The despatch states:

The columns were composed as follows:

Right Column, Brigadier-General F. E. Johnston—26th Indian Mountain Battery (less one section), Auckland Mounted Rifles, New Zealand Infantry Brigade, two Battalions 13th Division, and the Maori Contingent.

Centre and Left Columns—Major-General H. V. Cox—21st Indian Mountain
Battery (less one section), 4th Australian Brigade, 39th Infantry Brigade (less one
battalion), with 6th Battalion South Lancashire Regiment attached, and the 29th
Indian Infantry Brigade.

The right column was to climb up the Chunuk Bahr ridge; the left column
was to make for the prolongation of the ridge north-east to Koja Chemen Tepe,
the topmost peak of the range.

On August 8th the only important success was attained by the right column, which succeeded in occupying Chunuk Bahr, an important position,
though it was not one from which the Straits could be seen. The centre and
left columns met with such heavy opposition that they were unable to make
any material advance, and the left suffered so heavily that it had to be withdrawn to its original position.

On August 9th, 1915, the attack was renewed, with the troops again re-
arranged in three columns, whose constitution and objectives were thus
described:

The columns for the renewed attack were composed as follows:

No. 1 Column, Brigadier-General F. E. Johnston—26th Indian Mountain
Battery (less one section), the Auckland and Wellington Mounted Rifles
Regiments, the New Zealand Infantry Brigade, and two battalions of the 13th
Division.

No. 2 Column, Major-General H. V. Cox—21st Indian Mountain Battery (less
one section), 4th Australian Brigade, 39th Brigade (less the 7th Gloucesters,
relieved), with the 6th Battalion South Lancashire Regiment attached, and the
Indian Infantry Brigade.

No. 3 Column, Brigadier-General A. H. Baldwin, commanding 38th Infantry
Brigade—two battalions each from the 38th and 29th Brigades and one from
the 40th Brigade.

No. 1 Column was to hold and consolidate the ground gained on the 6th, and,
in co-operation with the other columns, to gain the whole of Chunuk Bahr, and
extend to the south-east. No. 2 Column was to attack Hill Q on the Chunuk
Bahr ridge, and No. 3 Column was to move from the Chailak Dere, also on Hill
Q. This last column was to make the main attack, and the others were to co-
operate with it.

A part of No. 1 Column, under the command of Major, now
Lieutenant-Colonel Allanson, consisting of a detachment of the 6th Gurkhas
and of the 6th South Lancashire Regiment (450 strong), succeeded in getting to a point on the ridge from which the Straits and the country on the
far side could be seen. The exact point which they reached is not quite
clearly ascertained, but it probably was at or near the top of the Chunuk
Bahr ridge, near the highest point, which is called Koja Chemen Tepe. From
this point the Narrows could be seen.

They were afterwards driven back by artillery fire to the trenches in which they had been the night before, and later in the day were counter-attacked by the Turks in force and driven down the hill.

The suggestion has been made that this artillery fire came from the British ships, and Lieutenant-Colonel Allanson inclined to this view. But Colonel Allanson's account is that the salvo [artillery attack] struck his men when they were pursuing the Turks a short distance down the reverse slope; and we accept Sir William Birdwood's opinion that, if the Gurkhas were on the reverse slope near the crest, it would have been impossible for naval guns to hit them. We do not think it possible to say whether the shells were Turkish or came from the high-angle fire of our howitzers putting a barrage on the reverse slopes. As Sir Alexander Godley remarks, it is often not possible in a modern battle to be quite certain as to particular facts.

No. 3 Column, under Brigadier-General Baldwin, which was attacking the same ridge from another direction, was unfortunately deflected to the left, in the direction of a place called The Farm, and never reached the ridge. In Sir Ian Hamilton's despatch it is said that Brigadier-General Baldwin, through no fault of his own, owing to the darkness and the awful country, lost his way. Sir Alexander Godley thinks it possible that General Baldwin did not exactly lose his way, but was driven rather to the left on to the lower slopes leading to The Farm by the heavy rifle and machine-gun fire which was sweeping the higher ground up which he should have gone. General Baldwin, with most of his staff, was killed very soon afterwards, and therefore it is impossible to ascertain what actually occurred.

No progress of any importance had been made from Suvla, and there was nothing in the operations in that area to divert the Turkish reinforcements from Sari Bahr. Thus the counter-attacks in that direction, which finally drove the British troops from the ridge, could be made in full strength.

General Baldwin, on arriving at The Farm, and finding that he could not reach the ridge according to the original plan, deployed his attack where he was, and some of his men charged up their side of the slope. The Turks, who were in overwhelming numbers, drove them back to The Farm, and then attacked the New Zealand troops which were holding Chunuk Bahr; but the New Zealanders, though much exhausted, continued to hold the position until relieved during the night.

On August 10th, 1915, the Turks, in great strength, attacked Chunuk Bahr and carried it. They also turned the flank of General Baldwin's column, and drove it from its position. It was in this fighting that General Baldwin and all his staff were killed. Reserves were sent up and the Turks driven back, but they kept their hold on Chunuk Bahr.

Sir Ian Hamilton says that he thought at one time of throwing his reserves into the Anzac battle, but was prevented from doing so because he feared that the water supply at Anzac would not be sufficient for a larger number of troops. Sir William Birdwood told us that he did not think he could have provided water for more troops; but it seems doubtful, in any case, if the reserves could have been put into the fighting line in time to save the situation.

REASONS FOR FAILURE

The country over which these operations were carried out was extremely difficult. General. Cox describes it in this way:

> It was an extraordinarily difficult bit of country and a confused country. There does not seem to be any reason why the hills should go where they do. It has been done by tremendous rushes of water. It is mad-looking country and very difficult.

The ground was very steep and without paths or tracks, broken up into gullies and tangled hollows, and covered with thick scrub. The weather, too, was very hot, and the climate very trying, even to the Australian and New Zealand troops, who had been acclimatised for several months; and much more so to the British troops, who had not been long out of England. A very hard task was therefore set to the troops. Sir William Birdwood, who presumably knew the country so far as it could be known, thought that the attack ought to succeed, and that the difficulties of the country would help him to surprise the Turks; and both he and Lieutenant-General Godley ascribe the failure to the Turks being in too strong force. Sir William Birdwood says: "They were too strong for us. They were just too strong, but only just, because we got up there in two places, but we could not maintain ourselves." Sir Alexander Godley says "The enemy was too strong for us."

THE OPERATIONS AT SUVLA

We think it is necessary to review in some detail the operations at Suvla, as these have given rise to controversy between the principal officers concerned, and led to the removal from their commands of the Commander of the IXth Corps, one of the Divisional Commanders, and one of the Brigade Commanders.

OBJECTIVES

The outline of Sir Ian Hamilton's plans for a landing at Suvla and subsequent operations is contained in a letter dated July 22nd, 1915, from the Chief of the General Staff of the Mediterranean Force to the General Officer Commanding the IXth Corps. In this letter the strength of the enemy north of Kilid Bahr was estimated at 30,000; 12,000 occupying trenches opposite the Anzac position and most of the remainder being in reserve at Boghali, Kojadere, and Eski-Keui. There were believed to be three battalions in the Anafarta villages, one battalion at Ismail Oglu Tepe, one battalion on Chocolate Hill, and outposts at Lala Baba and Ghazi Baba. The ridge of Karakol Dagh and Kiretch Tepe Sirt was understood to be held by gendarmerie. It was further stated that at or near Chocolate Hill and Ismail Oglu Tepe there were one 9.2 inch gun, one 4.7 inch gun, and three field guns, protected by wire entanglements and infantry trenches. Three field guns were reported later as having been seen moving into Anafarta Sagir.

On July 29th further instructions, which appear among the appendices to Sir Ian Hamilton's despatch, were issued to the General Officer Commanding the IXth Corps. Therein it was laid down that the primary objective would be to secure Suvla Bay as a base for all forces operating in the northern zone, and that, owing to the difficult nature of the terrain at

Suvla, the attainment of this objective might possibly require the use of all the troops at Sir Frederick Stopford's disposal. If, however, troops could be spared, his next step should be to assist the General Officer Commanding at Anzac in the latter's attack on Koja Chemen Tepe by an advance on Buyuk Anafarta. Subject only to his final approval, Sir Ian Hamilton gave Sir Frederick Stopford a free hand in regard to the plan of military operations at Suvla, and the latter was requested to submit a plan for approval as soon as possible.

The plan was submitted in a letter dated July 31st, 1915, and met with Sir Ian Hamilton's full approval. In this letter Sir Frederick Stopford recorded his conviction that to secure the reasonable immunity of Suvla Bay from shell fire, the occupation of the high ground from Ejelmer Bay to Anafarta Sagir and thence to Koja Chemen Tepe was essential. He also laid stress on the improbability of his being able to spare troops to assist the Anzac force in the attack on Koja Chemen Tepe.

THE OPERATION ORDER

On receipt of Sir Ian Hamilton's approval, Sir Frederick Stopford issued an Operation Order, dated August 3rd, 1915, in which the following task was assigned to General Hammersley:

(a) To safeguard the landing places.
(b) To occupy the enemy posts of Lala Baba and Ghazi Baba, and to establish a footing along the ridge from Ghazi Baba through Karakol Dagh and Kiretch Tepe Sirt to Hill 156, immediately overlooking Ejelmer Bay.
(c) To occupy Chocolate Hill and Ismail Oglu Tepe.
(d) To seize Baka Baba and establish connection northwards between that point and the troops advancing on Hill 156.

This was an extremely ambitious programme for one division, and only part of it was carried into effect. It is noticeable in this operation order that, although the two brigades of the 10th Division were mentioned in the list of available troops, no reference was made to the divisional commander, Sir Bryan Mahon, a Lieutenant-General of considerable seniority, nor was any duty assigned to these brigades.

General Braithwaite's letter and instructions of July 22nd and 29th, and Sir Frederick Stopford's Operation Order of August 3rd, give the following information in regard to the units detailed for the Suvla operations. According to the letter of July 22nd the force placed at Sir Frederick Stopford's disposal for the landing was to consist of the 11th Division under General Hammersley, the 10th Division (less the 29th Brigade) under Sir Bryan Mahon, two batteries of Highland Mountain Artillery, and the 1/4th Lowland Howitzer Brigade. The table appended to the letter includes, among the divisional troops of the 11th Division, two out of three Brigades of Field Artillery and one Heavy Battery, the third Brigade of Field Artillery having been landed at Helles. No mention is made in the table of the Divisional Artillery of the 10th Division.

In the instructions of July 29th the Lowland Howitzer Brigade was omitted, and three squadrons of the RN Armoured Car Division, RNAS, each armed with six machine guns, were added. It was stated that the following units were being despatched from Alexandria: the three squadrons of the RN Armoured Car Division, three Brigades of Field Artillery belonging to the 10th Division, one Brigade of Field Artillery belonging to the 11th Division, and two Brigades of Field Artillery belonging to the 13th Division. As one Brigade of Field Artillery belonging to the 11th Division had been landed at Helles, it would appear that only one Brigade of Field Artillery was actually attached at the time to that division.

In the Operation Order of August 3rd it was stated that one Brigade of Field Artillery belonging to the 11th Division and one Heavy Battery with their horses would land at Anzac, and proceed thence along the beach to join the division on its landing at Suvla. The two Highland Mountain Batteries and one squadron of the RN Armoured Car Division (motor cycles) were to land at Suvla. There is no record of the date and place of landing of the other two squadrons of the RN Armoured Car Division, which consisted of Ford cars and armoured cars.

Available artillery

The question of the artillery actually available at Suvla is discussed in a "Statement in connection with Sir Ian Hamilton's despatch of 11th December, 1915." This statement was drawn up by Sir Frederick Stopford by direction of the Adjutant-General, and is dated February 16th, 1916. The relevant paragraph is as follows:

> As regards other points in Sir Ian Hamilton's despatch which affect the IXth Corps, the description of the troops at my disposal is incorrectly stated. He states that at my disposal "was placed the IXth Army Corps, less the 13th Division and the 29th Brigade of the 10th Division." He should have stated that the 10th Division had no artillery, and that of the artillery of the 11th Division only one brigade of artillery was available until 12th August, and of it only one battery was available for the fighting of August 7th–8th.

Further information on the subject is given in General Braithwaite's instructions which were handed to General de Lisle on August 15th, when the latter called at Imbros on his way to replace Sir Frederick Stopford in the command of the IXth Corps. It would appear that at that date the artillery actually available at Suvla consisted of two mountain and two heavy batteries, and one brigade of field artillery.

Sir Frederick Stopford's contention as to the paucity of artillery is in substance supported by the evidence of General de Lisle.

Topography

And here it may be convenient to attempt some description of the ground in the vicinity of Suvla Bay. The area bordering the Salt Lake is low, and doubtless swampy in wet weather. In the dry season it is bare and open until the ground begins to rise. Then high grass and bush appear, the bush being mostly a prickly variety of *Ilex* [holly], very hard and tough. The bush in many cases increases in density and height as the hills get higher. The country can hardly be described as well watered during the dry season, but a moderate amount of water is procurable by those who know where to look for it and how to get it.

The following remarks by Sir Ian Hamilton on the nature of the ground at and near Suvla are of interest. In a letter to Lord Kitchener, dated August 12th, 1915, he wrote:

> The whole of the flattish plain east of Suvla Bay is covered with thick trees up high above your head, small and big dongas [gullies], long grass, etc. In these a very considerable number of Turkish snipers are concealed, sometimes up in the trees, sometimes down in hollows among the grass ... Supposing the Essex [161st Brigade of the 54th Division] make good their footing on the high hills north of Anafarta, there will always remain the problem of getting their mule convoys through this dense bush without being too much harried or losing too many mules.

Again, in a letter to Lord Kitchener, dated September 1st, 1915, he described the Suvla Bay country as "a jungle ringed round by high mountains." Again in his despatch of December 11th, 1915, he referred to Ismail Oglu Tepe as follows:

> The hill rises 350 feet from the plain with steep spurs jutting out to the west and south-west, the whole of it covered with dense holly oak scrub, so nearly impenetrable that it breaks up an attack and forces troops to move in single file along goat tracks between the bushes.

In the same despatch, describing an attack on August 12th by the 163rd Brigade on Kuchuk Anafarta Ova, about 2,000 yards north-east of the north-east corner of the Salt Lake, he records the mysterious disappearance of the commanding officer, 16 officers, and 250 men of the 1/5th Norfolk Regiment, who charged into the forest, were lost to sight or sound, and never reappeared.

In his evidence before us Sir Ian Hamilton gave the following description:

> The actual heights to get up were difficult. They were hills very thickly clothed with scrub and jungle with paths, but rather difficult for a man with his pack on to force his way through; but all the background of the bay was too open and too flat. It had one great advantage, that it was the only part of the peninsula where the guns of the ships could really command the ground.

Taking into consideration this and other evidence bearing on the subject, it may, we think, be concluded that the country in the vicinity of Suvla Bay must seriously have impeded military operations, more particularly in the way of breaking up concerted movements, and rendering night operations hazardous if not almost impracticable. The ground east of Anzac was more intricate and more broken, but the natural difficulties at Suvla were of a formidable character.

LANDING OPERATIONS ON AUGUST 6TH/7TH, 1915

The impression conveyed by the Intelligence reports which were communicated to Sir Frederick Stopford and Major-General Hammersley was that little opposition would be met with on landing except perhaps at Lala Baba, until the occupation of Chocolate Hill and Ismail Oglu Tepe was attempted. The time of landing was fixed for the evening of August 6th, and in drafting his divisional orders Major-General Hammersley had to consider whether Chocolate Hill and Ismail Oglu Tepe should be attacked from the north-west or south-west. He decided in favour of the former alternative. His orders to the three brigades of his division were as follows:

> The 34th Brigade on the left to land at the original Beach A 800 yards west of Hill 10; one battalion to move north towards Kiretch Tepe Sirt and occupy Suvla Point; one battalion to occupy Hill 10; the remaining two battalions to concentrate at Hill 10. These three battalions at Hill 10 then to move to the assault of Chocolate Hill, and if successful, to the assault of Ismail Oglu Tepe.
>
> The 32nd Brigade in the centre to land at Beach C; to assault and occupy Lala Baba, and then move north along the sand-spit in support of the 34th Brigade.
>
> The 33rd Brigade on the right to land at Beach B about a mile south-east of Nebrunesi Point; two battalions to hold the line from the south-east corner of the Salt Lake south-westerly to the shore. Two battalions to follow the 32nd Brigade along the sand-spit to a point 800 yards east of Hill 10, there to form the divisional reserve with the divisional Pioneer Battalion (6th East Yorkshire Regiment).
>
> The artillery to concentrate at Lala Baba, where the divisional report centre was to be established.

For the transport of the division from Imbros ten destroyers and ten lighters were allotted—three of each for each brigade, and one of each for divisional headquarters, signal section, cyclists, and engineers. From 500 to 550 men were embarked on each destroyer and lighter, and there was much congestion, especially on the lighters. The men went on board on the afternoon of the 6th, and were on board with no room to move about from six to eight hours before disembarking. Some reserve ammunition and water were carried on the lighters, but, for reasons mentioned in that portion of our report which deals with the water arrangements, the water was not distributed, and on the disembarkation of the men the lighters at once left the shore.

The flotilla was ready and started at 6.30 pm. The Pioneer Battalion, one battery of Royal Field Artillery, and the 4th Highland Mountain Brigade of two batteries followed later. At 10.30 pm the flotilla arrived opposite the points of disembarkation. The disembarkation of the 34th Brigade did not work smoothly. The original Beach A proved unsuitable for landing owing to reefs, and the brigade actually landed towards the south end of the sand spit instead of opposite Hill 10, the lighters grounding some 100 yards from shore. The landing was opposed by shrapnel fire from Hill 10 and rifle fire from Lala Baba and the sand spit. The 11th Manchester Regiment moved along the beach towards Suvla Point and Karakol Dagh, and carried out the task assigned to it.

Brigadier-General Sitwell, commanding the 34th Brigade, landed about 3.30 am on the 7th and directed the 9th Lancashire Fusiliers to assault Hill 10. The battalion proceeded after some delay and confusion in that direction, and occupied the highest sand dune north of the Cut, under the impression that this dune was Hill 10. The remaining two battalions of the 34th Brigade began to land on the sand spit about 2.30 am on the 7th and their landing was completed by 5 am.

At 11 pm on the 6th August the two leading battalions of the 32nd Brigade landed at a point between B and C beaches, and after considerable resistance Lala Baba was occupied. The remaining two battalions followed and concentrated at Lala Baba. This brigade was commanded by Brigadier-General Haggard.

Immediately after landing on the 7th Brigadier-General Sitwell asked for assistance from Brigadier-General Haggard, who sent a detachment from Lala Baba along the sand spit towards the Cut.

The 33rd Brigade, under Brigadier-General Maxwell, landed at Beach B without opposition. Two battalions took up and entrenched a line from the south-east corner of the Salt Lake south-westerly to the shore. The remaining two battalions of the 33rd Brigade proceeded to Lala Baba with a view to occupying subsequently their assigned position east of Hill 10 as a divisional reserve.

Shortly before daylight much desultory fighting took place between the Cut and Hill 10. Several isolated attempts to capture Hill 10 failed and the troops engaged fell back towards the Cut. Meanwhile, General Haggard had joined General Sitwell, the latter being the senior Brigade Commander in the division. By 6 am a fresh attack on Hill 10 was organised, the force being drawn from the 32nd and 34th Brigades. This attack succeeded, the Turks retiring in a north-easterly direction.

At 6.30 am General Sitwell reported to the Divisional Commander that his troops could not move eastward, this message apparently not reaching General Hammersley before 8 am.

We must now turn to the landing of the 10th Division, less one brigade detached to Anzac; this division being commanded by Lt.-General Sir Bryan Mahon.

It was originally intended that the two available brigades, the 30th and 31st, commanded respectively by Brigadier-Generals Nicol and Hill, together with the divisional Pioneer Battalion, should land at Beach A due west of Hill 10. This beach proved impracticable for landing, and a suitable place called New Beach A was eventually found in a cove about a mile east of Suvla Point and about 1,000 yards east of Ghazi Baba. On the arrival of the 10th Division from England between July 16th and 21st six battalions, namely, two battalions of the 30th Brigade and the whole of the 31st Brigade, had been sent to Mitylene under General Hill, the remaining two battalions of the 30th Brigade under General Nicol, plus the divisional Pioneer Battalion, being at Mudros, where the divisional Commander with his headquarters also was.

Sir Bryan Mahon received instructions about the Suvla landing on July 28th or 29th, but having failed to obtain a vessel to convey him to Mitylene he was unable to give any personal orders regarding disembarkation and subsequent action to General Hill, and his endeavour to communicate orders by cypher telegram failed. None of the artillery of the 10th Division landed until August 10th.

General Hill, followed by his six battalions, arrived at Suvla from Mitylene at daylight on August 7th, and was at once summoned to the *Jonquil*, where he saw Sir Frederick Stopford at about 6 am. He was directed by the latter to land at Beach C, to get in touch with the General Officer commanding the 11th Division, and to act under his orders. If he failed to get in touch, he was to advance and support the troops of the 11th Division and also to make good the occupation of Ghazi Baba and Karakol Dagh. Having selected a place west of Lala Baba for his troops to form up, General Hill went to the headquarters of the 11th Division and saw General Hammersley at about 8 am, who directed him, as soon as his troops were landed and concentrated, to move out along the sand-spit to the north-west corner of the Salt Lake, and thence to make an attack on Chocolate Hill, his right resting on the Salt Lake and his left being covered by troops of the 32nd and 34th Brigades, which would operate towards Ismail Oglu Tepe.

It must be mentioned here that only five out of the six battalions from Mitylene actually landed on August 7th at Beach C. One of the battalions of the 31st Brigade arrived too late on the 7th to join the force under General Hill and was sent across the bay to New Beach A, where it landed on the afternoon of the 7th or the morning of the 8th and came for the time being under the orders of General Nicol commanding the 30th Brigade. Sir Bryan Mahon with the headquarters of the 10th Division, General Nicol with his brigade staff, two battalions of the 30th Brigade, and the divisional Pioneer Battalion landed early on the morning of August 7th at New Beach A. Previous to landing Sir Bryan Mahon saw Sir Frederick Stopford, who ordered him to push on as far as possible along the ridge of Karakol Dagh and Kiretch Tepe Sirt in the direction of Ejelmer Bay. These orders were carried out so far as the small force at Sir Bryan Mahon's disposal would permit. The 11th Manchester Regiment, which was a battalion of the 34th Brigade, and which after occupying Suvla Point had advanced up Karakol Dagh before Sir Bryan Mahon's landing, took part in the movement along the ridge.

OPERATIONS ON AUGUST 7TH, 1915

From the foregoing account it will be seen that on the morning of August 7th the force at Suvla was allocated as follows by the Corps Commander: at the disposal of Major-General Hammersley, the whole of the 11th Division, less one battalion of the 34th Brigade (11th Manchester Regiment), plus five battalions of the 10th Division under Brigadier-General Hill; at the disposal of Lieutenant-General Sir Bryan Mahon two battalions of one of his brigades (the 30th Brigade) plus his divisional Pioneer Battalion, plus one battalion of the 34th Brigade of the 11th Division (the 11th Manchester Regiment). It will also be observed that the change in the scheme for distributing the troops when landed at Suvla on August 6th and 7th was largely due to the impracticability of disembarkation at the original Beach A and the unavoidable delay which occurred in finding the New Beach A.

It will further be noticed that the advance up Karakol Dagh and Kiretch Tepe Sirt, which had been assigned by the Corps Commander to Major-General Hammersley, was in fact undertaken by Sir Bryan Mahon.

At 8.45 am General Sitwell, whose report centre was south of Hill 10, received orders from General Hammersley for the 32nd and 34th Brigades to push on towards Chocolate Hill on the arrival of the 31st Brigade, which would operate on the left, moving with its own right on Ismail Oglu Tepe. This message apparently emanated from the divisional report centre at Lala Baba, at 8 am, at which hour General Hammersley had seen General Hill and told him to operate on the right of the 32nd and 34th Brigades with Chocolate Hill as his objective. At 8.55 am General Sitwell communicated the order he had just received to the commanders of three battalions of his own brigade, but gave no instructions to the 32nd Brigade, possibly because General Hammersley's orders had been repeated to General Haggard, the commander of that brigade.

Shortly afterwards General Sitwell, on his own initiative, directed two battalions of the 32nd Brigade to form an entrenchment from Hill 10 to the Cut. Their employment in this manner seems to us to have been inconsistent with General Hammersley's order, and to have shown on General Sitwell's part a lack of the offensive spirit necessary to success.

Meanwhile at about 10 am three battalions out of the five under General Hill's command had landed and concentrated near Lala Baba. Having given instructions to the commanding officers of these battalions, General Hill preceded them along the sand-spit for the purpose of arranging with General Haggard for the joint advance on Chocolate Hill and Ismail Oglu Tepe. He met General Haggard, who pointed out that he was under General Sitwell's orders and could only act under instructions from that officer. He next met General Sitwell to whom he explained the orders he had received from General Hammersley.

General Sitwell replied that he had himself received different orders from General Hammersley and, according to General Hill's account, that it was impossible for him to co-operate in the proposed advance on Chocolate Hill and Ismail Oglu Tepe. General Sitwell, however, states that he informed General Hill that he could only spare two battalions out of the 32nd and 34th Brigades in support of General Hill's three battalions. Be this as it may, General Hill, believing that he could get no support from General Sitwell, decided to return to General Hammersley's headquarters at Lala Baba and report the situation. About this time General Haggard was severely wounded and General Sitwell for the time being assumed the direct command of the 32nd Brigade in addition to that of the 34th Brigade. After General Hill had left, General Sitwell detailed two battalions of the 32nd Brigade and one battalion of the 34th Brigade to be in readiness to support General Hill's battalions as soon as they came up.

On his way back to divisional headquarters General Hill met his three battalions advancing along the sand-spit north of Lala Baba and ordered them to halt and await further orders. On reaching headquarters he found that General Hammersley was away, but a General Staff Officer of the division informed him that the instructions previously given him by General Hammersley were correct, and that General Sitwell would be so informed. General Hill thereupon returned to his troops and again set them in motion towards and across the Cut and thence to the east of Hill 10, with a view to an advance on Chocolate Hill. This was about 12.45 pm. General Hill did not personally accompany his first three battalions, but followed with his two remaining battalions which by that time had landed and were concentrating near Lala Baba.

On arrival in the vicinity of Hill 10 at about 2.45 pm, General Hill found that his three leading battalions had circled round the north-east corner of the Salt Lake and were ready to move on Chocolate Hill, but that no battalions of the 32nd or 34th Brigade had been sent to co-operate on his left towards Ismail Oglu Tepe. At 3 pm he telephoned to divisional headquarters to that effect, adding that he had seen General Sitwell, who told him that two battalions would be sent forward.

Just before the despatch of this message an order, timed 2.40 pm, was issued from divisional headquarters to the effect that the advance would be suspended for the present and resumed at 5.30 pm. Two battalions of the 33rd Brigade with the Brigade Commander, General Maxwell, would leave their position near Lala Baba and move with their right flank immediately north of the Salt Lake, so as to come on the right of General Hill's troops.

The general direction of the advance was to be on Chocolate Hill. The advance was to be supported by all the troops of the 32nd and 34th Brigades who had not suffered heavy casualties. General Sitwell was to command the attack, and these brigades, as well as the troops under General Hill, would act under General Sitwell's orders. The divisional artillery near Lala Baba would cover the attack, their fire beginning at 5.15 pm. This order, which was addressed to the 31st, 32nd and 34th Brigades, reached General Hill shortly after 3.15 pm, and was no doubt received by General Sitwell and General Maxwell at about the same time. General Hill states that General Sitwell supported the advance on the right flank with the two battalions of the 33rd Brigade under General Maxwell at about 4 pm and that the 32nd and 34th Brigades took no part in the attack on Chocolate Hill and Hill 70. On the other hand, General Sitwell states that one battalion of the 32nd Brigade and one battalion of the 34th Brigade followed General Hill's troops in support and a second battalion of the 32nd Brigade in reserve, and that he saw these three battalions engaged with the enemy. General Maxwell states that two battalions of the 34th Brigade operated on the left of General Hill's troops. The advance began somewhat earlier than had been ordered, but the artillery opened fire at the prescribed time, 5.15 pm. Chocolate Hill was captured, but no attempt was made to attack Ismail Oglu Tepe. It is not clear at what time and by what troops the capture of Chocolate Hill was effected. In the War Diary of the 31st Brigade it is recorded that Chocolate Hill was in the possession of that brigade at 5.30 pm, while General Hill, who commanded the brigade, states that Chocolate Hill was taken about dusk, and that in his opinion there was no reason why Ismail Oglu Tepe should not have been taken also, had the available battalions of the 32nd and 34th Brigades advanced more promptly on his left. He describes the Turkish opposition as not being very formidable. General Maxwell, who commanded the 33rd Brigade, ascribes the capture of Chocolate Hill solely to the action of his two battalions, and gives the time of its being taken as 7.20 pm. General Sitwell states that he was in telephonic communication with one of the two battalions of the 33rd Brigade, which reported at 11.30 pm that Chocolate Hill had been carried at 9.30 pm.

None of the three Brigadier-Generals concerned in the attack on Chocolate Hill—Generals Sitwell, Hill and Maxwell—accompanied the troops. They established their report centres to the south of Hill 10, about two miles distant from Chocolate Hill, and remained there. In view of the distance and the nature of the country they can have seen but little of what was going on, and though no doubt they may occasionally have been in telephonic communication with some of their battalion commanders, the latter's outlook was limited and their responsibility was confined to what concerned their respective battalions. In the absence of superior military control and guidance on the spot, a force of inexperienced troops, unacquainted with local conditions and consisting of a number of battalions drawn from five brigades—namely, two from the 30th, three from the 31st, two from the

32nd, two from the 33rd and one from the 34th—must have been lacking in cohesion and co-operation, and the evidence discloses the confusion and delay which resulted from this cause.

Apparently Brigadier-Generals Sitwell, Hill, and Maxwell remained near each other at their several report centres until just before midnight on August 7th. General Sitwell then decided that General Hill should proceed to Chocolate Hill in order personally to ascertain the situation, and the latter set out at the time mentioned. On his own initiative General Sitwell directed General Hill to send back the following battalions which had been employed in the attack on Chocolate Hill with a view to their rejoining their respective brigades: the two battalions of the 32nd Brigade to the sand dunes south of Hill 10; the two battalions of the 33rd Brigade to Lala Baba; and the one battalion of the 34th Brigade to the brigade reserve south of Hill 10. At 7.30 am on August 8th General Hammersley visited General Sitwell at the latter's report centre, informed him that there was no enemy in the direction of Baka Baba, and suggested his joining General Hill on Chocolate Hill. The suggestion, however, was not pressed, and General Sitwell remained where he was.

It may here be mentioned that in his account of the attack on Chocolate Hill, which differs in some respects from the accounts of the three brigade commanders concerned, General Hammersley states that when he issued his order for the attack at 2.40 pm on August 7th, it was his intention that Ismail Oglu Tepe as well as Chocolate Hill should be captured, though no reference was made in the order to the former objective. He also states that the battalion of the 34th Brigade which took part in the operation was seriously engaged and its commanding officer severely wounded; that Chocolate Hill was captured by 7.30 pm; that up to 700 yards from the Turkish position all the fighting was done by General Hill's troops; and that in the final stage of the attack the two battalions of the 33rd Brigade advanced with great steadiness.

On August 7th Sir Frederick Stopford remained with Admiral Christian on board the *Jonquil*, where he considered himself to be in the best position to communicate with General Headquarters and with his subordinate commanders on shore.

OPERATIONS ON AUGUST 8TH, 1915

The distribution of the troops of the 11th Division on the morning of August 8th is described by General Hammersley as follows. One field battery and two mountain batteries were at Lala Baba. The 32nd Brigade was concentrated near Hill 10, except a detachment of two companies on the southern slopes of Kiretch Tepe Sirt. Two battalions of the 33rd Brigade were south of the Salt Lake and two at Lala Baba. Two battalions of the 34th Brigade were near Hill 10, one battalion was east of Hill 10, and one (the 11th Manchester Regiment) was on Kiretch Tepe

Sirt. The divisional Pioneer Battalion (6th East Yorkshire Regiment) was at Lala Baba.

At this time the five Irish battalions under General Hill, which had been left in their advanced position when the other troops were withdrawn to the neighbourhood of the beach, appear to have been still holding Chocolate Hill and the ground in its vicinity.

The troops generally were much exhausted by the heat, thirst, and fighting of the previous day, besides which many men and parties were scattered owing partly to the mixing up of brigades and units in the attack on Chocolate Hill, and partly to straying in search of water, carrying and accompanying the wounded to the rear, and so on. We have, in fact, reason to believe that a considerable number of stragglers had collected at or near the shore.

The following movements took place on August 8th. One battalion of the 32nd Brigade, the 6th Yorkshire Regiment, owing to the losses which it had sustained, was replaced by the divisional Pioneer Battalion, the 6th East Yorkshire Regiment, and this brigade under the command of Colonel Minogue was ordered to take up a line running north and south through Sulajik, so as to get in touch on the north with a battalion of the 34th Brigade (the 5th Dorset Regiment), and on the south with the troops under General Hill. In the course of the afternoon, Hill 70 was occupied by the Pioneer Battalion, and the huts at Sulajik were put in a state of defence, with trenches surrounding them, by the 67th Field Company, RE.

The 5th Dorset Regiment and the 9th Lancashire Fusiliers, also belonging to the 34th Brigade, were put under the orders of Sir Bryan Mahon, and so remained until August 12th, when they rejoined the 11th Division.

The 11th Manchester Regiment of the 34th Brigade, which on the 7th was acting under Sir Bryan Mahon, rejoined its brigade from Kiretch Tepe Sirt.

The 7th South Staffordshire Regiment of the 33rd Brigade was sent to reinforce the troops under General Hill.

On August 8th, Sir Frederick Stopford had been anxious to push on, and had informed his two divisional commanders that he regarded it as being of the greatest importance to forestall the enemy on the high ground north of Anafarta Sagir and on the spur running thence to Ismail Oglu Tepe. The divisional commanders, however, represented that, though they would do what they could, they doubted the possibility of a further advance on that day, the troops being much exhausted by continuous fighting and lack of water. Sir Frederick Stopford was also influenced by the fact that the artillery at his disposal consisted of only one field battery and two mountain batteries, and that the troops of the 10th and 11th Divisions had been much scattered in the operations of August 7th.

He decided therefore to postpone the attack on Ismail Oglu Tepe and the Anafarta Sagir ridge until dawn on the 9th. It was arranged to attack Ismail Oglu Tepe from Chocolate Hill and the Anafarta Sagir ridge from the north-west between Baka Baba and Chocolate Hill, the 33rd Brigade with one battalion of the 31st Brigade on the right, the 32nd Brigade on the left, and two battalions of the 34th Brigade in reserve. It appears from Sir Frederick Stopford's report to Sir Ian Hamilton of the operations of the IXth Corps, dated October 26th, 1915, that on August 8th the former informed his two divisional commanders that, in view of the inadequate artillery support, he did not want them to let their men make frontal attacks on entrenched positions, but they were to push on as far as possible and try to turn any trenches they came across.

In his despatch to the Secretary of State for War, dated December 11th, 1915, Sir Ian Hamilton drew special attention to this passage in Sir Frederick Stopford's report and paraphrased it as follows: "General Stopford did not wish them to make frontal attacks on entrenched positions, but desired them, so far as was possible, to try and turn any trenches that were met with." He added: "Within the terms of this instruction lies the root of our failure to make use of the priceless daylight hours of August 8th." It is obvious that in one material respect the paraphrase differs from the instruction, which embodied three injunctions. First, to abstain from frontal attacks on entrenched positions; secondly, to push on as far as possible; and, thirdly, to try to turn any trenches which were encountered in pushing on. The second injunction is not mentioned by Sir Ian Hamilton, and the expression "as far as possible", which formed part of that injunction, is tacked on to the third.

Sir Ian Hamilton explains that in writing his despatch he had before him two documents from Sir Frederick Stopford—one, a memorandum to the Military Secretary, dated August 28th, written by Sir Frederick Stopford on board ship after he had been relieved of his command; the other, the report sent to Sir Ian Hamilton himself by General Stopford, dated October 26th— and that he inadvertently took up the former instead of the latter and quoted from it this sentence, which occurs textually in it as quoted, without the addition of "push on as far as possible." But in the early part of the paragraph in which the sentence occurs there is emphatic mention that Sir Frederick Stopford instructed his divisional generals to push on, and the sentence itself ends with a reiteration of the supreme importance of forestalling the enemy.

We think these facts show that there was some misunderstanding on the part of Sir Ian Hamilton as to the purport of the memorandum of August 28th and the report of October 26th, and we are of the opinion that his criticism is so worded as to obscure Sir Frederick Stopford's specific intention and injunction that the troops should push on as far as possible.

In the despatch Sir Ian Hamilton also referred to naval gunfire as compensating for the paucity of the available field and mountain artillery. Sir Frederick Stopford appears to have considered that, in the absence of a preparatory bombardment, the frontal attack of Turkish entrenchments would probably prove fruitless and entail heavy losses, and that as the trenches were not continuous the better course would be to push on between or past them, thus taking them in flank or reverse. As regards naval gunfire, Sir Frederick Stopford probably concurred with Admiral de Robeck in regarding such fire with its low trajectory as being ineffective against the deep trenches of the modern type, though effective enough against troops in the open or occupying shallow trenches. This view accords with much of the evidence which has been laid before us, while the importance of preparatory bombardment before making frontal attacks on deep entrenchments is confirmed not only by what repeatedly occurred on the Gallipoli Peninsula, but by the experience of our troops on the Western Front, where, the German trenches being continuous, attacks other than frontal are impossible.

Sir Ian Hamilton, who was at Imbros, received telegraphic reports of what was taking place at Suvla on August 7th from the commander of the IXth Corps. In particular there was a message despatched at 10 am on August 8th, reporting the position of the troops of the 11th Division at the time of despatch, and remarking that Major-General Hammersley and the force under his command deserved great credit for the results achieved. Presumably the capture of Chocolate Hill had been previously reported. The following message, despatched from Imbros at noon on August 8th, was sent by Sir Ian Hamilton to Sir Frederick Stopford:

> You and your troops have indeed done splendidly. Please tell Hammersley how much we hope from his able and rapid advance. Ian Hamilton.

With regard to this message, Sir Frederick Stopford informed us that the result of the operations on the night of the 6th and day of the 7th was not as satisfactory as he would have liked, but he gathered from Sir Ian Hamilton's congratulations that his dispositions and orders had met with the latter's approval.

Reverting to Sir Ian Hamilton's despatch of December 11th, 1915, we find it stated that the General Staff officer who had been sent from General Headquarters to Suvla early in the morning of the 8th reported by telegraph unfavourably as to the failure of our troops to take full advantage of the opportunities which were presenting themselves. But before this telegram was received, Sir Ian Hamilton had made up his mind from Sir Frederick Stopford's reports that all was not going well at Suvla, and he resolved himself to proceed thither, which he did, starting from Imbros at 4 pm and reaching Suvla an hour later. Sir Ian Hamilton's congratulatory telegram to Sir Frederick Stopford is hardly consistent with his conviction as recorded in the despatch, that all was not well at Suvla. It may, perhaps, have been written by Sir Ian Hamilton (as he said in his evidence) late on the 7th, or early on the 8th, as soon as the news of the capture of Chocolate Hill reached him; but if so we do not understand why its despatch from Imbros should have been delayed until noon on the 8th.

It is difficult to be certain as to the true explanation of this, but we do not consider the matter of great importance, as it is clear that for some reason Sir Ian Hamilton became dissatisfied on August 8th with the progress of operations, and consequently left Imbros for Suvla in the afternoon.

Sir Ian Hamilton's intervention

On arrival at Suvla Sir Ian Hamilton at once saw Sir Frederick Stopford on board HMS *Jonquil*, where, up to that time, the headquarters of the IXth Corps had been accommodated, pending their establishment on shore near Ghazi Baba. After a brief interview on the *Jonquil*, Sir Ian Hamilton's account of which is inconsistent with that of Sir Frederick Stopford, Sir Ian Hamilton proceeded to visit General Hammersley at Lala Baba. Sir Frederick Stopford did not accompany Sir Ian Hamilton to Lala Baba, and a good deal of conflicting evidence has been laid before us by these two officers with reference to his not doing so. The probable explanation of the incident is that Sir Frederick Stopford had only just returned from personally giving instructions to General Hammersley for the proposed operations at dawn on the 9th, and his attendance on shore not being requested by Sir Ian Hamilton, he saw no object in again visiting General Hammersley.

Sir Ian Hamilton arrived at Major-General Hammersley's headquarters about 6 pm, and in his despatch of December 11th, 1915, he describes the conversation which took place, and the extent to which he modified the orders previously given by Sir Frederick Stopford for the attack next morning. Sir Frederick Stopford and General Hammersley had decided against a night attack, but Sir Ian Hamilton thought that the advantages of such an attack in the matter of forestalling the enemy outweighed its disadvantages, and hearing that the 32nd Brigade was more or less concentrated and ready to move he gave General Hammersley a direct order that, even if it were only with this brigade, the advance should begin at the earliest possible moment instead of at dawn the next morning as previously arranged. Sir Ian Hamilton further directed that the 32nd Brigade should endeavour to occupy the heights north of Anafarta Sagir, presumably Tekke Tepe, but beyond giving these orders he states that he did nothing and said not a word calculated to affect the attack as originally planned. In his despatch he speaks of the 13 battalions detailed for the attack, but the correct number appears to be eleven, namely, four battalions of the 33rd Brigade, together with one from the 31st Brigade, on the right, with Ismail Oglu Tepe as the objective; four battalions of the 32nd Brigade on the left, with Anafarta Sagir as the objective; and two battalions of the 34th Brigade in reserve. It will be remembered that the remaining two battalions of the 34th Brigade had been placed at Sir Bryan Mahon's disposal on the morning of August 8th.

Sir Ian Hamilton's description of the nature and scope of his intervention is not fully corroborated by Sir Frederick Stopford and General Hammersley. Thus Sir Frederick Stopford points out in his report of October 26th, 1915, that his intention had been to make a concentrated attack upon the front stretching from Ismail Oglu Tepe to Anafarta Sagir, a distance of 4,100 yards, while under Sir Ian Hamilton's direct orders the front to be attacked was extended northward from Anafarta Sagir to Tekke Tepe, lengthening the front by an additional 2,200 yards. Moreover, the advance on this northern extension was through extremely difficult ground covered with dense bush, which had not been reconnoitred, and this greatly militated against the success of a night operation. Sir Frederick Stopford says in his report that, in view of the radical changes made by Sir Ian Hamilton in his plans and dispositions for the attack on the 9th, he repudiates any responsibility for the results of the action.

General Hammersley states that Sir Ian Hamilton's personal instructions quite upset the pre-arranged plans, and obliged him to re-issue his divisional orders late in the evening. Difficulty was experienced in communicating with the battalions of the 32nd Brigade, which were less concentrated than General Hammersley had supposed, and as a result only one battalion together with a section of engineers advanced in the direction of Tekke Tepe before 4 am on the 9th.

The change in the plan of operations approved by Sir Frederick Stopford was not communicated to him [Stopford] either by Sir Ian Hamilton or by General Hammersley. Sir Ian Hamilton states that he thought it would be reported by General Hammersley, and General Hammersley states that it did not occur to him at the time that he ought to report it. Later on, he imagines, the change was reported by some member of his staff to some member of the Corps staff. We think that this was an unfortunate omission. Sir Frederick Stopford might have expected to hear from the General Officer Commanding-in-Chief, and was entitled to hear from his divisional commander, in what respects his scheme of attack had been modified by direction of superior authority. If, however, Sir Frederick Stopford had accompanied Sir Ian Hamilton to Lala Baba, and been present at the latter's interview with General Hammersley, the alteration in the plan could not have been made without his knowledge.

At the end of the interview between Sir Ian Hamilton and Major-General Hammersley, the latter sent a General Staff officer to the commander of the 32nd Brigade with instructions to concentrate the brigade at Sulajik as soon as possible, and thence to occupy the high ground about Tekke Tepe before daybreak, at least one battalion being used for the purpose—preferably the 6th East Yorkshire Regiment. One battalion of the brigade was already at Sulajik; a second battalion reached that place without difficulty or delay; the third battalion, the 6th East Yorkshire Regiment, only got its orders to move from Hill 70 to Sulajik at 11 pm, and did not arrive until 3 am on the 9th; while the fourth battalion, the 9th West Yorkshire Regiment, had got out of touch in the thick bush near Abrikja at nightfall, never received the order to concentrate, and remained where it was.

OPERATIONS ON AUGUST 9TH, 1915

At 3.30 am on the 9th the brigade commander sent on the 6th East Yorkshire Regiment with the 67th Field Company, Royal Engineers (less one section), to secure Tekke Tepe, supporting the advance with another battalion, and retaining the third at Sulajik. On reaching a point about 1,000 yards south of Tekke Tepe, the head of the column was attacked by the Turks in superior strength; the commanding officers of the 6th East Yorkshire Regiment and the 67th Field Company, Royal Engineers, were killed; and many officers and men were killed or wounded. Shortly afterwards two machine guns were lost. Meanwhile the battalion in support, pushing up on the left of the 6th East Yorkshire Regiment, lost its commanding officer and suffered heavy loss. Eventually the 6th East Yorkshire Regiment and the battalion supporting it, the 8th West Riding Regiment, fell back, and continued their retirement until about noon, when they reached a point about 1,000 yards westward of Sulajik near the north-east corner of the Salt Lake. Here General Sitwell with two battalions of the 34th Brigade had taken up his position at 6 am and this served as a rallying point for the two retreating battalions of the 32nd Brigade.

The battalion of the 32nd Brigade which remained at Sulajik was joined at daybreak by the 9th West Yorkshire Regiment, which during the night had got out of touch near Abrikja. At 8 am the Turks made a strong attack against our left at Sulajik which was held by these two battalions, and continued all day to press this attack, endeavouring to work round the left flank. Their attempts were repulsed.

It will be remembered that according to the original plan the attack on Ismail Oglu Tepe was to be carried out by the four battalions of the 33rd Brigade with one battalion of the 31st Brigade under General Maxwell. In General Hammersley's revised written orders, which were issued after the interview with Sir Ian Hamilton, certain changes were made. One battalion of the 33rd Brigade, the 9th Sherwood Foresters, was directed to take up the long line from Chocolate Hill to Damakjelik Bahr, so as to connect the extreme left of the Anzac troops with the force under General Hill. The 33rd Brigade being thus reduced to three battalions, General Hill was directed to place two instead of one of his five battalions at General Maxwell's disposal, and the objective of General Maxwell's force of five battalions was enlarged so as to include not only Ismail Oglu Tepe but the ridge running thence to Anafarta Sagir.

General Maxwell had reconnoitred the ground during the afternoon of the 8th, and observed that Hill 70 was occupied by the 6th East Yorkshire Regiment. He determined to place three of his battalions in the front line, with one battalion in support of the centre and one in reserve. About 4.45 am on August 9th the battalions were concentrated, and moved off to their several points of deployment. As soon as this movement began, a heavy rifle fire broke out from the direction of Abrikja, and Chocolate Hill was shelled by the enemy. The right and centre battalions, however, pushed on towards the ridge near Ismail Oglu Tepe. The left battalion, on approaching Hill 70, found it occupied by the Turks instead of our own men, the 6th East Yorkshire not having been replaced when ordered away the previous evening. In aggravation of this mishap a considerable Turkish force from the north-east attacked the battalion at close quarters. From Hill 70 the centre battalion was taken in enfilade [from end to end], and lost heavily. General Maxwell's advance was brought to a standstill and his left seriously threatened. It now became a question not of pushing the attack, but of holding on at all costs.

Movements of the 53rd Division

A reference must now be made to the 53rd Division, under the command of Major-General Lindley, which on arrival at Mudros had been kept there as a general reserve for the combined operations which began on August 6th. This division was ordered to Suvla on August 8th. It consisted of three brigades—the 158th under Brigadier-General Cowans, the 159th under Brigadier-General Lloyd, and the 160th under Brigadier-General Hume. It had no artillery, only one Field Company of Royal Engineers without any stores, and only one field ambulance. The divisional Signal Company did not arrive until five or six days after the landing of its division, and when it did arrive it was attached to another division. The headquarters of the division with one battalion of the 159th Brigade were the first to arrive at Suvla, and landed at 7 pm on the 8th. The rest of the division landed during the night of the 8th and morning of the 9th. At 8.30 pm on the 8th Major-General Lindley received orders that two of his brigades, less one battalion for beach duty, were to be attached to the 11th Division for operations under General Hammersley on the following day. As soon as the troops became available they were pushed forward in the following order:

At 7 am [August 9th] one battalion, 160th Brigade, in support of the 33rd Brigade near Chocolate Hill.

At 9 am two battalions, 159th Brigade, to report to General Sitwell at Hill 10.

At 9.20 am one battalion, 160th Brigade, to reinforce the battalion already sent to Chocolate Hill.

At 10.55 am the remaining two battalions, 159th Brigade, under General Lloyd, to report to General Sitwell at Hill 10.

At 6.35 pm one battalion of the 158th Brigade, the 1/1 Hereford Regiment, to strengthen the right flank of the 9th Sherwood Foresters, who had been pushed back with heavy loss to a position between Kazlar Chair and Hetman Chair.

After the reinforcements from the 53rd Division had joined the troops already in action the fight continued in a somewhat desultory fashion during the rest of the day, no serious reverse being sustained and no appreciable success being achieved. In the afternoon the bush caught fire behind three battalions under General Maxwell's command near Hill 70, and these battalions had to fall back towards Hill 50 and Sulajik.

Distribution of troops on the evening of August 9th, 1915

At nightfall on the 9th the distribution of the troops was as follows:

The 9th Sherwood Foresters and 1/1 Hereford Regiment were near Hetman Chair.

Five battalions of the 10th Division under General Hill, with one field and one mountain battery, were on Chocolate Hill and Hill 50.

The 33rd Brigade, less the 9th Sherwood Foresters, plus two battalions of the 160th Brigade, under General Maxwell, were positioned from Hill 50 to the vicinity of Sulajik.

The 32nd Brigade, less one battalion, plus two battalions of the 159th Brigade, were at and to the north of Sulajik.

Two battalions of the 34th Brigade, with one battalion of the 32nd Brigade, were further to the north.

The remaining two battalions of the 34th Brigade were at Point 28, west of Kuchuk Anafarta Ova under the orders of the General Officer Commanding the 10th Division.

Two battalions of the 159th Brigade, presumably under General Lloyd, were near the north-east corner of the Salt Lake.

The 6th East Yorkshire Regiment (the Pioneer Battalion of the 11th Division), two field batteries and one mountain battery, were at Lala Baba.

It will be observed that the units were as much mixed up on the evening of August 9th as they had been on the previous evening, and organisation by brigades was practically non-existent. It would also appear that in the plan of operations for August 9th, which was initiated by Sir Frederick Stopford, more or less modified by Sir Ian Hamilton, and finally elaborated by General Hammersley, no reference was made to the troops of the 53rd Division, nor was any specific place or duty assigned to them. Yet presumably it must have been anticipated by each of these officers that the 53rd Division, or part of it, would have landed by the morning of the 9th, because General Lindley, who was the first to land, got an order from the IXth Corps at 8.30 pm on the 8th that he was to place two of his brigades, less one battalion, at General Hammersley's disposal for the operations on the 9th. Uncertainty as to the exact time of their landing may perhaps have led to the exclusion of these seven battalions from the plan of operations for August 9th, while the unfortunate repulse on both flanks on the morning of that day caused them to be hurried to the scene of action as soon as they could be got ready. They were much scattered in consequence, and removed from the control of their own divisional and brigade organisations, and this cannot have contributed to their fighting efficiency, especially as hardly any of their officers had been trained in the regular army or possessed previous war experience.

Position of the 10th Division

On August 8th and 9th Sir Bryan Mahon, commanding the 10th Division, but having with him of his own troops only two battalions of the 30th Brigade, one of the 31st Brigade, and his divisional Pioneer Battalion, supported by two battalions of the 34th Brigade which had been put under his orders, continued to push forward along Karakol Dagh and Kiretch Tepe Sirt, and entrenched a north and south line through a point marked on the map by a bench mark on the latter. Sir Frederick Stopford states that, taking into account the small force at his disposal and the lack of artillery support, the progress of Sir Bryan Mahon was as satisfactory as could be expected.

We think that it was unfortunate that the 10th Division had no opportunity of acting as a division under its own commander at the critical stages of these operations.

Orders from General Headquarters

Sir Ian Hamilton had spent the night of the 8th on board ship at Suvla and had watched General Hammersley's attack the next morning. After landing at Ghazi Baba at about 8 am he walked up the Karakol Dagh ridge as far as the headquarters of the 30th Brigade. He then appears to have returned to Imbros. At about 5 pm on the 9th Sir Frederick Stopford received a letter from General Braithwaite expressing the confident opinion that, if an attack of six or eight battalions could be organised under the command of a selected officer, and directed on Ismail Oglu Tepe and the ridge thence to Anafarta Sagir, the troops would attain their objective. The letter laid stress on the need for Sir Frederick Stopford's personal influence and driving power to get the operation driven through.

Sir Frederick Stopford regarded this letter as tantamount to an order from the General Officer Commanding-in-Chief. At the same time he was aware that the troops of the 11th Division and the seven battalions of the 53rd Division had lost heavily during the day's fighting and were considerably disorganised. There was, however, one brigade of the 53rd Division in reserve at Lala Baba which had not been engaged. Sir Frederick Stopford determined, therefore, to make the attack not with six or eight battalions only, as suggested in General Braithwaite's letter, but with the whole of the 53rd Division, less one battalion which had not yet landed, supported by the whole of the 11th Division.

OPERATIONS FROM AUGUST 10TH TO AUGUST 15TH, 1915

At 7.50 pm on August 9th, General Lindley received his orders for the attack which was to take place at 5 am on the following day. He found great difficulty in collecting his scattered battalions. In fact, two battalions of the 160th Brigade seem to have remained with the 33rd Brigade near Hill 50. There were three battalions of the Royal Welsh Fusiliers (158th Brigade) at Lala Baba, and these, with five other battalions (four of the 159th Brigade and one of the 160th Brigade), were eventually concentrated as two brigades near the position occupied by the 32nd Brigade at Sulajik. The right of this force moved south on Hill 70, but swung round to the west when about 200 yards from the top of the hill. It thus came under flank and reverse fire from the Turkish guns on Ismail Oglu Tepe and retreated, subsequently re-forming behind the 33rd Brigade. The centre and left of the force were at first more successful, but by about 10.30 am the left was rapidly driven back, and with the retirement of the centre the attack came to an end. Under the orders of the Corps Commander the attack was renewed, after some artillery preparation, at 5 pm, but the opposition being greater than in the morning no headway was made, and the troops fell back to the alignment held the previous evening.

On August 10th Sir Frederick Stopford received orders from General Headquarters to take up and entrench a line across the whole front extending from Azmak Dere on the south through the knoll east of Chocolate Hill, to the ground held by the 10th Division on Kiretch Tepe Sirt. In giving effect to this order on August 11th he took the opportunity of reorganising his divisions and brigades. The entrenchment of the line from Kazlar Chair to 600 yards south of Sulajik was assigned to the 11th Division, thence to the west of Kuchuk Anafarta Ova to the 53rd Division, and thence to Kiretch Tepe Sirt to the 10th Division. The length of this line was over 5 miles.

During this day the 54th Division arrived at Suvla and began to disembark at Beach A. It had no artillery, no divisional signal company, no field ambulances, no ammunition, and no mules. The division was commanded by Major-General F. S. Inglefield, and consisted of the 161st Brigade under Brigadier-General Daniell, the 162nd Brigade under Brigadier-General De Winton, and the 163rd Brigade under Brigadier-General Brunker. Sir Frederick Stopford was directed not to employ the division without instructions from General Headquarters.

On the morning of August 12th General Stopford received orders from General Headquarters that the 54th Division was to make a night march that night and at dawn the next day to attack the heights of Kavak Tepe and Tekke Tepe and thence to Anafarta Sagir. The feasibility of a night march through an intricate and wooded country depends upon the absence of opposition along the route to be traversed, but in this case Sir Frederick Stopford had reason to believe that from Kuchuk Anafarta Ova eastward the ground was held by the enemy. He therefore decided to send forward the 163rd Brigade in the afternoon for the purpose of occupying Kuchuk Anafarta Ova and securing an unopposed night march for the remainder of the Division, at any rate as far as that place. In spite of serious opposition the 163rd Brigade succeeded in establishing itself at the desired point in very difficult and enclosed country. It was on this occasion that the officer commanding the 1/5th Norfolk Regiment with 16 officers and 250 men pursued the enemy into the forest, from which none of them ever emerged.

In the course of the same afternoon General Headquarters enquired whether Sir Frederick Stopford was satisfied that the 54th Division could be supplied with food, water, ammunition, etc., if the troops succeeded in gaining the high ground which was their objective. Sir Frederick Stopford replied that he foresaw grave difficulty in supplying the division, as in such difficult and densely wooded country the convoys would be attacked and the mules shot or stampeded. Thereupon the orders for the night march and the attack on the heights were cancelled by General Headquarters.

On August 13th Sir Ian Hamilton informed Sir Frederick Stopford that, as soon as Sir William Birdwood was ready to co-operate, a simultaneous attack was to be made by the latter on Sari Bahr and by the 11th and 54th Divisions on Ismail Oglu Tepe. Sir Frederick Stopford prepared plans accordingly. As it appeared, however, that Sir William Birdwood could not then undertake a fresh attack on Sari Bahr the project was abandoned, and Sir Frederick Stopford was directed to confine his attention to strengthening the entrenched line across his front.

To straighten out the left of this line Sir Frederick Stopford on August 14th directed Sir Bryan Mahon to advance on the following day and gain possession of the whole of the top of Kiretch Tepe Sirt. The 54th Division was ordered to co-operate. On the morning of the 15th the two brigades of the 10th Division, the 30th and 31st, made a frontal attack along the ridge, while the 162nd Brigade of the 54th Division supported on the right. Gunfire from two men-of-war in the Gulf of Saros and from one mountain battery, one field battery, and one heavy battery was brought to bear on the Turkish position. At first the attack succeeded and the top of the ridge was captured by the 6th Dublin Fusiliers. The Turks, however, made a counterattack, and after severe fighting and heavy casualties our troops had to fall back to their original alignment.

The relief of Sir Frederick Stopford

On the evening of August 15th Sir Frederick Stopford was relieved of the command of the IXth Corps and replaced for the time being by Major-General de Lisle. On his way from Cape Helles to Suvla, Major-General de Lisle had called at Imbros, seen Sir Ian Hamilton, and received formal instructions from Major-General Braithwaite. In these instructions he was informed that his immediate and most urgent concern was to reorganise the IXth Corps, and to prepare as large a proportion of it as possible for a fresh attack on Ismail Oglu Tepe, and the ridge running thence to Anafarta Sagir. The force placed at his disposal consisted of the 10th Division, less the 29th Brigade, the 11th, 53rd and 54th Divisions, and the 2nd Mounted Division, composed of about 4,000 dismounted men, which was expected to reach Suvla from Egypt by August 18th. As regards artillery, two mountain batteries, two heavy batteries and one field artillery brigade had been landed at Suvla. One field artillery brigade and two batteries of 5-inch howitzers had been landed at Anzac and were at the disposal of the General Officer commanding the IXth Corps as soon as horses could be provided to mobilise them. Three more field artillery brigades and two batteries of 4–5 inch howitzers were at Mudros, ready to be brought up as soon as they could be landed, but they would have to be landed without horses and taken into position by the horses of other units.

OPERATIONS ON AUGUST 21st, 1915

On assuming command of the IXth Corps, Major-General de Lisle investigated the situation at Suvla and represented to General Headquarters the desirability of strengthening the force at his disposal by bringing over the 29th Division from Helles. This proposal commended itself to the General Officer Commanding-in-Chief and the 29th Division landed at Suvla on August 20th. The 2nd Mounted Division under Major-General Peyton had landed two days before. The attack was fixed for August 21st and Major-General de Lisle's plan, which met with Sir Ian Hamilton's approval, was as follows.

The 53rd and 54th Divisions were to hold the enemy from Sulajik to Kiretch Tepe Sirt; the 11th Division on the right and the 29th Division on the left were to attack Ismail Oglu Tepe and the ridge running thence to Anafarta Sagir; in support were to be the 2nd Mounted Division of Yeomanry, and in reserve were to be what remained of the two brigades of the 10th Division. It was arranged with Sir William Birdwood that a force of nine battalions should co-operate by advancing from Damakjelik Bahr so as to connect with the southern end of the outpost line of the IXth Corps near Kazlar Chair.

It had been decided to attack in the afternoon, and it so happened that a fog came on which seriously interfered with the preliminary bombardment of the enemy's position from 2.30 pm to 3 pm. The advance was begun at 3 pm by the 11th Division, the 34th Brigade rushing the Turkish trenches between Hetman Chair and Aire Kevak. In his despatch Sir Ian Hamilton states that this was done practically without loss, but Major-General Hammersley does not agree. He has informed us that one battalion lost five out of its seven officers before reaching the Turkish trenches and that by the end of the day the losses of this and of another battalion were extremely heavy.

The 32nd Brigade, moving directly against Hetman Chair and the communication trench thence eastward to Ismail Oglu Tepe, lost its proper direction by inclining too much to the north and came under a heavy enfilade fire. The brigade swung round to attack the communication trench from the north, but the attempt failed although successive lines advanced with conspicuous gallantry. Major-General Hammersley attributes this brigade's loss of direction to the fact that its right battalion lost all its officers within the first few hundred yards.

The 33rd Brigade, which was in divisional reserve, started from Lala Baba shortly after 3 pm towards Hetman Chair in support of the 34th and 32nd Brigades. During this movement some confusion arose from the 2nd Mounted Division, which was marching from Lala Baba to Chocolate Hill, cutting across the line of advance of the 33rd Brigade and temporarily separating the two battalions in front from the two battalions in the rear. The confusion was increased by a fierce bush fire which had started north of Hetman Chair. As a result the 33rd Brigade lost direction, part of it moving south-east towards Susak Kuyu and part to the north of the Turkish communication trench. So far as the 11th Division was concerned the operation had failed.

Meanwhile at 3.30 pm, the 29th Division attacked Hill 70. The trenches on the hill were carried by the 87th Brigade on the left, but the 86th Brigade was brought to a standstill by the bush fire. Moreover its right was not supported owing to the 32nd Brigade having deviated from the proper direction. Later on the 86th Brigade fell back to a point south-west of Hill 70, where a little cover was obtainable, and eventually the division withdrew to its previous position.

Later on in the afternoon the 2nd South Midland Brigade of the 2nd Mounted Division was sent forward from its position behind Chocolate Hill in the hope that some substantial success might yet be achieved. The bush fire and the enemy's opposition retarded the brigade's advance and it was almost nightfall before it reached the valley between Hill 70 and Hill 100 on Ismail Oglu Tepe. A knoll near the centre of this valley was captured by one of the regiments of the brigade as soon as it was dark, but as this knoll was commanded by the enemy's trenches and could not be held in the day-time unless we were in possession of Ismail Oglu Tepe, the regiment and the brigade to which it belonged were ordered back to Chocolate Hill. It appears therefore that so far as the 29th Division and 2nd Mounted Division were concerned, the operation had failed.

The casualties in the IXth Corps on August 21st were approximately as follows: in the 11th Division, 58 out of 129 officers and 2,300 other ranks out of 6,400. In the 29th Division a little under 5,000 officers and men. In the 2nd Mounted Division which was about 4,000 strong, 1,200 officers and men, or 30 per cent.

The force under Major-General Cox, which had been detailed to co-operate with the IXth Corps on August 21st, advanced in three sections, the left to establish connection with the outpost line of the 11th Division near Kazlar Chair, the centre on Kabak Kuyu where there was a good supply of water, and the right on the Turkish trenches at Kaiajik Aghala. The advance of the left and central sections was successful. The right section met with obstinate resistance, but effected a lodgment on Kaiajik Aghala before nightfall and held on during the night against a superior force. The next morning an additional battalion reinforced this section, and after several attacks and counter-attacks a line from Kaiajik Aghala northward to Susak Kuyu was taken up and strengthened and subsequently connected with the right of the IXth Corps.

A FINAL OFFENSIVE ON AUGUST 27TH, 1915

On August 27th, Sir William Birdwood again detailed a force under Major-General Cox to complete the capture of Hill 60, immediately north of Kaiajik Aghala. The troops consisted of detachments from the 4th and 5th Australian Brigades, the New Zealand Mounted Rifles Brigade, and the 5th Connaught Rangers. The advance was made at 5 pm and after severe fighting lasting through the night, the next day, and up to 1 am, on August 29th, the hill was captured. Our casualties on this occasion amounted to 1,000.

This was the last engagement of any serious importance at or in the vicinity of Suvla up to its evacuation.

CHANGE IN COMMAND AT SUVLA

We have already mentioned that Sir Frederick Stopford vacated the command of the IXth Corps on August 15th. Major-General Lindley resigned the command of the 53rd Division on August 17th. On August 18th Brigadier-General Sitwell was relieved of the command of the 34th Brigade on account of an adverse report on his capacity for command by Major-General Hammersley. Under orders from the War Office Major-General Hammersley was relieved of the command of the 11th Division on August 23rd. He received at the time a telegram from General Headquarters to the effect that no communication on the subject of his relief had emanated from Sir Ian Hamilton, but that presumably the War Office considered his age a bar. Major-General Hammersley was then nearly 57. On August 24th Major-General de Lisle vacated the temporary command of the IXth Corps and reverted to the command of the 29th Division, being replaced by Lieutenant-General the Hon. J. Byng. The reason for Lord Kitchener's action in regard to Sir Frederick Stopford and Major-General Hammersley appears to be as follows.

In a telegram to Lord Kitchener, dated August 14th, Sir Ian Hamilton reported that the result of his visit to the IXth Corps had bitterly disappointed him. He remarked:

> There is nothing for it but to allow them [the troops at Suvla] time to rest and re-organize, unless I force Stopford and his Divisional Commanders to undertake a general action, for which, in their present frame of mind, they have no heart. In fact, they are not fit for it.

Lord Kitchener replied on the same date, enquiring whether Sir Ian Hamilton had any competent generals to take the place of Sir Frederick Stopford, Sir Bryan Mahon and Major-General Hammersley. He added:

From your report I think Stopford should come home. This is a young man's war, and we must have commanding officers who will take full advantage of opportunities which occur but seldom. If, therefore, any Generals fail, do not hesitate to act promptly. Any Generals I have available I will send you.

Sir Ian Hamilton answered the foregoing telegram on the same date to the effect that the one man on the spot who could pull the IXth Corps together again was Major-General de Lisle. He remarked:

Unfortunately Mahon is senior to de Lisle, but I could not put him in command of the Corps at present, though as Divisional General he has done better than others, and I would ask him to accept the position . . . I hope you will agree to this and give de Lisle the temporary rank of Lieutenant-General.

Lord Kitchener again telegraphed on the same date to the effect that he was asking Sir John French to supply one Corps Commander and two Divisional Generals, and had suggested the name of Lieutenant-General Byng for the Corps Command, and that it was better not to act definitely until he had heard what Sir John French could do.

It will be observed that this telegraphic correspondence between Sir Ian Hamilton and Lord Kitchener hardly bears out the telegram received by Major-General Hammersley from General Headquarters when he was relieved of his Divisional Command.

Sir Ian Hamilton has urged us to investigate and express our opinion on certain incidents which occurred in connection with Sir Frederick Stopford's removal from his command.

Sir Frederick Stopford was replaced by Major-General de Lisle on August 15th, and left forthwith for England. He thereupon ceased to be under Sir Ian Hamilton's orders, and on his way home he wrote a memorandum, dated August 28th, in which he gave an account of the operations at Suvla from the landing up to the day of his departure. On reaching London he forwarded this memorandum to the Military Secretary at the War Office for Lord Kitchener's information.

On August 14th the telegraphic correspondence mentioned in the preceding paragraph had taken place between Sir Ian Hamilton and Lord Kitchener. This was followed by a telegram from Sir Ian Hamilton, dated August 17th, in which the operations at Anzac and Suvla were described and commented on. A telegram, dated August 22nd, was then sent by Lord Kitchener to Sir Ian Hamilton, desiring him to transmit the operation orders and other instructions relating to the Suvla operations; and Sir Ian Hamilton replied on the same date that these documents had been forwarded by the last King's Messenger, who had left three days before.

On receipt of the documents a synopsis was prepared, and Lord Kitchener decided to assemble a Committee of senior General Officers at the War Office for the purpose of considering them, together with Sir Ian

Hamilton's telegrams of August 14th and 17th and Sir Frederick Stopford's memorandum.

A copy of the memorandum was forwarded by the War Office to Sir Ian Hamilton on his return to England, and he does not appear to have taken exception to it at that time.

We understand Sir Ian Hamilton's present contention to be that Sir Frederick Stopford was not entitled to forward the memorandum of August 28th to the Military Secretary, except through himself as General Officer Commanding-in-Chief of the Mediterranean Expeditionary Force; and that the memorandum, being an irregular and *ex parte* [biased] statement, should have been debarred from consideration until he had been furnished with a copy and given an opportunity of expressing his views thereon.

The question raised by Sir Ian Hamilton being one of military discipline, and of administrative action on the part of Lord Kitchener as Secretary of State for War, its consideration appears to us to lie outside the scope of our enquiry.

REASONS FOR FAILURE AT SUVLA

Sir Beauvoir de Lisle attributes the failure on August 21st chiefly to the want of artillery. He states that there was not as much artillery on shore at Suvla as is normally assigned to a single division. About three-quarters of the artillery of one division had to support the attack of three divisions. Secondly, he is of the opinion that the troops landed at Suvla before the date of his assuming command of the IXth Corps had gone through a very trying experience, and that hardship, heat and thirst, coupled with futile attacks and repeated failures, had for the time being worn them out, shaken their self-reliance, and dulled their fighting spirit. Thirdly, he considers that the staff work generally had been indifferent and that consequently the troops had suffered more than they ought to have done.

Sir Beauvoir de Lisle gives no specific instance of this indifferent staff work as coming under his own observation, while he speaks in high terms of the professional qualifications of the Brigadier-General, General Staff, of the IXth Corps, Brigadier-General Reed, VC. He had no confidence in the fitness of Major-Generals Lindley and Hammersley for divisional commands in the field, and he thought that Major-General F. S. Inglefield, who at the time was 60, was too old for the command of the 54th Division. He was in favour of the evacuation of Suvla, which he regarded as the only thing to do when we had the factor of surprise no longer in our favour, and for the same reason he would have evacuated Helles and Anzac and abandoned the enterprise in June, as by that time there was no prospect of ultimate success. He described the operations planned by him for August 21st as having a defensive rather than an offensive object. He attacked in order to prevent the Turks from attacking.

Poor staff work

Sir Beauvoir de Lisle has spoken of the staff work in the IXth Corps as not being up to the proper standard, and certain incidents have come to our notice which support this allegation. General Hammersley put forward in his evidence a *précis* of the more important messages received at and issued from the headquarters of the 11th Division at Lala Baba, from 5 am to 5.40 pm, on August 7th. A message was sent by General Sitwell at 6.30 am that his troops were unable to move eastward from the vicinity of Hill 10, the order having been that they should so move for the capture of Chocolate Hill. To this message no reply was sent, but at 8 am another order was issued to General Sitwell that his troops and those of the 32nd Brigade were to advance on Chocolate Hill, supported on the left by the force under General Hill, which was to advance on Ismail Oglu Tepe.

At about the same time General Hill was told by General Hammersley that, when he reached the 32nd and 34th Brigades in the vicinity of Hill 10, he with the five battalions under his command was to operate on the right towards Chocolate Hill, the battalions of the 32nd and 34th Brigades operating on the left towards Ismail Oglu Tepe. Up to this time General Sitwell had shown no inclination to move forward, and the discrepancy between these orders, so far as concerned the tasks assigned to the several brigades, led to his neither taking action himself nor co-operating with General Hill. Again, when the final order for the combined attack on Chocolate Hill under General Sitwell's command was issued at 2.40 pm, no mention was made in it of Ismail Oglu Tepe as one of the objectives, though General Hammersley has informed us that he intended an attack on Ismail Oglu Tepe to form part of the operation. So far as we can judge, the orders emanating from General Hammersley's headquarters on August 7th were lacking in coherence and precision.

The unfortunate incident of the withdrawal of the 6th East Yorkshire Regiment from Hill 70 on the evening of August 8th, without its being replaced, also appears to indicate defective staff work. General Hammersley's account of this incident is far from clear. He tells us that he sent the 7th South Staffordshire Regiment belonging to the 33rd Brigade to reinforce General Hill at Chocolate Hill on the morning of the 8th, that General Hill ordered it forward at noon with directions to picket Hill 70 and entrench, but that Hill 70 was already occupied by the 6th East Yorkshire Regiment. Later on he tells us that the latter regiment advanced, under considerable fire, to the western slopes of Hill 70, that the fire became so intense that the Commanding Officer resolved to wait until dusk before occupying the hill, and that after dusk the hill was carried, and the troops began to entrench themselves. Later on, he tells us that, after his interview with Sir Ian Hamilton, he sent instructions to the Officer Commanding the 32nd Brigade at Sulajik, nominating the 6th East Yorkshire Regiment for the advance by night to Tekke Tepe, because he thought the battalion in question had been the least used so far, and was therefore the freshest. The battalion got orders to move from Hill 70 to Sulajik at 11 pm and, owing to the darkness and thick bush, did not arrive there until 3 am. No battalion was directed to replace the 6th East Yorkshire Regiment on its vacating Hill 70, which the Turks promptly re-occupied. In our opinion, General Hammersley did not know on August 8th that Hill 70 had been occupied, though this must have been known to General Hill, and is stated in evidence to have been observed by General Maxwell when he reconnoitred the ground east of Chocolate Hill. It would seem that these subordinate commanders or their staff took no steps to acquaint the divisional commander or his staff with what had occurred in regard to Hill 70.

The failure to replace the 6th East Yorkshire Regiment when ordered from Hill 70 to Sulajik entailed many fruitless attempts to recapture the hill and much unnecessary loss of life.

Lack of artillery

Again, it will be seen on reference to an earlier paragraph in this report that on July 29th the General Officer Commanding IXth Corps was led to expect that he would be supplied with a considerable force of artillery, including seven brigades of field artillery—namely, the three brigades belonging to the 10th Division, two out of the three brigades belonging to the 11th Division, and two out of the three brigades belonging to the 13th Division. Up to August 8th only one field battery was available at Suvla, from August 9th to August 15th only one brigade of field artillery was available, and for the operations of August 21st Major-General de Lisle states that he had at his disposal only about three-quarters of the artillery of a division to support the attack of three divisions.

We think that the absence of the artillery and horses available at Alexandria and Mudros must have materially contributed to the failure at Suvla.

Sir Ian Hamilton's intervention

We have already mentioned Sir Ian Hamilton's personal intervention on the afternoon of August 8th and the consequent alteration in the scheme of attack which Sir Frederick Stopford had previously decided on. We regard the intervention as well-intentioned but injudicious. In the modified scheme the scope of the operations was enlarged so as to include the high ground near Tekke Tepe, but the difficulties of reaching and holding this ground were not appreciated, and as a result the attack in that direction was repulsed with heavy loss. Moreover, the withdrawal of troops for the movement on Tekke Tepe prejudicially affected the attack on Ismail Oglu Tepe, which also failed. We cannot say whether the original scheme would have succeeded, but we think that it had more chance of success than the scheme which took its place.

The combined operations so carefully planned were a failure, and the losses incurred at Helles, Anzac, and Suvla had been extremely heavy. As regards Anzac, Sir Ian Hamilton remarks in his despatch:

> The grand coup had not come off. The Narrows were still out of sight, and beyond field-gun range. But this was not the fault of Sir William Birdwood, or any of the officers and men under his command.

As regards Suvla, he remarks that the units of the 10th and 11th Divisions had shown their mettle in the act of landing, when they stormed Lala Baba, when they tackled Chocolate Hill, and when they drove the enemy from Hill 10. He continues:

> Then had come hesitation. The advantage had not been pressed. The senior commanders at Suvla had had no personal experience of the new trench warfare; of the Turkish methods; of the paramount importance of time. Strong, clear leadership had not been promptly enough applied.

He concludes by stating that for these reasons he had replaced Sir Frederick Stopford by Major-General de Lisle.

Difficulties of hill warfare

It must be remembered that a great part of the fighting at both Anzac and Suvla was not trench warfare, but hill warfare. Hill warfare is not an easy business for troops unaccustomed to it, even when the hills are bare and the slopes normal, but its difficulties are greatly increased when the hills are covered with forest or dense bush, and the slopes are precipitous. The difficulties are further intensified if the operations are undertaken at night. Certain general principles for the guidance of commanders who may propose to undertake night operations have been authoritatively set forth in Field Service Regulations, 1914, Part I, Chapter IX, particular stress being laid on the importance of a complete preliminary reconnaissance. Local conditions at Anzac and Suvla did not allow the thorough reconnaissance prescribed in this chapter. Exceptional conditions may justify a departure from established tactical rules, and we do not doubt that Sir Ian Hamilton carefully balanced the advantages of surprise and immunity from hostile fire against the risk of misdirection, confusion, and delay. In the opinion of Sir William Birdwood and Sir Frederick Stopford night attacks were justified by the special circumstances. Still, having regard to the results, the history of the operations at Anzac and Suvla seems to us to substantiate the soundness of the regulations on this subject.

It may be mentioned, that in Lord Kitchener's telegram to Sir Ian Hamilton on April 2nd, Lord Kitchener had referred to night attacks without confessing any opinion thereon.

In his despatch, Sir Ian Hamilton describes Koja Chemen Tepe as the dominating point, the acquisition of which would necessarily lead to the capture of Maidos and Kaba Tepe, would enable the bulk of the Turkish Army to be cut off from land communication with Constantinople, and would give our artillery such a command as to stop all sea traffic between the Turkish Army and Constantinople or Asia. We suggest that these objects would not have been attained without a protracted struggle, the result of which cannot confidently be predicted.

THE INTERIM DECISION TO CONTINUE OPERATIONS

After the failure at Suvla on August 6th and the following days, the same question presented itself to the Dardanelles Committee and the Cabinet as in May, i.e., whether the Dardanelles operations were to be continued or abandoned, and, if continued, in what way.

The question was raised in a memorandum prepared by Colonel Swinton, the Assistant-Secretary to the Committee of Imperial Defence, and laid before the meeting of the Dardanelles Committee on the 19th August, 1915:

> There appear to be only two alternative courses to be adopted:
>
> (a)   Not to send out the additional troops asked for by the Commander-in-Chief, and, therefore, to abandon the attempt to force the Straits, for there appears to be no prospect of success in a further offensive if the troops out in Gallipoli are not so increased, and without advancing it appears to be impracticable to continue to occupy the portions of the peninsula already gained.
>
> (b)   To send out the troops asked for and to despatch them with the least possible delay so that the attempt which has just failed may be renewed. These reinforcements should be sent out at the earliest possible moment in view of the broken weather to be expected in the last half of September, which will render landing and supply impossible for considerable periods.

This was not quite exhaustive, for it was possible to send out smaller reinforcements which would enable Sir Ian Hamilton to maintain his position till a final decision was reached, and this was the plan adopted.

The reinforcements asked for were those which had been mentioned by Sir Ian Hamilton in a telegram of August 17th in which he stated that the Turks had 110,000 rifles on the peninsula to his 95,000; that his British divisions were 45,000 under establishment, exclusive of about 9,000 promised or on the way, and that he required—to give him the necessary superiority if the Turks were not largely reinforced—that this deficit should be made up and that new formations, totalling 50,000 rifles, should be sent.

The matter was discussed at many meetings of the Dardanelles Committee. Sir Ian Hamilton's views were considered, and appreciations were submitted by the General Staff, which had been reconstituted under Sir

Archibald Murray, and afterwards under Sir William Robertson. The final decision was not reached until December, 1915.

The position when Sir Ian Hamilton's telegram of August 17th was received was broadly this. It had been agreed at a joint Conference between the French and British authorities held at Calais in July, 1915, that no important offensive should be undertaken in the West until the spring of 1916. This would reduce the demands from the Western Front for men and munitions and might make it possible to move troops thence to the East.

It had become clear that no help could be looked for from Bulgaria, and that that country had become definitely hostile, and would probably join the Central Powers, as in fact she did very soon. It was likely that if Bulgaria joined the Central Powers an attack would be made on Serbia with the object of crushing that country and opening up communication with Constantinople. If this were done, the Turks could be supplied with guns and ammunition which they were known to want. The Russian reverses were still continuing.

It seemed to be agreed that it would not be wise to abandon the operations in the Dardanelles unless some operations in the Balkans or other operations against Turkey in some direction were undertaken, and there was undoubtedly a difference of opinion as to the course to be adopted.

On August 20th, Lord Kitchener pointed out that, owing to the situation in Russia, he could no longer maintain the attitude which was agreed upon in conjunction with the French at Calais (in July), namely, that a real serious offensive on a large scale in the West should be postponed until all the Allies were quite ready; and that the large divisional reinforcements asked for could not be sent to the Dardanelles, as they had been promised to France and could not be diverted. He said his inclination was to help Sir Ian Hamilton as far as was possible without interfering with the operations in France, at any rate until after the contemplated offensive there had taken place.

This was agreed to, and Sir Ian Hamilton was so informed. He replied that he would do the best he could with the forces at his disposal; and after giving an account of some fighting that had taken place, and pointing out that casualties, both from wounds and sickness, were very large, he said:

> Keeping these conditions in view, it appears inevitable that within the next fortnight I shall be compelled to relinquish either Suvla Bay or Anzac Cove, and must further envisage the possibility of a still further reduction of my front in the near future.

Later on, he reported that if Suvla or Anzac had to be given up, he thought it must be Suvla.

In answer, Lord Kitchener desired him to discuss the matter with his Corps Commanders, and referred to 47,000 drafts and reinforcements which had been sent since August 6th.

Sir Ian Hamilton replied that he did not understand the allusion to 47,000, as he had not been advised of any such number, and, in answer, Lord Kitchener said that he was sending the details. On this, Sir Ian Hamilton telegraphed that the welcome news of 47,000 reinforcements altered the whole situation, and that such a number would do much to complete his diminished cadres [units], and should materially lessen the sickness rate by giving more chance of taking tired troops out of the trenches. In fact, Sir Ian Hamilton appears to have received reinforcements amounting to 29,000, but of these 9,000 were not sufficiently trained for active service and had to be sent to Egypt, reducing the effective total to 20,000.

On August 27th, the Dardanelles Committee, after discussion, decided that no line of future policy could be framed for the present, but that Sir Ian Hamilton should do his best to hold the ground which he had gained, and be asked for his appreciation as to future policy and the requirements to carry it out. On the same date Lord Kitchener telegraphed to Sir Ian Hamilton accordingly.

Sir Ian Hamilton's appreciation was sent on September 2nd, and in it he pointed out that the drafts and reinforcements promised did not make up his deficit, and that he could not launch any grand attack unless or until his divisions could be brought up to establishment and new formations up to 50,000 were sent out. He also asked for reinforcements up to 20 per cent to be available in the theatre of operations to meet wastage. He concluded:

> To sum up, there is, in my opinion, no better alternative than to make fresh effort at Suvla and Anzac. You will understand that any appreciation I can send must inevitably alter from day to day, and that it must be again modified by any accession to my strength in the shape of fresh Allied troops or an alteration in the political situation in the Balkans. Meanwhile, all preparations are being made for a winter campaign.

When this came before the Dardanelles Committee on September 3rd, they were informed by Lord Kitchener that the French Government had decided to send four divisions against Turkey to the Asiatic side of the Dardanelles and wished their two divisions on the European side to be replaced by British troops. Lord Kitchener said that he proposed to instruct Sir John French to send two divisions from France for the purpose. This enterprise, if carried out by the French, might have materially assisted the operations in the Dardanelles, and in any case was inconsistent with the abandonment of the Gallipoli Expedition.

Preparations were made for carrying out this scheme, but the French troops could not be sent from the Western Front until the result of the contemplated offensive in that theatre was known. This offensive began on September 25th, and in the meantime the Bulgarians had mobilized, and evidently an attack on Serbia was probable. Another element was thus introduced into the problem, namely, the consideration of whether an Allied force should be sent to Salonica or elsewhere to help the Serbians. On September 23rd the Secretary of State for War was directed to prepare a military appreciation of the situation to be placed before the Dardanelles Committee on the morning of September 24th on the following lines:

The possibility of sending a British or Allied force to Salonica or farther in order to support Greece, if Greece should go to the assistance of Serbia in resisting an attack by the Austro-Germans and possibly the Bulgarians.

On September 24th Sir Ian Hamilton was asked what force could be spared from Gallipoli for Salonica. At the same time the attention of the Admiralty and War Office was to be drawn to the importance of pushing on arrangements for a winter campaign in the Gallipoli Peninsula.

The circumstances which led to the despatch of forces to Salonica do not come within the scope of our inquiry. It is sufficient to say that for a long time questions were raised and discussions took place about the matter, and eventually the British Government was committed to sending a large force to co-operate with the French in that theatre. The possibility of having to send this force again raised the question of the evacuation of Gallipoli.

There was a considerable division of opinion on the subject among the members of the Dardanelles Committee and, on October 11th, it was decided that immediate instructions should be given for the despatch, as soon as the pending operations on the Western Front were over, of an adequate force from France to Egypt, without prejudice to its ultimate destination, and that a specially selected General should proceed without delay to the Near East to consider and report as to the particular sphere and the particular objective to which we should direct our attention. Sir Charles Monro was the General selected, and he left England on October 22nd, and arrived at Gallipoli on October 31st.

THE DECISION TO EVACUATE

On October 14th the Government decided to recall Sir Ian Hamilton, and on October 20th General Sir Charles Monro was ordered to take over the command of the forces in the Mediterranean, and received written instructions from Lord Kitchener to report "fully and frankly" on the military position. He was instructed to consider the best means of removing the existing deadlock, and to report "whether, in his opinion, on purely military grounds, it was better to evacuate Gallipoli or to make another attempt to carry it." He was also asked to give his estimate of the loss which would be incurred in the course of an evacuation.

Sir Charles Monro left on October 22nd, arriving at Mudros on the 27th. After an inspection of the peninsula he came to the conclusion that the forces should be withdrawn. He never swerved from this opinion, which he communicated to Lord Kitchener in the following telegram on October 31st:

> With the exception of the Australian and New Zealand Army Corps the troops on the peninsula are not equal to a sustained effort, owing to inexperienced officers, the want of training of the men, and the depleted condition of many of the units.
>
> We merely hold the fringe of the shore, and are confronted by the Turks in very formidable entrenchments, with all advantages of position and power of observation of our movements. The beaches are exposed to observed artillery fire, and in the restricted areas all stores are equally exposed. We can no longer count upon any action by surprise as the Turks are in considerably stronger force than they were, and have had ample time to provide against surprise landings.
>
> Since the flanks of the Turks cannot be attacked, only a frontal attack is possible, and no room is afforded on any of the beaches for the distribution of

additional divisions should they be sent, nor is there sufficient space for the deployment of an adequate force of artillery, the action of which would be impaired by poverty of observation and good positions for searching or counter battery effects. Naval guns could only assist to a partial degree.

In fact an attack could only be prosecuted under the disadvantages of serious lack of depth, and of absence of power of surprise, seeing that our line is throughout dominated by the Turks' position. The uncertainty of weather might also seriously hinder the landing of reinforcements and regularity in providing the artillery ammunition to the amount which would be required.

It is therefore my opinion that another attempt to carry the Turkish lines would not offer any hope of success; the Turkish positions are being actively strengthened daily. Our information leads to the belief that heavy guns and ammunition are being sent to the peninsula from Constantinople. Consequently by the time fresh divisions, if available, could arrive, the task of breaking the Turkish line would be considerably more formidable than it is at present.

On purely military grounds, therefore, in consequence of the grave daily wastage of officers and men which occurs, and owing to the lack of prospect of being able to draw the Turks from their entrenched positions, I recommend the evacuation of the peninsula.

After adding that he was unable at that moment to give any definite estimate of the losses which would be incurred in a withdrawal, Sir Charles Monro concluded his telegram by saying:

> I have endeavoured in the expression of my opinion to give full weight to the effect which will be created in the East by our evacuation, and I consider that the force now in the peninsula, or such portion of it as we may be able to evacuate, would be more favourably placed in Egypt. This force stands in need of rest, re-organisation, and especially of training, before it can be usefully employed. The Corps and Divisional Commanders have done splendid work in the peninsula, but they do not possess the opportunity or time, as they now stand, to create the force into a reliable fighting machine. Hence I think loss of prestige caused by withdrawal would be compensated for in a few months by increased efficiency.

Sir Charles Monro told us that his opinion was strengthened by the state of health of the troops. The rate of sickness had been alarmingly high in the hot months of August and September. On August 23rd Sir Ian Hamilton had reported to Lord Kitchener that the average net wastage, even when there were no serious engagements, amounted, owing to sickness, to 24 per cent a month. In September the medical officers had reported that 50 per cent of the men in seven battalions of the old troops examined at Anzac had feeble hearts with shortness of breath, that 78 per cent of these had diarrhoea, and 64 per cent had sores on the skin. On the first three days of October over 1,800 sick were evacuated from the IXth Corps at Suvla, and at times the number of such evacuations from Suvla, Anzac, and Cape Helles amounted to 1,000 a day. In

August, September and October, the number of sick evacuated from the peninsula amounted to [★].

In addition the troops were continuously under fire, the beaches and rest trenches being shelled as much as the front lines. The men in reserve had to spend the night in getting up stores to the front and in making communications. Fatigue parties had to be constantly occupied in unloading the contents of the transports into lighters and from the lighters to the shore. Although there was a notable decline in the sick rate shortly after Sir Charles Monro's arrival, Sir William Birdwood on November 4th telegraphed to Lord Kitchener as follows:

> Byng and Davies and all their Divisional Commanders have very little faith in their troops' present power of endurance, and reply that with few exceptions none are at present capable of more than 24 hours of sustained offensive effort. The same applies to most of the Australians owing to amount of sickness we have had, from which they have by no means recovered.

On November 1st General Monro was asked by Lord Kitchener if his Corps Commanders were of the same opinion as himself. Sir Charles Monro accordingly consulted Sir William Birdwood, Sir Julian Byng and Sir Francis Davies, and asked them to submit their views in writing. He urged them "earnestly to give their opinions without paying any heed to his."

General Birdwood wrote:

> I agree with General Monro regarding the grave disadvantages of our position and the extreme difficulty of making any progress. But I consider that the Turks would look upon our evacuation as a complete victory. From Indian experience I fear the result on the Mahometan [Muslim] world in India, Egypt, Persia. I am therefore opposed to evacuation. I am of the opinion that, if we leave the peninsula, it is essential that the whole force must be launched immediately against the Turks elsewhere, and I fail to see where this can be done with confident hope of success. I am adverse to withdrawal which would enable Turkish forces to proceed to Caucasus or Mesopotamia; landing elsewhere than in Turkey would not have the same effect. I also fear that the morale effect on our troops of withdrawal would be bad, while the Turkish morale would proportionately rise. Season being so late and bad weather at hand, I think actual withdrawal fraught with difficulty and danger, as ample time and continuous fine weather essential. All embarkations must be done at night, and only four or five nights a week can now be counted on. Heavy loss might be caused by the advent of any continuous bad weather after withdrawal has been partially carried out.

General Byng replied:

> I consider evacuation desirable. As regards Suvla, a voluntary and not very costly retirement is feasible at the present time, but it seems possible that with German help to the enemy a compulsory and therefore costly retreat may be necessitated.

★ Figure not available at the time the report was signed.

General Davies replied:

> I agree with General Monro.

The opinions of these three officers were then fully communicated to Lord Kitchener by Sir Charles Monro in a telegram on November 2nd, in which he repeated his opinion as to the necessity of evacuating, and as a "rough estimate" stated that Admiral de Robeck and his Corps Commanders thought a loss of 30 to 40 per cent in personnel and material might be incurred, and that he was "inclined to agree with their estimate".

Sir Charles Monro's opinion in favour of evacuation made it necessary for the authorities at home to come to a decision of great gravity. On October 7th the War Committee had replaced the Dardanelles Committee, and on November 3rd both the War Committee and the Cabinet invited Lord Kitchener to go out to the Mediterranean in order to assist them in arriving at a final decision.

On the same day Lord Kitchener telegraphed to Sir William Birdwood:

> Very secret.
>
> You know the report sent in by Monro. I shall come out to you; am leaving tomorrow night. I have seen Captain Keyes, and I believe the Admiralty will agree to making naval attempt to force the passage of the Straits. We must do what we can to assist them, and I think that as soon as our ships are in the Sea of Marmora we should seize the Bulair isthmus and hold it so as to supply the Navy if the Turks still hold out.
>
> Examine very carefully the best position for landing near the marsh at the head of the Gulf of Xeros, so that we could get a line across the isthmus, with ships at both sides. In order to find the troops for this undertaking we should have to reduce the numbers in the trenches to the lowest possible, and perhaps evacuate positions at Suvla. All the best fighting men that could be spared, including your boys from Anzac and everyone I can sweep up in Egypt, might be concentrated at Mudros ready for this enterprise.
>
> There will probably be a change in the naval command, Wemyss being appointed in command to carry through the naval part of the work.
>
> As regards the military command, you would have the whole force, and should carefully select your commanders and troops. I would suggest Maude, Fanshawe, Marshall, Peyton, Godley, Cox, leaving others to hold the lines. Please work out plans for this, or alternative plans as you may think best. We must do it right this time.
>
> I absolutely refuse to sign orders for evacuation, which I think would be the gravest disaster and would condemn a large percentage of our men to death or imprisonment.
>
> Monro will be appointed to the command of the Salonica force.

In order to explain the telegram quoted above, it is necessary to state that after the failure of the military operations in August, a section of responsible naval officers, foremost among whom were Admiral Wemyss and Sir John de

Robeck's Chief of the Staff, Commodore Keyes, held very strongly that the fleet should renew the attempt to force the Straits in order to relieve the army. A plan of operations had been worked out, with the assent of Sir John de Robeck. It was thought by these officers that, if three or four battleships and six or eight destroyers could pass through the Straits, they would be able, in combination with the submarines, to dominate the Sea of Marmora, thus cutting the main Turkish lines of communication and supply, which ran from the Asiatic side of the peninsula.

Sir John de Robeck was not in favour of this project, which he thought underestimated the dangers and difficulties of the operation, and overrated the effect that a successful naval attack would produce. But he felt, nevertheless, that the contrary view should be fully put before the Admiralty, and towards the end of October he allowed Commodore Keyes to return home to do this. On arriving in England, Commodore Keyes discussed his plan of operations fully with Mr Balfour and the Sea Lords. He also had two interviews with Lord Kitchener on November 3rd and 4th. When he left for the Mediterranean on November 4th, Commodore Keyes told us he was under the impression that his suggestion had been regarded with favour.

Between November 3rd and 4th Lord Kitchener's proposal to seize the Bulair isthmus had been considered and adversely criticised by the Admiralty, by Sir William Birdwood, and by Commodore Keyes. On November 4th Lord Kitchener again telegraphed to Sir William Birdwood, intimating that a renewal of the naval attack might not be approved, and adding:

> I am coming as arranged, and shall be at Alexandria Monday night or Tuesday morning. Shall stay there one day without landing and without my presence being known. After seeing Maxwell and Macmahon, shall come on to you, leaving in the evening.
>
> The more I look at the problem the less I see my way through, so you had better very quietly and secretly work out any scheme for getting the troops off the peninsula.

Lord Kitchener left for the Mediterranean on the evening of November 4th. In the course of the following days he discussed the position with Sir John Maxwell, Sir Henry Macmahon and Sir Charles Monro, at Alexandria and Mudros. The telegrams which then passed between him and the Prime Minister show that Lord Kitchener was greatly concerned as to the difficulty of defending Egypt, in the event of an evacuation of the peninsula; and that he advocated a landing at Ayas Bay, in the neighbourhood of Alexandretta, with the object of cutting the Turkish railway communications. This project necessitated the withdrawal of forces from both Salonica and France, and the diversion of Indian divisions then on their way to Mesopotamia. It did not commend itself to the General Staff at the War Office, and was ultimately rejected at a joint conference between representatives of the British and French Governments held at Paris on November 17th.

On November 15th Lord Kitchener reported to the Prime Minister the result of his personal inspection of the positions on the peninsula:

To gain what we hold has been a most remarkable feat of arms. The country is much more difficult than I imagined, and the Turkish positions at Achi Baba and Kilid Bahr are natural fortresses of the most formidable nature, which, if not taken by surprise at first, could be held against very serious attack by larger forces than have been engaged, even if these forces had proper lines of communication to support them. This latter want is the main difficulty in carrying out successful operations on the peninsula.

The landings are precarious and often impossible through rough sea and want of harbours, and the enemy's positions are peculiarly suitable for making our communications more dangerous and difficult. The base at Mudros is too far detached from our forces in the field, and the proper co-ordination of the administrative services of a line of communications is prevented by distance and sea voyages dependable on the weather. This state of things, in my judgment, is the main cause of our troops not having been able to do better, and to attain really strategic points on the peninsula, which would have turned Kilid Bahr, and unless this were done I do not consider that the Fleet ever could have passed the Straits. Everyone has done wonders, both on sea and land, when the natural difficulties that have had to be surmounted are considered. Our present positions, in my opinion, can be held against the Turks even if they received increased ammunition.

The trenches have been well dug, and bomb-proof covering has been afforded for the men; supplies and water are on shore, and officers and men are confident that they can hold out against the Turks, but they are somewhat depressed at not being able to get through. I consider, however, the lines are not deep enough, if Germany sent a German force to attack, to allow proper arrangements for supports, and if the front line trenches were taken, these difficulties would increase. I consider that advances from our present positions are very difficult, particularly from Helles and Anzac. Suvla gives some opportunity for improving our positions, but it seems very doubtful whether this would enable us to push through.

About 125,000 Turks are immobilised by our occupation of the peninsula, and they are caused considerable loss, and, until the recent German operations in Serbia opened communications with Turkey and changed the situation, practically the whole Turkish Army had to be held in readiness to defend the capital if we succeeded on the peninsula. In present circumstances the *raison d'etre* of our forces on the Gallipoli Peninsula is no longer as important as it has been hitherto, and if another position in the neighbourhood of Alexandretta were occupied, where Turkish movements eastward could be effectively stopped, the realisation of the German objective against Egypt and the East would be prevented.

Careful and secret preparations for the evacuation of the peninsula are being made. If undertaken it would be an operation of extreme military difficulty and danger; but I have hopes that, given time and weather, which may be expected to be suitable until about the end of December, the troops will carry out this task with less loss than was previously estimated. My reason for this is that the distance they had to go to embark, and the contraction of the lines of defence to be held by a smaller force, gives them a better chance than I thought previously.

The Admiral and Generals Monro and Birdwood, to whom I have read the above, all agree.

Later in the same day Lord Kitchener telegraphed further to the Prime Minister that Admiral de Robeck would like to retain Cape Helles, even if Suvla and Anzac were evacuated.

On November 19th the Prime Minister telegraphed to Lord Kitchener that:

His Majesty's Government had decided against the proposed expedition to Ayas Bay as a result of their conference in Paris with the French Government, and Naval and Military authorities, and after consideration of the maritime position in the Mediterranean

and requested Lord Kitchener to give his "considered opinion as to the evacuation of the peninsula, in whole or in part," on the basis of the Ayas Bay scheme having been withdrawn.

In reply, Lord Kitchener telegraphed on November 22nd to the effect that, while our offensive had up to the present held up the Turkish Army, German assistance was now practically available, that this assistance would make our positions untenable, and that evacuation, therefore, seemed inevitable. He therefore recommended that the evacuation of Suvla and Anzac should be proceeded with, while Cape Helles should be held for the present. The retention of Cape Helles would enable the Navy to maintain the advantages already gained, still threaten the seizure of the Straits, and also give greater facilities for the evacuation of Suvla and Anzac.

On November 23rd the War Committee came to the decision that:

Having regard to the opinions expressed by Lord Kitchener in his telegram dated November 22nd, 1915, and by the General Staff in their memorandum dated November 22nd, 1915, the War Committee feel bound to advise the evacuation of the Gallipoli Peninsula on military grounds, notwithstanding the grave political disadvantages which may result from the decision. They have carefully examined the naval considerations in favour of the retention of Cape Helles as stated in a note by the Chief of the Admiralty War Staff, printed with the General Staff Memorandum referred to above. They are of the opinion, however, that the naval advantages to be gained by this course are not commensurate with the military disadvantages involved.

The proposal to evacuate was then discussed at a Cabinet Council on the following day. At this Council Lord Curzon told us that he "and several of his colleagues, anxious at least that the opposite side should be heard, and fearful of a decision fraught with such fearful possibilities, pleaded for a few hours' consideration", and that he "undertook to state the case to the best of his ability".

The case against evacuation was then elaborated by Lord Curzon in two memoranda dated November 25th and 30th, in which the military and political reasons in favour of and against evacuation were fully discussed. Lord Curzon's arguments were replied to by Mr Bonar Law in a memorandum circulated on December 4th, which ended as follows:

> So far I have considered the question from a military point of view, and my conclusions may be disputed, but there is another aspect of it which is not military, and which is not open to dispute. Recognising the seriousness of the position at the Dardanelles, the Government decided to send a military expert to report on the question of evacuation. For this purpose Sir Charles Monro was chosen. On the 31st October he reported in the strongest possible terms in favour of evacuation. He sent us also the opinions of three of the Generals on the spot—Generals Birdwood, Byng and Davies. Of these three General Birdwood alone was opposed to evacuation, but the reasons given by him for his opposition were entirely political, and he agreed with General Monro regarding the 'great disadvantages of our position and extreme difficulty of making any progress.' Afterwards he concurred in a telegram sent by Lord Kitchener on the 22nd November which contained these words: 'Our offensive on the peninsula has, up to the present, held up the Turkish Army, but with German assistance, which is now practically available, our positions there cannot be maintained, and evacuation seems inevitable.' Not satisfied with General Monro's report, the Government decided to send Lord Kitchener. In a telegram sent from Paris, on his way, Lord Kitchener showed clearly that he was entirely opposed to evacuation, and he has since told us that he held that view when he started for the Dardanelles. The actual examination of the situation, on the spot, however, changed his opinion, and he telegraphed to the Prime Minister in favour of evacuation in words which I have just quoted. We also consulted our General Staff on the subject. They gave us an opinion as definite as that of the other Generals in favour of evacuation. It is the fact, therefore, that every military authority, without a single exception, whom we have consulted, has reported in favour of evacuation.
>
> But this is not all. Some time ago the Cabinet unanimously came to the conclusion that the war could not be carried on by a body so large as the Cabinet. A War Committee was therefore appointed. The views of the military authorities came before this Committee, two of whose members, the Prime Minister and the First Lord of the Admiralty, were opposed in the strongest possible way to evacuation; yet this Committee reported unanimously in favour of acting upon the advice of our military advisers. Their recommendation was brought before the Cabinet, with the result that on a matter in regard to which delay must be dangerous and may be fatal, no decision has been reached.

I hope that my colleagues will agree with me that the war cannot be carried to a successful issue by methods such as these.

Meanwhile the condition of the forces on the peninsula was aggravated by a blizzard of exceptional severity which raged on November 26th, 27th, 28th and 29th. Two hundred and eighty men were drowned in the trenches at Suvla and many were frozen to death as they stood. Sixteen thousand cases of frost bite and exposure had to be evacuated: 12,000 from Suvla, where the positions were most exposed, and 2,700 and 1,200 from Anzac and Helles respectively. On December 1st Sir Charles Monro telegraphed to Lord Kitchener pressing for a decision and adding:

> There is, however, much to be done, and late season makes time a matter of great urgency. Detailed plans approach completion, but intricate arrangements have still to be made with regard to collection and clearing of shipping, distribution of small craft, embarkation and disposition of troops and material, accommodation on islands, disposal of reinforcements, etc., to say nothing of tactical arrangements. Experience of recent storms indicates that there is no time to lose. General Birdwood telegraphed yesterday that if evacuation is to be made possible it is essential to take advantage of every fine day from now. If a decision cannot be reached very shortly, it may be equivalent to deciding against evacuation.

It must here be mentioned that on November 25th Sir John de Robeck left the Mediterranean on sick leave, and his command was taken over by Vice-Admiral Wemyss. From November 25th to December 8th Vice-Admiral Wemyss, with remarkable pertinacity [obstinacy], advocated a renewal of the naval attack in a series of telegrams to the First Lord of the Admiralty.

On his return home Sir John de Robeck attended a meeting of the War Council on December 2nd, and his views as to the difficulties of a naval attack were placed before the members of the Council. The decision as to the policy to be pursued was then reserved for the Cabinet which met on the same day. Lord Kitchener, as the result of this Cabinet meeting, telegraphed to Sir Charles Monro:

> Private and secret.
>
> The Cabinet has been considering the Gallipoli situation all today. Owing to the political consequences there is a strong feeling against evacuation, even of a partial character. It is the general opinion that we should retain Cape Helles.
>
> If the Salonica troops are placed at your disposal (up to four divisions) for an offensive operation to improve the position at Suvla, could such operations be carried out in time with a view to making Suvla retainable by obtaining higher positions and greater depth? The Navy will also take the offensive in co-operation.

On December 3rd Sir Charles Monro telegraphed in reply to this proposal as follows:

I fully recognise the complexity of the situation which has arisen. I do not, however, think that the proposal to employ four fresh divisions in order to gain a more secure position at Suvla can be regarded as an operation offering a reasonable chance of success. We cannot expect the element of surprise which is so essential to make up for the disadvantages of position under which we labour. The Salonica Divisions could not be ready for active operations on the peninsula until storm weather sets in . . .

In respect of naval co-operation, the character of the terrain on the peninsula is such that naval guns cannot search the Turkish positions. The fire of howitzers would be needed to do so effectively. The many deep ravines and gullies are very favourable for the concealment and protection of the Turkish reserves, and for their rapid transference in case of bombardment. Nor do I think the supply of the Turks on the peninsula by the two lines of supply available to them could be prevented by naval action.

On December 7th the Cabinet decided to evacuate the positions at Suvla and Anzac only and to retain that at Cape Helles. This decision, Lord Curzon told us, was taken mainly on the advice of Lord Kitchener, who had then returned.

The decision of the Cabinet was communicated to Sir Charles Monro on December 7th, and to Vice-Admiral Wemyss on December 8th. The Vice-Admiral, in reply, persisted in recommending that the naval attack should be attempted, and in the course of his telegram to the First Lord of the Admiralty on December 8th stated:

The Navy is prepared to force the Straits and control them for an indefinite period, cutting off all Turkish supplies which now find their way to the peninsula either by sea from the Marmora or across the Dardanelles from Asiatic to European shore. The only line of communications left would be the road along the Isthmus of Bulair, which can be controlled almost entirely from the Sea of Marmora and the Gulf of Xeros. What is offered the Army, therefore, is the practical, complete severance of all Turkish lines of communication, accompanied by the destruction of the large supply depots on the shore of the Dardanelles.

In the first instance I strongly advocated that the naval attack should synchronize with an army offensive, and if the Army will be prepared to attack in the event of a favourable opportunity presenting itself, nothing more need be required of them. The Navy here is prepared to undertake this operation with every assurance of success. If the units as described in your letter of 24th November can be provided, these hopes of success are greatly increased, and the possible losses greatly diminished.

The unanimous military opinion referred to has, I feel certain, been greatly influenced, and naturally so, by the military appreciations of Sir Charles Monro. These I have not seen, but their purport I have gathered in course of conversations. The Corps Commanders, I know, view the evacuation with the greatest misgiving. The forcing of the Dardanelles, as outlined in my telegrams, has never been put before them, and I am convinced that, after considering the certain results which would follow a naval success, they would favour an attack on the lines indicated, especially in view of the undoubted low morale of the Turkish peninsula army, of which we have ample evidence ...

The very extensive German propaganda being pursued all over the Near East, accompanied by the expenditure of vast sums of money, is not, I feel convinced, being undertaken merely as a side issue to the European war.

A position of stalemate on both fronts of the principal theatres of war appears the natural outcome of the present situation. This opinion is freely expressed in the higher military circles in Greece, and would therefore appear to be fostered by the Germans—a significant point.

By surrendering our position here, when within sight of victory, we are aiding the enemy to obtain markets the possession of which may enable her to outlast the Allies in the war of exhaustion now commencing.

A successful attack would once and for all disperse those clouds of doubt, a large amount of shipping would be released, and the question of Greece and Egypt settled.

I do not know what has been decided about Constantinople, but if the Turks could be told that we were in the Marmora to prevent its occupation by the Germans, such a course would inevitably lead to disruption, and therefore weakness amongst them.

I fear the effect on the Navy would be bad.

Although no word of attack has passed my lips except to my immediate staff and admirals, I feel sure that every officer and man would feel that the campaign had been abandoned without sufficient use having been made of our greatest force, viz., the Navy.

The position is so critical that there is no time for standing on ceremony, and I suggest that General Birdwood, the officer who would now have to carry out the attack or evacuation which is now ordered, be asked for his appreciation.

The logical conclusion, therefore, is the choice of evacuation or forcing the Straits. I consider the former disastrous tactically and strategically, and the latter feasible, and, so long as troops remain at Anzac, decisive.

I am convinced that the time is ripe for a vigorous offensive, and I am confident of success.

To this strongly worded representation Mr Balfour, then First Lord of the Admiralty, replied on December 10th that, as the Admiralty were not prepared to authorise the Navy, single-handed, attempting to force the Narrows and acting in the Sea of Marmora, cut off from supplies, the decision of the Government to evacuate Suvla and Anzac would not be further questioned by the Admiralty in view of the individual and combined appreciation of the responsible Generals, and the great strain thrown on naval and military resources by the operations in Greece. The retention of Cape Helles and the mouth of the Straits would enable another attack to be started later, working on a different plan, should the Government decide to undertake it. And on the same day the then First Sea Lord, Sir Henry Jackson, telegraphed to Vice-Admiral Wemyss as follows:

Your telegram has been very carefully considered. I personally agree with your appreciation of German designs in the East, and I view with deepest regret the abandonment of Suvla and Anzac. But the military authorities, including Birdwood, are clear that they cannot be made tenable against an increased artillery fire, while the Admiralty hold that the naval arguments against forcing the Straits are overwhelming. Naval authorities here are convinced that, while success is most doubtful, very heavy losses are certain, and it must be remembered that nothing would have a worse effect on our Eastern position than a serious check to the Government.

The evacuation of Suvla and Anzac was at once proceeded with, men, guns, and stores being gradually withdrawn. The final embarkation was fixed for Saturday and Sunday, December 18th and 19th. On the Sunday a covering attack was made by the forces at Cape Helles, at a cost of 283 casualties. By 5.30 am on Monday, December 20th, the last man had quitted the trenches. That night the weather broke. A heavy gale blew from the south, accompanied by torrents of rain. Water rushed through the trenches at Suvla and Anzac, and the landing stages at Suvla, Anzac, and Cape Helles were washed away by heavy seas.

On December 20th Sir Charles Monro telegraphed to Lord Kitchener urging the evacuation of Cape Helles on the ground that this "would greatly facilitate the reorganisation of the Dardanelles army, would lead immediately to reduced expenditure, and would liberate a large quantity of freight"; and that this army, "when rested and reorganised, would constitute a valuable asset in a central position, ready to strike either in France or wherever demanded by the situation." On December 22nd evacuation was also recommended by the General Staff in a memorandum, in which they pointed out that:

The arrival of gun ammunition and of fresh guns to help the enemy will, moreover, greatly add to the difficulties in the way of holding on to Helles at all. Not only have munitions arrived from Germany, but artillery which had been previously opposed to Suvla and Anzac will be moved to act against our forces cooped up in the thoroughly bad position they now occupy at the southern end of the peninsula. Wastage, heavy before, will become greater. The troops, furthermore, are perfectly well aware that the Dardanelles undertaking has definitely failed, and, realising that they have no hope of advancing or of causing the enemy any serious injury, will become dispirited. There will be serious risk that the enemy will make a successful attack, and may, under the circumstances, cause us a disaster. The necessity of concentration of effort, if this war is to be brought to a successful conclusion, has been drawn attention to in recent papers prepared by the General Staff, and there is no object in labouring this point afresh; retention of Helles means dispersion, not concentration of effort. The General Staff therefore recommend that the Gallipoli Peninsula should be entirely evacuated, and with the least possible delay.

We have indicated that the retention of Cape Helles had been advocated mainly on naval grounds. Vice-Admiral Wemyss and Commodore Keyes held a different opinion, which was strengthened after the evacuation of Suvla and Anzac by the consideration of the heavy wastage occurring daily in the VIIIth Army Corps. From December 20th to January 7th the casualties incurred amounted to 345 killed and 1,178 wounded, a total of 1,523, or a daily average of 18 killed and 62 wounded. Vice-Admiral Wemyss therefore advised evacuation unless the Achi Baba position could be captured, and this Sir Charles Monro considered impracticable.

On December 23rd the War Committee decided to evacuate Cape Helles, and their decision was approved by the Cabinet on the 27th. The evacuation was completed on January 8th.

It is not, we think, necessary to give details of the evacuation, these being embodied in Sir Charles Monro's despatch of March 6th, 1916.

In the course of this despatch Sir Charles Monro wrote:

> The entire evacuation of the peninsula had now been completed. It demanded for its successful realisation two important military essentials, viz., good luck and skilled, disciplined organisation; and they were both forthcoming to a marked degree at the hour needed. Our luck was in the ascendant by the marvellous spell of calm weather which prevailed. But we were able to turn to the fullest advantage these accidents of fortune.
>
> Lieutenant-General Sir Wm. Birdwood and his Corps Commanders elaborated and prepared the orders in reference to the evacuation with a skill, competence, and courage which could not have been surpassed, and we had a further stroke of good fortune in being associated with Vice-Admiral Sir J. de Robeck, KCB, Vice-Admiral Wemyss, and a body of naval officers whose work remained throughout this anxious period at that standard of accuracy and professional ability which is beyond the power of criticism or cavil [objection].
>
> The line of communication staff, both military and naval, represented respectively by Lieutenant-General E. A. Altham, CB, CMG, Commodore M. S. Fitzmaurice, RN, principal Naval Transport Officer, and Captain H. V. Simpson, RN, Superintending Transport Officer, contributed to the success of the operation by their untiring zeal and conspicuous ability.
>
> The members of the Headquarters Staff showed themselves, without exception, to be officers with whom it was a privilege to be associated; their competence, zeal, and devotion to duty were uniform and unbroken.

In these words of well-deserved commendation of officers and men the name of Sir Charles Monro himself should be included.

ROLE OF THE FRENCH TROOPS

Our narrative of events would be incomplete without a reference to the important part taken by the French troops in the operations on the Gallipoli Peninsula.

On the afternoon of April 24th a regiment of the French division was disembarked at Kum Kale under the guns of the French fleet, and remained ashore till the morning of the the 26th, when it re-embarked. The French captured 500 prisoners, and their landing diverted the fire of the Asiatic guns from Morto Bay and Beach V to Kum Kale, thus contributing to the success of the British landings. On the evening of April 26th the main disembarkation of the French division was begun at Beach V, our Allies occupying the right of the Helles front. Sir Ian Hamilton's despatch, dated May 20th, 1915, describes the landings and subsequent operations up to May 6th. Therein he referred to the loyal and energetic support afforded him by Général d'Amade, who commanded the French force, and added:

> During the fighting which followed the landing of the French division at Sedd-el-Bahr no troops could have acquitted themselves more creditably under very trying circumstances and under very heavy losses than those working under the orders of M. le Général d'Amade.

In May a second French division reinforced the first, Général Gouraud relieving Général d'Amade on May 14th and assuming command of the whole of the French force. One brigade of this second division arrived at Helles on May 8th, and the other on May 12th. On the latter date Sir Ian Hamilton telegraphed to Lord Kitchener that the French casualties from April 25th to date amounted to 246 officers and 12,364 men out of a total strength engaged of 334 officers and 22,116 men.

There was severe fighting at Helles from June 4th to the end of the month, during which the French troops were conspicuous for their dash and gallantry. In one action on June 21st their losses amounted to 2,500. On June 30th Général Gouraud was wounded, and the command of the French force devolved upon Général Bailloud. In his despatch of August 26th, 1915, Sir Ian Hamilton referred to Général Gouraud in the following terms:

> Général Gouraud brought a great reputation to our help from the battlefields of the Argonne, and in so doing has added to its lustre. A happy mixture of daring in danger and of calm in crisis, full of energy and resource, he has worked hand in glove with his British comrades in arms, and has earned their respect and affection.

On July 12th and 13th the French troops again distinguished themselves in an attack on the enemy's trenches, capturing a machine gun and 200 prisoners. At this time Général Masnou, commanding the First Division, was mortally wounded.

During the operations early in August the French troops do not appear to have been seriously engaged.

In October one French division was transferred from the peninsula to Salonica, the other division being withdrawn soon afterwards.

While we do not think that the conduct of these troops comes within the scope of our inquiry, we feel bound to record their loyal and generous co-operation, their heavy losses, and their conspicuous gallantry.

WATER SUPPLY

The importance of sea-borne water was recognised by the authorities early in March, when it was known there was little or no water for the troops at Mudros, and provision was then made for supplying it, and also for providing distilling apparatus.

(1) The Headquarters Staff were responsible for providing the tanks to be placed on the beaches to receive the water; also for the necessary pumps and hoses for pumping out the lighters and for providing mules and water receptacles for carrying the water to the troops.
(2) Naval and military officers were appointed in charge of the beaches, responsible for the landing of all stores, including the water.

Sir William Birdwood had from the first realised the importance of water, and in March he sent Brigadier-General de Lotbinière from Egypt to Mudros to investigate the question of supply at that place. General de Lotbinière, who was the Chief Engineer of the Australian and New Zealand Division in Egypt, came to the conclusion, when the idea of the military expedition was contemplated in March, that sea-borne water would be a necessity. He also realised that piers would be required for landing on the peninsula at Anzac, and made arrangements, with the approval of Sir Ian Hamilton, to hire in Egypt four special steel pontoons to form a pier, and these were ballasted with water stowed in petrol tins.

Unfortunately three of these pontoons were lost on the voyage from Alexandria to Mudros. They were placed in the charge of Commander Mitchell, RN, who was attached to the Australian forces, and he arranged to have them towed by the transports carrying the troops. The weather was bad, and the pontoons, which were difficult to tow, broke adrift, and only one arrived at Mudros. This upset the arrangement so far as a landing pier was concerned, but as regards water supply General de Lotbinière, with the assistance of Admiral Wemyss, obtained at Mudros two large wooden lighters and had them filled with fresh water from the ships.

The arrangements for the supply of water during the operations of April 25th for the troops at Helles and Anzac were organised by General Headquarters in concert with the Generals commanding at Helles and Anzac.

At Helles a moderate supply of water was found on landing and subsequently there does not appear to have been any difficulty with the supply.

At Anzac the supply seems to have been barely sufficient. Surgeon-General Howse, VC, the Assistant Director of Medical Services of the 2nd Australian Division, gave evidence that the health of the men was very greatly impaired by the shortage of water. He thought that a great deal of the illness was attributable to the fact that the average ration of water, for many months at least, was not more than half a gallon a day. His evidence that there was a scarcity of water is corroborated by Lieutenant-Colonel Begg, commanding the New Zealand Field Ambulance, but he differs from General Howse as to the effect on the men's health. Sir William Birdwood had a special officer detailed to look after the water, Major Williams, of the Australian forces, as well as General de Lotbinière.

Search on shore was started immediately on landing, and by the evening three wells were found, yielding a small supply. Elaborate arrangements had to be made at Anzac for the supply of sea-borne water, as shore water was scarce. We think it may be stated that the actual operations at Anzac did not fail for want of water; but during the fighting early in August it is stated in Sir Ian Hamilton's despatch of December 11th, 1915, that all ranks were reduced to one pint a day, which is obviously an inadequate allowance for troops operating in a hot climate and difficult country. After the failure to take the heights at Sari Bahr, when Sir Ian Hamilton thought of sending his reserve troops to Sir William Birdwood to make a second attempt, he had to give up the idea on account of the shortage of water.

The water for the use of the troops at the first landing at Helles and Anzac was brought to the beaches by the Royal Navy. When it had been discharged on the beaches, the responsibility for its storage and distribution rested with the military authorities.

For the landing at Suvla detailed orders concerning the arrangements for water were issued by General Headquarters. The following additional information and directions were given to Sir Frederick Stopford, IXth Army Corps:

Water is plentiful throughout the Anafarta Valley, but pending the disembarkation of water carts, a number of mules with special 8-gallon water bags will be attached to the units of your command.

GOC [General Officer Commanding] IXth Army Corps will arrange for parties to pump water on shore from water lighters. Copy of the Director of Works memo on this subject is attached.

Two military landing officers and their assistant military landing officers will be placed at your disposal from units other than those under your command.

The strictest economy must be exercised in regard to drinking water. Under arrangements made by GHQ receptacles filled with water will be landed as early as possible from the ships carrying the mule corps, and will be conveyed to the troops as transport becomes available.

Waterproof tanks of 2,300 gallons capacity, lift and force pumps, will be available on the *Prah*—RE Store Ship—in Kephalos Harbour, and will be forwarded by the Deputy Quartermaster General, GHQ, on request of GOC Corps.

In his despatch of December 11th, 1915, Sir Ian Hamilton mentions that the War Office were asked to send with each division of the IXth Corps and with the 53rd and 54th Territorial Divisions water receptacles for pack transport at the rate of half a gallon per man. He also states that 3,700 mules, together with 1,750 water carts, were provided for the August operations at Anzac and Suvla—this in addition to 950 mules already at Anzac. We understand that no water carts were landed at Suvla, the ground being unsuitable for their use. No pack mules with water bags appear in the landing tables, but some mules were in fact sent.

In Sir Frederick Stopford's operation order of August 3rd the water question was dealt with as follows:

It is anticipated that sufficient water for drinking purposes will be found throughout the Anafarta Valley. This will be supplemented by tanks on shore, and water bags, but supply by these methods is limited. The General Officers commanding will issue instructions as regards the picketing [marking] of wells and springs, as may be found, the prevention of waste of water therefrom, and for the examination by Medical Officers before its issue. Too much stress cannot be laid on the importance of warning all ranks to observe the greatest care against waste of ammunition, food, or water.

For the landing at Suvla on the night of August 6th/7th provision was made for 450 tons of sea-borne fresh water to arrive during the early hours of August 7th as follows:

(a)	The steam water tank *Krini* with with a naval water lighter in tow	250 tons
(b)	Four wooden water lighters equipped with small wooden troughs, pumps and hoses provided by the Army and handed over to the Navy for transport to Suvla, 50 to 60 tons each	200 tons
		450 tons

The motor lighters in which the troops landed also had a certain amount of water on board in bulk, supplemented by water in petrol tins, with the idea that the troops should on landing, if necessary, refill their water-bottles.

The troops, before embarking in the destroyers and motor lighters at Imbros on the evening of the 6th, had their water-bottles (1½ pints) filled, and were told to husband [conserve] the water.

Arrangements were made for the troops to have tea from the destroyers before landing.

The failure of the troops to attain their objectives on August 7th, and especially on the 8th, is thought by some witnesses to be due to a large extent to the exhaustion of the troops from want of water, and on the 9th and 10th there was still difficulty in supplying sufficient water.

But the failure to obtain Hill 112, Ismail Oglu Tepe, on the 7th, the most favourable day for a surprise attack, was not primarily due to want of water, but is attributable to other causes, and is dealt with in another portion of the report.

General Hammersley, commanding the 11th Division, stated:

> The first water obtained from the water lighters was about 3 pm on the 8th. The want of water added very much to the exhaustion of the troops. They had nothing but their water-bottles with them. A certain quantity of water was found, but nothing like enough to assuage their thirst, and the troops were badly exhausted.

General Hammersley stated that he realised the great importance of water before the operations began, but did not take any steps to see where water was to be obtained. He knew that water was being sent ashore in lighters, but he was not informed and did not enquire as to the system of distribution of water when landed. He gathered that the men would have to depend on their water-bottles for 24 hours and upon any local supplies he might find.

General Sitwell, commanding 34th Brigade, stated that before he left Imbros on the evening of the 6th he did not know what the arrangements were for providing water. He informed us that he discovered two wells on August 7th and 8th, from which he watered his Brigade, and a considerable number after that date. From these a good supply of water was forthcoming. The position of the wells and springs seemed to him to be accurately marked on the map issued to the troops.

General Sitwell expressed the opinion that if a proper search had been made for water, sufficient would have been found to enable the attack to be pushed forward on the 8th.

General R. P. Maxwell, commanding 33rd Brigade, in his evidence stated:

> The want of water did not interfere with the operations up to the night of the 7th. The water-bottles were not touched before midday on the 7th.

On the 8th, even with a proper supply of water, he does not think his brigade could have done more, because they were so scattered. "My own men wanted water to recuperate, nothing worse than that."

General Haggard, commanding 32nd Brigade, stated:

> I have read Sir Ian Hamilton's despatch about the wonderful arrangements made for water, but nothing was ever communicated to me. The only thing on the subject of water that I remember is that either the Divisional Commander or his Chief Staff Officer told me I must particularly warn the men that they must husband the water in their water-bottles, because they probably would not get any for 48 hours.

He further stated there was no shortage up to the time he was wounded, which appears to have been in the forenoon [late morning] of the 7th. He did not know whose duty it was to see that water was supplied.

Sir Bryan Mahon, commanding 10th Division, stated that the men had their water-bottles full when they started. On the morning of the 7th they tried without success to get a further supply. Some was given to them by a destroyer which came inshore on the afternoon of that day. On the morning of the 8th they obtained a further quantity. A good well was discovered on the 8th about halfway down to the sea, but there was a difficulty in distributing it owing to the want of mules. The troops could not have operated on the 8th, but after that they could have gone on so far as water was concerned.

General Hill, commanding 31st Brigade, stated that his men got no water except what they had had in their water-bottles from the time that they landed at about 8 am on the 7th until 3 pm on the 8th, and they suffered very badly, and they could not advance on the 8th owing to that. The Dublin Fusiliers brought them up some water, about half a bottle per man. They found two wells, but the Turks were sniping most of the time. They had to get water under fire, and could not organise any good system of getting it. It was impossible to do more on the 8th, but they could have done more on the 7th. The men went out at night to the two wells and got a certain amount of water, enough to enable them to do some cooking, but it was not a big supply. If they had pushed on on the 7th they might very likely have reduced the sniping.

We think that want of water was not the sole cause of the failure of the troops to advance further on the 7th; but on the 8th, with the exception of the 34th Brigade, the troops had been so long without water that they could hardly have been expected to undertake any serious operation. There is some reason to suppose that if the objectives had been gained on the 7th more water would have been obtainable from wells and springs, and the sniping of the known wells would have been much reduced, if not stopped altogether.

The failure of the supply of sea-borne water for the troops is attributed by Sir Frederick Stopford and other military officers to the fact that only two of the five water lighters arrived on August 7th, that they grounded on a sandbank at 80–100 yards from the shore, and that as the hoses provided were not long enough to reach the beach, no water was available for use from them until the morning of the 8th. Colonel Western, the Principal Military Landing Officer, at 5.30 pm on August 7th, sent the following telegram to Sir Frederick Stopford:

> Water for troops essential to success of undertaking. None has been landed. Can you arrange with the Admiral that this be landed at Beach A? GHQ directs 1,000 water bags containing 8 gallons each be sent to Anzac. Suggest half be sent here and ship's balance be sent to Anzac. Casualty clearing station now at Beach C. I would add nothing has yet been landed except small arm ammunition.

In a statement by Admiral Keyes, Commander Ashby, Naval Transport Officer, informed us that the last water lighter left Kephalos at 4 am on the 7th, and should have arrived by 7 am. Further, Admiral Keyes stated:

> I cannot exactly say when the lighters reached the beaches, and I can produce no evidence to show that they were beached before the afternoon of the 7th. I can state quite definitely from my own observation that water lighters were delivering water to the shore at three different places on the afternoon of the 7th—namely, at one of the northern beaches (probably A west), under Mount Falcon (Lala Baba) in the south-east corner of Suvla Bay, and at C Beach, south of Nebrunesi Point.

This evidence is confirmed by statements by Captain Lambart, RN, and other naval officers. No doubt one lighter stranded on a rocky ledge under Lala Baba, as Admiral Keyes stated:

> The water lighter was some little distance from the shore, which its hose would not reach. I boarded it and used the picket [patrol] boat I was in to tow it into a position from which its hose would reach the shore. I remarked that the water was being wasted, as water bottles were being filled direct from the hose, and there was no proper control over the shore end of the hose.

Probably this stranded lighter may account for part of the evidence on this subject given by military witnesses, but we think the evidence of the naval officers is correct, and that on the afternoon of the 7th water was being discharged from three lighters to the beaches. This is confirmed by Colonel Western, Principal Military Landing Officer, who stated: "I think the supply was fairly tight, but it was getting the water from the beach to the troops where the block occurred. There were not sufficient receptacles."

From the evidence of Major White, commanding the 68th Field Company Royal Engineers, which was detailed to receive the water lighters, it appears possible that some of the lighters discharging water on August 7th were supplied by the Navy.

The original project as described by Sir Frederick Stopford was to use water carts as receptacles on the beach, but as none of these were landed this could not be done. Wooden tanks were provided by General de Lotbinière in each of the four water lighters. They were too small and leaked badly; eventually, naval carpenters made them water-tight, and the Navy supplied tanks and baths. In one instance the Commander of a Destroyer, *The Foxhound*, ordered one of his tanks to be cut out and taken ashore and it was used for the storage of water.

The evidence shows there was a great deal of confusion on the beaches. The men not being able to get water quickly enough, owing to the absence of receptacles, took out their knives and pricked holes in the hoses. Colonel Western considers there was a serious want of discipline, and a lack of power of command on the part of the regimental commanders and officers, and this is confirmed by naval officers, especially by Captain Carver, RN, who acted for a time as beach-master.

Major-General Poett, as Deputy Adjutant and Quartermaster-General, had the general responsibility for provision of water to the troops, but he states that with regard to sea-borne water he had no responsibility until it reached the beaches, because General Headquarters were, with the Navy, responsible for landing water and mules. He should have ascertained when the water was likely to be landed, and made arrangements for its reception and distribution. Sir Frederick Stopford states that General Poett did not write any appreciation in detail as to how the water was to be distributed and that he did not discuss the question verbally with General Poett. He [Stopford] said:

> I find it difficult to say exactly what was in my mind, knowing what has happened since, but my impression is that the water there did not cause me any anxiety because I was informed there was plenty of water. I was informed there were four lighters and mules coming, and I rather thought the mules would be wanted for getting it up country. When I found that water had failed, and had not been landed, to my great astonishment, I sent for General Poett and asked: 'How do we stand with regard to food?' He said: 'We have one day to go on with,' and I said: 'Very well, we must stop everything else for water.' My anxiety till then was more in connection with food, because I did not anticipate there would be any difficulty about water.

With regard to the distribution of water he said: "I did not go into it personally; perhaps I ought to have done." Water carts were brought by the ships which carried the mules, but they were not landed and Sir Frederick Stopford, in his evidence, stated that they could not have been used by reason of the nature of the country.

The arrangements made by General Headquarters for landing mules with water bags for the supply of troops in the first instance were impeded by the delay in landing the 10th Division and by the necessity of sending mules to Anzac owing to the urgent signal received from General Headquarters on the afternoon of August 7th. Sir Frederick Stopford and Admiral Christian think that this was the chief cause for the want of mules on that day.

According to Admiral Christian's evidence, only one ship with pack mules and 8-gallon water bags on board—the *Dundrennan*—arrived at Suvla Bay on August 7th. Admiral Keyes gives as the reason for this that big ships had to be berthed near the net to avoid the risk of being torpedoed.

Consequently, as the protected area was limited, it was arranged not to have at Suvla more ships than could be unloaded at the time.

The result was that sufficient mules were not landed, but Captain Unwin, RN, VC, who was in charge, states that they commenced to land mules at about 10 am on the 7th at A (New Beach), and they were hard at it the whole time; he was not able to give an estimate of the total number of mules landed on the 7th, but Sir Frederick Stopford says that 500 were landed. No effort, apparently, was made to organise fatigue parties to supplement the paucity of mules.

Water in bulk and in petrol tins was provided in the motor lighters, but we have been unable to ascertain whether orders were issued by the battalion and company officers to the men to refill their water-bottles before landing. In some cases the naval officers in the lighters warned the NCOs to have the water-bottles filled, but apparently nothing was done. There is no evidence, however, that the water-bottles were not full when the men landed.

Sir Frederick Stopford said that the lighters were ordered away at once before the water could be used for refilling the bottles. He said:

> The water, I think, in those lighters was not intended to be used on shore, but was intended for the troops while they were on board. It was never intended for a shore supply, that is my impression, or I never heard of it.

The steps to be taken to explore the local resources for water were entrusted to the Chief Engineer of the Corps. General Painter informed us in a telegram that he detailed parties to search and dig for water in the neighbourhood of the beaches, but we have no evidence as to what was done on August 7th by these parties.

Sir Beauvoir de Lisle, who relieved Sir Frederick Stopford on the 15th, stated that there he experienced no trouble about water.

> There were wells within a quarter of a mile of the shore, which I had opened out. On the hill Keritch Tepe Sirt, there were two wells 400 feet higher than the sea. But on this side, between Keritch Tepe Sirt and the Salt Lake, there were as many wells as you liked to dig. You had not to go more than 15 feet before you got as much water as you wanted. Inside the area which they occupied on the first day they had only to scratch the sand to get as much water as they wanted. On the shore, within 100 yards of high-water mark, you had only to dig the sand 4 feet down to get water. All that means bad staff work, because the Royal Engineers could have found that out as easily as I could. At one place, if they had only taken a mess tin and scraped it with their hands they would have come to water. The difficulties about water were very much exaggerated.

This is confirmed also by General Sitwell, who found sufficient water for his brigade (the 34th).

The discovery of water was, however, a gradual process, and we doubt whether on August 7th and 8th sufficient water could have been found from local resources alone to make good the deficiency of the sea-borne supply. The failure to supply sea-borne water to the troops is attributable to the fact that:

(1) The landing of the mules which were to supply the troops with water was much delayed.
(2) No arrangements had been made for the distribution of water in case of the failure of the mules to land in time.
(3) Suitable receptacles had not been provided on the beaches to receive the water from the lighters.
(4) No fatigue parties were organised to distribute such water as might be available in case of scarcity of mules.

We think that the Corps Commander and his Administrative Staff did not sufficiently realise the absolute importance of water, until Colonel Western sent a telegram to Sir Frederick Stopford at 5.15 pm on the 7th to say troops were short of water. This is corroborated by General Poett, who stated:

> When I left Sir Frederick Stopford at about 11 o'clock on the morning of the 7th he was not anxious about water, because he had been told definitely that water was plentiful, but he was most anxious that I should get the munitions on shore.

Possibly they may have been misled by information they had from the Headquarters Staff. General Stopford said:

> As regards the supply of water which came, till it was landed, I had nothing to do with it, and I assumed that the necessary arrangements had been made by the Commander-in-Chief, who was responsible for the plans.

He explained that when at Imbros he had made enquiries about the water, and found the Headquarters Staff were responsible for the water coming to Imbros and the Navy was responsible for getting it ashore.

> The General Officer who made the plan of the campaign was responsible for telling the Navy when and where the water was required. If I had been told it was a matter of duty to know what water I required, and get the mules and lighters, I should have done so, but I understood it was to be done by the Headquarters Staff.

He said that two lighters left Imbros with the troops and that he did not know whether Admiral Christian had any orders as to when he was to land the water, and did not talk it over with him. In another answer he said:

> According to my recollection the sole instructions I received about the water supply were in the secret instructions, 22nd July, that water was plentiful throughout the Anafarta Valley. I was never informed that water would be scarce, and the responsibility, according to the paper and instructions you get for such a supply of water as came from the sea, rested with the General Headquarters Staff.

General Poett stated:

> The orders for the landing of the personnel, the ammunition, the supplies, and the
> arrangement for providing sea-borne water were made by the General Headquarters
> Staff, presumably after consultation with the Admiral, and with his full approval.
> These orders were in great detail, and appear to cover the ground, assuming them to
> be carried out. Not only did General Headquarters assume all responsibility for the
> landing orders, but they appointed a special staff to assist in carrying them out. I am
> inclined to think the inaccurate information in General Headquarters' Orders that
> water was plentiful misled everybody. It must not be lost sight of that the food and
> ammunition had also to be considered. To the best of my recollection I received the
> detailed Orders, I think, on the 5th, but I will not be sure. We got them some days
> before the landing.

General Poett understood that the Navy was responsible for bringing the
water to the beaches, but he did not take any steps before the landing to get
into communication with the naval authorities in order to ascertain exactly
what was going to be done. He took it for granted that as the orders were
drafted by General Headquarters in concert with the Navy, and as they had
their own Principal Military Landing Officer and Beach Master, all details
would be arranged between those two officers. He considered that his
responsibility would begin with the distribution of the water.

We think that Sir Frederick Stopford and his staff failed to realise the
importance of having sea-borne water ready for issue to the troops early on
the 7th, they may have been misled by General Headquarters saying that
water was plentiful in the Anafarta Valley, but it was evident that until the valley was captured water would not be obtainable there.

The supply of sea-borne water was, however, specifically undertaken by
General Headquarters in concert with the Navy, and it rested with them to
place the lighters in positions from which water could be delivered on to the
beaches and to land the pack mules and filled water bags as required by the
Officer Commanding the IXth Corps.

FOOD

The circumstances in which the supply had to be made are described by Sir John Cowans, the Quartermaster-General to the Forces, as abnormal and peculiar. The details of the arrangements for the supply of stores, the amount shipped and the scale of daily rations are set out in the statement of Lieutenant-Colonel H. F. P. Percival, Assistant Director of Supplies. A large proportion of the meat supplied was preserved or tinned, and the precautions taken to secure that it was of good quality are described by Brigadier-General Long, then Director of Supplies and Transport.

These provided for an inspection of the meat before being shipped, and in order to secure a proper examination by competent persons it was arranged, with the consent of the Local Government Board, that it should be made by or with the assistance of the local authorities and their medical staff.

In the case of purchases from South America, the Local Government Board sent out some of their inspectors, who were at the factories during the whole of the time at the War Office expense, supervising the packing of meat and satisfying themselves as to its quality.

The only serious complaints which were brought to our notice are with regard to the absence of canteens, the deficient supply of condiments, and the quality of a certain brand of South American tinned meat.

When the hot weather began in Gallipoli there was a great deal of sickness, chiefly of the type of diarrhoea or dysentery, and a continued diet of tinned meat, even if of good quality, became distasteful. If it were salt and stringy, as was the case with some of the meat, it was still more distasteful, and, if eaten, made the men more liable to these diseases. As will be seen by the scale of rations set out in Lieutenant-Colonel Percival's statement, provision was made for the variation of the ration by giving equivalents, and these equivalents were provided. But this could only be done within limits, and a wider variation of the diet could only be attained by the establishment of canteens. If canteens had been established and this variation obtained at an earlier date, there would have been a reduction of the sickness.

The first request for canteens was made on May 27th, and it was suggested that they should be provided by the Canteen and Mess Co-operative Society.

It was proposed to finance them by using some money of the South African Garrison Institute Fund. Any money used would only be a loan, as it would be recouped from the sum paid by the men for supplies. It was alleged in evidence before us that obstacles were put in the way of supplying canteens by Sir Charles Harris, the Assistant Financial Secretary at the War Office, but we find there was no foundation for such statement.

At first Lord Kitchener was disinclined to send canteens, but after pressure from Sir John Cowans he consented to the use of £10,000. The Treasury later on advanced £50,000 for the same purpose. In the result ten ships carrying canteen stores to the value of about £90,000 went out to the peninsula between the 16th July and the 4th November, 1915. Sir John Cowans also told us that the troops were not getting the ordinary but a varied ration. He said: "It was a very good ration, and we had in addition fresh vegetables from Bulgaria and Greece and Egypt." There was also a complaint that more condiments and sauces were not supplied for the use of the Australian and New Zealand troops. Colonel Percival gave evidence that these articles would have been supplied if asked for by the Deputy Quartermaster-General of the force. They were not asked for, and we have no evidence that any request for them was ever conveyed to him.

The only complaint of the quality of food that we have had before us is in respect of a certain brand of South American tinned meat spoken of as "Fray Bentos". Two other brands of tinned meat were mentioned as not satisfactory, but there was not sufficient evidence about them to enable us to come to a conclusion.

The "Fray Bentos" meat is described by Sir Alexander Godley in the following terms:

> It was very, very salt, and very stringy bully. I think it was of inferior quality. I have eaten very much worse bully beef than that in previous campaigns. I have been campaigning and I have eaten much worse beef. Still it was not good, and certainly the men did not like it.

This agrees with all the other evidence in describing the meat as salt and stringy. When the weather was hot and the men inclined to suffer from diarrhoea and dysentery such meat was very distasteful, and they would not eat it. Many of them, while in hospital in England, stated that they could trace an increase of illness on the days when this brand and the other two mentioned were served out, and a decrease when they got other meat. No evidence except this was given as to the quality of the other two brands.

Lieutenant-Colonel Myers, the Assistant Director of Medical Services to the New Zealand forces, who took these statements from the men, was of the opinion that they would be able to trace such increase and diminution. Sir Alexander Godley, speaking not, of course, as a medical witness, said that he did not notice any difference in the health of the men if they had Fray Bentos one day and fresh meat the next; and Captain Ritchie, a medical officer with the New Zealand force, on being asked if he had noticed the change, said:

> The only marked change that I saw in that way was at Headquarters. Everyone of us had diarrhoea very bad the day after we were given fresh meat for the first time.

When asked if he had noticed anything of the ill-effects to the men's health from the Fray Bentos, he said: "No, it may not have been due to the meat that the men had diarrhoea, it may have been the combination of the meat, the method of living, and water; but the meat was not nice, it was a bit salt." He was serving as a sanitary officer and did not attend to the medical treatment of the men. Fray Bentos is a well-known brand, and we have ascertained from Colonel Percival that it has been issued to all troops in all theatres of war (including France) since the beginning of the War.

We think the result of this to be that there was nothing actively injurious to health in the meat; but it was of poor quality, and from being salt and stringy it caused some intestinal irritation, and so contributed to diarrhoea.

It must be remembered that the Australian and New Zealand troops had been some months at Anzac when the hot weather began, continually in the trenches, and without proper opportunities of rest, and that their energy and activity had been overtaxed. They were, therefore, probably very liable to ill-effects from food unsuitable to such weather.

We have no evidence that any complaint was made by the responsible military or medical authorities in Gallipoli while the meat was being issued, but a complaint was made to the Quartermaster-General's department in November, 1915, by the High Commissioner for New Zealand, and samples of that brand of meat were examined by experts, including the Principal Medical Officer of the inspection department of the Local Government Board, and found satisfactory.

In December, 1915, the complaint was renewed from the office of the High Commissioner for New Zealand, and it was stated that when preserved meat from New Zealand or Australia was supplied the health of the men improved. The Quartermaster-General's department agreed to consider offers of New Zealand meat, and also proposed a conference between representatives of the New Zealand Government, the Food Inspection Department of the Local Government Board, and representatives of the War Office to examine all brands of meat and discuss the whole question. In reply the War Office were informed by the High Commissioner for New Zealand that the only form of conference which could serve any useful purpose would be one at which actual samples of the meat buried by the troops or thrown overboard from the transports could be examined. It was, of course, impossible to get these samples, and so no conference was held.

After the examination in November, 1915, an alteration was made in the specification of the meat and the percentage of salt reduced.

These were the only complaints received about this meat, and since the alteration in the specification no complaints have been received by the Quartermaster-General's department.

MEDICAL ARRANGEMENTS

The medical arrangements for the Dardanelles Expedition were at first under the control of Surgeon-General Birrell, who was selected for the position by Sir Alfred Keogh, the Director-General of the Army Medical Service. Sir Alfred Keogh described the course adopted in such appointments as follows. When it became necessary to appoint a Director of Medical Services for a foreign expedition he examined the list of officers eligible for the position, and from his knowledge of their qualifications selected the one whom he considered most fitted for the position. This was the course adopted in the case of Surgeon-General Birrell, who had considerable experience of active service.

He was appointed Director of Medical Services on the 15th March, 1915, and arrived at Alexandria on April 1st, 1915. The Commander-in-Chief and the General Staff left in two or three days for Mudros, but the Director of Medical Services together with the rest of the Administrative Staff who were then at Alexandria were left behind. Lieutenant-Colonel Keble, one of Surgeon-General Birrell's subordinates, went with the General Staff to Mudros. There were matters connected with the provision of hospital accommodation in Egypt which had to be settled between Surgeon-General Birrell and Surgeon-General Ford, the Director of Medical Services in Egypt, under whose control they were to be.

On the whole we think it would have been better if Surgeon-General Birrell had gone to Mudros with the General Staff and left a subordinate to deal with hospital questions in Alexandria; but Colonel Keble, who went to Mudros, and from whose notes the scheme for dealing with the casualties was drafted, is spoken of by Sir Ian Hamilton as a very competent officer.

Before the Deputy Adjutant-General and Director of Medical Services arrived at Mudros, a scheme prepared by one of the officers of the

General Staff, based upon an estimate of 3,000 casualties, was shown to Lieutenant-Colonel Keble, who declined to consider it, as he thought that it was the duty of the Director of Medical Services and his Staff to prepare such a scheme and not that of the General Staff. He prepared notes of a scheme of evacuation based upon an estimate of 10,000 casualties. He had not been able before the arrival of the Administrative Staff to submit these notes to the Chief of the General Staff; and he handed them to the Deputy Adjutant-General and Director of Medical Services as soon as they arrived. There is some conflict of evidence as to whether the estimate of 10,000 was made in the first instance by the General Staff or by Lieutenant-Colonel Keble. We do not think that this is material, as the estimate was accepted by both the General and the Administrative Staffs, and Surgeon-General Birrell was so informed by an officer of the General Staff.

The Director of Medical Services arrived on April 18th, and Colonel Keble's notes were examined by him and the Deputy Adjutant-General. From these notes a draft scheme was made out and passed by the Chief of the General Staff on April 19th. This document is as follows:

The medical arrangements in connection with the landing of the British Force are at present as follows:

(1)   With each covering force the bearer sub-division of a field ambulance and one tent sub-division, with as much medical and surgical material as can be manhandled by the personnel; giving a total of 150 medical personnel with each covering force.

(2)   At 2 pm on the day of landing the personnel of the casualty clearing station (one for the 29th Division, one for the Australian and New Zealand Army Corps) will be landed with as much medical and surgical material as can be manhandled.

(3)   When the remainder of the division lands, the rest of the field ambulance and the equipment of the casualty clearing station will be put on shore as soon as it can be disembarked.

(4)   Two hospital ships will be available:
       With the 29th Division, *Sicilia*: accommodation, 400 serious cases.
       With the Australian and New Zealand Army Corps, *Gascon*:
       accommodation, 300 serious cases. The latter ship is expected here on Tuesday.

(5)   I understand from the Senior Naval Transport Officer that the Navy will commence the transport of wounded from the shore to the ships at about 2 pm. The means of evacuation are as follows:
       Three launches, each capable of holding 12 cots, are available for the 29th Division, and the same number for the Australian and New Zealand Army Corps. These launches are to be towed to the hospital ships and other ships in which the men are to be accommodated.

(6)   This provision for the evacuation of casualties from the Force appears to

be altogether inadequate, and I would strongly urge that the following proposals should be sanctioned:

(i)   B2 *Caledonia*   470 serious cases

       B7 *Aragon*   200 serious cases

       B9 *Dongola*   200 serious cases

       should be allotted to the 29th Division for the accommodation of their wounded.

I recommend:

(ii)   That the A25 *Lutzow*   200 serious cases

       A1 *Ionian*   100 serious cases

       some other ship (*Southland?*)   420 serious cases

       be allotted to the Australian and New Zealand Army Corps.

(iii)   That two more tows of three launches each— equals 72 additional cots—should be provided for the 29th Division and a similar number for the Australian and New Zealand Army Corps.

(7)   It has previously been proposed to provide the personnel and medical and surgical equipment for the above transports of the 29th Division from Nos 15 and 16 Stationary Hospitals, and the personnel for the transports of the Australian and New Zealand Army Corps from No. 2 Australian Stationary Hospital. These Stationary Hospitals have been wired for.

19th April, 1915

E. M. WOODWARD

Deputy Adjutant-General

This scheme, which was signed by General Woodward, mentions only one hospital ship, the *Sicilia*, for Helles, and one, the *Gascon*, for Anzac; and it will be observed that the number of serious cases for which accommodation was provided amounted to 2,290. No mention is made of the provision for slight cases. Surgeon-General Birrell, in a report to Sir Alfred Keogh, dated April 22nd, gives a fuller account of the arrangements.

REPORT ON MEDICAL ARRANGEMENTS IMPENDING OPERATIONS, GALLIPOLI PENINSULA

Hospital ships

(a)   With Naval Division which at the outset is not undertaking serious operations is the *Somali.*

(b)   With the Australian and New Zealand Army Corps is the HS *Gascon.*

(c)   With the 29th Division is the HS *Sicilia.*

This does not provide accommodation for anything like the expected casualties, and as for many days it may be impossible to open stationary hospitals ashore, I have, for the 29th Division, caused to be taken over, after evacuation by the fighting troops, the transports *Caledonia, Aragon* and *Dongola*, and have staffed them from the personnel of the 15th Stationary Hospital. The medical and surgical equipment has been divided equally between these three ships additional to the normal equipment carried. For the Australian and New Zealand Army Corps I have caused the *Lutzow, Ionian, Clan McGillivray*, and *Seang-Chung* to be taken over. They will be staffed by the personnel of the 2nd Australian Stationary Hospital when it arrives. It sailed from Alexandria on board the *Hindu* on the 20th April.

All these ships can make Alexandria in 48 hours and Malta in four days.

They can accommodate together with the regular hospital ships 1,995 serious cases, and at a pinch an additional 414 cases, or in all 2,409 cases, and 7,300 slightly wounded cases, or a grand total of 9,709 wounded.

If more transports are needed they are available and can be staffed by the 16th Stationary Hospital which sailed on 20th April on *Hindu*, and which is being held in reserve.

The hospital ship *Guildford Castle* has been wired for at Alexandria, and she sailed on 21st April; on arrival she will be used to evacuate the No. 1 Australian Stationary Hospital which is opened at Lemnos, and which is filled to overflowing.

Medical stores

No. 4 advanced depot of medical stores goes with the Australian and New Zealand Corps on the *Hymettus*, which, however, is ashore and may not be got off.

No. 5 advanced depot of medical stores sailed from Alexandria on 20th April on *Hindu*, and is for the supply of the 29th Division.

Evacuation

Evacuation of casualties will be direct to Egypt and Malta.

Casualty Clearing Stations

No. 11 Casualty Clearing Station goes ashore with the 29th Division, and operates near the beach, as does the Australian CCS with the Australian and New Zealand Army Corps.

Future proposals

After the initial operations the three hospital ships, *Sicilia, Gascon, Guildford Castle* and one other which is asked for, will act as ferry boats for sick and wounded between the three stationary hospitals which will be established according to regiments on the Gallipoli Peninsula and the bases at Alexandria and Malta. It is impossible to move the No. 1 Australian Stationary Hospital at Lemnos owing to the number of infectious cases therein, viz., small pox, 2; scarlet fever, 3; diphtheria, 1; measles, 14; mumps, 2.

Evacuation as affected by military operations

During the landing and the actions immediately subsequent thereto, the wounded may have to suffer hardships as it will be impossible to evacuate from shore to ships till the fighting troops have been landed, and even when they have been got aboard it may not be expedient to send the ships away to the bases till our foothold is secure, as during the first two or more days no wheeled transport can go ashore. The strain on the whole medical personnel will be exceedingly great.

Requirements

(1) I think the supply of dressings will not prove to be adequate if fighting is sustained, and therefore recommend that 100 boxes of reserve dressings be sent out.

(2) As the water on the Gallipoli Peninsula is not above suspicion filter water carts should be provided for the stationary hospitals at the rate of two per hospital. Eight will be required.

(3) One more hospital ship will be required to maintain the ferry service.

(4) To provide for casualties and to meet unexpected requirements, at least six medical officers should be sent here for attachment to the stationary hospitals.

Lemnos, April 22nd, 1915

W. G. Birrell,
Surgeon-General

This report mentions a larger number of hospital ships as available in the first two or three days and states the accommodation provided in all the ships mentioned to be: serious cases, 2,409; slight cases, 7,300; making a total of 9,709.

AVAILABILITY AND STAFFING OF HOSPITAL SHIPS

According to Surgeon-General Birrell's evidence the *Somali* and the *Sudan* were available at or immediately after the landing; while the *Guildford Castle* arrived on April 26th and the *Delta* on April 27th, making six hospital ships in all. In addition to these hospital ships, there were seven transports which were allotted, four to Anzac and three to Helles. If any further accommodation were required for the wounded, it had to be obtained by using other transports which had brought the troops to the peninsula.

This report states that the transports mentioned therein were taken up because it might be impossible to open stationary hospitals ashore for many days, and specifies the accommodation on the transports for serious cases. Both Surgeon-General Birrell and Lieutenant-Colonel Keble, however, gave evidence that, although there was accommodation for the estimated number of serious cases, the transports were not provided with the appliances necessary for the treatment of such cases, and also that such appliances could not be obtained at the time. It seems clear that, although this accommodation was provided, it was not expected that it would be required, as the medical staff shared the anticipation of all the military authorities that, if the landing were successfully effected, a rapid advance would be made and hospitals would soon be established on land.

In the actual circumstances of the landing the supply of hospital ships was insufficient, and if a landing in force on the peninsula had been contemplated when the expedition left England we think it would have been the duty of the Director of Medical Services to have arranged for a more ample supply. It has, however, been already pointed out that the instructions given to Sir Ian Hamilton by the Secretary of State for War did not contemplate such a landing, and the Director of Medical Services had no information before leaving England upon which he could base his requirements. In his evidence he stated that, if he had received earlier information that heavier casualties were expected, he could have made better preparation. We think that, if the Administrative Staff had accompanied General Headquarters to Mudros, the Director of Medical Services would have been in a better position to inform himself of the probable operations and to estimate the consequent requirements.

The Director of Medical Services, however, did make arrangements in Egypt for the provision of hospital accommodation for a large number of casualties, and we think that with a little more forethought he might have arranged for the supply of some of the equipment which was afterwards found to be wanting on the transports.

According to Lieutenant-Colonel Keble's evidence, each of the transports which were sent to Helles for the evacuation of the wounded was provided with at least four medical officers. Those which were sent to Anzac were not so provided on their leaving Mudros because the medical personnel intended for them was not available at the time. This personnel came to Mudros on a ship called the *Hindu*, which was unfortunately delayed. When she arrived a request was sent for a boat to transfer the medical staff to the transports, but one could not be obtained, and the transports left without the intended provision of medical officers. Colonel Keble said, however, that there was no reason why the number should not have been made up at Anzac, as the *Hindu* followed them there; and there were also medical officers of the units which could not be landed available for service on the transports.

TRANSPORT ARRANGEMENTS FOR THE SICK AND WOUNDED

At the time of the landing the bearer divisions and the field ambulances landed with the troops, and later the casualty clearing stations and a part of the tent divisions of the field ambulance. With the covering division one tent sub-division landed with the bearer divisions. The intention was that the stationary hospitals should be landed as soon as possible, and that from the first the cases should be sorted, the serious ones going to the hospital ships and the slighter ones to the seven allotted transports and the other transports which it was found necessary to employ.

Three classes of ships were employed for transporting the wounded to the main bases, Alexandria, Malta and England, namely:

Hospital ships

Hospital carriers

Transports, generally called "black ships".

In addition, sweepers and other craft were used to convey the wounded from the beaches to the ships.

The hospital ships were well equipped and gave every satisfaction, and took about five weeks to fit out.

The hospital carriers were hastily improvised; they were used because there was not time to fit them properly as hospital ships. Undoubtedly they were not adapted for the conveyance of serious cases for long distances, but they were fairly satisfactory for short distances. None of these vessels was available at the first landing.

The transports (black ships) which were only intended for the conveyance of light cases, were not properly equipped for serious cases. Many of them were used immediately after the troops had disembarked, and in some cases the horses were left on board. As a rule there were four medical officers on board, with some attendants and stores, but they had no arrangements for dealing with serious cases and were not meant to carry them. Unfortunately, owing to the difficulty of sorting the light from the serious cases, many of the latter were put on board these ships, and this entailed a great deal of suffering.

On the first days of the landing, April 25th, 26th and 27th, the Administrative Staff were again separated from the General Staff. The Commander-in-Chief and the greater part of the General Staff were on board the *Queen Elizabeth*, and the Administrative Staff, including the Director of Medical Services, were left on board the *Arcadian*. According to the evidence this was done because there was not room for the whole staff on board the *Queen Elizabeth*, but the result was that the Director of Medical Services, who was on the *Arcadian*, and was not allowed to use her wireless installation, was unable to give any directions as to the operations for evacuating the wounded. These directions were in consequence given by the General Staff. We think that this was unfortunate and should have been avoided, but we do not attach much importance to the incident, as Surgeon-General Birrell and Colonel Keble say that the General Staff were carrying out Surgeon-General Birrell's scheme, and that the fact of its being carried out by them, and not by himself, did not substantially interfere with the evacuation and the comfort of the wounded, or prejudicially affect the situation.

Difficulties of sorting the wounded

Hardly any advance was made after the landing, and it was found impossible to carry out the evacuation as intended. It therefore became necessary that all casualties should be evacuated by sea as soon as possible. The casualties began at the very outset of the landing, and many of them occurred in the boats before the men had disembarked. It was impossible to sort the cases as had been intended, and they could not be left on the beaches, which were under shell fire. The selection of serious cases for the hospital ships and lighter cases for the transports could not be carried out. The hospital ships received many slight cases, and what was more serious, many severe cases had, in consequence, to be taken to the transports.

According to General Woodward and Surgeon-General Birrell there were at one time 300 slight cases on the *Gascon*, a hospital ship intended for serious cases, and this probably occurred in other instances. The result was that much suffering was occasioned to the severely wounded men, who were carried on the partially fitted transports. These ships were not fitted or staffed for such cases, and there were no appliances for the surgical treatment or attendance required. Additional hardship sometimes was occasioned by reason of delay in transferring wounded men from the small craft which took them from the beach into a transport. Surgeon-General Howse said that he was informed that in one case the wounded were taken to four or five transports before one was found which could receive them, and a similar instance was mentioned by Admiral Keyes on the report of Admiral Phillimore.

Numbers of casualties

There is a conflict of evidence as to whether the number of casualties was greater than was expected. Sir Ian Hamilton and General Braithwaite say they were much greater, although the latter gave evidence that the General Staff estimated them at 10,000. Sir John Maxwell, speaking of course from hearsay, expresses the same opinion, and there is other evidence to the same effect. On the other hand, Surgeon-General Birrell says that in the first few days the casualties were not more than he had expected, and the estimate contained in his report to Sir Alfred Keogh bears out this statement. It may be that it was not the number of the casualties alone which was important, but that the number combined with the necessity of transporting them by sea, and the impossibility of sorting them into slight and serious cases, caused an unexpected confusion and crowding of the hospital ships and transports.

The conditions stated above prevailed at both Helles and Anzac during the early days following the landing. Throughout the months of May, June and July the evacuation of casualties continued, though, except in the attacks of May 5th and 6th, and June 4th and 28th, the number evacuated was much fewer, and the use of the transports much less. According to the evidence, matters began to improve after the first ten days.

There is no doubt that great difficulties were experienced in the first few days of the operations, and that the wounded suffered in consequence. To what extent this was due to bad arrangements and to what extent it was unavoidable is a difficult question to determine, the evidence being contradictory and too voluminous to be set out in full.

Inadequate medical care

The real substance of the complaints, in our opinion, is the want of medical and nursing attendance and equipment upon the transports. There is evidence as to the want of boats and barges in which to take the wounded from the beach and of tugs or pinnaces [rowing boats] to tow these craft when loaded to the hospital ships and transports, and also as to a want of organisation in ordering them to different hospital ships; but the real complaint seems to us to be the broad fact that men wounded on the peninsula were often many hours or days before their wounds were re-dressed, and did not receive proper medical attention in the meantime.

We think that, during the first few days after the landing in April, difficulty and confusion in collecting the wounded and removing them from the beaches were unavoidable, owing to the failure to push inland and the fact that the beaches and the small craft approaching or leaving the shore were under the enemy's fire. At Anzac, where the confusion appears to have been more pronounced than at Helles, the military situation immediately after the landing was so unfavourable that the withdrawal of the force at nightfall was contemplated by Sir William Birdwood and consequently orders were given to get every wounded man away at once. Surgeon-General Birrell and Lieutenant-Colonel Keble think that some of the confusion might have been avoided if the senior medical officers of the Australian and New Zealand Corps had remained with the headquarters of their divisions, leaving their subordinates to land and do the work on the beaches; and Lieutenant-Colonel Fenwick, DADMS, of the Australian and New Zealand Division, expresses that opinion in regard to his division. Possibly if they had done so they might have been able to exercise better control by being more in touch with the hospital ships, but we do not think that this would have materially affected the situation. In our opinion, the circumstances made confusion inevitable.

The difficulty and confusion mentioned above rapidly decreased after the first few days, and in the operations in August there were few complaints of the arrangements for the removal of the wounded from the beaches and their conveyance to the hospital ships, except on the first day of the fighting at Anzac, when, according to Lieutenant-Colonel Corbin, Medical Officer of the 1st Australian Clearing Station, and Lieutenant-Colonel Begg, Officer Commanding the New Zealand Field Ambulance, there were difficulties from want of transport from the beaches and from the delay in the arrival of two clearing stations which had been provided for that service. This delay was explained by Lieutenant-Colonel Corkery, Officer Commanding the 16th Casualty Clearing Station, one of the two under reference. It does not seem to have been occasioned by any fault in the arrangements of the medical staff.

NEW APPOINTMENTS

At the end of May, Surgeon-General Sir William Babtie was appointed Principal Director of Medical Services in the Mediterranean, and exercised a general supervision over all the medical arrangements for the Mediterranean Expeditionary Force, as well as for Egypt and Malta, Surgeon-General Birrell continuing in the position of Director of Medical Services of the Mediterranean Expeditionary Force until the latter part of August, when he was relieved by Surgeon-General Bedford.

In July, Surgeon-General Sir James Porter was sent out by the Admiralty to superintend the naval and military resources in respect of the sea hospital transport in the Mediterranean, under the title of Principal Hospital Transport Officer (Mediterranean). Up to this time this duty had been performed by Surgeon-General Birrell and Surgeon-General Ford, under the supervision of Surgeon-General Babtie, though all the movements of the vessels and other craft at sea were under the control of the naval authorities. In consequence of complaints received by Sir Arthur May, the Medical Director-General of the Navy, as to the condition of the wounded afloat and the defective arrangements for the direction of the transports, he represented to Sir Alfred Keogh that it would be well if a naval medical officer were sent out to supervise the shipping arrangements for the sick and wounded. Sir Alfred Keogh agreed to this, and Sir James Porter was accordingly sent out. Sir Ian Hamilton considered that the result would be dual control and consequent confusion, and represented his views to the War Office. Surgeon-General Babtie considered the appointment unnecessary, but he and Sir James Porter worked very well together. Sir James Porter remained there until December, 1915, when his appointment was terminated at the request of the War Office. There is a difference of opinion as to whether any benefit resulted from the appointment. Sir Arthur May thinks that there was an improvement. Sir Alfred Keogh thinks there was not. Vice-Admiral Wemyss told us that from the naval point of view there was a great improvement.

ARRANGEMENTS FOR CASUALTIES IN JULY, 1915

The question of dealing with casualties became very important in July, in view of the contemplated operations at Helles, Anzac and Suvla, and on July 13th Sir Ian Hamilton informed the War Office that he would need more medical assistance. He pointed out that 20,000 casualties was not an extravagant estimate judging from the results of fighting in the Dardanelles up to that date, and that such a number would require 30 transports converted into temporary hospital ships and 200 extra medical officers, with Royal Army Medical Corps rank-and-file and nurses in proportion.

The contemplated operations first came to the notice of the Director of Medical Services and General Woodward and General Winter at about the same time. Surgeon-General Birrell explained that it was only by accident that he heard of the operations, and that he repeated what he had heard to the other two officers. From another part of his evidence it seems that the telegram mentioned above was sent by Sir Ian Hamilton at his request; and as it did not entirely express what he wanted, another telegram, increasing the demand for orderlies and nurses, was sent. This demand was complied with.

There is the same conflict of evidence as to whether the estimate of the casualties on this occasion was made in the first instance by the General or by the Administrative Staff, but we do not think it necessary to investigate the matter.

Surgeon-General Birrell informed us that his final scheme for the evacuation of casualties from Helles, Anzac, and Suvla was based upon an estimate of 30,000 casualties; and this was also the estimate of Sir Ian Hamilton, after further considering the question. The scheme provided for the use of six hospital ships and 30 transports used as temporary hospital ships. The hospital ships were to take the serious cases and, when full, carry them to the bases and return to the peninsula. Sir James Porter disapproved of sending the hospital ships away from the battle area, and made out a plan of his own for the movement of the ships and other craft which is set out in his statement. This plan aimed at reserving the hospital ships more exclusively for serious cases and providing greater facilities for separating the light from the serious cases. The cases were then transferred from the hospital ships into transports for carriage to the bases and the hospital ships returned to the beaches.

Difficulties of communication

The evacuation was carried out in accordance with Sir James Porter's dispositions and, on the whole, the cases were better sorted than in the original landing, but there was still considerable confusion. This was increased, not only during these operations but throughout the whole time, by the difficulty of communication with, and inspection of, the hospital ships and transports when they arrived at Mudros. The Lines of Communication Staff, including the Deputy Director of Medical Services, were with the naval staff upon the SS *Aragon,* and for the purpose of communication with the shore or with any vessel in the bay, steam or motor launches or boats of some kind were necessary. Of these there was a great deficiency. The military staff on board the *Aragon* were in close touch with the naval authorities, and this advantage would have been lost without any compensating improvement in their means of communication with the vessels in harbour, had their headquarters been established on shore. Evidence to this effect was given by Major-General Altham, the Inspector-General of Communications, and we accept it.

Sir Frederick Treves in his evidence stated that great difficulty was occasioned because the Deputy Director of Medical Services at Mudros had no means of communication with Alexandria or Malta, and therefore did not know what accommodation there was at each place for the wounded, with the result that ships were sent to Alexandria, and then, finding no accommodation there, had to go on to Malta. We think that there is some misunderstanding about this. The statement is inconsistent with the evidence of Vice-Admiral Wemyss, Surgeon-General Birrell, Colonel Keble, Colonel Ryan, and other officers, and with the information given to us by Colonel Maher. Surgeon-General Ford also stated that he could at all times accommodate the wounded sent to him, though at times he sent on slight cases to Malta in order to keep beds available for serious cases.

Sickness from other causes

In addition to the casualties arising from wounds, there was much sickness, chiefly a form of dysentery and diarrhoea, and large numbers of men had to be removed from the peninsula to hospital. This was especially the case in the height of the summer. At the end of November, 1915, a very severe blizzard occurred, producing numerous cases of frost-bite, and also gangrene from the men's clothing being frozen to their bodies. There was much suffering during this time, and the storm came so suddenly and was so exceptional that no special provision had been made for it.

Conditions on board the black ships

We have had much evidence as to the treatment of the sick and wounded during the operations on the Gallipoli Peninsula. Some of it favourable to the medical organisation and arrangements, and some the reverse. The main complaints related to the condition of the wounded on the black ships, and the evidence as to them is contradictory.

Evidence as to the deficiencies of these ships and the consequent suffering of the wounded was given to us by many witnesses, amongst them Rear-Admiral Keyes, Surgeon-General Howse, Lieutenant-Colonel Begg, Fleet-Surgeon Levick, Lieutenant-Colonel Fenwick, Major Kent Hughes, Lieutenant-Colonel Corbin and Lieutenant-Colonel Ryan. Some of the information given to us by these witnesses was given from personal observation and some from reports and communications received by them. It is a subject on which hearsay information should be received with caution, as a natural sympathy with the sufferings of the wounded may lead to some exaggeration.

We think, too, that some of the witnesses have not made sufficient allowance for the inevitable hardships that must attend the evacuation and treatment of casualties under conditions such as existed at Gallipoli.

Colonel Warren Low said that in four or five days at Mudros and Anzac more big operations were performed than the total number performed in the twelve large hospitals in London in a week, and added: "If you are going to expect to have at a place like Anzac all the arrangements one expects at St Thomas's Hospital, you will not get them, and I cannot understand anyone expecting them." Sir Arthur May also said that where there is a very large number of casualties hospital ships cannot be provided for all, and black ships or carriers must be used to a certain extent, and that whenever these are used there must be a large amount of unnecessary suffering. The word "unnecessary" seems to mean suffering which would not result from the wound if treated under favourable conditions.

We think that great importance is to be attached to the evidence of Lieutenant-Colonel Ryan as to the condition of the transports, both because he had had experience of war before this campaign, and because he was Consulting Surgeon and Principal Medical Adviser to General Birdwood at Anzac, and for about a month, from April 25th, was constantly at work on the transports. This is the time during which the state of the transports was at its worst.

According to his [Lieutenant-Colonel Ryan's] evidence, he was on board about ten transports, and in half of them the supply of medical officers was insufficient and there was a want of equipment, such as bed pans, dressings, and clothing for the men. He also describes many of the transports as very dirty, because they had been carrying troops to the peninsula and there was not time to clean them properly. Great difficulty and discomfort was caused in some transports by the fact of horses having been carried on them to Gallipoli. When these ships were selected for the accommodation of wounded it was expected that the horses would have been disembarked before the wounded were put on board, but it was found impossible to disembark them, and on some occasions they were taken several times between Alexandria and Gallipoli. To carry horses and wounded on the same ship must occasion suffering to the latter. Lieutenant-Colonel Ryan stated that he did not think there was much loss of life, but that if all these transports had been fitted up as hospital ships more lives, but not a great many, would have been saved.

We think that this is in substance a fair account of the condition of the transports in the first days of the operations. Lieutenant-Colonel Ryan was only on board one of these transports for a second time and in that case he found a distinct improvement.

Lieutenant-Colonel Ryan also agrees with the evidence of many other witnesses that there was no possibility of separating the wounded into different classes on the beach, and that the cases had to be evacuated as they came without being sorted according to the nature of their wounds.

Sir John Maxwell and Sir Charles McGrigor described the state of the wounded when they arrived at Alexandria as most distressing, and ascribed it to want of medical and nursing attendance; and Lady Carnarvon, who was working amongst the sick at Alexandria, said that the black ships were deficient in nursing staff, and, she believed, in medical staff all the time. General Haggard and Corporal Ross speak of the want of attention and consequent hardships they themselves experienced, and there was other evidence to the same effect.

On the other hand, in answer to a telegram from the War Office of May 10th, 1915:

> Representations made here regarding inadequacy of arrangements for wounded. Insufficient doctors, nurses and dressings.

Sir John Maxwell answered, on May 11th, 1915:

> Please state the source of representations, which I believe to be unfounded. The rush of wounded could not be dealt with in fitted hospital ships, well supplied with everything, and, therefore, we had to use, and will have to use, ordinary transports. Under most difficult circumstances, the best possible surgical arrangements were made. Of course, as troops had to disembark, and the wounded embark on the same day, the transports could not be cleaned. More than 11,000 cases have been brought from the Dardanelles, all with their wounds dressed. With the exception of 2,000 sent to Malta, all of these were made comfortable in hospital, and within 80 hours of being wounded they were all attended to. The wounded arrived under circumstances well attended to, according to the report of the surgeons in all the hospitals.

Again, on May 23rd, 1915, he telegraphed:

> The wounded were all dressed on being put on board, and on arrival were reported by all the medical officers in charge of the hospitals as in a satisfactory condition, taking into consideration the military circumstances under which they were embarked.

This telegram was, apparently, sent after enquiry had been made by Surgeon-General Ford. Surgeon-General Birrell and Surgeon-General Babtie told us that adequate staffs were provided, and, so far as they knew, were on board the ships, though Surgeon-General Birrell admitted that in May the staffs were not sufficient at one time. It is remarkable that this is the time covered by Sir John Maxwell's telegrams.

Lieutenant-Colonel Thom, speaking of the time after July 1st, 1915, when he took over the office work of attending to the staffing of the hospital ships and black ships, said that there were always sufficient staffs available at Mudros, and that, so far as he knew, they were on board. Colonel Mayo Robson explained the deficiency of medical and nursing staffs by the fact that serious cases intended for hospital ships were put on the black ships, and he also explained some evidence which was given as to men arriving practically naked by saying that in the summer they fought in that way, and that the sunburnt condition in which they arrived was due to that cause and not to their having been exposed after being wounded, as was supposed by some of the witnesses. Colonel Warren Low also ascribed the condition of the black ships to the difficulties under which the work was done, but he had not much practical experience of those ships. Colonel Sir Courtauld Thomson, Chief Commissioner of the Red Cross

Society for Malta, Egypt and the Near East, had the opportunity of seeing many of the black ships, and travelled in some of them. He expressed the opinion that under the exceptional conditions the available resources were utilised to the best advantage.

The case of the *Saturnia*

In some instances transports were used as temporary hospital ships for the reception of wounded at Mudros when the hospital accommodation on shore was fully occupied. This occurred in the case of the *Saturnia*, described by Rear-Admiral Keyes, Fleet-Surgeon Levick and Major Purchas.

According to the evidence given by Major Purchas, Royal Army Medical Corps, he heard on June 29th, soon after his arrival at Mudros from Egypt, that there were a large number of wounded on board the *Saturnia* without sufficient medical attendance. He obtained this information from over-hearing a conversation between the captain of the *Minnewaska*, the vessel on which he had come from Egypt, and the captain of another transport. He at once asked for a boat and boarded the *Saturnia*, which he found filled with wounded. At this time, according to his evidence, the only medical officers on board were an Australian medical officer, who had arrived just before him, and Fleet-Surgeon Levick. The latter officer had boarded the *Saturnia* in consequence of a report made to him by a Roman Catholic chaplain that there were a large number of wounded on board the *Saturnia* and only one medical officer.

Soon after Fleet-Surgeon Levick went on board, surgeons from all the ships of the Fleet then lying in harbour were sent to the *Saturnia* in consequence of a general signal. Rear-Admiral Keyes, who took his information from a statement made by Naval Surgeon Lorimer and Fleet-Surgeon Levick, was under the impression that the *Saturnia* had brought these wounded men into Mudros and that the state of their wounds as described by them resulted from neglect on board of her. We see no reason to doubt the evidence of Fleet-Surgeon Levick and Major Purchas that there were a large number of wounded on board the *Saturnia* whose bandages had not been removed since the first dressing and were putrid, and that many of the wounds were in a very foul state and needed prompt attention.

It was not the fact that the *Saturnia* brought the wounded to Mudros from Helles. She was one of four transports taken up in anticipation of the fighting at Helles on June 28th to receive such wounded as could not be accommodated on shore. The other transports were the *Seeang Bee*, the *Minnewaska* and the *Nile*. The *Saturnia* was partly laden with ammunition and could not be used to carry wounded to Egypt, but only for their temporary accommodation at Mudros. The condition of the men's wounds was not produced by neglect on the *Saturnia*, but, according to the evidence of Major Purchas, was the result of the impossibility of bringing them to the dressing stations for some time after they were wounded and their consequent exposure. Major Purchas, however, stated that the condition was aggravated by the want of attention on the *Saturnia*, which he said was quite unprepared and unfitted for their reception. Major Purchas also stated in his evidence that he was informed that the wounded were put on board the *Saturnia* in consequence of a mistaken signal.

On June 30th Colonel Aspinall, who was serving on the General Staff under General Braithwaite, happened to be at Mudros and reported to General Headquarters at Imbros as follows:

> I was informed at Mudros yesterday that 1,350 wounded, including a large
> proportion of stretcher cases, had arrived there in fleet sweepers and trawlers,
> including Isle of Man paddle steamers. Two hundred and fifty additional cases arrived
> during the day in similar ships. There was insufficient accommodation for these men
> on arrival, with the result that 600 cases were yesterday morning transferred to the
> ammunition ship *Saturnia*. Yesterday afternoon it was reported to the naval
> authorities by the Roman Catholic chaplain that there were 800 sick and wounded
> on the *Saturnia* and only two doctors to look after them. Admiral Wemyss
> accordingly ordered each man-of-war in harbour to send a surgeon on board.

This report on receipt at General Headquarters was referred to Surgeon-General Birrell, who the next day, July 1st, sent Colonel Keble to Mudros to enquire into the matter. Colonel Maher was at that time Deputy Director of Medical Services on the Lines of Communication at Mudros, and was responsible under the Director of Medical Services, who was at Imbros, for the medical arrangements at Mudros. Colonel Keble stated in evidence that on reaching Mudros he was informed by Colonel Maher that the wounded had been put on board the *Saturnia* by the mistake of the master of a fleet sweeper, and that they had been removed as soon as Colonel Maher heard of it. Colonel Keble did not make any further enquiry. Having regard to the specific allegations in Colonel Aspinall's report it appears to us that Colonel Keble's enquiry was perfunctory and insufficient.

We think that the evidence establishes that the wounded were put on board at some time on June 29th and that they were removed, some on June 30th to the *Nile* and the remainder on July 1st to the *Minnewaska*, both of which were properly fitted to receive them.

Major Purchas stated that on June 30th he was not in want of more medical assistance.

It is difficult to be certain as to the number of wounded on the *Saturnia*, but we think Major Purchas's evidence is probably correct. He stated the number as about 800, and as he was in charge of their removal from the *Saturnia* to the *Nile* and the *Minnewaska*, and was afterwards in charge of the *Minnewaska* while taking those transferred to that ship from Mudros to Alexandria, he had good opportunities of estimating the number.

After hearing the evidence of Fleet-Surgeon Levick and Major Purchas, we at once communicated with Colonel Maher. He is at present on duty with the Egyptian Expeditionary Force and has not given evidence before us, but we caused enquiries to be made from him by cable as to circumstances connected with the *Saturnia*. His answer is in direct contradiction of most of the evidence stated above. It is in substance as follows:

When the fighting on June 28th was anticipated he was told to expect a certain number of wounded, and took up and got ready the transports already mentioned for their reception. It was intended that the more serious cases should be put on board the hospital ships at Helles, only the less serious being brought to Mudros. By some mistake at Helles, many cases intended for the hospital ships were not put on board of them, but were brought to Mudros, and more accommodation than had been contemplated was required at that place. When the accommodation on shore was exhausted it was necessary to put the wounded on board the transports mentioned, and he ordered some of them to be put on board the *Saturnia*. Only 300 cases were put on board of her, and eight military medical officers and other medical personnel with medical and surgical equipments were put on board at once. The wounded were not left without sufficient medical attention, and help was given on this, as on many other occasions, by naval surgeons. On June 30th all the serious cases were transferred to the *Nile*, and on July 1st the remainder were transferred to the *Minnewaska*. Colonel Maher also stated that on June 29th and 30th he went on board the *Saturnia* and satisfied himself that the sick were well cared for.

Towards the end of August, 1915, in consequence of a complaint made to the War Office about the treatment of the wounded on board the *Saturnia*, Colonel Maher sent a report to Surgeon-General Babtie, the Principal Director of Medical Services in the Mediterranean, in which he gave substantially the same account of the circumstances as that contained in his cable sent in answer to our enquiry. He also stated that Major Purchas, an Australian surgeon of wide experience, was in charge and was assisted by several other competent surgeons. Major Purchas, in fact, comes from New Zealand and not from Australia. It appears from War Office records that Surgeon-General Babtie informed the War Office on August 31st that he had personally visited the *Saturnia* on July 1st, and that on that day there were eight medical officers on board, while a number of naval medical officers were also assisting as voluntary helpers. He stated that the number of wounded on board was about 500 and that the *Saturnia* was quite a suitable ship for the purpose to which she was put, but could not be used as a carrier, as she was loaded with ammunition.

We must point out, however, that on July 1st all the more serious cases had been removed to the *Nile* and medical and other assistance had been obtained, so that Surgeon-General Babtie's statement is no guide to the state of things on June 29th. His statement of the number of cases then on board as 500 is more consistent with Major Purchas's estimate of number than with Colonel Maher's statement that only 300 were put on board.

We are of the opinion that no definite conclusion can be formed on this matter in the absence of the evidence of Colonel Maher and any witnesses whom he might wish to be called. Colonel Maher is at present on active service with the Egyptian Expeditionary Force. We have communicated with the War Office and are informed that for military reasons the Army Council strongly deprecate the recall of Colonel Maher to England at the present time. Under these circumstances, in order fully to investigate the matter, it would be necessary to postpone the presentation of our report for an indefinite period. We do not feel justified in taking such a course, as a decision upon this particular incident would not affect the general conclusions at which we have arrived on the medical arrangements.

In view, however, of the serious nature of the evidence recorded in the present case, especially as affecting the conduct and capacity of Colonel Maher, we recommend that, as soon as the exigencies of the public service permit, steps should be taken by the Army Council definitely to ascertain with whom the responsibility rests for the deplorable state of things which has been represented to us as existing on board the *Saturnia* on June 29th.

SUMMARY

As regards the medical arrangements generally, although the evidence in several material respects is conflicting, we consider that a fair inference to be drawn from it is that much suffering was caused to the wounded during their evacuation from the peninsula, and that some part of it might have been avoided. Much of this suffering and discomfort was occasioned by the use of the black ships for serious cases. This, in our opinion, arose not so much from a miscalculation of the actual number of casualties as from a miscalculation of the circumstances under which they would be handled. All arrangements were made on the assumption that much more ground would be gained, that the hospitals would be landed, and that there would be an opportunity of sorting the casualties which did not exist on beaches constantly under fire. The difficulties which arose in evacuating the wounded were largely due to an under-estimate of the opposition which would be encountered, and too confident an anticipation of rapid and substantial success. The conditions on shore were, as we have said, aggravated by the impossibility of any proper inspection and regulation of the ships at Mudros by reason of the want of facilities of communication.

Though a great deal of discomfort, amounting in many cases to actual suffering, was occasioned to the wounded by the deficiency in medical attendance and the want of proper appliances on board the transports, we think that the result of the evidence is that the loss of life in consequence was small.

In our opinion, most of the suffering was due to the causes here mentioned, but we also think that there was, in some instances, a lack of organisation and supervision. Evidence of this was given by Admiral Keyes, Major Kent Hughes, and Surgeon-General Howse. The last-named witness described the conditions as "extremely difficult" and exceptional, and said: "We were in the unfortunate position of having no history to guide us of a previous landing on such a large scale in modern times, so that we could get no idea of what medical arrangements should have been made." We think that many of the difficulties might have been avoided if a general plan of the operations had been carefully worked out before the expedition was undertaken.

Many of the wounded after evacuation were taken to hospitals in Egypt and at Malta, and others were sent to England, Australia, New Zealand, or India. We consider the hospitals in England, Australia, New Zealand, and India to be outside the scope of our inquiry. We had some evidence laid before us as to the condition of the hospitals in Egypt and Malta, but we do not propose to discuss it at any length. Our conclusion is that, though there may have been some difficulties at first, especially in Egypt, which were the inevitable result of the large development of hospital accommodation, the provision and management of the hospitals were, under the circumstances, satisfactory. At times stores were not readily obtainable, but this resulted from the general difficulties of transport, and not from anything specially connected with the medical arrangements.

There were also hospitals for the lighter cases established at Mudros and Imbros. At Mudros their establishment was hampered by the want of piers and roads and other facilities of a port; and at one time, in order to be near the landing places and the water supply, the hospitals were placed too near to the general camp, but this was afterwards rectified. There was also evidence that the ground on which the hospitals stood became infected, and that they should have been moved on that account. On this subject there seems to be a difference of opinion. On the whole, we think that the position of the hospitals at Mudros is fairly described by Surgeon-General Babtie. The effect of this evidence is that at first there was not sufficient accommodation and, owing to the absence of water, roads and piers, its provision was very difficult; but that, as the size of the force increased, the supply of medical officers and attendants increased in proportion. It is possible that from time to time there was a shortage of medical attendance, but we do not think it existed to any serious extent.

When the weather became hot, there was a great increase of sickness, chiefly dysentery, diarrhoea, and para-typhoid, and these diseases were carried by the enormous number of flies. It was, therefore, very important that the sanitation of the camps and trenches should be properly carried out. On the whole, so far as conditions permitted, we think this was done. Surgeon-General Babtie states that the difficulties in remedying defects were almost insuperable owing to the cramped positions held and the lack of materials, such as wood and corrugated iron to enclose the latrines and make them fly-proof and to provide fly-proof kitchen-shelters. Some materials sent for the purpose were lost or damaged by accident of war, but one of the main causes of the deficiency was the anticipation that the operations would be very short, and the consequent omission to make provision for a long occupation of the peninsula.

Effective sanitation of the whole area was made impossible by the fact that our trenches were very near to those of the Turks, who took no sanitary measures at all. In July, a Sanitary Advisory Committee was appointed, which arrived in the peninsula after the fighting in August. The members of this Committee were all men of acknowledged scientific position, and their reports were of great service. A bacteriological laboratory was established at Mudros, and did good work.

There does not seem to be any complaint as to the supply of medicine, except in the case of Australian and New Zealand troops, who were said to have been short of the ordinary medicines, especially castor oil, and of the variety of food required for men suffering from illness. There is no dispute as to the fact that, at one time, the supply of castor oil ran short, the explanation put forward being that the supply was sufficient to meet ordinary demands, but that for some reason these troops required and consumed more drugs than the normal supply. This is probably correct, for there are no complaints of a lack of drugs in any other quarter.

POSTAL ARRANGEMENTS

The postal arrangements for letters and parcels sent to the Mediterranean Expeditionary Force were complicated, and increased in difficulty as the number of troops increased. The arrangements also changed from time to time. The statements of Lieutenant-Colonel Williamson, Director of Army Postal Service, Major McClintock, Director Army Postal Service Mediterranean Expeditionary Force, and Captain McCurdy, Officer Commanding New Zealand Base Post Office, set out all the details of the system, and will be found elsewhere.

Various complaints as to the service were brought before us. They were chiefly concerned with the non-delivery or late delivery of letters and parcels to the New Zealand troops, but we think what happened with regard to them may be taken as fairly representing the facts as to the whole of the force. The only material difference is that the mails for the New Zealand troops were passed through a very efficient New Zealand Post Office under Captain McCurdy, but they remained always under the control of the General Post Office.

Complaints were made by General R. P. Maxwell, General Cox and Colonel Mayo Robson.

The two former complained that parcels regularly despatched from England were only delivered in rare instances, and the latter that letters addressed to him were delivered on board the *Aragon*, where the naval and part of the administrative staff were quartered. Colonel Mayo Robson on more than one occasion went on board and asked for his letters, and was told there were none for him, and eventually they were all found in the hold in another part of the *Aragon*. He said they consisted of letters and newspapers extending over a period from July to October, 1915, and contained several orders which had been sent to him by Surgeon-General Babtie and others.

We have not been able to get any explanation of this incident. The letters had been carried and delivered at the place to which they were addressed and, in the absence of explanation, we can only conclude that it was owing to the negligence or stupidity of some postal clerk on board the *Aragon* that they were not given to Colonel Mayo Robson.

It must be remembered that the Post Office was not the only agency by which parcels were sent to the Mediterranean Expeditionary Force. A great many were sent by the Army Service Corps Parcels Transit Service, and the Post Office was sometimes held responsible for the delay or non-delivery of parcels which were not entrusted to them. Speaking generally, parcels up to 11 lbs were sent by post and parcels above that weight by the military forwarding office. There was a good deal of looting of parcels sent by the military forwarding office, probably because they were not sent in sealed bags, as Post Office parcels were.

Still, it cannot be doubted that there were delays and failures in the delivery of letters and parcels which were sent by the Post Office. In considering the amount of blame, if any, to be attached to the department, it is necessary not to lose sight of two main considerations.

(1) The number of letters and parcels was very large, and increased very rapidly, and a failure to deliver a very small percentage of the letters and parcels would amount to a formidable figure and give rise to many complaints. The amount of letters is stated to have grown to 1,000,000 a week, and the parcels are variously stated as from 40,000 or 90,000 a week. The difference is probably accounted for by a difference in the estimate of the number of parcels to a bag.

(2) The service was performed under circumstances of great difficulty, and for this reason the delivery of mails cannot fairly be compared with delivery in ordinary circumstances or to the troops in France.

The system of checking the bags was elaborate and efficient, as is shown by the fact that every bag except one could be traced and accounted for, and that cases in which the bags had been tampered with were also discovered. This checking continued up to the time when the mails were delivered to the post orderlies of the different units. After they had been so delivered the responsibility of the Post Office ceased.

In consequence of complaints as to the postal service, Colonel Williamson was sent out specially to make enquiries and report, which he did in October, 1915. His report is substantially in accordance with the evidence of other witnesses.

From this report it appears that the Post Office probably had to bear some of the responsibility which properly attached to the Army Service Corps Parcels Transit Service as well as its own.

The Post Office sent the letters via Marseilles and the parcels by P&O packets from the Thames. The result was that a letter advising the despatch of a parcel often arrived a considerable time before the parcel, and complaints were made of its non-arrival because the addressee of the letter did not appreciate that they were not sent together.

In cases where the addressee had become a casualty or for some other reason was not with his unit, there were great difficulties in finding where he was and in delivering his letters or parcels, even if they arrived safe and were not distributed to other men. The names of several men whose letters were not delivered were supplied to us by the Office of the High Commissioner of New Zealand. These cases were investigated so far as was possible by Captain McCurdy, and the result is given by him in his statement. They illustrate the difficulty experienced in delivering mails when the addressees were not with their unit.

Many parcels were destroyed through insufficient packing. The bags were handled and transhipped several times, and could not always be carefully handled, the result being that parcels were burst open and their contents crushed so as to be quite indistinguishable. Colonel Williamson described in his evidence the state of a large number of bags of parcels which had been sent up to the Front and returned to Alexandria because they could not be delivered. He says:

> The state in which these parcels arrived was absolutely deplorable. It was a deplorable sight. There was hardly a vestige of a resemblance to a parcel left. The contents were often ground to powder. The packing was all gone, the address was illegible, and one would simply get a bagful of *disjecta membra* [dismembered objects] of a parcel which it was impossible to reassemble and send on. That must have accounted for a very large proportion.

It is improbable that all this damage was done on their return from the Front to Alexandria, and it may therefore be concluded that many parcels arrived at the Front in the state described by Colonel Williamson. In many cases where the addressee was not present with his unit, the parcels, rightly or wrongly, were treated as common property, and distributed amongst his comrades.

In the case of letters which arrived at intervals over a considerable period and were not delivered as they arrived, but all together at a later date, the fault may have been that of the unit to which the addressee belonged and not that of the Post Office, whose duty was discharged when the letter was delivered to the post orderly. In one case that was investigated by Captain McCurdy this proved to have been the case. It does not seem to have been so in the case of Colonel Mayo Robson.

Parcels sent to General Cox were packed by the Army and Navy Stores and forwarded by Parcel Post. Presumably, they would be properly packed. We have not been able to ascertain anything further with regard to this case or that of General Maxwell.

The causes mentioned above account for a very large proportion of the complaints, but they do not explain them all. There must have been cases in which the Post Office was at fault. Considering the difficulties of the service and the amount of letters and parcels which had to be handled, we think that some miscarriage was inevitable, and we are of opinion that, on the whole, no blame attaches to those responsible for the organization and conduct of the service.

THE ZION MULE CORPS

The Zion Mule Corps was raised in Alexandria from a number of Jewish refugees from Syria. They or their fathers had gone to Syria following the principle of Zionism and at the outbreak of war they came to Egypt and were under the charge of a Mr Hornblower, Inspector of Refugees in the Ministry of the Interior, Egypt. The Corps, when raised, was put under the command of Lieutenant-Colonel Patterson, and did good work in Gallipoli as a transport Corps.

The only question raised before us was as to the terms of service and pension on which they were engaged. We doubt if this question is strictly within our reference, but we think it well to represent the facts as stated to us. Evidence was given to us by Lieutenant-Colonel Patterson and Captain Trumpeldor. Lieutenant-Colonel Patterson spoke in a great measure from hearsay, and the important evidence was that of Captain Trumpeldor. We consider him quite a trustworthy witness.

Lieutenant-Colonel Patterson said that there were two meetings held at which officials of the British Government addressed the men and told them that they would be treated in all respects in the same way as British soldiers and would receive the same pay and everything else, and that the men agreed to serve in the Corps on those terms.

Captain Trumpeldor said that they wished to raise a fighting unit to fight for Palestine and the Zion ideal, and did not want to serve as a transport unit because they did not think it so honourable. He said that he and a committee of prominent Israelites saw Sir John Maxwell and discussed the question of forming a fighting or a transport unit, and that afterwards a meeting of the men was held at which they were addressed by Mr Hornblower and a staff officer who spoke in Sir John Maxwell's name. This staff officer was Captain (now Lieutenant-Colonel) H. V. Holdich, DSO.

The landing at Suvla in Gallipoli, 1915. The battle between the Allied forces and the Turkish army on the Gallipoli Peninsula was to prove a disastrous military campaign for the Allies. Archive: Corbis.

The British Division at Gully Beach, Gallipoli. The 42nd (East Lancashire) Division of the British army was encamped at Gully Beach on the Gallipoli Peninsula in 1915. Archive: Corbis.

Troops landing at Anzac Cove on the Gallipoli Peninsula in 1915. Archive: Corbis.

Australian troops charge towards a Turkish trench just before the evacuation at Anzac in 1915. When they reached it the Turks had fled. Archive: Corbis.

V Beach, Gallipoli, showing the River Clyde. *Public Record Office.*

The Turkish fortifications at Medijieh near Chanak, 1915. Public Record Office.

The British statesman and author, Winston Churchill, c. 1915. Hulton Archive.

Lord Kitchener (1850–1916), British military leader. Archive: Corbis.

Sir Ian Standish Monteith Hamilton (1853–1947), who was given command of the British forces in Gallipoli. Hulton Archive.

Herbert Henry Asquith (1852–1928), British Liberal statesman and Prime Minister (1908–16). Hulton Archive.

Group of British military commanders. From left to right, top to bottom: Field Marshal Lord Roberts; Field Marshal Sir John French; General Sir H. Smith-Dorrien; General Sir Ian Hamilton; Lord Horatio Kitchener; General Robert Baden-Powell; Major General Murray; General Douglas Haig; General William Douglas. Archive: Corbis.

British General Frederick William Stopford (1854–1929), centre, at Crystal Palace in London. General Stopford was relieved of his command at Gallipoli by Sir Ian Hamilton. Hulton Archive.

British Secretary of War Lord Kitchener visits the trenches at Gallipoli in Turkey. Hulton Archive.

Wartime politicians: in October 1915 Lloyd George, Minister of Munitions (left), and Winston Churchill, First Lord of the Admiralty, walk down Whitehall in London.
Hulton Archive.

French trench on the western front.
Archive: Corbis.

German soldiers fire
from a trench on the
Belgian frontier during
World War I.
Archive: Corbis.

French trench on the
western front during
World War I.
Archive: Corbis.

According to Captain Trumpeldor's evidence the men were told by Mr Hornblower and Captain Holdich that a transport and a fighting unit in the British Army were equally honourable and served on the same conditions. Some of the men who were married and had families asked what would happen to their families if they were killed or wounded, and in answer they were told that like the families of soldiers they would receive a pension and allowance. Captain Trumpeldor said that he did not remember the expression "pensions" being used, as Mr Hornblower and Captain Holdich spoke in English and he did not understand it very well, but that what they said was translated into Hebrew by Mr Gordon, a clerk in Mr Hornblower's office. Captain Trumpeldor spoke English fairly well and gave his evidence in English.

Lieutenant-Colonel Holdich is on active service in Egypt. We made enquiries from him by telegraph, and received an answer that to the best of his recollection no mention specifically was made of any gratuities or pensions, as it was understood that any question regarding them would be settled later by the General Officer Commanding-in-Chief of the Mediterranean Force, according to the nature of the work on which the Corps was employed; and that he believes an agreement was made between Sir J. Maxwell and the General Officer Commanding-in-Chief of the Mediterranean Force. He also stated that the terms, so far as he made them, were defined in writing to the War Office in a letter at the beginning of April, 1915, as 1s. a day and khaki uniform, without any other conditions. The letter mentioned is one from Sir John Maxwell, of April 10th, 1915. The War Office have not been able to find it, but we are informed by General Headquarters in Egypt that it contained no mention of gratuities or pensions.

We referred Captain Trumpeldor's evidence to Sir John Maxwell and received in answer a letter in which he stated:

> My staff officer was Captain [now Lieutenant-Colonel] Holdich, DSO, and he drew
> up the terms of service. As far as my recollection goes Colonel Patterson has
> correctly stated the case. The terms of service of the men must be available in Egypt;
> they accepted the conditions and were taken on the strength of the Mediterranean
> Expeditionary Force.

On receiving this letter we communicated with Lieutenant-Colonel Holdich, and received the answer mentioned above.

Some of the Corps were killed and wounded, and a question as to the payment of pensions arose. In August, 1915, Sir John Maxwell wrote to the War Office:

> Although no promise or agreement of any sort was made regarding pensions, the
> men were evidently quite under the impression that in case of their death, pensions
> or compensation of some sort would be granted to their widows.

He recommended the payment of a gratuity in lieu of a pension, owing to the difficulties that might arise in the payment of pensions.

In September, 1915, he again wrote to the War Office and explained that the men were not attested [enlisted], but had entered into a voluntary agreement to serve at the pay of ls. a day, their families being maintained in refuge camps during their absence. He concluded: "No authorised mention of pension was made to them before joining, but they undoubtedly consider themselves eligible for the same consideration as soldiers," and again recommended gratuities rather than pensions.

Authority has been obtained from the Treasury to issue gratuities to the Zion Mule Corps men if disabled or to their dependants if they die.

Some of the men sent a petition to Lieutenant-Colonel Patterson complaining that they only received gratuities instead of pensions, and said that it was not fair after what had been said to them when they joined.

We suggest for the favourable consideration of the War Office the question whether, under the circumstances, the men of this Corps should not be treated as to pensions similarly to British soldiers regularly enlisted.

GENERAL REVIEW

Before setting out the conclusions to which we have come, it seems desirable briefly to review the salient features of the Dardanelles Expedition in their broad military aspect. We would first refer to the paper on the possibility of a joint naval and military attack upon the Dardanelles, drawn up by the General Staff at the War Office for the consideration of the Committee of Imperial Defence and dated December 19th, 1906, in which the following statement appears:

> The successful conclusion of a military enterprise directed against the Gallipoli Peninsula must hinge upon the ability of the Fleet not only to dominate the Turkish defences with gun fire, and crush their field troops during that period of helplessness which exists while an army is in actual process of disembarkation, but also to cover the advance of the troops once ashore until they could gain a firm foothold, and establish themselves upon the high ground in rear of the coast defences of the Dardanelles. However brilliant as a combination of war and, however fruitful in its consequences such an operation would be, were it crowned with success, the General Staff, in view of the risks involved, are not prepared to recommend its being attempted.

These words were written before the recent development of deep trenches flanked by hidden machine guns, concealed howitzer batteries, and the other appliances of modern defensive warfare. Sir John de Robeck pointed out to Sir Ian Hamilton at their first interview on March 17th, 1915, that the peninsula was rapidly being fortified, that all the landing places were now defended by lines of trenches and effectively commanded by field guns and howitzers which could not be located from the sea, that the Turks possessed searchlights of the latest pattern which were skilfully handled, and that their troops were so ably disposed and heavily entrenched that they had not much to fear from the flat trajectory guns of the Navy. Sir John de Robeck subsequently sent a telegram on May 9th, 1915, to the Admiralty, in which he remarked:

> The Navy is of small assistance when it is a matter of trenches and machine guns, and the check of the Army is due to these factors.

It will be seen that the condition which the General Staff had laid down in 1906 as being essential to the success of a military enterprise on the Gallipoli Peninsula was incapable of fulfilment; and though Sir John de Robeck's views about naval gunfire were of great importance, we cannot find that they were taken into serious consideration or communicated to the War Office.

Landings took place at Helles and Anzac with disappointing results. The troops not only suffered heavy loss during disembarkation, but subsequently were unable to advance beyond a short distance from the beach, or to establish themselves on the high ground which the Turks had occupied and entrenched. Our forces on the peninsula were in the position of isolated garrisons confined to small areas on the fringe of the shore, and engaged in trench warfare against an enemy possessing freedom of movement, advantages of ground, and the power of concentration and rapid reinforcement. Our garrisons fought bravely and lost heavily, but were unable to make any substantial advance.

Sir Ian Hamilton made an effort to extricate his troops from the trench warfare in which they were entangled by means of the combined operations at the beginning of August. These operations failed, partly because the Turks were too strong, partly because some of our troops and their leaders were unequal to the task assigned them, partly through shortage of water, and partly because the plan was defective. The descriptions of the ground on the northern and north-western slopes of Sari Bahr, and of the hills to the north and east of Suvla Bay, lead us to the conclusion that in the plan of operations too little importance was attached to natural difficulties. We doubt whether it was prudent or advantageous to order night advances through so difficult a country, especially when no complete preliminary reconnaissance had been or could have been made. In hardly any case, either at Anzac or Suvla, were the troops able to reach the specified objectives at or near the time mentioned in the plan.

Thus from the beginning the execution of the plan was delayed, and this delay caused a loss of cohesion and co-operation among the attacking units. In spite of heat, want of water and difficulties of ground, the troops with very few exceptions appear to have fought well and in some instances heroically; but after successive nights and days of strenuous effort they became exhausted and in urgent need of rest and reorganisation. The losses, too, had been so heavy that without large reinforcements nothing further could be attempted. Even with large reinforcements it had become increasingly evident that no substantial success could be achieved without an overwhelming preponderance of high angle and high explosive fire upon the Turkish entrenchments which confronted our positions on the shore.

Viewed as a military enterprise which was undertaken not as a surprise, but after ample warning had been given to the enemy of the probability of a land attack, we are of the opinion that from the outset the risks of failure attending the expedition outweighed its chances of success. The conditions of the problem, so far as we can judge, were not fully investigated in the first instance by competent experts, and no correct appreciation of the nature and difficulties of the task involved was arrived at. In the absence of such appreciation the authorities responsible for the expedition confidently expected that military action on the peninsula would be short and decisive and, that after the Turkish defences had been destroyed and the Turkish guns dismounted, the force which had been landed would be available for such operations in the vicinity of Constantinople as might seem appropriate.

The strength of the opposition to our landing on the peninsula and the failure of our troops to make any material impression on the Turkish entrenchments which hemmed them in came, therefore, as a surprise. The heavy losses and the repeated checks that were experienced up to the end of July caused the authorities considerable anxiety, but they were naturally reluctant to abandon a project, the realisation of which would have had such far-reaching effects. The failure of the combined attack early in August, from which much had been hoped and for which large reinforcements had been despatched from England, was a severe disappointment to the Government and the country. Doubts arose as to the ultimate success of the expedition, and alternative courses of action came under consideration. It was open to the Government, if the requisite resources in the way of men, guns, and munitions were forthcoming, promptly to strengthen the Expeditionary Force to such an extent as would enable it to drive the Turks out of the peninsula, or at least to attempt to do so. Or our garrisons on the shore of the peninsula might be maintained in the positions they were then occupying until the spring of 1916, provided that the Turks did not bring heavy guns into play and render these positions untenable; or steps might be taken for the evacuation of the peninsula before the winter set in.

There was much divergence of opinion in regard to these different courses, the General Staff at the War Office, which by this time was in process of resuscitation, being strongly in favour of evacuation. To Sir Ian Hamilton such a step as evacuation was unthinkable, and he informed Lord Kitchener accordingly. On October 11th Lord Kitchener also told the Dardanelles Committee that in his opinion the abandonment of the Gallipoli Peninsula would be disastrous. On the other hand, Sir Charles Monro strongly urged its expediency and feasibility, and this view, though at first distasteful to Lord Kitchener, was afterwards accepted by him. At last the Government resolved to withdraw from the peninsula. We think that this was a wise and courageous decision. It was generally recognised that the evacuation would in all probability involve heavy loss in men and material. Besides this, stress had been laid on the irreparable damage to our prestige in the Eastern world which would attend our abandonment of the expedition. Fortunately, however, in the result our losses proved to be inappreciable and hitherto our prestige appears to have remained unimpaired.

It has been represented in some of the evidence which has come before us that from a military point of view the Dardanelles Expedition, even if unsuccessful, was justified by the fact that it neutralised or contained a large number of Turkish troops who otherwise would have been free to operate elsewhere. Lord Kitchener estimated this number as being nearly 300,000. But in containing the Turkish force we employed on the peninsula and at Lemnos and Imbros 385,700 officers and soldiers, besides Indian soldiers— a total of at least 400,000. Our casualties amounted to 31,389 killed, 78,749 wounded and 9,708 missing, making a total of 119,846. The expedition also involved heavy financial expenditure and the employment of a considerable naval force and of a large amount of merchant shipping.

Taking these factors into consideration, we do not think that from a military standpoint our gain in one direction compensated for our losses in other directions. On the other hand, certain important political advantages were secured.

Our attention has been called to the fact that in our first report, we quoted an extract from a statement made to us by Mr Churchill in which he referred to the changed attitude of Lord Fisher towards the operations at the Dardanelles. Mr Churchill's statement was in fact given as relating not to the period "shortly after January 13th" but to a much later period.

While we gladly make this correction, we wish to add that the conclusions stated are in our opinion established by the evidence and are in no way vitiated [undermined] by this correction.

We regret that the official duties of Mr Fisher as High Commissioner of Australia became latterly so exacting as to deprive us to a large extent of his help. For this reason, as explained in his separate memorandum, he considers it inadvisable to sign the report.

It will be noticed that Sir Thomas Mackenzie has added a memorandum dealing with certain aspects of the inquiry on which he takes a stronger view than the general body of the Commissioners.

GENERAL CONCLUSIONS

We think that, when it was decided to undertake an important military expedition to the Gallipoli Peninsula, sufficient consideration was not given to the measures necessary to carry out such an expedition with success. We have already pointed out that it had been apparent in February, 1915, that serious military operations might be necessary. Under these circumstances we think that the conditions of a military attack on the peninsula should have been studied and a general plan prepared by the Chief of the Imperial General Staff, Sir James Wolfe Murray, special attention being paid to the probable effect of naval gun-fire in support of the troops; and that it was the duty of the Secretary of State for War to ensure that this was done.

We think that the difficulties of the operations were much underestimated. At the outset all decisions were taken and all provisions based on the assumption that, if a landing were effected, the resistance would be slight and the advance rapid. We can see no sufficient ground for this assumption. The short naval bombardment in November, 1914, had given the Turks warning of a possible attack, and the naval operations in February and March of 1915 led naturally to a great strengthening of the Turkish defences. The Turks were known to be led by German officers, and there was no reason to think that they would not fight well, especially in defensive positions. These facts had been reported by Admiral de Robeck and Sir Ian Hamilton.

We think that the position which, in fact, existed after the first attacks in April and the early days of May should have been regarded from the outset as possible and the requisite means of meeting it considered. This would have made it necessary to examine and decide whether the demands of such extended operations could be met consistently with our obligations in other theatres of war. In fact those obligations made it impossible in May, June, and

July to supply the forces with the necessary drafts, gun ammunition, high explosives and other modern appliances of war.

We are of the opinion that, with the resources then available, success in the Dardanelles, if possible, was only possible upon condition that the Government concentrated their efforts upon the enterprise and limited their expenditure of men and material in the Western theatre of war. This condition was never fulfilled.

After the failure of the attacks which followed the first landing there was undue delay in deciding upon the course to be pursued in the future. Sir Ian Hamilton's appreciation was forwarded on May 17th, 1915. It was not considered by the War Council or the Cabinet until June 7th. The reconstruction of the Government which took place at this most critical period was the main cause of the delay. As a consequence the despatch of the reinforcements asked for by Sir Ian Hamilton in his appreciation was postponed for six weeks.

We think that the plan of attack from Anzac and Suvla in the beginning of August was open to criticism. The country over which the attack had to be made was very difficult, especially at Anzac. In order to obtain if possible the element of surprise, the main advance of the Anzac force up the north-western spurs of Sari Bahr was undertaken at night, the risk of misdirection and failure being much increased thereby. The plan, however, was decided upon after a consideration of other plans, and with the concurrence of the Commander of the Anzac Corps, who had been in command since the first landing.

The operations at Suvla were a severe trial for a force consisting of troops who had never been under fire, but we think that after taking into consideration and making every allowance for the difficulties of the attack and the inexperience of the troops, the attack was not pressed as it should have been at Suvla on the 7th and 8th August, and we attribute this in a great measure to a want of determination and competence in the Divisional Commander and one of his Brigadiers. The leading of the 11th Division and the attached battalions of the 10th Division, which constituted the main body of the attack, was not satisfactory. As explained previously, the orders given by General Hammersley were confused and the work of his staff defective. Major-General Hammersley's health had in the past been such that it was dangerous to select him for a divisional command in the field, although he seemed to have recovered. We think that the defects that we have mentioned in his leading probably arose from this cause. General Sitwell, the senior Brigade Commander, did not, in our opinion, show sufficient energy and decision.

Sir Frederick Stopford was hampered by the want of effective leadership referred to above, and the inexperience of his troops, but we do not think he took sufficient means to inform himself of the progress of operations. On August 7th, when he became aware that the troops had not advanced as rapidly as had been intended, we think that he should have asked for some explanation from General Hammersley. In that case he would have been informed of the difference which had arisen between General Sitwell and General Hill, and of General Sitwell's lack of vigour and energy in leading. We think that at this point his intervention was needed.

We think that he and his staff were partly responsible for the failure to supply the troops with water on August 7th and 8th. Our detailed conclusions on the water supply will be found below.

We cannot endorse Sir Ian Hamilton's condemnation of the orders given by Sir Frederick Stopford on the morning of August 8th, 1915, whether the account of them given in Sir Ian Hamilton's despatch or that in Sir Frederick Stopford's report to him be accepted. According to the evidence of Sir Bryan Mahon and General Hammersley, they were not deterred from advancing by those orders.

On the evening of August 8th we think that Sir Frederick Stopford's difficulties were increased by the intervention of Sir Ian Hamilton. Sir Ian Hamilton seems to have considered Sir Frederick Stopford lacking in energy in the operations between August 9th and August 15th. As this opinion is based more upon general conduct than upon any specific acts or omissions, we are not in a position to pronounce upon it. We realise, however, that importance attaches to the impressions of a Commander-in-Chief on such a subject.

As regards Sir Ian Hamilton it is inevitable that the capabilities of a commander in war should be judged by the results he achieves, even though, if these results are disappointing, his failure may be due to causes for which he is only partially responsible.

In April, 1915, Sir Ian Hamilton succeeded in landing his troops at the places which he had chosen; but the operations that were intended immediately to follow the landing were abruptly checked owing to a miscalculation of the strength of the Turkish defences and the fighting qualities of the Turkish troops. This rebuff should have convinced Sir Ian Hamilton that the Turkish entrenchments were skilfully disposed and well armed, and that naval gun-fire was ineffective against trenches and entanglements of the modern type. We doubt, however, whether the failure of these operations sufficiently impressed Sir Ian Hamilton and the military authorities at home with the serious nature of the opposition likely to be encountered.

During May, June, and July severe fighting took place, but its results were not commensurate with the efforts made and the losses incurred.

During July a plan of combined operations was elaborated, which was carried into effect early in August. Sir Ian Hamilton was confident of success, but was again baffled by the obstinacy of the Turkish resistance. Moreover, the failure of night advances in a difficult and unexplored country, which formed part of the plan, led to heavy casualties and temporarily disorganised the forces employed.

Sir Ian Hamilton was relieved of his command on October 15th.

We recognise Sir Ian Hamilton's personal gallantry and energy, his sanguine disposition, and his determination to win at all costs. We recognise also that the task entrusted to him was one of extreme difficulty, the more so as the authorities at home at first misconceived the nature and duration of the operations, and afterwards were slow to realise that to drive the Turks out of their entrenchments and occupy the heights commanding the Straits was a formidable and hazardous enterprise which demanded a concentration of force and effort. It must further be borne in mind that Lord Kitchener, whom Sir Ian Hamilton appears to have regarded as a Commander-in-Chief rather than as a Secretary of State, pressed upon him the paramount importance, if it were by any means possible, of carrying out the task assigned to him.

Though from time to time Sir Ian Hamilton represented the need of drafts, reinforcements, guns and munitions, which the Government found it impossible to supply, he was nevertheless always ready to renew the struggle with the resources at his disposal, and to the last was confident of success. For this it would be hard to blame him; but viewing the expedition in the light of events it would, in our opinion, have been well had he examined the situation as disclosed by the first landings in a more critical spirit, impartially weighed the probabilities of success and failure, having regard to the resources in men and material which could be placed at his disposal, and submitted to the Secretary of State for War a comprehensive statement of the arguments for and against a continuance of the operations.

The failure at Anzac was due mainly to the difficulties of the country and the strength of the enemy. The failure at Suvla also prevented any pressure being put upon the Turkish force in that direction, and success at Suvla might have lessened the resistance at Anzac.

We think that after the attacks ending on August 9th had failed, the operations contemplated could not have been successfully carried out without large reinforcements. The fighting after General de Lisle replaced Sir Frederick Stopford was really of a defensive character.

We think that after the advice of Sir Charles Monro had been confirmed by Lord Kitchener the decision to evacuate should have been taken at once. We recognise, however, that the question of evacuation was connected with other questions of high policy which do not appear to us to come within the scope of our inquiry.

We think that the decision to evacuate when taken was right.

We think that the operations were hampered throughout by the failure to supply sufficient artillery and munitions, and to keep the original formations up to strength by the provision of adequate drafts as well as reinforcements. In our opinion this was not owing to any neglect on the part of the Heads of Departments charged with such provision, but to the demands proving much larger than was expected when the operations were undertaken and to demands which had to be met in other theatres of war.

On the other hand, a considerable amount of artillery was available in Egypt and at Mudros for the Suvla operations, but it was not utilised.

Many minor frontal attacks were made without adequate artillery preparation, which produced little or no material advantage. Evidence was given that these attacks entailed an unnecessary loss of life. Without a more intimate knowledge of the locality and conditions than it is possible for us to obtain, we cannot express an opinion as to whether it was right to undertake such attacks. We think that the evidence disproves the allegation made before us that useless attacks were made because of the neglect on the part of superior commanders and staff officers to visit and inspect the trenches and positions.

There was full co-operation between the Navy and Army and the two services worked well and harmoniously together.

WATER SUPPLY

As regards the landings at Helles and Anzac in April, 1915, and the subsequent operations up to the end of July, we consider that the water arrangements at Helles were satisfactory, but that the daily allowance at Anzac was barely sufficient.

As regards the operations at Anzac in August, 1915, we find that, owing in some measure to the breakdown of a pumping engine and the collision of a vessel carrying 80,000 gallons of water with another vessel, there was a serious shortage of water, the allowance to each man being restricted to one pint a day. This may not have checked the action of the troops, but, as stated earlier, it precluded the sending of reserves when the attack was brought to a standstill.

As regards the landing at Suvla in August, 1915, we consider that:

(1) General Headquarters undertook the responsibility of arranging for the supply of sea-borne water and for the necessary equipment for its storage and distribution.

(2) Sufficient attention was not paid by Sir Frederick Stopford and his Administrative Staff to these arrangements, which should have been more thoroughly discussed between the Administrative Staff at General Headquarters and the Corps Administrative Staff before the landing. For the absence of such adequate consultation neither staff can be exonerated from responsibility.

(3) Besides the foregoing arrangements the questions which demanded special consideration on the part of Sir Frederick Stopford and his Administrative Staff were the action to be taken on the spot for the reception, storage and distribution of sea-borne water, including the provision of working parties to pump the water from the lighters; the expedients to be adopted in the event of delay in the landing of the pack mules, together with the filled water bags which they were to carry; and the instructions to be given for the discovery and development of local sources of supply.

It appears to us that these questions were not sufficiently considered, and that Major-General Poett, Deputy Adjutant and Quartermaster-General of the IXth Corps, must be held to be primarily responsible for the lack of due consideration.

(4) The water shortage at Suvla abated after August 8th, but this fact does not excuse the want of organisation and prevision [foresight] which was apparent during the first two days, and which largely contributed to the inaction of the troops on the second day, and to the failure of the operations.

We are of the opinion that throughout the operations the Navy carried out their duties with regard to the supply of sea-borne water in an efficient manner, and were always ready to render any assistance in their power.

As regards the operations generally, and having in view the vital importance of water on the Gallipoli Peninsula, we consider that the question of water supply would have been more efficiently handled throughout if, following the analogy of food supply, a staff officer with the requisite qualifications had been appointed Director of Water Supply under the Quartermaster-General at General Headquarters, with a Deputy Director on the staff of each Corps Commander and an Assistant Director on the staff of each Divisional Commander.

FOOD

We think that, on the whole, the supply of food to the troops in Gallipoli was satisfactory.

MEDICAL

The provision for the evacuation of the wounded, especially in the matter of hospital ships, proved insufficient to meet the emergencies which actually arose. We think that, if the operations to be undertaken in landing on the peninsula had been considered before the expedition started and a general plan prepared, further provision of hospital ships might, and probably would, have been made.

We do not think that the Director of Medical Services, Surgeon-General Birrell, before leaving England had any opportunity of estimating the number of hospital ships required, as he did not know what operations were contemplated.

We think that the separation of the Administrative Staff, including the Deputy Adjutant-General and Director of Medical Services, from the rest of the Headquarters Staff during the time immediately preceding the landing was a mistake, and that it would have been better if the Director of Medical Services had been kept more fully informed of the operations which were proposed. The time was very short in which to make preparations, and we doubt if it was then possible to obtain a sufficient number of hospital ships to accommodate the casualties which actually occurred. If Surgeon-General

Birrell had been able to discuss matters with the General Staff he might have seen the necessity of, and been able to obtain, a fuller supply of appliances and equipment for the transports.

We think, however, that it would have been well if, while in Egypt, where he was arranging for hospital accommodation on a large scale, he had made requisition for appliances such as would probably be required for even the less serious cases on the transports, such as bed pans, blankets, pillows, and clothing. We recognise, however, that at that time he was separated from General Headquarters, and therefore not possessed of adequate information as to the intended operations.

The scheme of evacuation drawn up by the Director of Medical Services was based on an estimate of casualties which was approximately correct, and would probably have worked satisfactorily if the anticipation of a rapid advance after the landing had been fulfilled. The failure of the scheme was mainly due to the fact that no substantial advance was effected, and that no hospitals could therefore be established on the land. This necessitated the immediate evacuation by sea of all casualties without any possibility of separating the serious cases from those of a slighter nature. The transports or black ships were therefore used for cases for which they were not intended, and for which they were not adequately staffed or equipped.

In these circumstances the greater part of the sufferings of the wounded in the first days after the landing seem to us to have been inevitable, but there appears to have been some want of organisation in the control of the boats and barges carrying wounded to the hospital ships and transports, which occasioned delay in their embarkation.

For the dislocation of the arrangements for evacuation, owing to the non-fulfilment of the expectations of the military authorities, the Director of Medical Services cannot be held responsible. He could not do otherwise than be guided by the views entertained by the Commander-in-Chief, and conveyed to the latter's subordinates in the operation orders and instructions for the landings issued by General Headquarters. It may indeed be contended that a prudent administrator, even though assured by a superior military authority of the probability of success, would do well not to leave out of account the possibility of failure; but to be prepared alike for either contingency demands a flexibility of organisation and an adaptability of resources, which in war are seldom attainable.

After the first two or three weeks, until the heavy fighting in August, there was an improvement in the condition of the transports, though some of them continued to be unsatisfactory. The transports required close supervision, which was, however, much hampered by the want of means of communication between the several ships and between the ships and shore.

The scheme for the evacuation of the wounded in the August operations was based upon an approximately correct estimate of casualties, and the supply of hospital ships was much larger than at the first landing. On the whole, this scheme worked well, though again there were cases in which the transports were not satisfactory and the organisation for transferring the wounded to the ships was imperfect.

After the middle of May the evacuation was made more difficult by the presence of enemy submarines. The transports were then unable to come to the beaches, the wounded being conveyed to them on trawlers and mine-sweepers, some of which were not suitable for their accommodation.

The field ambulances and clearing-stations were, on the whole, efficient, considering the great difficulties under which the work in them had to be done.

The executive work of the medical officers and staff of the Royal Army Medical Corps and the Dominion Forces, and of the physicians and surgeons who placed their services at the disposal of the War Office, was performed with great energy, courage, and skill under very trying conditions.

The supply of medicines and other medical requisites was, on the whole, adequate, though at times there was a shortage of some drugs at some places. The food also was on the whole satisfactory, but at times it was not possible to give the sick and wounded all the variety of food which was desired, and at times the supply of water was insufficient.

The difficulties under which the evacuation of the wounded was carried out, especially in the early part of the operations, were exceptional and not easily surmountable. We think that in some cases there was a want of organisation and supervision. The Director of Medical Services, Surgeon-General Birrell, did his best; we are of the opinion, however, that he was not equal to the task of grappling with the exceptional conditions which arose.

Great help was given by the naval surgeons on the transports as well as on the trawlers and sweepers, and they were always ready to do everything in their power. It was not, however, possible to employ them on the transports during their voyage to Alexandria or Malta, as they could not leave their ships for an indefinite time. The naval officers concerned in the evacuation of the wounded gave every assistance and rendered excellent service.

We have pleasure in recording our obligations to the Foreign Office, the Admiralty, the War Office, and the secretarial staff of the Committee of Imperial Defence, who have given us full information and every assistance in their power.

Finally we wish to express our high appreciation of the services rendered by our Secretary, Sir Grimwood Mears, to whom we are greatly indebted for the ability, tact, and industry which he has displayed throughout the course of the inquiry.

W. PICKFORD
NICHOLSON
W. H. MAY
THOMAS MACKENZIE
STEPHEN L. GWYNN
WALTER ROCHE

GRIMWOOD MEARS
Secretary
December 4th 1917

SUPPLEMENTARY REPORT
BY THE HONOURABLE SIR
THOMAS MACKENZIE, KCMG

It is to be regretted that, for diplomatic reasons, a full report of the evidence cannot be given to the public, as the narrative must necessarily be inadequate. For this reason, although I am substantially in agreement with the findings of the Commission, I desire to supplement some of the conclusions reached by my colleagues, and in addition I hold stronger views upon certain of the findings which I feel it my duty to put forward.

Preparations for the campaign

In my opinion, which I express with all deference, the forcing of the Dardanelles was a practicable proposition had the authorities approached the problem with a recognition of the nature and extent of the difficulties which confronted them, and made adequate provision and exhibited the necessary strength of purpose to carry the operations through to the desired end. History has demonstrated, and expert opinion supported, the view that a combined naval and military attack would ultimately offer the only chance of a favourable issue. The authorities should, I consider, have launched this combined attack only after thorough preparation, and I regard the preliminary bombardment of the outer forts on November 3rd, 1914—ordered by the Admiralty without consultation with the War Council—as an almost irreparable mistake. Its effect was to draw the attention of the Turks to the possibility of an attack in force on the peninsula, and there is no doubt it prompted them to make good use of the time which intervened between the November bombardment and the military landing on April 25th, 1915, in the way of improving their defences, etc.

Regarding the conduct of the military operations as a whole, it will be asked: "Was Sir Ian Hamilton the right man to command the expedition?" This question, in my opinion, we shall never be able to answer because he was hurriedly despatched, imperfectly instructed, and inadequately provided with men, artillery and munitions. Later on the deficiency in men was rectified, but although Lord Kitchener had said this was a young man's war, some generals were sent out to Sir Ian Hamilton who were unequal to the task. In this connection, let us glance for a moment at the methods of the War Office. General Sir James Wolfe Murray was the Chief of the Imperial General Staff. He was also a member of the War Council, and though he attended their meetings he expressed no opinions and tendered no advice, nor did he clearly understand that a decision was arrived at on January 13th to prepare for a naval attack on the Dardanelles in February.

Questioned later on as to whether it was not his duty, when the amphibious attack was decided on, to instruct the General Staff as to the preparation of plans, he admitted that under ordinary circumstances it was; and when asked to account for not doing so, he said in effect that he was overshadowed by Lord Kitchener.

Such a state of affairs at Headquarters did not presage a favourable inauguration or effective prosecution of the campaign, and the following statement of the position appears to me to be unassailable:

The Cabinet, having determined upon amphibious operations against Constantinople, necessarily left the preparations for and conduct of the military attack to the War Department. That system seems to be at fault which permitted:

(a) The outbreak of war to find the Imperial General Staff unprepared for operations against the Dardanelles and the Bosphorus—always of vital strategic interest for the British Empire in the East.

(b) The General Staff to remain inactive in that respect after August 4th, 1914.

(c) The General Staff to allow Sir Ian Hamilton to proceed to the Mediterranean without either a worked-out plan of attack or such primary requirements as verified or complete maps of the peninsula.

(d) The General Staff, notwithstanding their knowledge of the difficulties and lack of preparation, to silently acquiesce in this state of affairs.

To this breakdown of the War Office system on the testing ground of war may, in my opinion, be traced some of the vital factors of the Gallipoli disaster.

The attack at Suvla

The brief period from August 6th to 10th was, to my mind, the vital time in the history of the later Dardanelles operations, for on the wise and determined use of those few days depended the success or failure of the campaign.

The objective was the range of hills controlling the Straits and the Narrows, the highest point of which was about 1,000 feet, three miles distant from the disembarkation point, the first two miles being easy, open country, the last mile rough and scrub-covered. Few Turks were then in the locality—estimates varied from 2,000 to 4,000—and prompt, decisive action was absolutely essential.

By daylight on August 7th General Stopford had landed over 13,000 men, and by the evening of that day 26,750 men. But the golden opportunity was thrown away by him and some of his officers, and the necessary swift advance—which military and naval witnesses thought quite possible—was not delivered, so that the Turks had time to bring up their reinforcements.

During the first four days, but mainly on the 9th and 10th August, General Stopford suffered 400 officer casualties and about 8,000 men killed and wounded. The failure at Suvla he attributes, not to the initial opposition of the Turks, but largely to the lack of water. He maintains that he relied on arrangements made by General Headquarters for the supply of water; but while that might have relieved him of the administrative work, it did not, to my mind, free him from the responsibility of seeing that the arrangements were carried out, and there is no doubt that the responsibility of distributing the water to his troops, if not of having it landed, rested with General Stopford and his subordinates. Nevertheless, until August 8th he took no active personal interest in this all-important question.

Captain Carver, of the Royal Navy, did his best to encourage prompt action, but this was regarded by the military as undue interference, and he was withdrawn. No one seems to have been immediately answerable for supplying water, though undoubtedly General Poett's duties included its distribution. Except for General Sitwell's men, the troops were suffering severely from thirst, which impeded their operations. At the same time a barge of water was lying stranded within 100 yards of the beach, and the maps, captured from the Turks, showed that there were wells and springs within a quarter of a mile. We have General de Lisle's statement that:

> There were wells within a quarter of mile of the shore, which I had opened out. On the hill Kiretch Tepe Sirt there were two wells 400 feet higher than the sea, but on this side, between Kiretch Tepe Sirt and the Salt Lake, there were as many wells as you liked to dig.

Colonel Aspinall, too, states that he saw "a tremendous lot of water trickling down from the cliffs," and other witnesses declare that water was to be found. Yet General Poett neither made an attempt to procure water from the barge, nor to institute any search for water ashore. When questioned as to why he took no action, he disclaimed responsibility, contending that it was the duty of the Navy to get the water ashore, and of the Divisional Commanders to find it on land.

It is true that Sir Ian Hamilton cabled to General Stopford on the evening of August 7th–8th an appreciation of his work, but, as he afterwards explained, this cable was despatched before he visited Suvla, and when he was under the impression that everything was going well in connection with the operations.

Operations at Helles

In reference to Helles, attention should, I think, be directed to the evidence of some of the witnesses as to the frittering away of life through frontal attacks repeatedly carried out by General Hunter-Weston, in spite, it is alleged, of the absence of adequate artillery preparation and the lack of promise of substantial results. Lord Nicholson questioned Lieutenant-Colonel Wilson upon this matter, saying, "I suggest that in order to evade, so to speak, the necessity for an adequate artillery preparation, or the provision of artillery and ammunition, lives had to be sacrificed."

Colonel Wilson answered, "Yes."

Lord Nicholson continued, "In order to make good the deficiency of artillery and ammunition—that is the upshot of it?"

Colonel Wilson replied, "Yes, lives had to be sacrificed."

Lord Nicholson asked, "And almost with futility?"

"Yes, that is what I mean," said Colonel Wilson.

General Cox, too, considered that these frontal attacks fulfilled no useful function whatever, as at Helles the situation was hopeless tactically; but in reply to this, General Hunter-Weston stated that such attacks as were made were made for some reason which may not have been known to General Cox.

General Sir Ian Hamilton admitted to Lord Nicholson that lives were used instead of shells. He said:

> The vital thing was to make good, and to make good we ought to have had ample artillery, especially howitzers. We had not, and there was nothing for it but to try and get on, as you say, by a sacrifice of human life.

This matter is so serious that it seems to me to call for further enquiry, and this I recommend should be carried out by military experts.

Evidence of witnesses

With reference to the evidence tendered, whilst undoubtedly it was, in many respects, full and complete, yet one felt that some of the officers called as witnesses could have disclosed a great deal more than they did. Probably their reticence arose from a sense of loyalty to the Service and a disinclination to say anything against their comrades. As a consequence of this and the natural desire of the Commission to give those chiefly concerned the benefit of any doubt, some of the conclusions arrived at may be somewhat different from what they otherwise might have been.

Treatment of wounded

Until August, 1915, the arrangements for dealing with the transport of the wounded were in a very unsatisfactory state, and, indeed, the medical side of the campaign does not seem to have ever been thoroughly thought out. The treatment of the wounded ashore on the peninsula appears to have been as satisfactory as circumstances would permit, but in the transport of men to the ships and overseas many of the complaints were justifiable. The Medical Authorities contend that from the information supplied by the military commanders, they expected the Turks would be driven back and room would be made for establishing hospitals ashore. This, however, presupposed success, but better provision ought also to have been made for the contingency of failure.

A great strain was imposed on the arrangements— hospital ships were insufficient, and troop ships had to be rapidly converted into carriers and ambulance vessels; during the early days of the campaign undoubtedly a great deal of acute suffering resulted to the wounded from this cause. The extemporised [hastily prepared] hospital ships were insufficiently staffed, and there were not nearly enough medical officers of junior ranks, or female nurses, to attend to the patients. Although the medical personnel did their utmost, we hear of cases where men had to shift for themselves [manage] as best they could, and in fact some were left during the voyage to Alexandria in their first field dressings. General Maxwell testified that on some of the black ships the wounded were exposed to the sun and heat, with nothing to eat or drink, for 60 or 70 hours. Sir Frederick Treves gave evidence as to the absence of arrangements for the despatch of hospital ships, and the want of decision as to their destination.

There was also a general shortage of pillows, mattresses, fresh clothing, etc., and in some instances medical supplies and appliances were sadly lacking. In addition, the sanitary arrangements on the converted trawlers were lamentably deficient: the almost entire absence of such conveniences as bed pans, for instance, reduced the wounded to a deplorable condition.

That the medical arrangements must have been lamentably inadequate and the organisation seriously defective is confirmed by the fact that Surgeon-General Howse, VC, was impelled to give the following matured opinion:

> That he personally would recommend his Government, when this war is over, under no conceivable conditions to trust to the medical arrangements that may be made by the Imperial Authorities for the care of the Australian sick and wounded.

This is doubtless a strongly expressed view, and I think it is beyond question that a great improvement has been brought about since that time; but it is impossible to hold Surgeon-General Birrell free from a great deal of the responsibility for the serious condition of affairs to which Surgeon-General Howse and other witnesses drew attention.

The *Saturnia* case

Then we have the terrible story of the *Saturnia*—a most extraordinary indication of the absence of organisation. Father Barry first drew attention to the fact that 800 wounded men had been placed on that vessel, and the conditions which he brought to light as existing for a time, approximate to some of the revelations in connection with the Mesopotamian Medical Service. As the evidence stands I am unable to accept Colonel Maher's statement, sent by cable to the Committee, as giving an accurate description of the circumstances surrounding the case. I believe that Admiral Keyes, Fleet-Surgeon Levick, and Major Purchas gave the Commission the correct account of the conditions prevailing, and I concur in the suggestion that this matter should be further investigated. In this connection I should like to refer to the excellent work done by Fleet-Surgeon Levick and Major Purchas, and to the straightforward manner in which the evidence of all these officers was tendered.

The work of the Army

Coming now to the work of the troops, I endorse the Majority Report that the men fought bravely and often heroically; and although there were certain phases of the conduct of the operations which led to misfortune and entailed great suffering, it is gratifying to know that there were in the Army on the peninsula men whose actions have not been surpassed by any deeds performed by the British Army. This applies to officers, NCOs and men. In my opinion, the outstanding figure in the campaign is General Birdwood, although many approached him in the excellence of their work, and shared with him in patient endurance the long and trying period of the Gallipoli operations. I should like to draw attention to the concluding work of General Birdwood and of those serving under him, in connection with the evacuation.

The opinion of experts who had studied the situation was that the evacuation might cost anything from 20 to 40 per cent in personnel and *matériel* [equipment]. The total number of the force evacuated was 125,000 men, and the whole operation was successfully carried out without the loss of a single life, and with only three men wounded—an achievement surely unsurpassed in the annals of history.

Conclusion

The Dardanelles Campaign with all its distressing circumstances and disappointments is now past history, and, without doubt, under the vigorous direction of Sir William Robertson, the haphazard, uncertain methods have largely disappeared and a good deal of the inefficiency which formerly prevailed has been swept away. If, however, the result of our investigations should assist in the bringing about of such an improvement in organisation and management as will render impossible a recurrence of events as sad as those with which we have had to deal, the work of the Commission will not have been in vain.

THOS. MACKENZIE

BRITISH BATTLES OF WORLD WAR I, 1914–15

MILITARY DESPATCHES FROM THE COMMANDERS AT THE FRONT

CONTENTS

MAPS

When Britain declared war on Germany on 4th August 1914, the Germans had already begun their invasion of Belgium. The 100,000-strong British Expeditionary Force (BEF), under the general leadership of Sir John French, was soon mobilised, but unfortunately was far too small to stem the flow of the one-and-a-half-million Germans who were pouring into France. According to the German plan devised by Count Schlieffen, the German army was to sweep through Belgium and encircle Paris in one huge, pincer-like movement, thereby knocking France out of the war quite quickly. However, the German commander Helmuth von Moltke failed to adhere to the Schlieffen plan, partly because of the resistance shown by the BEF at Mons, and the determined counter-attack of the French and British forces at the battle of the Marne in September 1914.

The first part of this book reproduces the despatches that were written by Sir John French while at the front during the first nine months of the war. The later chapters are of the despatches written by generals involved in other parts of the globe where the British were engaged in combat at this time. These include the capture of a German cruiser off the Cocos Islands in the Indian Ocean, a description of a daring air raid on Friedrickshafen in Germany, and an account of the landing of the troops at Gallipoli in 1915.

Sketch map of the area covered by despatches (northern France and Belgium)

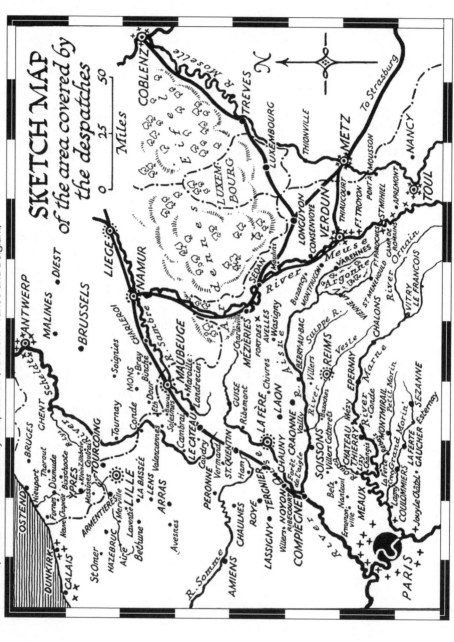

SKETCH MAP
of the area covered by
the despatches

Miles
0   25   50

MILITARY OPERATIONS IN NORTHERN FRANCE AND BELGIUM, AUGUST 1914 TO MAY 1915

MONS AND LE CATEAU, AUGUST 1914

From the Field Marshal Commanding in Chief, British Forces in the Field, to the Secretary of State for War

7th September, 1914

My Lord,

I have the honour to report the proceedings of the field force under my command up to the time of rendering this despatch.

The transport of the troops from England both by sea and by rail was effected in the best order and without a check. Each unit arrived at its destination in this country well within the scheduled time.

The concentration was practically complete on the evening of Friday, the 21st August, and I was able to make dispositions to move the force during Saturday, the 22nd, to positions I considered most favourable from which to commence operations which the French Commander-in-Chief, General Joffre, requested me to undertake in pursuance of his plans in prosecution of the campaign.

The line taken up extended along the line of the canal from Condé on the west, through Mons and Binche on the east. This line was taken up as follows:

From Condé to Mons inclusive was assigned to the Second Corps, and to the right of the Second Corps from Mons the First Corps was posted. The 5th Cavalry Brigade was placed at Binche.

In the absence of my Third Army Corps I desired to keep the Cavalry Division as much as possible as a reserve to act on my outer flank, or move in support of any threatened part of the line. The forward reconnaissance was

Mons and Le Cateau, 1914

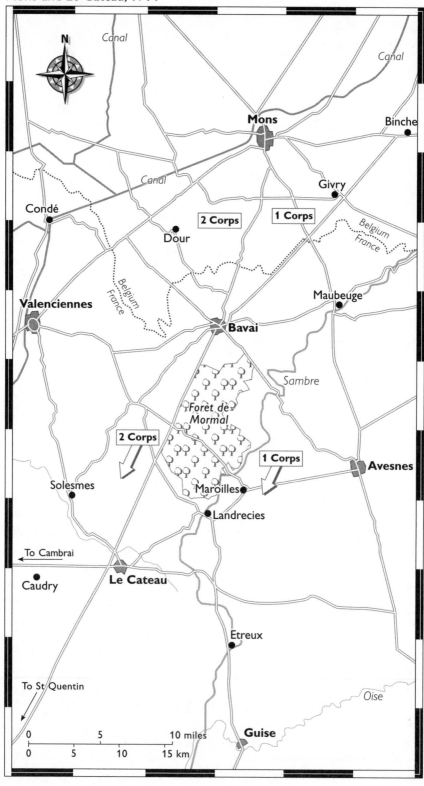

N

Canal

Canal

Mons

Binche

Givry

Canal

Condé

2 Corps

1 Corps

Belgium
France

Dour

Valenciennes

Belgium
France

Maubeuge

Bavai

Sambre

Forêt de
Mormal

2 Corps

1 Corps

Avesnes

Solesmes

Maroilles

Landrecies

To Cambrai

Caudry

Le Cateau

Etreux

To St Quentin

Oise

Guise

0   5   10 miles

0   5   10   15 km

entrusted to Brigadier-General Sir Philip Chetwode with the 5th Cavalry Brigade, but I directed General Allenby to send forward a few squadrons to assist in this work.

During the 22nd and 23rd these advanced squadrons did some excellent work, some of them penetrating as far as Soignies, and several encounters took place in which our troops showed to great advantage.

At 6 a.m., on August 23rd, I assembled the Commanders of the First and Second Corps and Cavalry Division at a point close to the position, and explained the general situation of the Allies, and what I understood to be General Joffre's plan. I discussed with them at some length the immediate situation in front of us.

From information I received from French Headquarters I understood that little more than one, or at most two, of the enemy's Army Corps, with perhaps one Cavalry Division, were in front of my position; and I was aware of no attempted outflanking movement by the enemy. I was confirmed in this opinion by the fact that my patrols encountered no undue opposition in their reconnoitring operations. The observation of my aeroplanes seemed also to bear out this estimate.

About 3 p.m. on Sunday, the 23rd, reports began coming in to the effect that the enemy was commencing an attack on the Mons line, apparently in some strength, but that the right of the position from Mons and Bray was being particularly threatened.

The Commander of the First Corps had pushed his flank back to some high ground south of Bray, and the 5th Cavalry Brigade evacuated Binche, moving slightly south: the enemy thereupon occupied Binche.

The right of the 3rd Division, under General Hamilton, was at Mons, which formed a somewhat dangerous salient; and I directed the Commander of the Second Corps to be careful not to keep the troops on this salient too long, but, if threatened seriously, to draw back the centre behind Mons. This was done before dark. In the meantime, about 5 p.m., I received a most unexpected message from General Joffre by telegraph, telling me that at least three German Corps, viz., a reserve corps, the 4th Corps and the 9th Corps, were moving on my position in front, and that the Second Corps was engaged in a turning movement from the direction of Tournay. He also informed me that the two reserve French divisions and the 5th French Army on my right were retiring, the Germans having on the previous day gained possession of the passages of the Sambre between Charleroi and Namur.

In view of the possibility of my being driven from the Mons position, I had previously ordered a position in rear to be reconnoitred. This position rested on the fortress of Maubeuge on the right and extended west to Jenlain, south-east of Valenciennes, on the left. The position was reported difficult to hold, because standing crops and buildings made the siting of trenches very difficult and limited the field of fire in many important localities. It nevertheless afforded a few good artillery positions.

When the news of the retirement of the French and the heavy German threatening on my front reached me, I endeavoured to confirm it by aeroplane reconnaissance; and as a result of this I determined to effect a retirement to the Maubeuge position at daybreak on the 24th.

A certain amount of fighting continued along the whole line throughout the night, and at daybreak on the 24th the 2nd Division from the neighbourhood of Harmignies made a powerful demonstration as if to retake Binche. This was supported by the artillery of both the 1st and 2nd Divisions, whilst the 1st Division took up a supporting position in the neighbourhood of Peissant. Under cover of this demonstration the Second Corps retired on the line Dour–Quarouble–Frameries. The 3rd Division on the right of the Corps suffered considerable loss in this operation from the enemy, who had retaken Mons.

The Second Corps halted on this line, where they partially entrenched themselves, enabling Sir Douglas Haig with the First Corps gradually to withdraw to the new position; and he effected this without much further loss, reaching the line Bavai–Maubeuge about 7 p.m. Towards midday the enemy appeared to be directing his principal effort against our left. I had previously ordered General Allenby with the Cavalry to act vigorously in advance of my left front and endeavour to take the pressure off.

About 7.30 a.m. General Allenby received a message from Sir Charles Fergusson, commanding 5th Division, saying that he was very hard pressed and in urgent need of support. On receipt of this message General Allenby drew in the Cavalry and endeavoured to bring direct support to the 5th Division.

During the course of this operation General De Lisle, of the 2nd Cavalry Brigade, thought he saw a good opportunity to paralyse the further advance of the enemy's infantry by making a mounted attack on his flank. He formed up and advanced for this purpose, but was held up by wire about 500 yards from his objective, and the 9th Lancers and 18th Hussars suffered severely in the retirement of the brigade.

The 19th Infantry Brigade, which had been guarding the Line of Communications, was brought up by rail to Valenciennes on the 22nd and 23rd. On the morning of the 24th they were moved out to a position south of Quarouble to support the left flank of the Second Corps. With the assistance of the cavalry Sir Horace Smith-Dorrien was enabled to effect his retreat to a new position; although, having two corps of the enemy on his front and one threatening his flank, he suffered great losses in doing so.

At nightfall the position was occupied by the Second Corps to the west of Bavai, the First Corps to the right. The right was protected by the fortress of Maubeuge, the left by the 19th Brigade in position between Jenlain and Bry, and the cavalry on the outer flank.

The French were still retiring, and I had no support except such as was afforded by the fortress of Maubeuge; and the determined attempts of the enemy to get round my left flank assured me that it was his intention to hem me against that place and surround me. I felt that not a moment must be lost in retiring to another position.

I had every reason to believe that the enemy's forces were somewhat exhausted, and I knew that they had suffered heavy losses. I hoped, therefore, that his pursuit would not be too vigorous to prevent me effecting my object. The operation, however, was full of danger and difficulty, not only owing to the very superior force in my front, but also to the exhaustion of the troops.

The retirement was recommenced in the early morning of the 25th to a position in the neighbourhood of Le Cateau, and rearguards were ordered to be clear of the Maubeuge–Bavai–Eth Road by 5.30 a.m.

Two cavalry brigades, with the divisional cavalry of the Second Corps, covered the movement of the Second Corps. The remainder of the Cavalry Division with the 19th Brigade, the whole under the command of General Allenby, covered the west flank.

The 4th Division commenced its detrainment at Le Cateau on Sunday, the 23rd, and by the morning of the 25th eleven battalions and a brigade of artillery with divisional staff were available for service.

I ordered General Snow to move out to take up a position with his right south of Solesmes, his left resting on the Cambrai–Le Cateau Road south of La Chaprie. In this position the division rendered great help to the effective retirement of the Second and First Corps to the new position. Although the troops had been ordered to occupy the Cambrai–Le Cateau–Landrecies position, and the ground had, during the 25th, been partially prepared and entrenched, I had grave doubts—owing to the information I received as to the accumulating strength of the enemy against me—as to the wisdom of standing there to fight.

Having regard to the continued retirement of the French on my right, my exposed left flank, the tendency of the enemy's western corps (II) to envelop me, and, more than all, the exhausted condition of the troops, I determined to make a great effort to continue the retreat till I could put some substantial obstacle, such as the Somme or the Oise, between my troops and the enemy, and afford the former some opportunity of rest and re-organisation. Orders were, therefore, sent to the Corps Commanders to continue their retreat as soon as they possibly could towards the general line Vermand–St Quentin–Ribemont. The cavalry, under General Allenby, were ordered to cover the retirement.

Throughout the 25th and far into the evening, the First Corps continued its march on Landrecies, following the road along the eastern border of the Forêt De Mormal, and arrived at Landrecies about 10 o'clock. I had intended that the corps should come further west so as to fill up the gap between Le Cateau and Landrecies, but the men were exhausted and could not get further in without rest.

The enemy, however, would not allow them this rest, and about 9.30 p.m. a report was received that the 4th Guards Brigade in Landrecies was heavily attacked by troops of the 9th German Army Corps who were coming through the forest on the north of the town. This brigade fought most gallantly and caused the enemy to suffer tremendous loss in issuing from the forest into the narrow streets of the town. The loss has been estimated from reliable sources at from 700 to 1,000. At the same time information reached me from Sir Douglas Haig that his 1st Division was also heavily engaged south and east of Maroilles. I sent urgent messages to the Commander of the two French Reserve Divisions on my right to come up to the assistance of the First Corps, which they eventually did. Partly owing to this assistance, but mainly to the skilful manner in which Sir Douglas Haig extricated his corps from an exceptionally difficult position in the darkness of the night, they were able at dawn to resume their march south towards Wessigny on Guise.

By about 6 p.m. the Second Corps had got into position with their right on Le Cateau, their left in the neighbourhood of Caudry, and the line of defence was continued thence by the 4th Division towards Seranvillers, the left being thrown back.

During the fighting on the 24th and 25th the Cavalry became a good deal scattered, but by the early morning of the 26th General Allenby had succeeded in concentrating two brigades to the south of Cambrai. The 4th Division was placed under the orders of the General Officer Commanding the Second Army Corps.

On the 24th the French Cavalry Corps, consisting of three divisions, under General Sordêt, had been in billets north of Avesnes. On my way back from Bavai, which was my "Poste de Commandement" during the fighting of the 23rd and 24th, I visited General Sordêt, and earnestly requested his co-operation and support. He promised to obtain sanction from his Army Commander to act on my left flank, but said that his horses were too tired to move before the next day. Although he rendered me valuable assistance later on in the course of the retirement, he was unable for the reasons given to afford me any support on the most critical day of all, viz., the 26th.

At daybreak it became apparent that the enemy was throwing the bulk of his strength against the left of the position occupied by the Second Corps and the 4th Division. At this time the guns of four German Army Corps were in position against them, and Sir Horace Smith-Dorrien reported to me that he judged it impossible to continue his retirement at daybreak (as ordered) in the face of such an attack.

I sent him orders to use his utmost endeavours to break off the action and retire at the earliest possible moment, as it was impossible for me to send him any support, the First Corps being at the moment incapable of movement.

The French Cavalry Corps, under General Sordêt, was coming up on our left rear early in the morning, and I sent an urgent message to him to do his utmost to come up and support the retirement of my left flank; but, owing to the fatigue of his horses he found himself unable to intervene in any way. There had been no time to entrench the position properly, but the troops showed a magnificent front to the terrible fire which confronted them. The artillery, although outmatched by at least four to one, made a splendid fight, and inflicted heavy losses on their opponents.

At length it became apparent that, if complete annihilation was to be avoided, a retirement must be attempted; and the order was given to commence it about 3.30 p.m. The movement was covered with the most devoted intrepidity and determination by the artillery, which had itself suffered heavily, and the fine work done by the cavalry in the further retreat from the position assisted materially in the final completion of this most difficult and dangerous operation. Fortunately the enemy had himself suffered too heavily to engage in an energetic pursuit.

I cannot close the brief account of this glorious stand of the British troops without putting on record my deep appreciation of the valuable services rendered by General Sir Horace Smith-Dorrien. I say without hesitation that the saving of the left wing of the Army under my command on the morning of the 26th August could never have been accomplished unless a commander of rare and unusual coolness, intrepidity, and determination had been present to personally conduct the operations.

The retreat was continued far into the night of the 26th and through the 27th and 28th, on which date the troops halted on the line Noyon–Chauny–La Fère, having then thrown off the weight of the enemy's pursuit.

On the 27th and 28th I was much indebted to General Sordêt and the French Cavalry Division which he commands for materially assisting my retirement and successfully driving back some of the enemy on Cambrai. General D'Amade also, with the 61st and 62nd French Reserve Divisions, moved down from the neighbourhood of Arras on the enemy's right flank and took much pressure off the rear of the British forces.

This closes the period covering the heavy fighting which commenced at Mons on Sunday afternoon, 23rd August, and which really constituted a four days' battle. At this point, therefore, I propose to close the present despatch.

I deeply deplore the very serious losses which the British forces have suffered in this great battle; but they were inevitable in view of the fact that the British Army—only two days after a concentration by rail—was called upon to withstand a vigorous attack of five German Army Corps.

It is impossible for me to speak too highly of the skill evinced by the two General Officers commanding Army Corps; the self-sacrificing and devoted exertions of their staffs; the direction of the troops by divisional, brigade and regimental leaders; the command of the smaller units by their officers; and the magnificent fighting spirit displayed by non-commissioned officers and men.

I wish particularly to bring to your Lordship's notice the admirable work done by the Royal Flying Corps under Sir David Henderson. Their skill, energy and perseverance have been beyond all praise. They have furnished me with the most complete and accurate information which has been of incalculable value in the conduct of the operations. Fired at constantly both by friend and foe, and not hesitating to fly in every kind of weather, they have remained undaunted throughout. Further, by actually fighting in the air, they have succeeded in destroying five of the enemy's machines.

I wish to acknowledge with deep gratitude the incalculable assistance I received from the General and Personal Staffs at Headquarters during this trying period. Lieutenant-General Sir Archibald Murray, Chief of the General Staff; Major-General Wilson, Sub-Chief of the General Staff; and all under them have worked day and night unceasingly with the utmost skill, self-sacrifice, and devotion; and the same acknowledgment is due by me to Brigadier-General Hon. W. Lambton my Military Secretary, and the Personal Staff.

In such operations as I have described, the work of the Quartermaster-General is of an extremely onerous nature. Major-General Sir William Robertson has met what appeared to be almost insuperable difficulties with his characteristic energy, skill and determination; and it is largely owing to his exertions that the hardships and sufferings of the troops—inseparable from such operations—were not much greater.

Major-General Sir Nevil Macready, the Adjutant-General, has also been confronted with most onerous and difficult tasks in connection with disciplinary arrangements and the preparation of casualty lists. He has been indefatigable in his exertions to meet the difficult situations which arose.

I have not yet been able to complete the list of officers whose names I desire to bring to your Lordship's notice for services rendered during the period under review; and, as I understand it is of importance that this despatch should no longer be delayed, I propose to forward this list, separately, as soon as I can.

J. D. P. FRENCH
Field-Marshal,
Commander-in-Chief,
British Forces in the Field

FIRST BATTLE OF THE MARNE, SEPTEMBER 1914

From the Field Marshal Commanding in Chief, British Forces in the Field,
to the Secretary of State for War

17th September, 1914

My Lord,

In continuation of my despatch of September 7th, I have the honour to report the further progress of the operations of the forces under my command from August 28th.

Battle of the Marne, 1914

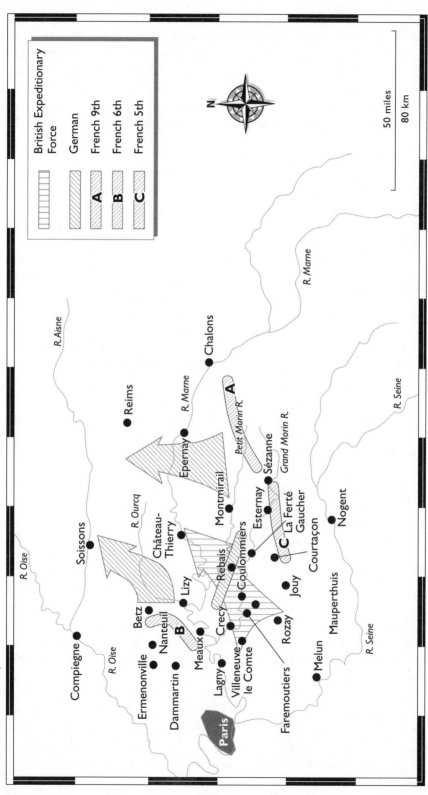

On that evening the retirement of the force was followed closely by two of the enemy's cavalry columns, moving south-east from St Quentin.

The retreat in this part of the field was being covered by the 3rd and 5th Cavalry Brigades. South of the Somme General Gough, with the 3rd Cavalry Brigade, threw back the Uhlans of the Guard with considerable loss.

General Chetwode, with the 5th Cavalry Brigade, encountered the eastern column near Cérizy, moving south. The brigade attacked and routed the column, the leading German regiment suffering very severe casualties and being almost broken up.

The 7th French Army Corps was now in course of being railed up from the south to the east of Amiens. On the 29th it nearly completed its detrainment, and the French 6th Army got into position on my left, its right resting on Roye. The 5th French Army was behind the line of the Oise between La Fère and Guise.

The pursuit of the enemy was very vigorous; some five or six German corps were on the Somme, facing the 5th Army on the Oise. At least two corps were advancing towards my front, and were crossing the Somme east and west of Ham. Three or four more German corps were opposing the 6th French Army on my left. This was the situation at 1 o'clock on the 29th, when I received a visit from General Joffre at my headquarters.

I strongly represented my position to the French Commander-in-Chief, who was most kind, cordial, and sympathetic, as he has always been. He told me that he had directed the 5th French Army on the Oise to move forward and attack the Germans on the Somme, with a view to checking pursuit. He also told me of the formation of the 6th French Army on my left flank, composed of the 7th Army Corps, four Reserve Divisions, and Sordêt's Corps of Cavalry.

I finally arranged with General Joffre to effect a further short retirement towards the line Compiègne–Soissons, promising him, however, to do my utmost to keep always within a day's march of him. In pursuance of this arrangement the British forces retired to a position a few miles north of the line Compiègne–Soissons on the 29th.

The right flank of the German Army was now reaching a point which appeared seriously to endanger my line of communications with Havre. I had already evacuated Amiens, into which place a German reserve division was reported to have moved.

Orders were given to change the base to St Nazaire, and establish an advance base at Le Mans. This operation was well carried out by the Inspector-General of Communications.

In spite of a severe defeat inflicted upon the Guard 10th and Guard Reserve Corps of the German Army by the 1st and 3rd French Corps on the right of the 5th Army, it was not part of General Joffre's plan to pursue this advantage, and a general retirement on to the line of the Marne was ordered, to which the French forces in the more eastern theatre were directed to conform.

A new Army (the 9th) had been formed from three corps in the south by General Joffre, and moved into the space between the right of the 5th and left of the 4th Armies.

Whilst closely adhering to his strategic conception to draw the enemy on at all points until a favourable situation was created from which to assume the offensive, General Joffre found it necessary to modify from day to day the methods by which he sought to attain this object, owing to the development of the enemy's plans and changes in the general situation.

In conformity with the movements of the French forces, my retirement continued practically from day to day. Although we were not severely pressed by the enemy, rearguard actions took place continually.

On the 1st September, when retiring from the thickly wooded country to the south of Compiègne, the 1st Cavalry Brigade was overtaken by some German cavalry. They momentarily lost a Horse Artillery battery, and several officers and men were killed and wounded. With the help, however, of some detachments from the 3rd Corps operating on their left, they not only recovered their own guns but succeeded in capturing twelve of the enemy's.

Similarly, to the eastward, the 1st Corps, retiring south, also got into some very difficult forest country, and a somewhat severe rearguard action ensued at Villers-Cotterets, in which the 4th Guards Brigade suffered considerably.

On September 3rd the British forces were in position south of the Marne between Lagny and Signy-Signets. Up to this time I had been requested by General Joffre to defend the passages of the river as long as possible, and to blow up the bridges in my front. After I had made the necessary dispositions, and the destruction of the bridges had been effected, I was asked by the French Commander-in-Chief to continue my retirement to a point some 12 miles in rear of the position I then occupied, with a view to taking up a second position behind the Seine. This retirement was duly carried out. In the meantime the enemy had thrown bridges and crossed the Marne in considerable force, and was threatening the Allies all along the line of the British forces and the 5th and 9th French Armies. Consequently several small outpost actions took place.

On Saturday, September 5th, I met the French Commander-in-Chief at his request, and he informed me of his intention to take the offensive forthwith, as he considered conditions were very favourable to success. General Joffre announced to me his intention of wheeling up the left flank of the 6th Army, pivoting on the Marne and directing it to move on the Ourcq; cross and attack the flank of the 1st German Army, which was then moving in a south-easterly direction east of that river. He requested me to effect a change of front to my right—my left resting on the Marne and my right on the 5th Army—to fill the gap between that army and the 6th. I was then to advance against the enemy in my front and join in the general offensive movement.

These combined movements practically commenced on Sunday, September 6th, at sunrise; and on that day it may be said that a great battle opened on a front extending from Ermenonville, which was just in front of the left flank of the 6th French Army, through Lizy on the Marne, Mauperthuis, which was about the British centre, Courtacon, which was the left of the 5th French Army, to Esternay and Charleville, the left of the 9th Army under General Foch, and so along the front of the 9th, 4th, and 3rd French Armies to a point north of the fortress of Verdun. This battle, in so far as the 6th French Army, the British Army, the 5th French Army and the 9th French Army were concerned, may be said to have concluded on the evening of September 10th, by which time the Germans had been driven back to the line Soissons–Reims, with a loss of thousands of prisoners, many guns, and enormous masses of transport.

About the 3rd September the enemy appears to have changed his plans and to have determined to stop his advance south direct upon Paris; for on the 4th September air reconnaissances showed that his main columns were moving in a south-easterly direction generally east of a line drawn through Nanteuil and Lizy on the Ourcq.

On the 5th September several of these columns were observed to have crossed the Marne; whilst German troops, which were observed moving south-east up the left bank of the Ourcq on the 4th, were now reported to be halted and facing that river. Heads of the enemy's columns were seen crossing at Changis, La Ferté, Nogent, Château Thierry and Mezy.

Considerable German columns of all arms were seen to be converging on Montmirail, whilst before sunset large bivouacs of the enemy were located in the neighbourhood of Coulommiers, south of Rebais, La Ferté-Gaucher and Dagny.

I should conceive it to have been about noon on the 6th September, after the British forces had changed their front to the right and occupied the line Jouy–Le Chatel–Faremoutiers–Villeneuve Le Comte, and the advance of the 6th French Army north of the Marne towards the Ourcq became apparent, that the enemy realised the powerful threat that was being made against the flank of his columns moving south-east, and began the great retreat which opened the battle above referred to.

On the evening of the 6th September, therefore, the fronts and positions of the opposing armies were roughly as follows:

ALLIES

6th French Army—Right on the Marne at Meaux, left towards Betz.
British Forces—On the line Lagny–Coulommiers–Maison.
5th French Army—At Courtacon, right on Esternay.
Conneau's Cavalry Corps—Between the right of the British and the left of the French 5th Army.

GERMANS

4th Reserve and 2nd Corps—East of the Ourcq and facing that river.
9th Cavalry Division—West of Crecy.
2nd Cavalry Division—North of Coulommiers.

4th Corps—Rebais.
3rd and 7th Corps—South-west of Montmirail.

All the German troops [listed above] constituted the 1st German Army, which was directed against the French 6th Army on the Ourcq, and the British forces, and the left of the 5th French Army south of the Marne.

The 2nd German Army (IX, X, XR and Guard) was moving against the centre and right of the 5th French Army and the 9th French Army.

On the 7th September both the 5th and 6th French Armies were heavily engaged on our flank. The 2nd and 4th Reserve German Corps on the Ourcq vigorously opposed the advance of the French towards that river, but did not prevent the 6th Army from gaining some headway, the Germans themselves suffering serious losses. The French 5th Army threw the enemy back to the line of the Petit Morin river after inflicting severe losses upon them, especially about Montceaux, which was carried at the point of the bayonet.

The enemy retreated before our advance, covered by his 2nd and 9th and Guard Cavalry Divisions, which suffered severely. Our cavalry acted with great vigour, especially General De Lisle's brigade with the 9th Lancers and 18th Hussars.

On the 8th September the enemy continued his retreat northward, and our Army was successfully engaged during the day with strong rearguards of all arms on the Petit Morin River, thereby materially assisting the progress of the French Armies on our right and left, against whom the enemy was making his greatest efforts. On both sides the enemy was thrown back with very heavy loss. The First Army Corps encountered stubborn resistance at La Trétoire (north of Rebais). The enemy occupied a strong position with infantry and guns on the northern bank of the Petit Morin River; they were dislodged with considerable loss. Several machine guns and many prisoners were captured, and upwards of 200 German dead were left on the ground.

The forcing of the Petit Morin at this point was much assisted by the cavalry and the 1st Division, which crossed higher up the stream. Later in the day a counter-attack by the enemy was well repulsed by the First Army Corps, a great many prisoners and some guns again falling into our hands.

On this day (8th September) the Second Army Corps encountered considerable opposition, but drove back the enemy at all points with great loss, making considerable captures. The Third Army Corps also drove back considerable bodies of the enemy's infantry and made some captures.

On the 9th September the First and Second Army Corps forced the passage of the Marne and advanced some miles to the north of it. The Third Corps encountered considerable opposition, as the bridge at La Ferté was destroyed and the enemy held the town on the opposite bank in some strength, and thence persistently obstructed the construction of a bridge; so the passage was not effected until after nightfall.

During the day's pursuit the enemy suffered heavy loss in killed and wounded, some hundreds of prisoners fell into our hands and a battery of eight machine guns was captured by the 2nd Division.

On this day the 6th French Army was heavily engaged west of the River Ourcq. The enemy had largely increased his force opposing them; and very heavy fighting ensued, in which the French were successful throughout.

The left of the 5th French Army reached the neighbourhood of Château Thierry after the most severe fighting, having driven the enemy completely north of the river with great loss. The fighting of this Army in the neighbourhood of Montmirail was very severe.

The advance was resumed at daybreak on the 10th up to the line of the Ourcq, opposed by strong rearguards of all arms. The 1st and 2nd Corps, assisted by the Cavalry Division on the right, the 3rd and 5th Cavalry Brigades on the left, drove the enemy northwards. Thirteen guns, seven machine guns, about 2,000 prisoners, and quantities of transport fell into our hands. The enemy left many dead on the field. On this day the French 5th and 6th Armies had little opposition.

As the 1st and 2nd German Armies were now in full retreat, this evening marks the end of the battle which practically commenced on the morning of the 6th instant; and it is at this point in the operations that I am concluding the present despatch.

Although I deeply regret to have had to report heavy losses in killed and wounded throughout these operations, I do not think they have been excessive in view of the magnitude of the great fight, the outlines of which I have only been able very briefly to describe, and the demoralisation and loss in killed and wounded which are known to have been caused to the enemy by the vigour and severity of the pursuit.

In concluding this despatch I must call your Lordship's special attention to the fact that from Sunday, August 23rd, up to the present date (September 17th), from Mons back almost to the Seine, and from the Seine to the Aisne, the Army under my command has been ceaselessly engaged without one single day's halt or rest of any kind.

Since the date to which in this despatch I have limited my report of the operations, a great battle on the Aisne has been proceeding. A full report of this battle will be made in an early further despatch.

It will, however, be of interest to say here that, in spite of a very determined resistance on the part of the enemy, who is holding in strength and great tenacity a position peculiarly favourable to defence, the battle which commenced on the evening of the 12th instant has, so far, forced the enemy back from his first position, secured the passage of the river, and inflicted great loss upon him, including the capture of over 2,000 prisoners and several guns.

J. D. P. FRENCH
Field-Marshal,
Commanding-in-Chief,
The British Forces in the Field

BATTLE OF THE AISNE, SEPTEMBER 1914

From the Field-Marshal Commanding-in-Chief, British Forces in the Field,
to the Secretary of State for War

8th October, 1914

My Lord,

I have the honour to report the operations in which the British forces in France have been engaged since the evening of the 10th September.

In the early morning of the 11th the further pursuit of the enemy was commenced; and the three corps crossed the Ourcq practically unopposed, the cavalry reaching the line of the Aisne River; the 3rd and 5th Brigades south of Soissons, the 1st, 2nd and 4th on the high ground at Couvrelles and Cerseuil.

On the afternoon of the 12th from the opposition encountered by the 6th French Army to the west of Soissons, by the 3rd Corps south-east of that place, by the 2nd Corps south of Missy and Vailly, and certain indications all along the line, I formed the opinion that the enemy had, for the moment at any rate, arrested his retreat and was preparing to dispute the passage of the Aisne with some vigour.

South of Soissons the Germans were holding Mont de Paris against the attack of the right of the French 6th Army when the 3rd Corps reached the neighbourhood of Buzancy, south-east of that place. With the assistance of the artillery of the 3rd Corps the French drove them back across the river at Soissons, where they destroyed the bridges. The heavy artillery fire which was visible for several miles in a westerly direction in the valley of the Aisne showed that the 6th French Army was meeting with strong opposition all along the line.

On this day the cavalry under General Allenby reached the neighbourhood of Braine and did good work in clearing the town and the high ground beyond it of strong hostile detachments. The Queen's Bays are particularly mentioned by the General as having assisted greatly in the success of this operation. They were well supported by the 3rd Division, which on this night bivouacked at Brenelle, south of the river.

The 5th Division approached Missy, but were unable to make headway. The 1st Army Corps reached the neighbourhood of Vauxcéré without much opposition. In this manner the battle of the Aisne commenced.

The Aisne Valley runs generally east and west, and consists of a flat-bottomed depression of width varying from half a mile to two miles, down which the river follows a winding course to the west at some points near the southern slopes of the valley and at others near the northern. The high ground both on the north and south of the river is approximately 400 feet above the bottom of the valley and is very similar in character, as are both slopes of the valley itself, which are broken into numerous rounded spurs and re-entrants. The most prominent of the former are the Chivre spur on

Battle of the Aisne, 1914

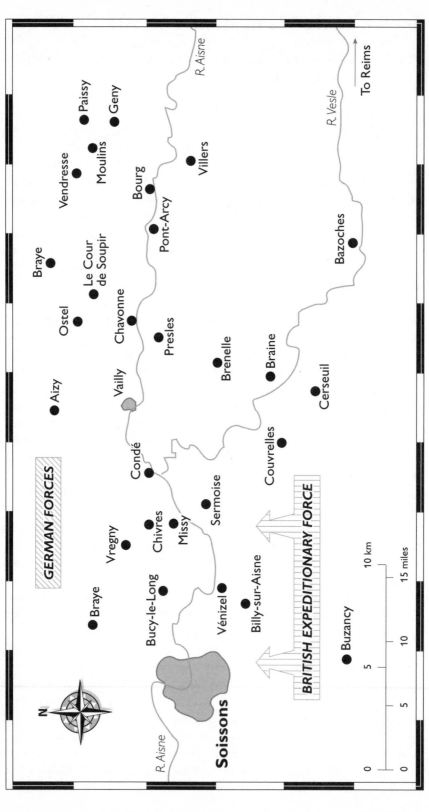

the right bank and Sermoise spur on the left. Near the latter place the general plateau on the south is divided by a subsidiary valley of much the same character, down which the small River Vesle flows to the main stream near Sermoise. The slopes of the plateau overlooking the Aisne on the north and south are of varying steepness, and are covered with numerous patches of wood, which also stretch upwards and backwards over the edge on to the top of the high ground. There are several villages and small towns dotted about in the valley itself and along its sides, the chief of which is the town of Soissons.

The Aisne is a sluggish stream of some 170 feet in breadth, but, being 15 feet deep in the centre, it is unfordable. Between Soissons on the west and Villers on the east (the part of the river attacked and secured by the British forces) there are eleven road bridges across it. On the north bank a narrow-gauge railway runs from Soissons to Vailly, where it crosses the river and continues eastward along the south bank. From Soissons to Sermoise a double line of railway runs along the south bank, turning at the latter place up the Vesle Valley towards Bazoches.

The position held by the enemy is a very strong one, either for a delaying action or for a defensive battle. One of its chief military characteristics is that from the high ground on neither side can the top of the plateau on the other side be seen except for small stretches. This is chiefly due to the woods on the edges of the slopes. Another important point is that all the bridges are under either direct or high-angle artillery fire.

The tract of country above described, which lies north of the Aisne, is well adapted to concealment, and was so skilfully turned to account by the enemy as to render it impossible to judge the real nature of his opposition to our passage of the river, or to accurately gauge his strength; but I have every reason to conclude that strong rearguards of at least three army corps were holding the passages on the early morning of the 13th.

On that morning I ordered the British forces to advance and make good the Aisne. The 1st Corps and the Cavalry advanced on the river. The 1st Division was directed on Chanouille via the canal bridge at Bourg, and the 2nd Division on Courtecon and Presles via Pont-Arcy and on the canal to the north of Braye via Chavonne. On the right the cavalry and 1st Division met with slight opposition, and found a passage by means of the canal which crosses the river by an aqueduct. The division was therefore able to press on, supported by the Cavalry Division on its outer flank, driving back the enemy in front of it.

On the left the leading troops of the 2nd Division reached the river by 9 o'clock. The 5th Infantry Brigade were only enabled to cross, in single file and under considerable shell fire, by means of the broken girder of the bridge which was not entirely submerged in the river. The construction of a pontoon bridge was at once undertaken, and was completed by 5 o'clock in the afternoon.

On the extreme left the 4th Guards Brigade met with severe opposition at Chavonne, and it was only late in the afternoon that it was able to establish a foothold on the northern bank of the river by ferrying one battalion across in boats. By nightfall the 1st Division occupied the area Moulins–Paissy–Geny, with posts in the village of Vendresse.

The 2nd Division bivouacked as a whole on the southern bank of the river, leaving only the 5th Brigade on the north bank to establish a bridge head.

The Second Corps found all the bridges in front of them destroyed, except that of Condé, which was in possession of the enemy, and remained so until the end of the battle.

In the approach to Missy, where the 5th Division eventually crossed, there is some open ground which was swept by heavy fire from the opposite bank. The 13th Brigade was, therefore, unable to advance; but the 14th, which was directed to the east of Venizel at a less exposed point, was rafted across, and by night established itself with its left at St Marguérite. They were followed by the 15th Brigade; and later on both the 14th and 15th supported the 4th Division on their left in repelling a heavy counter-attack on the Third Corps.

On the morning of the 13th the Third Corps found the enemy had established himself in strength on the Vregny Plateau. The road bridge at Venizel was repaired during the morning, and a reconnaissance was made with a view to throwing a pontoon bridge at Soissons. The 12th Infantry Brigade crossed at Venizel, and was assembled at Bucy Le Long by 1 p.m., but the bridge was so far damaged that artillery could only be man-handled across it. Meanwhile the construction of a bridge was commenced close to the road bridge at Venizel.

At 2 p.m. the 12th Infantry Brigade attacked in the direction of Chivres and Vregny with the object of securing the high ground east of Chivres, as a necessary preliminary to a further advance northwards. This attack made good progress, but at 5.30 p. m. the enemy's artillery and machine-gun fire from the direction of Vregny became so severe that no further advance could be made. The positions reached were held till dark.

The pontoon bridge at Venizel was completed at 5.30 p.m., when the 10th Infantry Brigade crossed the river and moved to Bucy Le Long.

The 19th Infantry Brigade moved to Billy Sur Aisne, and before dark all the artillery of the division had crossed the river, with the exception of the heavy battery and one brigade of field artillery.

During the night the positions gained by the 12th Infantry Brigade to the east of the stream running through Chivres were handed over to the 5th Division.

The section of the Bridging Train allotted to the Third Corps began to arrive in the neighbourhood of Soissons late in the afternoon, when an attempt to throw a heavy pontoon bridge at Soissons had to be abandoned, owing to the fire of the enemy's heavy howitzers. In the evening the enemy retired at all points and entrenched himself on the high ground about two miles north of the river along which runs the Chemin-des-Dames. Detachments of Infantry, however, strongly entrenched in commanding points down slopes of the various spurs, were left in front of all three corps with powerful artillery in support of them.

During the night of the 13th and on the 14th and following days the field companies were incessantly at work night and day. Eight pontoon bridges and one footbridge were thrown across the river under generally very heavy artillery fire, which was incessantly kept up on to most of the crossings after completion. Three of the road bridges, i.e., Venizel, Missy and Vailly, and the railway bridge east of Vailly were temporarily repaired so as to take foot traffic and the Villers bridge made fit to carry weights up to six tons. Preparations were also made for the repair of the Missy, Vailly and Bourg bridges so as to take mechanical transport.

The weather was very wet and added to the difficulties by cutting up the already indifferent approaches, entailing a large amount of work to repair and improve.

The operations of the field companies during this most trying time are worthy of the best traditions of the Royal Engineers.

On the evening of the 14th it was still impossible to decide whether the enemy was only making a temporary halt, covered by rearguards, or whether he intended to stand and defend the position. With a view to clearing up the situation, I ordered a general advance.

The action of the First Corps on this day under the direction and command of Sir Douglas Haig was of so skilful, bold and decisive a character that he gained positions which alone have enabled me to maintain my position for more than three weeks of very severe fighting on the north bank of the river. The corps was directed to cross the line Moulins–Moussy by 7 a.m.

On the right the General Officer Commanding the 1st Division directed the 2nd Infantry Brigade (which was in billets and bivouacked about Moulins), and the 25th Artillery Brigade (less one battery), under General Bulfin, to move forward before day-break, in order to protect the advance of the division sent up the valley to Vendresse. An officers' patrol sent out by this brigade reported a considerable force of the enemy near the factory north of Troyon, and the Brigadier accordingly directed two regiments (the King's Royal Rifles and the Royal Sussex Regiment) to move at 3 a.m. The Northamptonshire Regiment was ordered to move at 4 a.m. to occupy the spur east of Troyon. The remaining regiment of the brigade (the Loyal North Lancashire Regiment) moved at 5.30 a.m. to the village of Vendresse. The factory was found to be held in considerable strength by the enemy, and the Brigadier ordered the Loyal North Lancashire Regiment to support the King's Royal Rifles and the Sussex Regiment. Even with this support the force was unable to make headway, and on the arrival of the 1st Brigade the Coldstream Guards were moved up to support the right of the leading brigade (the 2nd), while the remainder of the 1st Brigade supported its left.

About noon the situation was, roughly, that the whole of these two brigades were extended along a line running east and west, north of the line Troyon and south of the Chemin-des-Dames. A party of the Loyal North Lancashire Regiment had seized and were holding the factory. The enemy held a line of entrenchments north and east of the factory in considerable strength, and every effort to advance against this line was driven back by heavy shell and machine-gun fire. The morning was wet and a heavy mist hung over the hills, so that the 25th Artillery Brigade and the divisional artillery were unable to render effective support to the advanced troops until about 9 o'clock.

By 10 o'clock the 3rd Infantry Brigade had reached a point one mile south of Vendresse, and from there it was ordered to continue the line of the 1st Brigade and to connect with and help the right of the 2nd Division. A strong hostile column was found to be advancing, and by a vigorous counter-stroke with two of his battalions the Brigadier checked the advance of this column and relieved the pressure on the 2nd Division. From this period until late in the afternoon the fighting consisted of a series of attacks and counter-attacks. The counter-strokes by the enemy were delivered at first with great vigour, but later on they decreased in strength, and all were driven off with heavy loss.

On the left the 6th Infantry Brigade had been ordered to cross the river and to pass through the line held during the preceding night by the 5th Infantry Brigade and occupy the Courtecon Ridge, whilst a detached force, consisting of the 4th Guards Brigade and the 36th Brigade, Royal Field Artillery, under Brigadier-General Perceval, were ordered to proceed to a point east of the village of Ostel.

The 6th Infantry Brigade crossed the river at Pont-Arcy, moved up the valley towards Braye, and at 9 a.m. had reached the line Tilleul–La Buvelle. On this line they came under heavy artillery and rifle fire, and were unable to advance until supported by the 34th Brigade, Royal Field Artillery, and the 44th Howitzer Brigade and the heavy artillery.

The 4th Guards Brigade crossed the river at 10 a.m. and met with very heavy opposition. It had to pass through dense woods; field artillery support was difficult to obtain; but one section of a field battery pushed up to and within the firing line. At 1 p.m. the left of the brigade was south of the Ostel Ridge.

At this period of the action the enemy obtained a footing between the First and Second Corps, and threatened to cut the communications of the latter.

Sir Douglas Haig was very hardly pressed and had no reserve in hand. I placed the Cavalry Division at his disposal, part of which he skilfully used to prolong and secure the left flank of the Guards Brigade. Some heavy fighting ensued, which resulted in the enemy being driven back with heavy loss.

About 4 o'clock the weakening of the counter-attacks by the enemy and other indications tended to show that his resistance was decreasing, and a general advance was ordered by the Army Corps Commander. Although meeting with considerable opposition and coming under very heavy artillery and rifle fire, the position of the corps at the end of the day's operations extended from the Chemin-des-Dames on the right, through Chivy, to Le Cour de Soupir, with the 1st Cavalry Brigade extending to the Chavonne–Soissons road.

On the right the corps was in close touch with the French Moroccan troops of the 18th Corps, which were entrenched in échelon to its right rear. During the night they entrenched this position.

Throughout the battle of the Aisne this advanced and commanding position was maintained, and I cannot speak too highly of the valuable services rendered by Sir Douglas Haig and the Army Corps under his command. Day after day and night after night the enemy's infantry has been hurled against him in violent counter-attack which has never on any one occasion succeeded, whilst the trenches all over his position have been under continuous heavy artillery fire.

The operations of the First Corps on this day resulted in the capture of several hundred prisoners, some field pieces, and machine guns. The casualties were very severe, one brigade alone losing three of its four Colonels.

The 3rd Division commenced a further advance and had nearly reached the plateau of Aizy when they were driven back by a powerful counter-attack supported by heavy artillery. The division, however, fell back in the best order, and finally entrenched itself about a mile north of Vailly Bridge, effectively covering the passage. The 4th and 5th Divisions were unable to do more than maintain their ground.

On the morning of the 15th, after close examination of the position, it became clear to me that the enemy was making a determined stand; and this view was confirmed by reports which reached me from the French armies fighting on my right and left, which clearly showed that a strongly entrenched line of defence was being taken up from the north of Compiègne, eastward and south-eastward, along the whole valley of the Aisne up to and beyond Reims.

A few days previously the fortress of Maubeuge fell, and a considerable quantity of siege artillery was brought down from that place to strengthen the enemy's position in front of us.

During the 15th shells fell in our position which have been judged by experts to be thrown by eight-inch siege guns with a range of 10,000 yards. Throughout the whole course of the battle our troops have suffered very heavily from this fire, although its effect latterly was largely mitigated by more efficient and thorough entrenching, the necessity for which I impressed strongly upon Army Corps Commanders. In order to assist them in this work all villages within the area of our occupation were searched for heavy entrenching tools, a large number of which were collected.

In view of the peculiar formation of the ground on the north side of the river between Missy and Soissons, and its extraordinary adaptability to a force on the defensive, the 5th Division found it impossible to maintain its position on the southern edge of the Chivres Plateau, as the enemy in possession of the village of Vregny to the west was able to bring a flank fire to bear upon it. The division had, therefore, to retire to a line the left of which was the village of Marguérite, and thence ran by the north edge of Missy back to the river to the east of that place.

With great skill and tenacity Sir Charles Fergusson maintained this position throughout the whole battle, although his trenches were necessarily on lower ground than that occupied by the enemy on the southern edge of the plateau, which was only 400 yards away.

General Hamilton with the 3rd Division vigorously attacked to the north, and regained all the ground he had lost on the 15th, which throughout the battle has formed a most powerful and effective bridge head.

On the 16th the 6th Division came up into line.

It had been my intention to direct the First Corps to attack and seize the enemy's position on the Chemin-des-Dames, supporting it with this new reinforcement. I hoped from the position thus gained to bring effective fire to bear across the front of the 3rd Division, which, by securing the advance of the latter, would also take the pressure off the 5th Division and the Third Corps.

But any further advance of the First Corps would have dangerously exposed my right flank. And, further, I learned from the French Commander-in-Chief that he was strongly reinforcing the 6th French Army on my left, with the intention of bringing up the Allied left to attack the enemy's flank and thus compel his retirement. I therefore sent the 6th Division to join the Third Corps with orders to keep it on the south side of the river, as it might be available in general reserve.

On the 17th, 18th and 19th the whole of our line was heavily bombarded, and the First Corps was constantly and heavily engaged. On the afternoon of the 17th the right flank of the 1st Division was seriously threatened. A counter-attack was made by the Northamptonshire Regiment in combination with the Queen's, and one battalion of the Divisional Reserve was moved up in support. The Northamptonshire Regiment, under cover of mist, crept up to within a hundred yards of the enemy's trenches and charged with the bayonet, driving them out of the trenches and up the hill. A very strong force of hostile infantry was then disclosed on the crest line. This new line was enfiladed by part of the Queen's and the King's Royal Rifles, which wheeled to their left on the extreme right of our infantry line, and were supported by a squadron of cavalry on their outer flank. The enemy's attack was ultimately driven back with heavy loss.

On the 18th, during the night, the Gloucestershire Regiment advanced from their position near Chivy, filled in the enemy's trenches and captured two maxim guns. On the extreme right the Queen's were heavily attacked, but the enemy was repulsed with great loss. About midnight the attack was renewed on the First Division, supported by artillery fire, but was again repulsed.

Shortly after midnight an attack was made on the left of the 2nd Division with considerable force, which was also thrown back.

At about 1 p.m. on the 19th the 2nd Division drove back a heavy infantry attack strongly supported by artillery fire. At dusk the attack was renewed and again repulsed.

On the 18th I discussed with the General Officer Commanding the Second Army Corps and his Divisional Commanders the possibility of driving the enemy out of Condé, which lay between his two divisions, and seizing the bridge which has remained throughout in his possession.

As, however, I found that the bridge was closely commanded from all points on the south side and that satisfactory arrangements were made to prevent any issue from it by the enemy by day or night, I decided that it was not necessary to incur the losses which an attack would entail, as, in view of the position of the Second and Third Corps, the enemy could make no use of Condé, and would be automatically forced out of it by any advance which might become possible for us.

On this day information reached me from General Joffre that he had found it necessary to make a new plan, and to attack and envelop the German right flank. It was now evident to me that the battle in which we had been engaged since the 12th instant must last some days longer until the effect of this new flank movement could be felt and a way opened to drive the enemy from his positions.

It thus became essential to establish some system of regular relief in the trenches, and I have used the infantry of the 6th Division for this purpose with good results. The relieved brigades were brought back alternately south of the river, and, with the artillery of the 6th Division, formed a general reserve on which I could rely in case of necessity.

The cavalry has rendered most efficient and ready help in the trenches, and have done all they possibly could to lighten the arduous and trying task which has of necessity fallen to the lot of the infantry.

On the evening of the 19th and throughout the 20th the enemy again commenced to show considerable activity. On the former night a severe counter-attack on the 3rd Division was repulsed with considerable loss, and from early on Sunday morning various hostile attempts were made on the trenches of the 1st Division. During the day the enemy suffered another severe repulse in front of the 2nd Division, losing heavily in the attempt. In the course of the afternoon the enemy made desperate attempts against the trenches all along the front of the First Corps, but with similar results. After dark the enemy again attacked the 2nd Division, only to be again driven back.

Our losses on these two days were considerable, but the number, as obtained, of the enemy's killed and wounded vastly exceeded them.

As the troops of the First Army Corps were much exhausted by this continual fighting, I reinforced Sir Douglas Haig with a brigade from the reserve, and called upon the 1st Cavalry Division to assist them.

On the night of the 21st another violent counter-attack was repulsed by the 3rd Division, the enemy losing heavily.

On the 23rd the four six-inch howitzer batteries, which I had asked to be sent from home, arrived. Two batteries were handed over to the Second Corps and two to the First Corps. They were brought into action on the 24th with very good results.

Our experiences in this campaign seem to point to the employment of more heavy guns of a larger calibre in great battles which last for several days, during which time powerful entrenching work on both sides can be carried out.

These batteries were used with considerable effect on the 24th and the following days.

On the 23rd the action of General de Castelnau's Army on the Allied left developed considerably, and apparently withdrew considerable forces of the enemy away from the centre and east. I am not aware whether it was due to this cause or not, but until the 26th it appeared as though the enemy's opposition in our front was weakening. On that day, however, a very marked renewal of activity commenced. A constant and vigorous artillery bombardment was maintained all day, and the Germans in front of the 1st Division were observed to be "sapping" up to our lines and trying to establish new trenches. Renewed counter-attacks were delivered and beaten off during the course of the day, and in the afternoon a well-timed attack by the 1st Division stopped the enemy's entrenching work.

During the night of 27th–28th the enemy again made the most determined attempts to capture the trenches of the 1st Division, but without the slightest success. Similar attacks were reported during these three days all along the line of the Allied front, and it is certain that the enemy then made one last great effort to establish ascendency. He was, however, unsuccessful everywhere, and is reported to have suffered heavy losses. The same futile attempts were made all along our front up to the evening of the 28th, when they died away, and have not since been renewed.

On former occasions I have brought to your Lordship's notice the valuable services performed during this campaign by the Royal Artillery. Throughout the battle of the Aisne they have displayed the same skill, endurance and tenacity, and I deeply appreciate the work they have done.

Sir David Henderson and the Royal Flying Corps under his command have again proved their incalculable value. Great strides have been made in the development of the use of aircraft in the tactical sphere by establishing effective communication between aircraft and units in action.

It is difficult to describe adequately and accurately the great strain to which officers and men were subjected almost every hour of the day and night throughout this battle.

I have described above the severe character of the artillery fire which was directed from morning till night, not only upon the trenches, but over the whole surface of the ground occupied by our forces. It was not until a few days before the position was evacuated that the heavy guns were removed and the fire slackened. Attack and counter-attack occurred at all hours of the night and day throughout the whole position, demanding extreme vigilance, and permitting only a minimum of rest.

The fact that between the 12th September to the date of this despatch the total numbers of killed, wounded and missing reached the figures amounting to 561 officers, 12,980 men, proves the severity of the struggle. The tax on the endurance of the troops was further increased by the heavy rain and cold which prevailed for some ten or twelve days of this trying time. The battle of the Aisne has once more demonstrated the splendid spirit, gallantry and devotion which animates the officers and men of His Majesty's Forces.

With reference to the last paragraph of my despatch of September 7th, I append the names of officers, non-commissioned officers and men brought forward for special mention by Army Corps commanders and heads of departments for services rendered from the commencement of the campaign up to the present date. I entirely agree with these recommendations and beg to submit them for your Lordship's consideration.

I further wish to bring forward the names of the following officers who have rendered valuable service: General Sir Horace Smith-Dorrien and Lieutenant-General Sir Douglas Haig (commanding First and Second Corps respectively) I have already mentioned in the present and former despatches for particularly marked and distinguished service in critical situations. Since the commencement of the compaign they have carried out all my orders and instructions with the utmost ability.

Lieutenant-General W. P. Pulteney took over the command of the Third Corps just before the commencement of the battle of the Marne. Throughout the subsequent operations he showed himself to be a most capable commander in the field and has rendered very valuable services.

Major-General E. H. H. Allenby and Major-General H. de la P. Gough have proved themselves to be Cavalry leaders of a high order, and I am deeply indebted to them. The undoubted moral superiority which our Cavalry has obtained over that of the enemy has been due to the skill with which they have turned to the best account the qualities inherent in the splendid troops they command.

In my despatch of 7th September I mentioned the name of Brigadier-General Sir David Henderson and his valuable work in command of the Royal Flying Corps; and I have once more to express my deep appreciation of the help he has since rendered me.

Lieutenant-General Sir Archibald Murray has continued to render me invaluable help as Chief of the Staff; and in his arduous and responsible duties he has been ably assisted by Major-General Henry Wilson, Sub-Chief.

Lieutenant-General Sir Nevil Macready and Lieutenant-General Sir William Robertson have continued to perform excellent service as Adjutant-General and Quartermaster-General respectively.

The Director of Army Signals, Lieutenant-Colonel J. S. Fowler, has materially assisted the operations by the skill and energy which he has displayed in the working of the important department over which he presides.

My Military Secretary, Brigadier-General the Hon. W. Lambton, has performed his arduous and difficult duties with much zeal and great efficiency.

I am anxious also to bring to your Lordship's notice the following names of officers of my Personal Staff, who throughout these arduous operations have shown untiring zeal and energy in the performance of their duties:

Aides-de-Camp
Lieutenant-Colonel Stanley Barry
Lieutenant-Colonel Lord Brooke
Major Fitzgerald Watt

Extra Aide-de-Camp
Captain the Hon. F. E. Guest

Private Secretary
Lieutenant-Colonel Brindsley Fitzgerald

Major His Royal Highness Prince Arthur of Connaught, KG, joined my Staff as Aide-de-Camp on the 14th September. His Royal Highness's intimate knowledge of languages enabled me to employ him with great advantage on confidential missions of some importance, and his services have proved of considerable value.

I cannot close this despatch without informing your Lordship of the valuable services rendered by the Chief of the French Military Mission at my Headquarters, Colonel Victor Huguet, of the French Artillery. He has displayed tact and judgment of a high order in many difficult situations, and has rendered conspicuous service to the Allied cause.

J. D. P. FRENCH
Field-Marshal,
Commanding-in-Chief,
The British Army in the Field

In October 1914, with the Germans firmly entrenched on the River Aisne, the Allies withdrew their forces to the north in an attempt to outflank the enemy and compel them to evacuate. Thus the British Expeditionary Force moved to the area just inside Belgium around Ypres, where they were close to Calais and their vital lines of supply.

Meanwhile the Germans, realising the significance of the Channel ports, moved first on Antwerp, which surrendered on 10th October 1914.

ANTWERP, OCTOBER 1914

From Sir J. D. P. French, Field-Marshal, Commanding-in-Chief, to the Secretary of the Admiralty

5th December, 1914

In forwarding this report to the Army Council at the request of the Lords Commissioners of the Admiralty, I have to state that, from a comprehensive review of all the circumstances, the force of marines and naval brigades which assisted in the defence of Antwerp was handled by General Paris with great skill and boldness.

Although the results did not include the actual saving of the fortress, the action of the force under General Paris certainly delayed the enemy for a considerable time, and assisted the Belgian Army to be withdrawn in a condition to enable it to reorganize and refit, and regain its value as a fighting force. The destruction of war material and ammunition—which, but for the intervention of this force, would have proved of great value to the enemy—was thus able to be carried out.

The assistance which the Belgian Army has rendered throughout the subsequent course of the operations on the canal and the Yeser river has been a valuable asset to the Allied cause, and such help must be regarded as an outcome of the intervention of General Paris's force. I am further of opinion that the morale effect produced on the minds of the Belgian Army by this necessarily desperate attempt to bring them succour, before it was too late, has been of great value to their use and efficiency as a fighting force.

J. D. P. FRENCH
Field-Marshal,
Commanding-in-Chief

From Major-General A. Paris, CB, Commanding Royal Naval Division, to the Secretary of the Admiralty

31st October, 1914

Regarding the operations round Antwerp from 3rd to 9th October, I have the honour to report as follows:

The Brigade (2,200 all ranks) reached Antwerp during the night 3rd–4th October, and early on the 4th occupied, with the 7th Belgian Regiment, the trenches facing Lierre, with advanced post on the River Nethe, relieving some exhausted Belgian troops.

The outer forts on this front had already fallen and bombardment of the trenches was in progress. This increased in violence during the night and early morning of 5th October, when the advanced posts were driven in and the enemy effected a crossing of the river, which was not under fire from the trenches.

About midday the 7th Belgian Regiment was forced to retire, thus exposing my right flank. A vigorous counter-attack, gallantly led by Colonel Tierchon, 2nd Chasseurs, assisted by our aeroplanes, restored the position late in the afternoon. Unfortunately, an attempt made by the Belgian troops during the night (5th–6th October) to drive the enemy across the river failed, and resulted in the evacuation of practically the whole of the Belgian trenches.

The few troops now capable of another counter-attack were unable to make any impression, and the position of the Marine Brigade became untenable. The bombardment, too, was very violent, but the retirement of the brigade was well carried out, and soon after midday (6th October) an intermediate position, which had been hastily prepared, was occupied.

The two naval brigades reached Antwerp during the night, 5th–6th October. The 1st Brigade moved out in the afternoon of 5th to assist the withdrawal to the main 2nd Line of Defence. The retirement was carried out during the night, 6th–7th October, without opposition, and the Naval Division occupied the intervals between the forts on the 2nd Line of Defence.

The bombardment of the town, forts and trenches began at midnight, 7th–8th October, and continued with increasing intensity until the evacuation of the fortress. As the water supply had been cut, no attempt could be made to subdue the flames, and soon 100 houses were burning. Fortunately, there was no wind, or the whole town and bridges must have been destroyed.

During the day (8th October) it appeared evident that the Belgian Army could not hold the forts any longer. About 5.30 p.m. I considered that if the Naval Division was to avoid disaster an immediate retirement under cover of darkness was necessary. General De Guise, the Belgian Commander, was in complete agreement. He was most chivalrous and gallant, insisting on giving orders that the roads and bridges were to be cleared for the passage of the British troops. The retirement began about 7.30 p.m., and was carried out under very difficult conditions.

The enemy were reported in force (a Division plus a Reserve Brigade) on our immediate line of retreat, rendering necessary a detour of 15 miles to the north. All the roads were crowded with Belgian troops, refugees, herds of cattle, and all kinds of vehicles, making inter-communication a practical impossibility. Partly for these reasons, partly on account of fatigue, and partly from at present unexplained causes large numbers of the 1st Naval Brigade became detached, and I regret to say are either prisoners or interned in Holland.

Marching all night (8th to 9th October), one battalion of 1st Brigade, the 2nd Brigade and Royal Marine Brigade, less one battalion, entrained at St Gillies Waes and effected their retreat without further incident.

The Battalion (Royal Marine Brigade) Rear Guard of the whole force also entrained late in the afternoon together with many hundreds of refugees, but at Morbeke the line was cut, the engine derailed, and the enemy opened fire.

There was considerable confusion. It was dark and the agitation of the refugees made it difficult to pass any orders. However, the battalion behaved admirably, and succeeded in fighting its way through, but with a loss in missing of more than half its number. They then marched another 10 miles to Selzaate and entrained there.

Colonel Seely and Colonel Bridges were not part of my command, but they rendered most skilful and helpful services during the evacuation.

The casualties are approximately:

1st Naval Brigade and 2nd Naval Brigade, 5 killed, 64 wounded, 2,040 missing.

Royal Marine Brigade, 23 killed, 103 wounded, 388 missing.

A. PARIS
Major General,
Commanding Royal Naval Division

In October 1914 the Germans bore down heavily on the Ypres front in their attempt to recapture Ypres from the British. The first battle of Ypres (also known as the battle of Ypres-Armentieres) raged for more than three weeks, and saw some of the fiercest fighting of the war. The British held on grimly to Ypres, but at a cost in excess of 50,000 lives. The German losses were even greater, at over 150,000.

As winter set in, the two sides came to a standstill in the north, just as they had on the Aisne. Both armies went to ground, digging themselves into trenches that were to form a ragged, almost permanent line stretching from the Channel in the north to the Swiss border in the south.

TRENCH WARFARE: YPRES AND LA BASSÉE, DECEMBER 1914 TO JANUARY 1915

From the Field-Marshal Commanding-in-Chief, British Forces in the Field,
to the Secretary of State for War

General Headquarters, 5th December, 1914

My Lord,

I have the honour to forward a further report on the operations of the Army under my command.

In the period under review the salient feature was the presence of His Majesty the King in the field. His Majesty arrived at Headquarters on the 30th November, and left on the 5th December.

At a time when the strength and endurance of the troops had been tried to the utmost throughout the long and arduous battle of Ypres-Armentières the presence of His Majesty in their midst was of the greatest possible help and encouragement. His Majesty visited all parts of the extensive area of operations and held numerous inspections of the troops behind the line of trenches.

On the 16th November Lieutenant His Royal Highness the Prince of Wales, K.G., Grenadier Guards, joined my Staff as Aide-de-Camp.

Since the date of my last report the operations of the Army under my command have been subject almost entirely to the limitations of weather. History teaches us that the course of campaigns in Europe, which have been actively prosecuted during December and January, have been largely influenced by weather conditions. It should, however, be thoroughly understood throughout the country that the most recent development of armaments and the latest methods of conducting warfare have added greatly to the difficulties and drawbacks of a vigorous winter campaign.

To cause anything more than a waste of ammunition long-range artillery fire requires constant and accurate observation; but this most necessary condition is rendered impossible of attainment in the midst of continual fog and mist. Again, armies have now grown accustomed to rely largely on aircraft reconnaissance for accurate information of the enemy; but the effective performance of this service is materially influenced by wind and weather.

The deadly accuracy, range and quick-firing capabilities of the modern rifle and machine gun require that a fire-swept zone be crossed in the shortest possible space of time by attacking troops. But if men are detained under the enemy's fire by the difficulty of emerging from a water-logged trench, and by the necessity of passing over ground knee-deep in holding mud and slush, such attacks become practically prohibitive owing to the losses they entail.

During the exigencies of the heavy fighting which ended in the last week of November the French and British forces had become somewhat mixed up, entailing a certain amount of difficulty in matters of supply and in securing unity of command.

By the end of November I was able to concentrate the Army under my command in one area, and, by holding a shorter line, to establish effective reserves.

By the beginning of December there was a considerable falling off in the volume of artillery fire directed against our front by the enemy. Reconnaissance and reports showed that a certain amount of artillery had been withdrawn. We judged that the cavalry in our front, with the exception of one division of the Guard, had disappeared. There did not, however, appear to have been any great diminution in the numbers of infantry holding the trenches.

Although both artillery and rifle fire were exchanged with the enemy every day, and sniping went on more or less continuously during the hours of daylight, the operations which call for special record or comment are comparatively few.

During the last week in November some successful minor night operations were carried out in the 4th Corps.

On the night of the 23rd–24th November a small party of the 2nd Lincolnshire Regiment, under Lieutenant E. H. Impey, cleared three of the enemy's advanced trenches opposite the 25th Brigade and withdrew without loss.

On the night of the 24th–25th Captain J. R. Minshull Ford, Royal Welsh Fusiliers, and Lieutenant E. L. Morris, Royal Engineers, with 15 men of the Royal Engineers and Royal Welsh Fusiliers, successfully mined and blew up a group of farms immediately in front of the German trenches on the Touquet–Bridoux Road which had been used by German snipers.

On the night of the 26th–27th November a small party of the 2nd Scots Guards, under Lieutenant Sir E. H. W. Hulse, Bt., rushed the trenches opposite the 20th Brigade; and after pouring a heavy fire into them returned with useful information as to the strength of the Germans and the position of machine guns.

The trenches opposite the 25th Brigade were rushed the same night by a patrol of the 2nd Rifle Brigade, under Lieutenant E. Durham.

On the 23rd November the 112th Regiment of the 14th German Army Corps succeeded in capturing some 800 yards of the trenches held by the Indian Corps, but the General Officer Commanding the Meerut Division organized a powerful counter-attack, which lasted throughout the night. At daybreak on the 24th November the line was entirely re-established. The operation was a costly one, involving many casualties, but the enemy suffered far more heavily. We captured over 100 prisoners, including 3 officers, as well as 3 machine guns and 2 trench mortars.

On December 7th the concentration of the Indian Corps was completed by the arrival of the Sirhind Brigade from Egypt.

On December 9th the enemy attempted to commence a strong attack against the 3rd Corps, particularly in front of the trenches held by the Argyll and Sutherland Highlanders and the Middlesex Regiment. They were driven back with heavy loss, and did not renew the attempt. Our casualties were very slight.

During the early days of December certain indications along the whole front of the Allied Line induced the French Commanders and myself to believe that the enemy had withdrawn considerable forces from the Western theatre.

Arrangements were made with the Commander of the 8th French Army for an attack to be commenced on the morning of December 14th. Operations began at 7 a.m. by a combined heavy artillery bombardment by the two French and the 2nd British Corps. The British objectives were the Petit Bois and the Maedelsteed Spur, lying respectively to the west and south-west of the village of Wytschaete.

At 7.45 a.m. the Royal Scots, with great dash, rushed forward and attacked the former, while the Gordon Highlanders attacked the latter place. The Royal Scots, commanded by Major F. J. Duncan, D.S.O., in face of a terrible machine-gun and rifle fire, carried the German trench on the west edge of the Petit Bois, capturing two machine-guns and 53 prisoners, including one officer.

The Gordon Highlanders, with great gallantry, advanced up the Maedelsteed Spur, forcing the enemy to evacuate their front trench. They were, however, losing heavily, and found themselves unable to get any further. At nightfall they were obliged to fall back to their original position.

Captain C. Boddam-Whetham and Lieutenant W. F. R. Dobie showed splendid dash, and with a few men entered the enemy's leading trenches; but they were all either killed or captured. Lieutenant G. R. V. Hume-Gore and Lieutenant W. H. Paterson also distinguished themselves by their gallant leading. Although not successful, the operation was most creditable to the fighting spirit of the Gordon Highlanders, most ably commanded by Major A. W. F. Baird, DSO.

As the 32nd French Division on the left had been unable to make any progress, the further advance of our infantry into the Wytschaete Wood was not practicable. Possession of the western edge of the Petit Bois was, however, retained. The ground was devoid of cover and so water-logged that a rapid advance was impossible, the men sinking deep in the mud at every step they took.

The artillery throughout the day was very skilfully handled by the CRAs of the 3rd, 4th and 5th Divisions: Major-General F. D. V. Wing, CB, Brigadier-General G. F. Milne, CB, DSO, and Brigadier-General J. E. W. Headlam, CB, DSO.

The casualties during the day were about 17 officers and 407 other ranks. The losses of the enemy were very considerable, large numbers of dead being found in the Petit Bois and also in the communicating trenches in front of the Gordon Highlanders, in one of which a hundred were counted by a night patrol.

On this day the artillery of the 4th Division, 3rd Corps, was used in support of the attack, under orders of the General Officer Commanding 2nd Corps. The remainder of the 3rd Corps made demonstrations against the enemy with a view to preventing him from detaching troops to the area of operations of the 2nd Corps.

From the 15th to the 17th December the offensive operations which were commenced on the 14th were continued, but were confined chiefly to artillery bombardment. The infantry advance against Wytschaete Wood was not practicable until the French on our left could make some progress to afford protection to that flank.

On the 17th it was agreed that the plan of attack as arranged should be modified, but I was requested to continue demonstrations along my line in order to assist and support certain French operations which were being conducted elsewhere.

In his desire to act with energy up to his instructions to demonstrate and occupy the enemy, the General Officer Commanding the Indian Corps decided to take the advantage of what appeared to him a favourable opportunity to launch attacks against the advanced trenches in his front on the 18th and 19th December.

The attack of the Meerut Division on the left was made on the morning of the 19th with energy and determination, and was at first attended with considerable success, the enemy's advanced trenches being captured. Later on, however, a counter-attack drove them back to their original position with considerable loss.

The attack of the Lahore Division commenced at 4.30 a.m. It was carried out by two companies each of the 1st Highland Light Infantry and the 1st Battalion, 4th Gurkha Rifles, of the Sirhind Brigade, under Lieutenant-Colonel R. W. H. Ronaldson. This attack was completely successful, two lines of the enemy's trenches being captured with little loss. Before daylight the captured trenches were filled with as many men as they would hold. The front was very restricted, communication to the rear impossible.

At daybreak it was found that the position was practically untenable. Both flanks were in the air, and a supporting attack, which was late in starting, and, therefore, conducted during daylight, failed; although attempted with the greatest gallantry and resolution. Lieutenant-Colonel Ronaldson held on till dusk, when the whole of the captured trenches had to be evacuated, and the detachment fell back to its original line. By the night of the 19th December nearly all the ground gained during the day had been lost.

From daylight on the 20th December the enemy commenced a heavy fire from artillery and trench mortars on the whole front of the Indian Corps. This was followed by infantry attacks, which were in especial force against Givenchy, and between that place and La Quinque Rue.

At about 10 a.m. the enemy succeeded in driving back the Sirhind Brigade, and capturing a considerable part of Givenchy, but the 57th Rifles and 9th Bhopals, north of the canal, and the Connaught Rangers, south of it, stood firm.

The 15th Sikhs of the Divisional Reserve were already supporting the Sirhind Brigade. On the news of the retirement of the latter being received, the 47th Sikhs were also sent up to reinforce General Brunker. The 1st Manchester Regiment, 4th Suffolk Regiment, and two battalions of French Territorials under General Carnegy were ordered to launch a vigorous counter-attack from Pont Fixe through Givenchy to retake by a flank attack the trenches lost by the Sirhind Brigade.

Orders were sent to General Carnegy to divert his attack on Givenchy village, and to re-establish the situation there. A battalion of the 58th French Division was sent to Annequin in support.

About 5 p.m. a gallant attack by the 1st Manchester Regiment and one company of the 4th Suffolk Regiment had captured Givenchy, and had cleared the enemy out of the two lines of trenches to the north-east. To the east of the village the 9th Bhopal Infantry and 57th Rifles had maintained their positions, but the enemy were still in possession of our trenches to the north of the village.

General Macbean, with the Secunderabad Cavalry Brigade, 2nd Battalion, 8th Gurkha Rifles, and the 47th Sikhs, was sent up to support General Brunker, who at 2 p.m. directed General Macbean to move to a position of readiness in the second line trenches from Maris northward, and to counter-attack vigorously if opportunity offered. Some considerable delay appears to have occurred, and it was not until 1 a.m. on the 21st that the 47th Sikhs and the 7th Dragoon Guards under the command of Lieutenant-Colonel H. A. Lemprière, DSO, of the latter regiment, were launched in counter-attack. They reached the enemy's trenches, but were driven out by enfilade fire, their gallant Commander being killed. The main attack by the remainder of General Macbean's force, with the remnants of Lieutenant-Colonel Lemprière's detachment (which had again been rallied), was finally pushed in at about 4.30 a.m., and also failed.

In the northern section of the defensive line the retirement of the 2nd Battalion, 2nd Gurkha Rifles, at about 10 a.m. on the 20th, had left the flank of the 1st Seaforth Highlanders, on the extreme right of the Meerut Division line, much exposed. This battalion was left shortly afterwards completely in the air by the retirement of the Sirhind Brigade. The 58th Rifles, therefore, were ordered to support the left of the Seaforth Highlanders, to fill the gap created by the retirement of the Gurkhas.

During the whole of the afternoon strenuous efforts were made by the Seaforth Highlanders to clear the trenches to their right and left. The 1st Battalion, 9th Gurkha Rifles, reinforced the 2nd Gurkhas near the orchard where the Germans were in occupation of the trenches abandoned by the latter regiment. The Garhwal Brigade was being very heavily attacked, and their trenches and loopholes were much damaged; but the brigade continued to hold its front and attack, connecting with the 6th Jats on the left of the Dehra Dun Brigade. No advance in force was made by the enemy, but the troops were pinned to their ground by heavy artillery fire, the Seaforth Highlanders especially suffering heavily.

Shortly before nightfall the 2nd Royal Highlanders on the right of the Seaforth Highlanders had succeeded in establishing touch with the Sirhind Brigade; and the continuous line (though dented near the orchard) existed throughout the Meerut Division.

Early in the afternoon of December 20th orders were sent to the 1st Corps, which was then in general army reserve, to send an infantry brigade to support the Indian Corps. The 1st Brigade was ordered to Béthune, and reached that place at midnight on 20th–21st December. Later in the day Sir Douglas Haig was ordered to move the whole of the 1st Division in support of the Indian Corps.

The 3rd Brigade reached Béthune between 8 a.m. and 9 a.m. on the 21st, and on the same date the 2nd Brigade arrived at Lacon at 1 p.m.

The 1st Brigade was directed on Givenchy, via Pont Fixe, and the 3rd Brigade, through Gorre, on the trenches evacuated by the Sirhind Brigade. The 2nd Brigade was directed to support; the Dehra Dun Brigade being placed at the disposal of the General Officer Commanding Meerut Division.

At 1 p.m. the General Officer Commanding 1st Division directed the 1st Brigade in attack from the west of Givenchy in a north-easterly direction, and the 3rd Brigade from Festubert in an east-north-easterly direction, the object being to pass the position originally held by us and to capture the German trenches 400 yards to the east of it. By 5 p.m. the 1st Brigade had obtained a hold in Givenchy, and the ground south as far as the canal; and the 3rd Brigade had progressed to a point half a mile west of Festubert.

By nightfall the 1st South Wales Borderers and the 2nd Welsh Regiment of the 3rd Brigade had made a lodgment in the original trenches to the north-east of Festubert, the 1st Gloucestershire Regiment continuing the line southward along the track east of Festubert. The 1st Brigade had established itself on the east side of Givenchy.

By 3 p.m. the 3rd Brigade was concentrated at Le Touret, and was ordered to retake the trenches which had been lost by the Dehra Dun Brigade. By 10 p.m. the support trenches west of the orchard had been carried, but the original fire trenches had been so completely destroyed that they could not be occupied. This operation was performed by the 1st Loyal North Lancashire Regiment and the 1st Northamptonshire Regiment, supported by the 2nd King's Royal Rifle Corps, in reserve.

Throughout this day the units of the Indian Corps rendered all the assistance and support they could in view of their exhausted condition.

At 1 p.m. on the 22nd Sir Douglas Haig took over command from Sir James Willcocks. The situation in the front line was then approximately as follows:

South of the La Bassée Canal the Connaught Rangers of the Ferozepore Brigade had not been attacked. North of the canal a short length of our original line was still held by the 9th Bhopals and the 57th Rifles of the same brigade. Connecting with the latter was the 1st Brigade holding the village of Givenchy and its eastern and northern approaches. On the left of the 1st Brigade was the 3rd Brigade. Touch had been lost between the left of the former and the right of the latter. The 3rd Brigade held a line along, and in places advanced to, the east of the Festubert Road. Its left was in communication with the right of the Meerut Division line, where troops of the 2nd Brigade had just relieved the 1st Seaforth Highlanders. To the north, units of the 2nd Brigade held an indented line west of the orchard, connecting with half of the 2nd Royal Highlanders, half of the 41st Dogras and the 1st Battalion, 9th Gurkha Rifles. From this point to the north the 6th Jats and the whole of the Garhwal Brigade occupied the original line which they had held from the commencement of the operations.

The relief of most units of the southern sector was effected on the night of 22nd December. The Meerut Division remained under the orders of the 1st Corps, and was not completely withdrawn until the 27th December. In the evening the position at Givenchy was practically re-established, and the 3rd Brigade had re-occupied the old line of trenches. During the 23rd the enemy's activities ceased, and the whole position was restored to very much its original condition.

In my last despatch I had occasion to mention the prompt and ready help I received from the Lahore Division, under the command of Major-General H. B. B. Watkis, CB, which was thrown into action immediately on arrival, when the British forces were very hard pressed during the battle of Ypres-Armentières.

The Indian troops have fought with the utmost steadfastness and gallantry whenever they have been called upon. Weather conditions were abnormally bad, the snow and floods precluding any active operations during the first three weeks of January.

At 7.30 a.m. on the 25th January the enemy began to shell Béthune, and at 8 a.m. a strong hostile infantry attack developed south of the canal, preceded by a heavy bombardment of artillery, minenwerfers, and, possibly, the explosion of mines, though the latter is doubtful.

The British line south of the canal formed a pronounced salient from the canal on the left, thence running forward toward the railway triangle and back to the main La Bassée–Bethune Road, where it joined the French. This line was occupied by half a battalion of the Scots Guards, and half a battalion of the Coldstream Guards, of the 1st Infantry Brigade. The trenches in the salient were blown in almost at once; and the enemy's attack penetrated this line. Our troops retired to a partially prepared second line, running approximately due north and south from the canal to the road, some 500 yards west of the railway triangle. This second line had been strengthened by the construction of a keep half way between the canal and the road. Here the other two half battalions of the above-mentioned regiments were in support.

These supports held up the enemy who, however, managed to establish himself in the brick stacks and some communication trenches between the keep, the road and the canal—and even beyond the west of the keep on either side of it.

The London Scottish had in the meantime been sent up in support, and a counter-attack was organised with the 1st Royal Highlanders, part of the 1st Cameron Highlanders, and the 2nd King's Royal Rifle Corps, the latter regiment having been sent forward from the Divisional Reserve. The counter-attack was delayed in order to synchronise with a counter-attack north of the canal which was arranged for 1 p.m.

At 1 p.m. these troops moved forward, their flanks making good progress near the road and the canal, but their centre being held up. The 2nd Royal Sussex Regiment was then sent forward, late in the afternoon, to reinforce. The result was that the Germans were driven back far enough to enable a somewhat broken line to be taken up, running from the culvert on the railway, almost due south to the keep, and thence south-east to the main road.

The French left near the road had also been attacked and driven back a little, but not to so great an extent as the British right. Consequently, the French left was in advance of the British right and exposed to a possible flank attack from the north. The Germans did not, however, persevere further in their attack.

The above-mentioned line was strengthened during the night; and the 1st Guards Brigade, which had suffered severely, was withdrawn into reserve and replaced by the 2nd Infantry Brigade.

While this was taking place another, an equally severe attack was delivered north of the canal against the village of Givenchy. At 8.15 a.m., after a heavy artillery bombardment with high explosive shells, the enemy's infantry advanced under the effective fire of our artillery, which, however, was hampered by the constant interruption of telephonic communication between the observers and batteries. Nevertheless, our artillery fire, combined with that of the infantry in the fire trenches, had the effect of driving the enemy from his original direction of advance, with the result that his troops crowded together on the north-east corner of the village and broke through into the centre of the village as far as the keep, which had been previously put in a state of defence. The Germans had lost heavily, and a well-timed local counter-attack, delivered by the reserves of the 2nd Welsh Regiment and 1st South Wales Borderers, and by a company of the 1st Royal Highlanders (lent by the 1st Brigade as a working party—this company was at work on the keep at the time), was completely successful, with the result that, after about an hour's street fighting, all who had broken into the village were either captured or killed; and the original line round the village was re-established by noon. South of the village, however, and close to the canal, the right of the 2nd Royal Munster Fusiliers fell back in conformity with the troops south of the canal; but after dark that regiment moved forward and occupied the old line.

During the course of the attack on Givenchy the enemy made five assaults on the salient at the north-east of the village about French Farm, but was repulsed every time with heavy loss.

On the morning of the 29th January attacks were made on the right of the 1st Corps, south of the canal in the neighbourhood of La Bassée. The enemy (part of the 14th German Corps), after a severe shelling, made a violent attack with scaling ladders on the keep, also to the north and south of it. In the keep and on the north side the Sussex Regiment held the enemy off, inflicting on him serious losses. On the south side the hostile infantry succeeded in reaching the Northamptonshire Regiment's trenches; but were immediately counter-attacked and all killed. Our artillery cooperated well with the infantry in repelling the attack.

In this action our casualties were inconsiderable, but the enemy lost severely, more than 200 of his killed alone being left in front, of our position.

On the 1st February a fine piece of work was carried out by the 4th Brigade in the neighbourhood of Cuinchy. Some of the 2nd Coldstream Guards were driven from their trenches at 2.30 a.m., but made a stand some twenty yards east of them in a position which they held till morning.

A counter-attack, launched at 3.15 a.m. by one company of the Irish Guards and half a company of the 2nd Coldstream Guards, proved unsuccessful, owing to heavy rifle fire from the east and south.

At 10.05 a.m., acting under orders of the 1st Division, a heavy bombardment was opened on the lost ground for ten minutes; and this was followed immediately by an assault by about 50 men of the 2nd Coldstream Guards with bayonets, led by Captain A. Leigh Bennett, followed by 30 men of the Irish Guards, led by Second Lieutenant F. F. Graham, also with bayonets. These were followed by a party of Royal Engineers with sand bags and wire.

All the ground which had been lost was brilliantly retaken; the 2nd Coldstream Guards also taking another German trench and capturing two machine guns. Thirty-two prisoners fell into our hands.

The General Officer Commanding 1st Division describes the preparation by the artillery as "splendid, the high explosive shells dropping in the exact spot with absolute precision."

In forwarding his report on this engagement, the General Officer Commanding First Army writes as follows:

Special credit is due:

(i) To Major-General Haking, Commanding 1st Division, for the prompt manner in which he arranged this counter-attack and for the general plan of action, which was crowned with success.

(ii) To the General Officer Commanding the 4th Brigade (Lord Cavan) for the thorough manner in which he carried out the orders of the General Officer Commanding the Division.

(iii) To the regimental officers, non-commissioned officers and men of the 2nd Coldstream Guards and Irish Guards, who, with indomitable pluck, stormed two sets of barricades, captured three German trenches, two machine guns, and killed or made prisoners many of the enemy.

During the period under report the Royal Flying Corps has again performed splendid service. Although the weather was almost uniformly bad and the machines suffered from constant exposure, there have been only thirteen days on which no actual reconnaissance has been effected. Approximately, one hundred thousand miles have been flown.

In addition to the daily and constant work of reconnaissance and co-operation with the artillery, a number of aerial combats have been fought, raids carried out, detrainments harassed, parks and petrol depôts bombed, etc.

Various successful bomb-dropping raids have been carried out, usually against the enemy's aircraft material. The principle of attacking hostile aircraft whenever and wherever seen (unless highly important information is being delivered) has been adhered to, and has resulted in the morale fact that enemy machines invariably beat immediate retreat when chased.

Five German aeroplanes are known to have been brought to the ground, and it would appear probable that others, though they have managed to reach their own lines, have done so in a considerably damaged condition.

In my despatch of 20th November, 1914 [not included], I referred to the reinforcements of Territorial Troops which I had received, and I mentioned several units which had already been employed in the fighting line.

In the positions which I held for some years before the outbreak of this war I was brought into close contact with the Territorial Force, and I found every reason to hope and believe that, when the hour of trial arrived, they would justify every hope and trust which was placed in them.

The Lords Lieutenant of Counties and the Associations which worked under them bestowed a vast amount of labour and energy on the organization of the Territorial Force; and I trust it may be some recompense to them to know that I, and the principal Commanders serving under me, consider that the Territorial Force has far more than justified the most sanguine hopes that any of us ventured to entertain of their value and use in the field. Commanders of Cavalry Divisions are unstinted in their praise of the manner in which the Yeomanry regiments attached to their brigades have done their duty, both in and out of action. The service of Divisional Cavalry is now almost entirely performed by Yeomanry, and Divisional Commanders report that they are very efficient.

Army Corps Commanders are loud in their praise of the Territorial Battalions which form part of nearly all the brigades at the front in the first line, and more than one of them have told me that these battalions are fast approaching—if they have not already reached—the standard of efficiency of Regular Infantry.

I wish to add a word about the Officers Training Corps. The presence of the Artists' Rifles (28th Battalion, The London Regiment) with the Army in France enabled me also to test the value of this organization. Having had some experience in peace of the working of the Officers Training Corps, I determined to turn the Artists' Rifles (which formed part of the Officers Training Corps in peace time) to its legitimate use. I therefore established the battalion as a Training Corps for officers in the field.

The cadets pass through a course, which includes some thoroughly practical training as all cadets do a tour of 48 hours in the trenches, and afterwards write a report on what they see and notice. They also visit an observation post of a battery or group of batteries, and spend some hours there.

A Commandant has been appointed, and he arranges and supervises the work, sets schemes for practice, administers the school, delivers lectures, and reports on the candidates. The cadets are instructed in all branches of military training suitable for platoon commanders. Machine gun tactics, a knowledge of which is so necessary for all junior officers, is a special feature of the course of instruction. When first started the school was able to turn out officers at the rate of 75 a month. This has since been increased to 100. Reports received from Divisional and Army Corps Commanders on officers who have been trained at the school are most satisfactory.

Since the date of my last report I have been able to make a close personal inspection of all the units in the command. I was most favourably impressed by all I saw.

The troops composing the Army in France have been subjected to as severe a trial as it is possible to impose upon any body of men. The desperate fighting described in my last despatch had hardly been brought to a conclusion when they were called upon to face the rigours and hardships of a winter campaign. Frost and snow have alternated with periods of continuous rain.

The men have been called upon to stand for many hours together almost up to their waists in bitterly cold water, only separated by one or two hundred yards from a most vigilant enemy. Although every measure which science and medical knowledge could suggest to mitigate these hardships was employed, the sufferings of the men have been very great. In spite of all this they presented, at the inspections to which I have referred, a most soldier-like, splendid, though somewhat war-worn appearance. Their spirit remains high and confident; their general health is excellent, and their condition most satisfactory.

I regard it as most unfortunate that circumstances have prevented any account of many splendid instances of courage and endurance, in the face of almost unparalleled hardship and fatigue in war, coming regularly to the knowledge of the public.

Reinforcements have arrived from England with remarkable promptitude and rapidity. They have been speedily drafted into the ranks, and most of the units I inspected were nearly complete when I saw them. In appearance and quality the drafts sent out have exceeded my most sanguine expectations, and I consider the Army in France is much indebted to the Adjutant-General's Department at the War Office for the efficient manner in which its requirements have been met in this most essential respect.

With regard to these inspections, I may mention in particular the fine appearance presented by the men of the 27th and 28th Divisions, composed principally of battalions which had come from India. Included in the former division was the Princess Patricia's Royal Canadian Regiment. They are a magnificent set of men, and they have since done some excellent work in the trenches.

It was some three weeks after the events recorded that I made my inspection of the Indian Corps, under Sir James Willcocks. The appearance they presented was most satisfactory, and fully confirmed my first opinion that the Indian troops only required rest, and a little acclimatizing, to bring out all their fine inherent fighting qualities.

I saw the whole of the Indian Cavalry Corps, under Lieutenant-General Rimington, on a mounted parade soon after their arrival. They are a magnificent body of cavalry, and will, I feel sure, give the best possible account of themselves when called upon.

In the meantime, at their own particular request, they have taken their turn in the trenches and performed most useful and valuable service.

The Rt. Rev. Bishop Taylor Smith, CVO, DD, Chaplain-General to the Forces, arrived at my Headquarters on 6th January, on a tour of inspection throughout the command. The Cardinal Archbishop of Westminster has also visited most of the Irish Regiments at the front and the principal centres on the Line of Communications.

In a quiet and unostentatious manner the chaplains of all denominations have worked with devotion and energy in their respective spheres. The number with the forces in the field at the commencement of the war was comparatively small, but towards the end of last year the Rev. J. M. Simms, DD, KHC, Principal Chaplain, assisted by his Secretary, the Rev. W. Drury, reorganised the branch, and placed the spiritual welfare of the soldier on a more satisfactory footing. It is hoped that the further increase of personnel may be found possible. I cannot speak too highly of the devoted manner in which all chaplains, whether with the troops in the trenches, or in attendance on the sick and wounded in casualty clearing stations and hospitals on the line of communications, have worked throughout the campaign.

Since the commencement of hostilities the work of the Royal Army Medical Corps has been carried out with untiring zeal, skill and devotion. Whether at the battle front under conditions such as obtained during the fighting on the River Aisne, when casualties were heavy and accommodation for their reception had to be improvised, or on the line of communications, where an average of some 11,000 patients have been daily under treatment, the organisation of the Medical Services has always been equal to the demands made upon it.

The careful system of sanitation introduced into the Army has, with the assistance of other measures, kept the troops free from any epidemic, in support of which it is to be noticed that since the commencement of the war some 500 cases only of enteric have occurred.

The organisation for the first time in war of Motor Ambulance Convoys is due to the initiative and organising powers of Surgeon-General T. J. O'Donnell, DSO, ably assisted by Major P. Evans, Royal Army Medical Corps. Two of these convoys, composed entirely of Red Cross Society personnel, have done excellent work under the superintendence of Regular Medical Officers.

Twelve hospital trains ply between the front and the various bases. I have visited several of the trains when halted in stations, and have found them conducted with great comfort and efficiency. During the more recent phase of the campaign the creation of Rest Depôts at the front has materially reduced the wastage of men to the Line of Communications.

Since the latter part of October, 1914, the whole of the medical arrangements have been in the hands of Surgeon-General Sir A. T. Sloggett, CMG, KHS, under whom Surgeon-General T. P. Woodhouse and Surgeon-General T. J. O'Donnell have been responsible for the organisation on the Line of Communications and at the front respectively.

The exceptional and peculiar conditions brought about by the weather have caused large demands to be made upon the resources and skill of the Royal Engineers. Every kind of expedient has had to be thought out and adopted to keep the lines of trenches and defence work effective. The Royal Engineers have shown themselves as capable of overcoming the ravages caused by violent rain and floods as they have been throughout in neutralising the effect of the enemy's artillery.

In this connection I wish particularly to mention the excellent services performed by my Chief Engineer, Brigadier-General G. H. Fowke, who has been indefatigable in supervising all such work. His ingenuity and skill have been most valuable in the local construction of the various expedients which experience has shown to be necessary in prolonged trench warfare.

I have once more gratefully to acknowledge the valuable help and support I have received throughout this period from General Foch, General D'Urbal and General Maud'huy of the French Army.

J. D. P. FRENCH
Field-Marshal,
Commanding-in-Chief,
The British Army in the Field

NEUVE CHAPELLE AND ST ELOI, FEBRUARY TO MARCH 1915

From the Field-Marshal Commanding-in-Chief, British Forces in the Field, to the Secretary of State for War

General Headquarters, 5th April, 1915

My Lord,
I have the honour to report the operations of the forces under my command since the date of my last despatch, 2nd February, 1915.

The event of chief interest and importance which has taken place is the victory achieved over the enemy at the battle of Neuve Chapelle, which was fought on the 10th, 11th and 12th of March. The main attack was delivered by troops of the First Army under the command of General Sir Douglas Haig, supported by a large force of heavy artillery, a division of cavalry and some infantry of the general reserve.

Secondary and holding attacks and demonstrations were made along the front of the Second Army under the direction of its Commander, General Sir Horace Smith-Dorrien.

Whilst the success attained was due to the magnificent bearing and indomitable courage displayed by the troops of the 4th and Indian Corps, I consider that the able and skilful dispositions which were made by the General Officer Commanding First Army contributed largely to the defeat of the enemy and to the capture of his position. The energy and vigour with which General Sir Douglas Haig handled his command show him to be a leader of great ability and power.

Another action of considerable importance was brought about by a surprise attack of the Germans made on the 14th March against the 27th Division holding the trenches east of St Eloi. A large force of artillery was concentrated in this area under cover of mist, and a heavy volume of fire was suddenly brought to bear on the trenches at 5 p.m. This artillery attack was accompanied by two mine explosions; and, in the confusion caused by these and the suddenness of the attack, St Eloi was captured and held for some hours by the enemy.

Well directed and vigorous counter-attacks, in which the troops of the 5th Army Corps showed great bravery and determination, restored the situation by the evening of the 15th.

A more detailed account of these operations will appear in subsequent pages of this despatch.

On the 6th February a brilliant action by troops of the 1st Corps materially improved our position in the area south of the La Bassée Canal. During the previous night parties of Irish Guards and of the 3rd Battalion Coldstream Guards had succeeded in gaining ground whence converging fire could be directed on the flanks and rear of certain "brickstacks" occupied by the Germans, which had been for some time a source of considerable annoyance.

At 2 p.m. the affair commenced with a severe bombardment of the "brickstacks" and the enemy trenches. A brisk attack by the 3rd Coldstream Guards and Irish Guards from our trenches west of the "brickstacks" followed, and was supported by fire from the flanking positions which had been seized the previous night by the same regiments. The attack succeeded, the "brickstacks" were occupied by our men without difficulty, and a line was established running north and south through a point about forty yards east of the "brickstacks."

The casualties suffered by the 5th Corps throughout the period under review, and particularly during the month of February, have been heavier than those in other parts of the line. I regret this; but I do not think, taking all the circumstances into consideration, that they were unduly numerous. The position then occupied by the 5th Corps has always been a very vulnerable part of our line; the ground is marshy, and trenches are most difficult to construct and maintain. The 27th and 28th Divisions of the 5th Corps have had no previous experience of European warfare, and a number of the units composing it had only recently returned from service in tropical climates. In consequence, the hardships of a rigorous winter campaign fell with greater weight upon these divisions than upon any other in the command.

Chiefly owing to these causes, the 5th Corps, up to the beginning of March, was constantly engaged in counter-attacks to retake trenches and ground which had been lost. In their difficult and arduous task, however, the troops displayed the utmost gallantry and devotion; and it is most creditable to the skill and energy of their leaders that I am able to report how well they have surmounted all their difficulties, that the ground first taken over by them is still intact, and held with little greater loss than is incurred by troops in all other parts of the line.

On the 14th February the 82nd Brigade of the 27th Division was driven from its trenches east of St Eloi; but by 7 a.m. on the 15th all these trenches had been recaptured, fifteen prisoners taken, and sixty German dead counted in front of the trenches. Similarly in the 28th Division trenches were lost by the 85th Brigade and retaken the following night.

During the month of February the enemy made several attempts to get through all along the line, but he was invariably repulsed with loss. A particularly vigorous attempt was made on the 17th February against the trenches held by the Indian Corps, but it was brilliantly repulsed.

On February 28th a successful minor attack was made on the enemy's trenches near St Eloi by small parties of the Princess Patricia's Canadian Light Infantry. The attack was divided into three small groups, the whole under the command of Lieutenant Crabbe: No. 1 Group under Lieutenant Papineau, No. 2 Group under Sergeant Patterson, and No. 3 Group under Company Sergeant-Major Lloyd. The head of the party got within fifteen or twenty yards of the German trench and charged; it was dark at the time (about 5.15 a.m.).

Lieutenant Crabbe, who showed the greatest dash and *élan*, took his party over everything in the trench until they had gone down it about eighty yards, when they were stopped by a barricade of sandbags and timber. This party, as well as the others, then pulled down the front face of the German parapet. A number of Germans were killed and wounded, and a few prisoners were taken.

The services performed by this distinguished corps have continued to be very valuable since I had occasion to refer to them in my last despatch. They have been most ably organised, trained and commanded by Lieutenant-Colonel F. D. Farquhar, DSO, who, I deeply regret to say, was killed while superintending some trench work on the 20th March. His loss will be deeply felt.

A very gallant attack was made by the 4th Battalion of the King's Royal Rifle Corps of the 80th Brigade on the enemy's trenches in the early hours of March 2nd. The Battalion was led by Major Widdrington, who launched it at 12.30 a.m. (he himself being wounded during its progress), covered by an extremely accurate and effective artillery fire. About sixty yards of the enemy's trench were cleared, but the attack was brought to a standstill by a strong barricade, in attempting to storm which several casualties were incurred.

During the month of February I arranged with General Foch to render the 9th French Corps, holding the trenches on my left, some much-needed rest by sending the three divisions of the British Cavalry Corps to hold a portion of the French trenches, each division for a period of ten days alternately.

It was very gratifying to me to note once again in this campaign the eager readiness which the cavalry displayed to undertake a rôle which does not properly belong to them in order to support and assist their French comrades. In carrying out this work leaders, officers and men displayed the same skill and energy which I have had reason to comment upon in former despatches. The time passed by the cavalry in the French trenches was, on the whole, quiet and uneventful, but there are one or two incidents calling for remark.

At about 1.45 a.m. on 16th February a half-hearted attack was made against the right of the line held by the 2nd Cavalry Division, but it was easily repulsed by rifle fire, and the enemy left several dead in front of the trenches. The attack was delivered against the second and third trenches from the right of the line of this division.

At 6 a.m. on the 21st the enemy blew up one of the 2nd Cavalry Division trenches, held by the 16th Lancers, and some adjoining French trenches. The enemy occupied forty yards of our trench and tried to advance, but were stopped. An immediate counter-attack by the supporting squadron was stopped by machine-gun fire. The line was established opposite the gap, and a counter-attack by two squadrons and one company of French reserve was ordered. At 5.30 p.m. 2nd Cavalry Division reported that the counter-attack did not succeed in retaking the trench blown in, but that a new line had been established forty yards in rear of it, and that there was no further activity on the part of the enemy. At 10 p.m. the situation was unchanged.

The Commander of the Indian Cavalry Corps expressed a strong desire that the troops under his command should gain some experience in trench warfare. Arrangements were made, therefore, with the General Officer Commanding the Indian Corps, in pursuance of which the various units of the Indian Cavalry Corps have from time to time taken a turn in the trenches, and have thereby gained some valuable experience.

About the end of February many vital considerations induced me to believe that a vigorous offensive movement by the forces under my command should be planned and carried out at the earliest possible moment.

Amongst the more important reasons which convinced me of this necessity were: the general aspect of the Allied situation throughout Europe, and particularly the marked success of the Russian Army in repelling the violent onslaughts of Marshal Von Hindenburg; the apparent weakening of the enemy in my front, and the necessity for assisting our Russian Allies to the utmost by holding as many hostile troops as possible in the Western theatre; the efforts to this end which were being made by the French forces at Arras and Champagne; and, perhaps the most weighty consideration of all, the need of fostering the offensive spirit in the troops under my command after the trying and possibly enervating experiences which they had gone through of a severe winter in the trenches.

In a former despatch I commented upon the difficulties and drawbacks which the winter weather in this climate imposes upon a vigorous offensive. Early in March these difficulties became greatly lessened by the drying up of the country and by spells of brighter weather. I do not propose in this despatch to enter at length into the considerations which actuated me in deciding upon the plan, time and place of my attack, but Your Lordship is fully aware of these.

As mentioned above, the main attack was carried out by units of the First Army, supported by troops of the Second Army and the general reserve. The object of the main attack was to be the capture of the village of Neuve Chapelle and the enemy's position at that point, and the establishment of our line as far forward as possible to the east of that place.

The object, nature and scope of the attack, and instructions for the conduct of the operation were communicated by me to Sir Douglas Haig in a secret memorandum dated 19th February.

The main topographical feature of this part of the theatre is a marked ridge which runs south-west from a point two miles south-west of Lille to the village of Fournes, whence two spurs run out, one due west to a height known as Haut Pommereau, the other following the line of the main road to Illies.

The buildings of the village of Neuve Chapelle run along the Rue du Bois–Fauquissart Road. There is a triangle of roads just north of the village. This area consists of a few big houses, with walls, gardens, orchards, etc., and here, with the aid of numerous machine guns, the enemy had established a strong post which flanked the approaches to the village.

The Bois du Biez, which lies roughly south-east of the village of Neuve Chapelle, influenced the course of this operation. Full instructions as to assisting and supporting the attack were issued to the Second Army.

The battle opened at 7.30 a.m. on the 10th March by a powerful artillery bombardment of the enemy's position at Neuve Chapelle. The artillery bombardment had been well prepared and was most effective, except on the extreme northern portion of the front of attack.

At 8.05 a.m. the 23rd (left) and 25th (right) Brigades of the 8th Division assaulted the German trenches on the north-west of the village. At the same hour the Garhwal Brigade of the Meerut Division, which occupied the position to the south of Neuve Chapelle, assaulted the German trenches in its front.

Neuve Chapelle, 1915

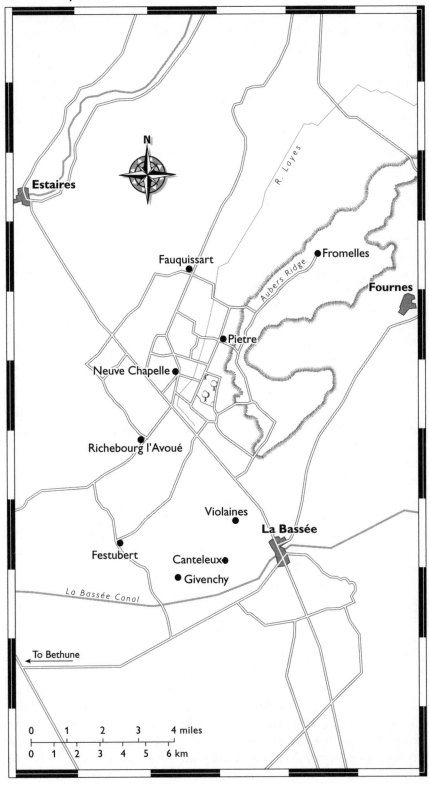

The Garhwal Brigade and the 25th Brigade carried the enemy's lines of entrenchments where the wire entanglements had been almost entirely swept away by our shrapnel fire. The 23rd Brigade, however, on the north-east, was held up by the wire entanglements, which were not sufficiently cut.

At 8.05 a.m. the artillery turned on to Neuve Chapelle, and at 8.35 a.m. the advance of the infantry was continued. The 25th and Garwhal Brigades pushed on eastward and north-eastward respectively, and succeeded in getting a footing in the village. The 23rd Brigade was still held up in front of the enemy's wire entanglements, and could not progress. Heavy losses were suffered, especially in the Middlesex Regiment and the Scottish Rifles. The progress, however, of the 25th Brigade into Neuve Chapelle immediately to the south of the 23rd Brigade had the effect of turning the southern flank of the enemy's defences in front of the 23rd Brigade.

This fact, combined with powerful artillery support, enabled the 23rd Brigade to get forward between 10 and 11 a.m., and by 11 a.m. the whole of the village of Neuve Chapelle and the roads leading northward and south-westward from the eastern end of that village were in our hands.

During this time our artillery completely cut off the village and the surrounding country from any German reinforcements which could be thrown into the fight to restore the situation by means of shrapnel fire. Prisoners subsequently reported that all attempts at reinforcing the front line were checked. Steps were at once taken to consolidate the position won.

Considerable delay occurred after the capture of the Neuve Chapelle position. The infantry was greatly disorganised by the violent nature of the attack and by its passage through the enemy's trenches and the buildings of the village. It was necessary to get units to some extent together before pushing on. The telephonic communication being cut by the enemy's fire rendered communication between front and rear most difficult. The fact of the left of the 23rd Brigade having been held up had kept back the 8th Division, and had involved a portion of the 25th Brigade in fighting to the north out of its proper direction of advance. All this required adjustment. An orchard held by the enemy north of Neuve Chapelle also threatened the flank of an advance towards the Aubers Ridge.

I am of the opinion that this delay would not have occurred had the clearly expressed order of the General Officer Commanding First Army been more carefully observed. The difficulties above enumerated might have been overcome at an earlier period of the day if the General Officer Commanding 4th Corps had been able to bring his reserve brigades more speedily into action. As it was, the further advance did not commence before 3.30 p.m.

The 21st Brigade was able to form up in the open on the left without a shot being fired at it, thus showing that at the time the enemy's resistance had been paralysed. The brigade pushed forward in the direction of Moulin de Pietre. At first it made good progress, but was subsequently held up by the machine-gun fire from the houses and from a defended work in the line of the German entrenchments opposite the right of the 22nd Brigade.

Further to the south the 24th Brigade, which had been directed on Pietre, was similarly held up by machine-guns in the houses and trenches at the road junction six hundred yards north-west of Pietre.

The 25th Brigade, on the right of the 24th, was also held up by machine-guns from a bridge held by the Germans, over the River des Layes, which is situated to the north-west of the Bois du Biez.

Whilst the two brigades of the Meerut Division were establishing themselves on the new line, the Dehra Dun Brigade, supported by the Jullundur Brigade of the Lahore Division, moved to the attack of the Bois du Biez, but were held up on the line of the River des Layes by the German post at the bridge which enfiladed them and brought them to a standstill.

The defended bridge over the River des Layes and its neighbourhood immediately assumed considerable importance. Whilst artillery fire was brought to bear, as far as circumstances would permit, on this point, Sir Douglas Haig directed the 1st Corps to despatch one or more battalions of the 1st Brigade in support of the troops attacking the bridge. Three battalions were thus sent to Richebourg St Vaast. Darkness coming on, and the enemy having brought up reinforcements, no further progress could be made, and the Indian Corps and 4th Corps proceeded to consolidate the position they had gained.

Whilst the operations which I have thus briefly recorded were going on, the 1st Corps in accordance with orders, delivered an attack in the morning from Givenchy, simultaneously with that against Neuve Chapelle; but as the enemy's wire was insufficiently cut, very little progress could be made, and the troops at this point did little more than hold fast the Germans in front of them.

On the following day, March 11th, the attack was renewed by the 4th and Indian Corps, but it was soon seen that a further advance would be impossible until the artillery had dealt effectively with the various houses and defended localities which held up the troops along the entire front. Efforts were made to direct the artillery fire accordingly; but owing to the weather conditions, which did not permit of aerial observation, and the fact that nearly all the telephonic communications between the artillery observers and their batteries had been cut, it was impossible to do so with sufficient accuracy. Even when our troops which were pressing forward occupied a house here and there, it was not possible to stop our artillery fire, and the infantry had to be withdrawn. The two principal points which barred the advance were the same as on the preceding day—namely, the enemy's position about Moulin de Pietre and at the bridge over the River des Layes.

On the 12th March the same unfavourable conditions as regards weather prevailed, and hampered artillery action.

Although the 4th and Indian Corps most gallantly attempted to capture the strongly fortified positions in their front, they were unable to maintain themselves, although they succeeded in holding them for some hours.

Operations on this day were chiefly remarkable for the violent counter-attacks, supported by artillery, which were delivered by the Germans, and the ease with which they were repulsed.

As most of the objects for which the operations had been undertaken had been attained and as there were reasons why I considered it inadvisable to continue the attack at that time, I directed Sir Douglas Haig on the night of the 12th to hold and consolidate the ground which had been gained by the 4th and Indian Corps, and to suspend further offensive operations for the present.

On the morning of the 12th I informed the General Officer Commanding 1st Army that he could call on the 2nd Cavalry Division, under General Gough, for immediate support in the event of the successes of the First Army opening up opportunities for its favourable employment. This Division and a Brigade of the North Midland Division, which was temporarily attached to it, was moved forward for this purpose.

The 5th Cavalry Brigade, under Sir Philip Chetwode, reached the Rue Bacquerot at 4 p.m., with a view to rendering immediate support; but he was informed by the General Officer Commanding 4th Corps that the situation was not so favourable as he had hoped it would be, and that no further action by the cavalry was advisable. General Gough's command, therefore, retired to Estaires.

The artillery of all kinds was handled with the utmost energy and skill, and rendered invaluable support in the prosecution of the attack.

The losses during these three days' fighting were, I regret to say, very severe, numbering:

190 officers and 2,337 other ranks, killed.
359 officers and 8,174 other ranks, wounded.
23 officers and 1,728 other ranks, missing.

But the results attained were, in my opinion, wide and far reaching.

The enemy left several thousand dead on the battlefield which were seen and counted; and we have positive information that upwards of 12,000 wounded were removed to the north-east and east by train. Thirty officers and 1,657 other ranks of the enemy were captured.

I can best express my estimate of this battle by quoting an extract from a Special Order of the Day which I addressed to Sir Douglas Haig and the First Army at its conclusion:

> I am anxious to express to you personally my warmest appreciation of the skilful manner in which you have carried out your orders, and my fervent and most heartfelt appreciation of the magnificent gallantry and devoted, tenacious courage displayed by all ranks whom you have ably led to success and victory.

Some operations in the nature of holding attacks, carried out by troops of the Second Army, were instrumental in keeping the enemy in front of them occupied, and preventing reinforcements being sent from those portions of the front to the main point of attack.

At 12.30 a.m. on the 12th March the 17th Infantry Brigade of the 4th Division, 3rd Corps, engaged in an attack on the enemy which resulted in the capture of the village of L'Epinette and adjacent farms. Supported by a brisk fire from the 18th Infantry Brigade, the 17th Infantry Brigade, detailed for the attack, assaulted in two columns converging, and obtained the first houses of the village without much loss. The remainder of the village was very heavily wired, and the enemy got away by means of communication trenches while our men were cutting through the wire. The enemy suffered considerable loss; our casualties being 5 officers and 30 other ranks, killed and wounded.

The result of this operation was that an advance of 300 yards was made on a front of half a mile. All attempts to retake this position have been repulsed with heavy loss to the enemy.

The General Officer Commanding the Second Corps arranged for an attack on a part of the enemy's position to the south-west of the village of Wytschaete which he had timed to commence at 10 a.m. on the 12th March. Owing to dense fog, the assault could not be made until 4 o'clock in the afternoon. It was then commenced by the Wiltshire and Worcestershire Regiments, but was so hampered by the mist and the approach of darkness that nothing more was effected than holding the enemy to his ground.

The action of St Eloi referred to in the first paragraph of this despatch commenced at 5 p.m. on the 14th March by a very heavy cannonade which was directed against our trenches in front of St Eloi, the village itself and the approaches to it. There is a large mound lying to the south-east of the village. When the artillery attack was at its height a mine was exploded under this mound, and a strong hostile infantry attack was immediately launched against the trenches and the mound.

Our artillery opened fire at once, as well as our infantry, and inflicted considerable losses on the enemy during their advance; but, chiefly owing to the explosion of the mine and the surprise of the overwhelming artillery attack, the enemy's infantry had penetrated the first line of trenches at some points. As a consequence the garrisons of other works which had successfully resisted the assault were enfiladed and forced to retire just before it turned dark.

A counter-attack was at once organised by the General Officer Commanding 82nd Brigade, under the orders of the General Officer Commanding 27th Division, who brought up a reserve brigade to support it. The attack was launched at 2 a.m., and the 82nd Brigade succeeded in recapturing the portion of the village of St Eloi which was in the hands of the enemy and a portion of the trenches east of it. At 3 a.m. the 80th Brigade in support took more trenches to the east and west of the village. The counter-attack, which was well carried out under difficult conditions, resulted in the recapture of all lost ground of material importance.

It is satisfactory to be able to record that, though the troops occupying the first line of trenches were at first overwhelmed, they afterwards behaved very gallantly in the counter-attack for the recovery of the lost ground; and the following units earned and received the special commendation of the Army Commander: the 2nd Royal Irish Fusiliers, the 2nd Duke of Cornwall's Light Infantry, the 1st Leinster Regiment, the 4th Rifle Brigade and the Princess Patricia's Canadian Light Infantry.

A vigorous attack made by the enemy on the 17th to recapture these trenches was repulsed with great loss. Throughout the period under review night enterprises by smaller or larger patrols, which were led with consummate skill and daring, have been very active along the whole line. A moral superiority has thus been established, and valuable information has been collected.

I cannot speak too highly of the invincible courage and the remarkable resource displayed by these patrols. The troops of the 3rd Corps have particularly impressed me by their conduct of these operations.

The work of the Royal Flying Corps throughout this period, and especially during the operations of the 10th, 11th, and 12th March, was of the greatest value. Though the weather on March 10th and on the subsequent days was very unfavourable for aerial work, on account of low-lying clouds and mist, a remarkable number of hours flying of a most valuable character were effected, and continuous and close reconnaissance was maintained over the enemy's front.

In addition to the work of reconnaissance and observation of artillery fire, the Royal Flying Corps was charged with the special duty of hampering the enemy's movements by destroying various points on his communications. The railways at Menin, Courtrai, Don and Douai were attacked, and it is known that very extensive damage was effected at certain of these places. Part of a troop train was hit by a bomb, a wireless installation near Lille is believed to have been effectively destroyed, and a house in which the enemy had installed one of his Headquarters was set on fire. These afford other instances of successful operations of this character. Most of the objectives mentioned were attacked at a height of only 100 to 150 feet. In one case the pilot descended to about 50 feet above the point he was attacking.

Certain new and important forms of activity, which it is undesirable to specify, have been initiated and pushed forward with much vigour and success.

There have been only eight days during the period under review on which reconnaissances have not been made. A total of approximately 130,000 miles have been flown—almost entirely over the enemy's lines.

No great activity has been shown over our troops on the part of the enemy's aircraft, but they have been attacked whenever and wherever met with, and usually forced down or made to seek refuge in their own lines.

In my last despatch I referred to the remarkable promptitude and rapidity with which reinforcements arrived in this country from England. In connection with this it is of interest to call attention to the fact that, in spite of the heavy casualties incurred in the fighting between the 10th and 15th March, all deficiencies, both in officers and rank and file, were made good within a few days of the conclusion of the battle.

The drafts for the Indian Contingents have much improved of late, and are now quite satisfactory.

Since the date of my last report the general health of the Army has been excellent; enteric has decreased, and there has been no recurrence on any appreciable scale of the "foot" trouble which appeared so threatening in December and January. These results are due to the skill and energy which have characterised in a marked degree the work of the Royal Army Medical Corps throughout the campaign, under the able supervision of Surgeon-General T. J. O'Donnell, DSO, Deputy Director-General, Medical Services. But much credit is also due to Divisional, Brigade, Regimental and Company Commanders for the close supervision which has been kept over the health of their men by seeing that the precautions laid down for the troops before entering and after leaving the trenches are duly observed, and by the establishment and efficient maintenance of bathing-places and wash-houses, and by the ingenious means universally employed throughout the forces to maintain the cleanliness of the men, having regard both to their bodies and their clothing. I have inspected most of these houses and establishments, and consider them models of careful organisation and supervision.

I would particularly comment upon the energy displayed by the Royal Army Medical Corps in the scientific efforts they have made to discover and check disease in its earliest stages by a system of experimental research, which I think has never before been so fully developed in the field. In this work they have been ably assisted by those distinguished members of the medical profession who are now employed as Military Medical Officers, and whose invaluable services I gratefully acknowledge.

The actual strength of the force in the field has been increased and the health of the troops improved by a system of "convalescent" hospitals. In these establishments slight wounds and minor ailments are treated, and men requiring attention and rest are received.

By these means efficient soldiers, whose services would otherwise be lost for a long time, are kept in the country, whilst a large number of men are given immediate relief and rest when they require it without removing them from the area of operations. This adds materially to the fighting efficiency of the forces.

The principal convalescent hospital is at St Omer. It was started and organised by Colonel A. F. L. Bate, Army Medical Service, whose zeal, energy, and organising power have rendered it a model hospital of its kind, and this example has materially assisted in the efficient organisation of similar smaller establishments at every Divisional Headquarters.

I have already commented upon the number and severity of the casualties in action which have occurred in the period under report. Here once again I have to draw attention to the excellent work done by Surgeon-General O'Donnell and his officers. No organisation could excel the efficiency of the arrangements—whether in regard to time, space, care and comfort, or transport—which are made for the speedy evacuation of the wounded.

I wish particularly to express my deep sense of the loss incurred by the Army in general, and by the forces in France in particular, in the death of Brigadier-General J. E. Gough, VC, CMG, ADC, late Brigadier-General, General Staff, First Army, which occurred on 22nd February as a result of a severe wound received on the 20th February when inspecting the trenches of the 4th Corps. I always regarded General Gough as one of our most promising military leaders of the future. His services as a Staff Officer throughout the campaign have been invaluable, and I had already brought his name before Your Lordship for immediate promotion.

I can well understand how deeply these casualties are felt by the nation at large, but each daily report shows clearly that they are being endured on at least an equal scale by all the combatants engaged throughout Europe, friends and foes alike.

In war as it is today between civilised nations, armed to the teeth with the present deadly rifle and machine-gun, heavy casualties are absolutely unavoidable. For the slightest undue exposure the heaviest toll is exacted.

The power of defence conferred by modern weapons is the main cause of the long duration of the battles of the present day, and it is this fact which mainly accounts for such loss and waste of life.

Both one and the other can, however, be shortened and lessened if attacks can be supported by the most efficient and powerful force of artillery available; but an almost unlimited supply of ammunition is necessary and a most liberal discretionary power as to its use must be given to the Artillery Commanders.

I am confident that this is the only means by which great results can be obtained with a minimum of loss.

On the 15th February the Canadian Division began to arrive in this country. I inspected the Division, which was under the command of Lieutenant-General E. A. H. Alderson, C.B., on 20th February. They presented a splendid and most soldier-like appearance on parade. The men were of good physique, hard and fit. I judged by what I saw of them that they were well trained, and quite able to take their places in the line of battle. Since then the Division has thoroughly justified the good opinion I formed of it.

The troops of the Canadian Division were first attached for a few days by brigades for training in the 3rd Corps trenches under Lieutenant-General Sir William Pulteney, who gave me such an excellent report of their efficiency that I was able to employ them in the trenches early in March.

During the battle of Neuve Chapelle they held a part of the line allotted to the First Army, and, although they were not actually engaged in the main attack, they rendered valuable help by keeping the enemy actively employed in front of their trenches.

All the soldiers of Canada serving in the Army under my command have so far splendidly upheld the traditions of the Empire, and will, I feel sure, prove to be a great source of additional strength to the forces in this country.

In former despatches I have been able to comment very favourably upon the conduct and bearing of the Territorial Forces throughout the operations in which they have been engaged. As time goes on, and I see more and more of their work, whether in the trenches or engaged in more active operations, I am still further impressed with their value. Several battalions were engaged in the most critical moments of the heavy fighting which occurred in the middle of March, and they acquitted themselves with the utmost credit.

Up till lately the troops of the Territorial Force in this country were only employed by battalions, but for some weeks past I have seen formed divisions working together, and I have every hope that their employment in the larger units will prove as successful as in the smaller. These opinions are fully borne out by the result of the close inspection which I have recently made of the North Midland Division, under Major-General Hon. Montague-Stuart-Wortley, and the 2nd London Division, under Major-General Barter.

General Baron Von Kaulbars, of the Russian General Staff, arrived at my Headquarters on the 18th March. He was anxious to study our aviation system, and I gave him every opportunity of doing so.

The Bishop of London arrived here with his Chaplain on Saturday, March 27th, and left on Monday, April 5th. During the course of his visit to the Army His Lordship was at the front every day, and I think I am right in saying that there was scarcely a unit in the command which was not at one time or another present at his services or addresses. Personal fatigue and even danger were completely ignored by His Lordship. The Bishop held several services virtually under shell fire, and it was with difficulty that he could be prevented from carrying on his ministrations under rifle fire in the trenches.

I am anxious to place on record my deep sense of the good effect produced throughout the Army by this self-sacrificing devotion on the part of the Bishop of London, to whom I feel personally very deeply indebted. I have once more to remark upon the devotion to duty, courage and contempt of danger which has characterised the work of the chaplains of the Army throughout this campaign.

The increased strength of the force and the gradual exhaustion of the local resources have necessitated a corresponding increase in our demands on the Line of Communications, since we are now compelled to import many articles which in the early stages could be obtained by local purchase. The Directorates concerned have, however, been carefully watching the situation, and all the Administrative Services on the Line of Communications have continued to work with smoothness and regularity, in spite of the increased pressure thrown upon them. In this connection I wish to bring to notice the good service which has been rendered by the staff of the base ports.

The work of the Railway Transport Department has been excellently carried out, and I take this opportunity of expressing my appreciation of the valuable service rendered by the French railway authorities generally, and especially by Colonel Ragueneau, late Directeur des Chemins de Fer, Lieutenant-Colonel Le Hénaff, Directeur des Chemins de Fer, Lieutenant-Colonel Dumont, Commissaire Militaire, Chemin de Fer du Nord, and Lieutenant-Colonel Frid, Commissaire Regulateur, Armée Anglaise.

The Army Postal Service has continued to work well, and at the present time a letter posted in London is delivered at General Headquarters or at the Headquarters of the Armies and Army Corps on the following evening, and reaches an addressee in the trenches on the second day after posting. The delivery of parcels has also been accelerated, and is carried out with regularity and despatch.

His Majesty the King of the Belgians visited the British lines on February 8th and inspected some of the units in reserve behind the trenches.

During the last two months I have been much indebted to His Majesty and his gallant Army for valuable assistance and co-operation in various ways.

His Royal Highness the Prince of Wales is the bearer of this despatch. His Royal Highness continues to make most satisfactory progress. During the battle of Neuve Chapelle he acted on my General Staff as a Liaison Officer. Reports from the General Officers Commanding Corps and Divisions to which he has been attached agree in commending the thoroughness in which he performs any work entrusted to him. I have myself been very favourably impressed by the quickness with which His Royal Highness has acquired knowledge of the various branches of the service, and the deep interest he has always displayed in the comfort and welfare of the men. His visits to the troops, both in the field and in hospitals, have been greatly appreciated by all ranks. His Royal Highness did duty for a time in the trenches with the battalion to which he belongs.

In connection with the battle of Neuve Chapelle I desire to bring to Your Lordship's special notice the valuable services of General Sir Douglas Haig, KCB, KCIE, KCVO, ADC, Commanding the First Army. I am also much indebted to the able and devoted assistance I have received from Lieutenant-General Sir William Robertson, KCB, KCVO, DSO, Chief of the General Staff, in the direction of all the operations recorded in this despatch.

I have many other names to bring to notice for valuable, gallant and distinguished service during the period under review, and these will form the subject of a separate report at an early date.

J. D. P. FRENCH
Field-Marshal,
Commanding-in-Chief,
The British Army in the Field

SECOND BATTLE OF YPRES AND THE BATTLE OF FESTUBERT, APRIL TO MAY 1915

From the Field-Marshal Commanding-in-Chief, British Forces in the Field,
to the Secretary of State for War

General Headquarters, 15th June, 1915

My Lord,

I have the honour to report that since the date of my last despatch (5th April, 1915) the Army in France under my command has been heavily engaged opposite both flanks of the line held by the British forces.

In the north the town and district of Ypres have once more in this campaign been successfully defended against vigorous and sustained attacks made by large forces of the enemy, and supported by a mass of heavy and field artillery, which, not only in number, but also in weight and calibre, is superior to any concentration of guns which has previously assailed that part of the line.

In the south a vigorous offensive has again been taken by troops of the First Army, in the course of which a large area of entrenched and fortified ground has been captured from the enemy, whilst valuable support has been afforded to the attack which our Allies have carried on with such marked success against the enemy's positions to the east of Arras and Lens.

I much regret that during the period under report the fighting has been characterised on the enemy's side by a cynical and barbarous disregard of the well-known usages of civilised war and a flagrant defiance of the Hague Convention.

All the scientific resources of Germany have apparently been brought into play to produce a gas of so virulent and poisonous a nature that any human being brought into contact with it is first paralysed and then meets with a lingering and agonising death.

The enemy has invariably preceded, prepared and supported his attacks by a discharge in stupendous volume of these poisonous gas fumes whenever the wind was favourable. Such weather conditions have only prevailed to any extent in the neighbourhood of Ypres, and there can be no doubt that the effect of these poisonous fumes materially influenced the operations in that theatre, until experience suggested effective counter-measures, which have since been so perfected as to render them innocuous.

Second battle of Ypres, 1915

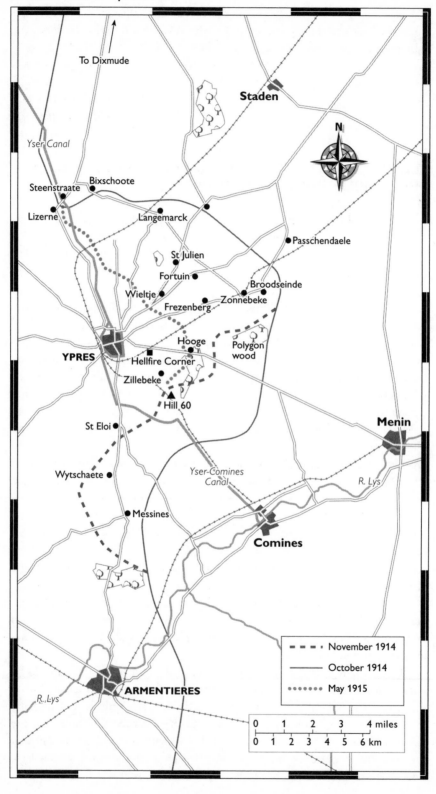

To Dixmude

Yser Canal

Staden

Bixschoote

Steenstraate

Lizerne

Langemarck

Passchendaele

St Julien

Fortuin

Broodseinde

Wieltje

Zonnebeke

Frezenberg

YPRES

Hooge

Polygon wood

Hellfire Corner

Zillebeke

Hill 60

St Eloi

Menin

Wytschaete

Yser-Comines Canal

R. Lys

Messines

Comines

ARMENTIERES

R. Lys

— — — November 1914

———— October 1914

•••••• May 1915

0	1	2	3	4 miles
0	1 2 3 4 5	6 km		

The brain power and thought which has evidently been at work before this unworthy method of making war reached the pitch of efficiency which has been demonstrated in its practice shows that the Germans must have harboured these designs for a long time.

As a soldier I cannot help expressing the deepest regret and some surprise that an Army which hitherto has claimed to be the chief exponent of the chivalry of war should have stooped to employ such devices against brave and gallant foes.

On the night of Saturday, April 17th, a commanding hill which afforded the enemy excellent artillery observation toward the west and north-west was successfully mined and captured. This hill, known as Hill 60, lies opposite the northern extremity of the line held by the 2nd Corps.

The operation was planned and the mining commenced by Major-General Bulfin before the ground was handed over to the troops under Lieutenant-General Sir Charles Fergusson, under whose supervision the operation was carried out.

The mines were successfully fired at 7 p.m. on the 17th instant, and immediately afterwards the hill was attacked and gained, without difficulty, by the 1st Battalion, Royal West Kent Regiment, and the 2nd Battalion, King's Own Scottish Borderers. The attack was well supported by the Divisional Artillery, assisted by French and Belgian batteries.

During the night several of the enemy's counter-attacks were repulsed with heavy loss, and fierce hand-to-hand fighting took place; but on the early morning of the 18th the enemy succeeded in forcing back the troops holding the right of the hill to the reverse slope, where, however, they hung on throughout the day.

On the evening of the 18th these two battalions were relieved by the 2nd Battalion, West Riding Regiment, and the 2nd Battalion, King's Own Yorkshire Light Infantry, who again stormed the hill under cover of heavy artillery fire, and the enemy was driven off at the point of the bayonet. In this operation 53 prisoners were captured, including four officers. On the 20th and following days many unsuccessful attacks by the enemy were made on Hill 60, which was continuously shelled by heavy artillery.

On May 1st another attempt to recapture Hill 60 was supported by great volumes of asphyxiating gas, which caused nearly all the men along a front of about 400 yards to be immediately struck down by its fumes.

The splendid courage with which the leaders rallied their men and subdued the natural tendency to panic (which is inevitable on such occasions), combined with the prompt intervention of supports, once more drove the enemy back.

A second and more severe "gas" attack, under much more favourable weather conditions, enabled the enemy to recapture this position on May 5th. The enemy owes his success in this last attack entirely to the use of asphyxiating gas. It was only a few days later that the means, which have since proved so effective, of counteracting this method of making war were put into practice. Had it been otherwise, the enemy's attack on May 5th would most certainly have shared the fate of all the many previous attempts he had made.

It was at the commencement of the second battle of Ypres on the evening of the 22nd April, referred to earlier in this report, that the enemy first made use of asphyxiating gas.

Some days previously I had complied with General Joffre's request to take over the trenches occupied by the French, and on the evening of the 22nd the troops holding the lines east of Ypres were posted as follows:

> From Steenstraate to the east of Langemarck, as far as the Poelcappelle Road, a French Division.

> Thence, in a south-easterly direction toward the Passchendaele–Becelaere Road, the Canadian Division.

> Thence a division took up the line in a southerly direction east of Zonnebeke to a point west of Becelaere, whence another division continued the line south-east to the northern limit of the corps on its right.

Of the 5th Corps there were four battalions in Divisional Reserve about Ypres; the Canadian Division had one battalion in Divisional Reserve and the 1st Canadian Brigade in Army Reserve. An Infantry Brigade, which had just been withdrawn after suffering heavy losses on Hill 60, was resting about Vlamertinghe.

Following a heavy bombardment, the enemy attacked the French Division at about 5 p.m., using asphyxiating gases for the first time. Aircraft reported that at about 5 p.m. thick yellow smoke had been seen issuing from the German trenches between Langemarck and Bixschoote. The French reported that two simultaneous attacks had been made east of the Ypres-Staden Railway, in which these asphyxiating gases had been employed.

What follows almost defies description. The effect of these poisonous gases was so virulent as to render the whole of the line held by the French Division mentioned above practically incapable of any action at all. It was at first impossible for anyone to realise what had actually happened. The smoke and fumes hid everything from sight, and hundreds of men were thrown into a comatose or dying condition, and within an hour the whole position had to be abandoned, together with about 50 guns. I wish particularly to repudiate any idea of attaching the least blame to the French Division for this unfortunate incident.

After all the examples our gallant Allies have shown of dogged and tenacious courage in the many trying situations in which they have been placed throughout the course of this campaign, it is quite superfluous for me to dwell on this aspect of the incident, and I would only express my firm conviction that, if any troops in the world had been able to hold their trenches in the face of such a treacherous and altogether unexpected onslaught, the French Division would have stood firm.

The left flank of the Canadian Division was thus left dangerously exposed to serious attack in flank, and there appeared to be a prospect of their being overwhelmed and of a successful attempt by the Germans to cut off the British troops occupying the salient to the east.

In spite of the danger to which they were exposed the Canadians held their ground with a magnificent display of tenacity and courage; and it is not too much to say that the bearing and conduct of these splendid troops averted a disaster which might have been attended with the most serious consequences. They were supported with great promptitude by the reserves of the divisions holding the salient and by a brigade which had been resting in billets.

Throughout the night the enemy's attacks were repulsed, effective counter-attacks were delivered, and at length touch was gained with the French right, and a new line was formed.

The 2nd London Heavy Battery, which had been attached to the Canadian Division, was posted behind the right of the French Division, and, being involved in their retreat, fell into the enemy's hands. It was recaptured by the Canadians in their counter-attack, but the guns could not be withdrawn before the Canadians were again driven back.

During the night I directed the Cavalry Corps and the Northumbrian Division, which was then in general reserve, to move to the west of Ypres, and placed these troops at the disposal of the General Officer Commanding the Second Army. I also directed other reserve troops from the 3rd Corps and the First Army to be held in readiness.

In the confusion of the gas and smoke the Germans succeeded in capturing the bridge at Steenstraate and some works south of Lizerne, all of which were in occupation by the French.

The enemy having thus established himself to the west of the Ypres Canal, I was somewhat apprehensive of his succeeding in driving a wedge between the French and Belgian troops at this point. I directed, therefore, that some of the reinforcements sent north should be used to support and assist General Putz, should he find difficulty in preventing any further advance of the Germans west of the canal.

At about 10 o'clock on the morning of the 23rd connection was finally ensured between the left of the Canadian Division and the French right, about eight hundred yards east of the canal; but as this entailed the maintenance by the British troops of a much longer line than that which they had held before the attack commenced on the previous night, there were no reserves available for counter-attack until reinforcements, which were ordered up from the Second Army, were able to deploy to the east of Ypres.

Early on the morning of the 23rd I went to see General Foch, and from him I received a detailed account of what had happened, as reported by General Putz. General Foch informed me that it was his intention to make good the original line and regain the trenches which the French Division had lost. He expressed the desire that I should maintain my present line, assuring me that the original position would be re-established in a few days. General Foch further informed me that he had ordered up large French reinforcements, which were now on their way, and that troops from the north had already arrived to reinforce General Putz.

I fully concurred in the wisdom of the General's wish to re-establish our old line, and agreed to co-operate in the way he desired, stipulating, however, that if the position was not re-established within a limited time I could not allow the British troops to remain in so exposed a situation as that which the action of the previous twenty-four hours had compelled them to occupy.

During the whole of the 23rd the enemy's artillery was very active, and his attacks all along the front were supported by some heavy guns which had been brought down from the coast in the neighbourhood of Ostend. The loss of the guns on the night of the 22nd prevented this fire from being kept down, and much aggravated the situation. Our positions, however, were well maintained by the vigorous counter-attacks made by the 5th Corps.

During the day I directed two brigades of the 3rd Corps, and the Lahore Division of the Indian Corps, to be moved up to the Ypres area and placed at the disposal of the Second Army.

In the course of these two or three days many circumstances combined to render the situation east of the Ypres Canal very critical and most difficult to deal with.

The confusion caused by the sudden retirement of the French Division, and the necessity for closing up the gap and checking the enemy's advance at all costs, led to a mixing up of units and a sudden shifting of the areas of command, which was quite unavoidable. Fresh units, as they came up from the south, had to be pushed into the firing line in an area swept by artillery fire which, owing to the capture of the French guns, we were unable to keep down.

All this led to very heavy casualties; and I wish to place on record the deep admiration which I feel for the resource and presence of mind evinced by the leaders actually on the spot. The parts taken by Major-General Snow and Brigadier-General Hull were reported to me as being particularly marked in this respect.

An instance of this occurred on the afternoon of the 24th when the enemy succeeded in breaking through the line at St Julien.

Brigadier-General Hull, acting under the orders of Lieutenant-General Alderson, organised a powerful counter-attack with his own brigade and some of the nearest available units. He was called upon to control, with only his brigade staff, parts of battalions from six separate divisions which were quite new to the ground. Although the attack did not succeed in retaking

St Julien, it effectually checked the enemy's further advance. It was only on the morning of the 25th that the enemy were able to force back the left of the Canadian Division from the point where it had originally joined the French line.

During the night, and the early morning of the 25th, the enemy directed a heavy attack against the division at Broodseinde crossroads which was supported by a powerful shell fire, but he failed to make any progress.

During the whole of this time the town of Ypres and all the roads to the east and west were uninterruptedly subjected to a violent artillery fire, but in spite of this the supply of both food and ammunition was maintained throughout with order and efficiency.

During the afternoon of the 25th many German prisoners were taken, including some officers. The hand-to-hand fighting was very severe, and the enemy suffered heavy loss.

During the 26th the Lahore Division and a Cavalry Division were pushed up into the fighting line, the former on the right of the French, the latter in support of the 5th Corps. In the afternoon the Lahore Division, in conjunction with the French right, succeeded in pushing the enemy back some little distance toward the north, but their further advance was stopped owing to the continual employment by the enemy of asphyxiating gas.

On the right of the Lahore Division the Northumberland Infantry Brigade advanced against St Julien and actually succeeded in entering, and for a time occupying, the southern portion of that village. They were, however, eventually driven back, largely owing to gas, and finally occupied a line a short way to the south. This attack was most successfully and gallantly led by Brigadier-General Riddell, who, I regret to say, was killed during the progress of the operation.

Although no attack was made on the south-eastern side of the salient, the troops operating to the east of Ypres were subjected to heavy artillery fire from this direction which took some of the battalions, which were advancing north to the attack, in reverse.

Some gallant attempts made by the Lahore Division on the 27th, in conjunction with the French, pushed the enemy further north; but they were partially frustrated by the constant fumes of gas to which they were exposed. In spite of this, however, a certain amount of ground was gained.

The French had succeeded in retaking Lizerne, and had made some progress at Steenstraate and Het Sas; but up to the evening of the 28th no further progress had been made toward the recapture of the original line. I sent instructions therefore, to Sir Herbert Plumer, who was now in charge of the operation, to take preliminary measures for the retirement to the new line which had been fixed upon.

On the morning of the 29th I had another interview with General Foch, who informed me that strong reinforcements were hourly arriving to support General Putz, and urged me to postpone issuing orders for any retirement until the result of his attack, which was timed to commence at daybreak on the 30th, should be known. To this I agreed, and instructed Sir Herbert Plumer accordingly.

No substantial advance having been made by the French, I issued orders to Sir Herbert Plumer at one o'clock on May 1st to commence his withdrawal to the new line. The retirement was commenced the following night, and the new line was occupied on the morning of May 4th.

I am of the opinion that this retirement, carried out deliberately with scarcely any loss, and in the face of an enemy in position, reflects the greatest possible credit on Sir Herbert Plumer and those who so efficiently carried out his orders.

The successful conduct of this operation was the more remarkable from the fact that on the evening of May 2nd, when it was only half completed, the enemy made a heavy attack, with the usual gas accompaniment, on St Julien and the line to the west of it. An attack on a line to the east of Fortuin was made at the same time under similar conditions.

In both cases our troops were at first driven from their trenches by gas fumes, but on the arrival of the supporting battalions and two brigades of a Cavalry Division, which were sent up in support from about Potijze, all the lost trenches were regained at night.

On the 3rd May, while the retirement was still going on, another violent attack was directed on the northern face of the salient. This was also driven back with heavy loss to the enemy. Further attempts of the enemy during the night of the 3rd to advance from the woods west of St Julien were frustrated entirely by the fire of our artillery.

During the whole of the 4th the enemy heavily shelled the trenches we had evacuated, quite unaware that they were no longer occupied. So soon as the retirement was discovered the Germans commenced to entrench opposite our new line and to advance their guns to new positions. Our artillery, assisted by aeroplanes, caused him considerable loss in carrying out these operations.

Up to the morning of the 8th the enemy made attacks at short intervals, covered by gas, on all parts of the line to the east of Ypres, but was everywhere driven back with heavy loss.

Throughout the whole period since the first break of the line on the night of April 22nd all the troops in this area had been constantly subjected to violent artillery bombardment from a large mass of guns with an unlimited supply of ammunition. It proved impossible whilst under so vastly superior fire of artillery to dig efficient trenches, or to properly reorganise the line, after the confusion and demoralisation caused by the first great gas surprise and the subsequent almost daily gas attacks. Nor was it until after this date (May 8th) that effective preventatives had been devised and provided. In these circumstances a violent bombardment of nearly the whole of the 5th Corps front broke out at 7 a.m. on the morning of the 8th, which gradually concentrated on the front of the division between north and south of Frezenberg. This fire completely obliterated the trenches and caused enormous losses. The artillery bombardment was shortly followed by a heavy infantry attack, before which our line had to give way.

I relate what happened in Sir Herbert Plumer's own words:

The right of one brigade was broken about 10.15 a.m.; then its centre, and then part of the left of the brigade in the next section to the south. The Princess Patricia's Canadian Light Infantry, however, although suffering very heavily, stuck to their fire or support trenches throughout the day. At this time two battalions were moved to General Headquarters 2nd line astride the Menin Road to support and cover the left of their division.

At 12.25 p.m. the centre of a brigade further to the left also broke; its right battalion, however, the 1st Suffolks, which had been refused to cover a gap, still held on and were apparently surrounded and overwhelmed. Meanwhile, three more battalions had been moved up to reinforce, two other battalions were moved up in support to General Headquarters line, and an infantry brigade came up to the grounds of Vlamertinghe Chateau in Corps Reserve.

At 11.30 a.m. a small party of Germans attempted to advance against the left of the British line, but were destroyed by the 2nd Essex Regiment.

A counter-attack was launched at 3.30 p.m. by the 1st York and Lancaster Regiment, 3rd Middlesex Regiment, 2nd East Surrey Regiment, 2nd Royal Dublin Fusiliers and the 1st Royal Warwickshire Regiment. The counter-attack reached Frezenberg, but was eventually driven back and held up on a line running about north and south through Verlorenhoek, despite repeated efforts to advance. The 12th London Regiment on the left succeeded at great cost in reaching the original trench line, and did considerable execution with their machine gun.

The 7th Argyll and Sutherland Highlanders and the 1st East Lancashire Regiment attacked in a north-easterly direction towards Wieltje, and connected the old trench line with the ground gained by the counter-attack, the line being consolidated during the night.

During the night orders were received that two cavalry divisions would be moved up and placed at the disposal of the 5th Corps, and a territorial division would be moved up to be used if required.

On the 9th the Germans again repeated their bombardment. Very heavy shell fire was concentrated for two hours on the trenches of the 2nd Gloucestershire Regiment and 2nd Cameron Highlanders, followed by an infantry attack which was successfully repulsed. The Germans again bombarded the salient, and a further attack in the afternoon succeeded in occupying 150 yards of trench. The Gloucesters counter-attacked, but suffered heavily, and the attack failed. The salient being very exposed to shell fire from both flanks, as well as in front, it was deemed advisable not to attempt to retake the trench at night, and a retrenchment was therefore dug across it.

At 3 p.m. the enemy started to shell the whole front of the centre division, and it was reported that the right brigade of this division was being heavily punished, but continued to maintain its line.

The trenches of the brigades on the left centre were also heavily shelled during the day and attacked by infantry. Both attacks were repulsed.

On the 10th instant the trenches on either side of the Menin–Ypres Road were shelled very severely all the morning. The 2nd Cameron Highlanders, 9th Royal Scots, and the 3rd and 4th King's Royal Rifles, however, repulsed an attack made, under cover of gas, with heavy loss. Finally, when the trenches had been practically destroyed and a large number of the garrison buried, the 3rd King's Royal Rifles and 4th Rifle Brigade fell back to the trenches immediately west of Bellewaarde Wood. So heavy had been the shell fire that the proposal to join up the line with a switch through the wood had to be abandoned, the trees broken by the shells forming an impassable entanglement.

After a comparatively quiet night and morning (10th–11th) the hostile artillery fire was concentrated on the trenches of the 2nd Cameron Highlanders and 1st Argyll and Sutherland Highlanders at a slightly more northern point than on the previous day. The Germans attacked in force and gained a footing in part of the trenches, but were promptly ejected by a supporting company of the 9th Royal Scots. After a second short artillery bombardment the Germans again attacked about 4.15 p.m., but were again repulsed by rifle and machine-gun fire. A third bombardment followed and this time the Germans succeeded in gaining a trench—or rather what was left of it—a local counter-attack failing. However, during the night the enemy were again driven out. The trench by this time being practically non-existent, the garrison found it untenable under the very heavy shell fire the enemy brought to bear upon it, and the trench was evacuated. Twice more did the German snipers creep back into it, and twice more they were ejected. Finally, a retrenchment was made, cutting off the salient which had been contested throughout the day. It was won owing solely to the superior weight and number of the enemy's guns, but both our infantry and our artillery took a very heavy toll of the enemy, and the ground lost has proved of little use to the enemy. On the remainder of the front the day passed comparatively quietly, though most parts of the line underwent intermittent shelling by guns of various calibres.

With the assistance of the Royal Flying Corps the 31st Heavy Battery scored a direct hit on a German gun, and the North Midland Heavy Battery got on to some German howitzers with great success. With the exception of another very heavy burst of shell fire against the right division early in the morning, the 12th passed uneventfully.

On the night of the 12th–13th the line was re-organised, the centre division retiring into Army Reserve to rest, and their places being taken in the trenches by the two cavalry divisions; the artillery and engineers of the centre division forming with them what was known as the "Cavalry Force" under the command of General De Lisle.

On the 13th the various reliefs having been completed without incident, the heaviest bombardment yet experienced broke out at 4.30 a.m. and continued with little intermission throughout the day. At about 7.45 a.m. the cavalry brigade astride the railway, having suffered very severely, and their trenches having been obliterated, fell back about 800 yards. The North Somerset Yeomanry on the right of the brigade, although also suffering severely, hung on to their trenches throughout the day, and actually advanced and attacked the enemy with the bayonet. The brigade on its right also maintained its position; as did also the Cavalry Division, except the left squadron which, when reduced to sixteen men, fell back. The 2nd Essex Regiment, realising the situation, promptly charged and retook the trench, holding it till relieved by the cavalry. Meanwhile a counter-attack by two cavalry brigades was launched at 2.30 p.m., and succeeded, in spite of very heavy shrapnel and rifle fire, in regaining the original line of trenches, turning out the Germans who had entered it, and in some cases pursuing them for some distance. But a very heavy shell fire was again opened on them, and they were again compelled to retire to an irregular line in rear, principally the craters of shell holes. The enemy in their counter-attack suffered very severe losses.

The fighting in other parts of the line was little less severe. The 1st East Lancashire Regiment were shelled out of their trenches, but their support company and the 2nd Essex Regiment, again acting on their own initiative, won them back. The enemy penetrated into the farm at the north-east corner of the line, but the 1st Rifle Brigade, after a severe struggle, expelled them. The 1st Hampshire Regiment also repelled an attack, and killed every German who got within fifty yards of their trenches. The 5th London Regiment, despite very heavy casualties, maintained their position unfalteringly.

At the southern end of the line the left brigade was once again heavily shelled, as indeed was the whole front. At the end of a very hard day's fighting our line remained in its former position, with the exception of the short distance lost by one cavalry division. Later, the line was pushed forward, and a new line was dug in a less exposed position, slightly in rear of that originally held. The night passed quietly.

Working parties of from 1,200 to 1,800 men have been found every night by a territorial division and other units for work on rear lines of defence, in addition to the work performed by the garrisons in reconstructing the front line trenches which were daily destroyed by shell fire.

The work performed by the Royal Flying Corps has been invaluable. Apart from the hostile aeroplanes actually destroyed, our airmen have prevented a great deal of aerial reconnaissance by the enemy, and have registered a large number of targets with our artillery.

There have been many cases of individual gallantry. As instances may be given the following:

During one of the heavy attacks made against our infantry, gas was seen rolling forward from the enemy's trenches. Private Lynn of the 2nd Lancashire Fusiliers at once rushed to the machine gun without waiting to adjust his respirator. Single-handed he kept his gun in action the whole time the gas was rolling over, actually hoisting it on to the parapet to get a better field of fire. Although nearly suffocated by the gas, he poured a stream of lead into the advancing enemy and checked their attack. He was carried to his dug-out, but, hearing another attack was imminent, he tried to get back to his gun. Twenty-four hours later he died in great agony from the effects of the gas.

A young subaltern in a cavalry regiment went forward alone one afternoon to reconnoitre. He got into a wood, 1,200 yards in front of our lines, which he found occupied by Germans, and came back with the information that the enemy had evacuated a trench and were digging another—information which later proved most valuable to the artillery as well as to his own unit.

A patrol of two officers and a non-commissioned officer of the 1st Cambridgeshires went out one night to reconnoitre a German trench 350 yards away. Creeping along the parapet of the trench, they heard sounds indicating the presence of six or seven of the enemy. Further on they heard deep snores, apparently proceeding from a dug-out immediately beneath them. Although they knew that the garrison of the trench outnumbered them, they decided to procure an identification. Unfortunately, in pulling out a clasp knife with which to cut off the sleeper's identity disc, one of the officer's revolvers went off. A conversation in agitated whispers broke out in the German trench, but the patrol kept safely away, the garrison being too startled to fire.

Despite the very severe shelling to which the troops had been subjected, which obliterated trenches and caused very many casualties, the spirit of all ranks remains excellent. The enemy's losses, particularly on the 10th and 13th, have unquestionably been serious. On the latter day they evacuated trenches (in face of the cavalry counter-attack) in which were afterwards found quantities of equipment and some of their own wounded. The enemy have been seen stripping our dead, and on three occasions men in khaki have been seen advancing.

The fight went on by the exchange of desultory shell and rifle fire, but without any remarkable incident until the morning of May 24th. During this period, however, the French on our left had attained considerable success. On the 15th instant they captured Steenstraate and the trenches in Het Sas, and on the 16th they drove the enemy headlong over the canal, finding two thousand German dead. On the 17th they made a substantial advance on the east side of the canal, and on the 20th they repelled a German counter-attack, making a further advance in the same direction, and taking one hundred prisoners.

On the early morning of the 24th a violent outburst of gas against nearly the whole front was followed by heavy shell fire, and the most determined attack was delivered against our position east of Ypres. The hour the attack commenced was 2.45 a.m. A large proportion of the men were asleep, and the attack was too sudden to give them time to put on their respirators.

The 2nd Royal Irish and the 9th Argyll and Sutherland Highlanders, overcome by gas fumes, were driven out of a farm held in front of the left division, and this the enemy proceeded to hold and fortify.

All attempts to retake this farm during the day failed, and during the night of the 24th–25th the General Officer Commanding the Left Division decided to take up a new line which, although slightly in rear of the old one, he considered to be a much better position. This operation was successfully carried out.

Throughout the day the whole line was subjected to one of the most violent artillery attacks which it had ever undergone; and the 5th Corps and the Cavalry Divisions engaged had to fight hard to maintain their positions. On the following day, however, the line was consolidated, joining the right of the French at the same place as before, and passing through Wieltje (which was strongly fortified) in a southerly direction on to Hooge, where the cavalry have since strongly occupied the chateau, and pushed our line further east.

In pursuance of a promise which I made to the French Commander-in-Chief to support an attack which his troops were making on the 9th May between the right of my line and Arras, I directed Sir Douglas Haig to carry out on that date an attack on the German trenches in the neighbourhood of Rougebanc (north-west of Fromelles) by the 4th Corps, and between Neuve Chapelle and Givenchy, by the 1st and Indian Corps.

The bombardment of the enemy's positions commenced at 5 a.m. Half-an-hour later the 8th Division of the 4th Corps captured the first line of German trenches about Rougebanc, and some detachments seized a few localities beyond this line. It was soon found, however, that the position was much stronger than had been anticipated, and that a more extensive artillery preparation was necessary to crush the resistance offered by his numerous fortified posts. Throughout the 9th and 10th repeated efforts were made to make further progress. Not only was this found to be impossible, but the violence of the enemy's machine-gun fire from his posts on the flanks rendered the captured trenches so difficult to hold that all the units of the 4th Corps had to retire to their original position by the morning of the 10th.

The 1st and Indian Divisions south of Neuve Chapelle met with no greater success, and on the evening of the 10th I sanctioned Sir Douglas Haig's proposal to concentrate all our available resources on the southern point of attack.

The 7th Division was moved round from the 4th Corps area to support this attack, and I directed the General Officer Commanding the First Army to delay it long enough to ensure a powerful and deliberate artillery preparation.

The operations of the 9th and 10th formed part of a general plan of attack which the Allies were conjointly conducting on a line extending from the north of Arras to the south of Armentières; and, although immediate progress was not made during this time by the British forces, their attack assisted in securing the brilliant successes attained by the French forces on their right, not only by holding the enemy in their front but by drawing off a part of the German reinforcements which were coming up to support their forces east of Arras.

It was decided that the attack should be resumed on the night of the 12th instant, but the weather continued very dull and misty, interfering much with artillery observation. Orders were finally issued, therefore, for the action to commence on the night of the 15th instant.

On the 15th May I moved the Canadian Division into the 1st Corps area and placed them at the disposal of Sir Douglas Haig.

The infantry of the Indian Corps and the 2nd Division of the 1st Corps advanced to the attack of the enemy's trenches which extended from Richebourg L'Avoué in a south-westerly direction.

Before daybreak the 2nd Division had succeeded in capturing two lines of the enemy's trenches, but the Indian Corps were unable to make any progress owing to the strength of the enemy's defences in the neighbourhood of Richebourg L'Avoué.

At daybreak the 7th Division, on the right of the 2nd, advanced to the attack, and by 7 a.m. had entrenched themselves on a line running nearly north and south, half-way between their original trenches and La Quinque Rue, having cleared and captured several lines of the enemy's trenches, including a number of fortified posts.

As it was found impossible for the Indian Corps to make any progress in face of the enemy's defences Sir Douglas Haig directed the attack to be suspended at this point and ordered the Indian Corps to form a defensive flank. The remainder of the day was spent in securing and consolidating positions which had been won, and endeavouring to unite the inner flanks of the 7th and 2nd Divisions, which were separated by trenches and posts strongly held by the enemy. Various attempts which were made throughout the day to secure this object had not succeeded at nightfall in driving the enemy back.

The German communications leading to the rear of their positions were systematically shelled throughout the night. About two hundred prisoners were captured on the 16th instant.

Fighting was resumed at daybreak; and by 11 o'clock the 7th Division had made a considerable advance, capturing several more of the enemy's trenches. The task allotted to this division was to push on in the direction of Rue D'Ouvert, Chateau St Roch and Canteleux. The 2nd Division was directed to push on when the situation permitted towards the Rue de Marais and Violaines. The Indian Division was ordered to extend its front far enough to enable it to keep touch with the left of the 2nd Division when they advanced.

On this day I gave orders for the 51st (Highland) Division to move into the neighbourhood of Estaires to be ready to support the operations of the First Army. At about noon the enemy was driven out of the trenches and posts which he occupied between the two divisions, the inner flanks of which were thus enabled to join hands. By nightfall the 2nd and 7th Divisions had made good progress, the area of the captured ground being considerably extended to the right by the successful operations of the latter.

The state of the weather on the morning of the 18th much hindered an effective artillery bombardment, and further attacks had, consequently, to be postponed. Infantry attacks were made throughout the line in the course of the afternoon and evening; but, although not very much progress was made, the line was advanced to the La Quinque Rue–Béthune Road before nightfall.

On the 19th May the 7th and 2nd Divisions were drawn out of the line to rest. The 7th Division was relieved by the Canadian Division and the 2nd Division by the 51st (Highland) Division. Sir Douglas Haig placed the Canadian and 51st Divisions, together with the artillery of the 2nd and 7th Divisions, under the command of Lieutenant-General Alderson, whom he directed to conduct the operations which had hitherto been carried on by the General Officer Commanding First Corps; and he directed the 7th Division to remain in Army Reserve.

During the night of the 19th–20th a small post of the enemy in front of La Quinque Rue was captured.

During the night of the 20th–21st the Canadian Division brilliantly carried on the excellent progress made by the 7th Division by seizing several of the enemy's trenches and pushing forward their whole line several hundred yards. A number of prisoners and some machine guns were captured.

On the 22nd instant the 51st (Highland) Division was attached to the Indian Corps, and the General Officer Commanding the Indian Corps took charge of the operations at La Quinque Rue, Lieutenant-General Alderson with the Canadians conducting the operations to the north of that place. On this day the Canadian Division extended their line slightly to the right and repulsed three very severe counter-attacks.

On the 24th and 25th May the 47th Division (2nd London Territorials) succeeded in taking some more of the enemy's trenches and making good the ground gained to the east and north.

I had now reason to consider that the battle, which was commenced by the First Army on the 9th May and renewed on the 16th, having attained for the moment the immediate object I had in view, should not be further actively proceeded with; and I gave orders to Sir Douglas Haig to curtail his artillery attack and to strengthen and consolidate the ground he had won.

In the battle of Festubert above described the enemy was driven from a position which was strongly entrenched and fortified, and ground was won on a front of some four miles to an average depth of 600 yards.

The enemy is known to have suffered very heavy losses, and in the course of the battle 785 prisoners and 10 machine guns were captured. A number of machine guns were also destroyed by our fire.

During the period under report the Army under my command has taken over trenches occupied by some other French Divisions. I am much indebted to General d'Urbal, commanding the 10th French Army, for the valuable and efficient support received throughout the battle of Festubert from three groups of French 75 centimetre guns. In spite of very unfavourable weather conditions, rendering observation most difficult, our own artillery did excellent work throughout the battle.

During the important operations described above, which were carried on by the First and Second Armies, the 3rd Corps was particularly active in making demonstrations with a view to holding the enemy in its front and preventing reinforcements reaching the threatened area.

As an instance of the successful attempts to deceive the enemy in this respect it may be mentioned that on the afternoon of the 24th instant a bombardment of about an hour was carried out by the 6th Division with the object of distracting attention from the Ypres salient. Considerable damage was done to the enemy's parapets and wire; and that the desired impression was produced on the enemy is evident from the German wireless news on that day, which stated "West of Lille the English attempts to attack were nipped in the bud."

In previous reports I have drawn attention to the enterprise displayed by the troops of the 3rd Corps in conducting night reconnaissances, and to the courage and resource shown by officers' and other patrols in the conduct of these minor operations.

Throughout the period under report this display of activity has been very marked all along the 3rd Corps front, and much valuable information and intelligence have been collected.

I have much pleasure in again expressing my warm appreciation of the admirable manner in which all branches of the Medical Services now in the field, under the direction of Surgeon-General Sir Arthur Sloggett, have met and dealt with the many difficult situations resulting from the operations during the last two months.

The medical units at the front were frequently exposed to the enemy's fire, and many casualties occurred amongst the officers of the regimental Medical Service. At all times the officers, non-commissioned officers and men, and nurses carried out their duties with fearless bravery and great devotion to the welfare of the sick and wounded.

The evacuation of casualties from the front to the base and to England was expeditiously accomplished by the Administrative Medical Staffs at the front and on the Lines of Communication. All ranks employed in units of evacuation and in base hospitals have shown the highest skill and untiring zeal and energy in alleviating the condition of those who passed through their hands.

The whole organisation of the Medical Services reflects the highest credit on all concerned.

I have once more to call your Lordship's attention to the part taken by the Royal Flying Corps in the general progress of the campaign, and I wish particularly to mention the invaluable assistance they rendered in the operations described in this report, under the able direction of Major-General Sir David Henderson.

The Royal Flying Corps is becoming more and more an indispensable factor in combined operations. In co-operation with the artillery, in particular, there has been continuous improvement both in the methods and in the technical material employed. The ingenuity and technical skill displayed by the officers of the Royal Flying Corps, in effecting this improvement, have been most marked.

Since my last despatch there has been a considerable increase both in the number and in the activity of German aeroplanes in our front. During this period there have been more than sixty combats in the air, in which not one British aeroplane has been lost. As these fights take place almost invariably over or behind the German lines, only one hostile aeroplane has been brought down in our territory. Five more, however, have been definitely wrecked behind their own lines, and many have been chased down and forced to land in most unsuitable ground.

In spite of the opposition of hostile aircraft, and the great number of anti-aircraft guns employed by the enemy, air reconnaissance has been carried out with regularity and accuracy.

I desire to bring to your Lordship's notice the assistance given by the French Military Authorities, and in particular by General Hirschauer, Director of the French Aviation Service, and his assistants, Colonel Bottieaux and Colonel Stammler, in the supply of aeronautical material, without which the efficiency of the Royal Flying Corps would have been seriously impaired.

In this despatch I wish again to remark upon the exceptionally good work done throughout the whole of this campaign by the Army Service Corps and by the Army Ordnance Department, not only in the field, but also on the Lines of Communication and at the base ports.

To foresee and meet the requirements in the matter of Ammunition, Stores, Equipment, Supplies and Transport has entailed on the part of the officers, non-commissioned officers and men of these services a sustained effort which has never been relaxed since the beginning of the war, and which has been rewarded by the most conspicuous success.

The close co-operation of the Railway Transport Department, whose excellent work, in combination with the French Railway Staff, has ensured the regularity of the maintenance services, has greatly contributed to this success. The degree of efficiency to which these services have been brought was well demonstrated in the course of the second battle of Ypres.

The roads between Poperinghe and Ypres, over which transport, supply and ammunition columns had to pass, were continually searched by hostile heavy artillery during the day and night; whilst the passage of the canal through the town of Ypres, and along the roads east of that town, could only be effected under most difficult and dangerous conditions as regards hostile shell fire. Yet, throughout the whole five or six weeks during which these conditions prevailed, the work was carried on with perfect order and efficiency.

Since the date of my last report some divisions of the "New" Army have arrived in this country. I made a close inspection of one division, formed up on parade, and have at various times seen several units belonging to others. These divisions have as yet had very little experience in actual fighting; but, judging from all I have seen, I am of the opinion that they ought to prove a valuable addition to any fighting force.

As regards the Infantry, their physique is excellent, whilst their bearing and appearance on parade reflects great credit on the officers and staffs responsible for their training. The units appear to be thoroughly well officered and commanded. The equipment is in good order and efficient. Several units of artillery have been tested in the firing line behind the trenches, and I hear very good reports of them. Their shooting has been extremely good, and they are quite fit to take their places in the line.

The Pioneer Battalions have created a very favourable impression, the officers being keen and ingenious and the men of good physique and good diggers. The equipment is suitable. The training in field works has been good, but, generally speaking, they require the assistance of Regular Royal Engineers as regards laying out of important works. Man for man in digging the battalions should do practically the same amount of work as an equivalent number of sappers, and in rivetting, entanglement, etc., a great deal more than the ordinary infantry battalions.

During April and May several divisions of the Territorial Force joined the Army under my command. Experience has shown that these troops have now reached a standard of efficiency which enables them to be usefully employed in complete divisional units.

Several divisions have been so employed; some in the trenches, others in the various offensive and defensive operations reported in this despatch. In whatever kind of work these units have been engaged, they have all borne an active and distinguished part, and have proved themselves thoroughly reliable and efficient.

The opinion I have expressed in former despatches as to the use and value of the Territorial Force has been fully justified by recent events.

The Prime Minister was kind enough to accept an invitation from me to visit the Army in France, and arrived at my Headquarters on the 30th May. Mr Asquith made an exhaustive tour of the front, the hospitals and all the administrative arrangements made by the Corps Commanders for the health and comfort of men behind the trenches. It was a great encouragement to all ranks to see the Prime Minister amongst them; and the eloquent words which on several occasions he addressed to the troops had a most powerful and beneficial effect.

As I was desirous that the French Commander-in-Chief should see something of the British troops, I asked General Joffre to be kind enough to inspect a division on parade. The General accepted my invitation, and on the 27th May he inspected the 7th Division, under the command of Major-General H. de la P. Gough, CB, which was resting behind the trenches. General Joffre subsequently expressed to me in a letter the pleasure it gave him to see the British troops, and his appreciation of their appearance on parade. He requested me to make this known to all ranks.

The Moderator of the Church of Scotland, the Right Reverend Dr Wallace Williamson, Dean of the Order of the Thistle, visited the Army in France between the 7th and 17th May, and made a tour of the Scottish regiments with excellent results.

In spite of the constant strain put upon them by the arduous nature of the fighting which they are called upon to carry out daily and almost hourly, the spirit which animates all ranks of the Army in France remains high and confident. They meet every demand made upon them with the utmost cheerfulness. This splendid spirit is particularly manifested by the men in hospital, even amongst those who are mortally wounded. The invariable question which comes from lips hardly able to utter a sound is, "How are things going on at the front?"

In conclusion, I desire to bring to Your Lordship's special notice the valuable services rendered by General Sir Douglas Haig in his successful handling of the troops of the First Army throughout the battle of Festubert, and Lieutenant-General Sir Herbert Plumer for his fine defence of Ypres throughout the arduous and difficult operations during the latter part of April and the month of May.

J. D. P. FRENCH
Field-Marshal Commanding-in-Chief,
The British Army in France

The Cocos Islands (Keeling Islands)

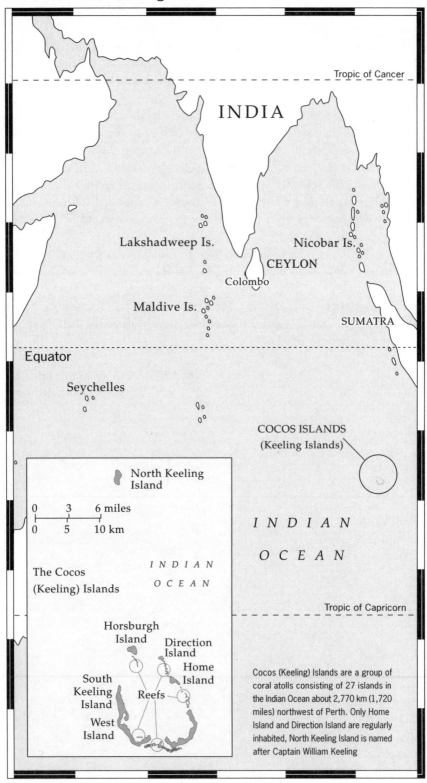

Tropic of Cancer

INDIA

Lakshadweep Is.

Nicobar Is.

CEYLON

Colombo

Maldive Is.

SUMATRA

Equator

Seychelles

COCOS ISLANDS
(Keeling Islands)

North Keeling
Island

0   3   6 miles

0   5   10 km

I N D I A N

O C E A N

The Cocos
(Keeling) Islands

I N D I A N

O C E A N

Tropic of Capricorn

Horsburgh
Island

Direction
Island

Home
Island

South
Keeling
Island

Reefs

West
Island

Cocos (Keeling) Islands are a group of
coral atolls consisting of 27 islands in
the Indian Ocean about 2,770 km (1,720
miles) northwest of Perth. Only Home
Island and Direction Island are regularly
inhabited, North Keeling Island is named
after Captain William Keeling

NAVAL AND AIR OPERATIONS, NOVEMBER TO DECEMBER 1914

At the outbreak of war, several German cruisers were on the high seas, even though the British fleet commanded superiority. The Emden *was one such cruiser, and she had inflicted much damage on British ships in the Pacific. The following report describes her capture in the Indian Ocean in November 1914.*

CAPTURE OF THE GERMAN CRUISER *EMDEN* BY HMAS *SYDNEY*

Despatch from Captain John C. T. Glossop
HMAS *Sydney* at Colombo, 15th November, 1914

Sir,

I have the honour to report that whilst on escort duty with the Convoy under the charge of Captain Silver, HMAS *Melbourne*, at 6.30 a.m., on Monday, 9th November, a wireless message from Cocos was heard reporting that a foreign warship was off the entrance. I was ordered to raise steam for full speed at 7.00 a.m. and proceed thither. I worked up to 20 knots, and at 9.15 a.m. sighted land ahead and almost immediately the smoke of a ship, which proved to be HIGMS *Emden* coming out towards me at a great rate. At 9.40 a.m. fire was opened, she firing the first shot. I kept my distance as much as possible to obtain the advantage of my guns. Her fire was very accurate and rapid to begin with, but seemed to slacken very quickly, all casualties occurring in this ship almost immediately. First the foremost funnel of her went, secondly the foremast, and she was badly on fire aft, then the second funnel went, and lastly the third funnel, and I saw she was making for the beach on North Keeling Island, where she grounded at 11.20 a.m. I gave her two more broadsides and left her to pursue a merchant ship which had come up during the action.

Although I had guns on this merchant ship at odd times during the action I had not fired, and as she was making off fast I pursued and overtook her at 12.10, firing a gun across her bows, and hoisting International Code Signal to stop, which she did. I sent an armed boat and found her to be the SS *Buresk*, a captured British collier, with 18 Chinese crew, 1 English Steward, 1 Norwegian Cook, and a German Prize Crew of 3 Officers, 1 Warrant Officer and 12 men. The ship unfortunately was sinking, the Kingston knocked out and damaged to prevent repairing, so I took all on board, fired 4 shells into her and returned to *Emden*, passing men swimming in the water, for whom I left 2 boats I was towing from *Buresk*.

On arriving again off *Emden* she still had her colours up at mainmast head. I enquired by signal, International Code, "Will you surrender?" and received a reply in Morse "What signal? No signal books." I then made in Morse "Do you surrender?" and subsequently "Have you received my signal?" to neither of which did I get an answer. The German Officers on board gave me to understand that the Captain would never surrender, and therefore, though reluctantly, I again fired at her at 4.30 p.m., ceasing at 4.35, as she showed white flags and hauled down her ensign by sending a man aloft.

I then left *Emden* and returned and picked up the *Buresk's* two boats, rescuing 2 sailors (5.00 p.m.), who had been in the water all day. I returned and sent in one boat to *Emden*, manned by her own prize crew from *Buresk*, and 1 Officer, and stating I would return to their assistance next morning. This I had to do, as I was desirous to find out the condition of cables and Wireless Station at Direction Island. On the passage over I was again delayed by rescuing another sailor (6.30 p.m.), and by the time I was again ready and approaching Direction Island it was too late for the night.

I lay on and off all night and communicated with Direction Island at 8.00 a.m., 10th November, to find that the *Emden's* party consisting of 3 officers and 40 men, 1 launch and 2 cutters had seized and provisioned a 70 tons schooner (the *Ayesha*), having 4 Maxims, with 2 belts to each. They left the previous night at six o'clock. The Wireless Station was entirely destroyed, 1 cable cut, 1 damaged, and 1 intact. I borrowed a Doctor and 2 Assistants, and proceeded as fast as possible to *Emden's* assistance.

I sent an officer on board to see the Captain, and in view of the large number of prisoners and wounded and lack of accommodation, etc., in this ship, and the absolute impossibility of leaving them where they were, he agreed that if I received his officers and men and all wounded, "then as for such time as they remained in *Sydney* they would cause no interference with ship or fittings, and would be amenable to the ship's discipline." I therefore set to work at once to tranship them—a most difficult operation, the ship being on weather side of Island and the send alongside very heavy. The conditions in the *Emden* were indescribable. I received the last from her at 5.00 p.m., then had to go round to the lee side to pick up 20 more men who had managed to get ashore from the ship.

Darkness came on before this could be accomplished, and the ship again stood off and on all night, resuming operations at 5.00 a.m. on 11th November, a cutter's crew having to land with stretchers to bring wounded round to embarking point. A German officer, a doctor, died ashore the previous day. The ship in the meantime ran over to Direction Island to return their doctor and assistants, send cables, and was back again at 10.00 a.m., embarked the remainder of wounded, and proceeded for Colombo by 10.35 a.m. Wednesday, 11th November.

Total casualties in *Sydney*: killed 3, severely wounded (since dead) 1, severely wounded 4, wounded 4, slightly wounded 4. In the *Emden* I can only approximately state the killed at 7 officers and 108 men from the Captain's statement. I had on board 11 officers, 9 warrant officers, and 191 men, of whom 3 officers and 53 men were wounded, and of this number 1 Officer and 3 men have since died of wounds.

The damage to *Sydney*'s hull and fittings was surprisingly small; in all about 10 hits seem to have been made. The engine and boiler rooms and funnels escaped entirely.

I have great pleasure in stating that the behaviour of the ship's company was excellent in every way, and with such a large proportion of young hands and people under training it is all the more gratifying. The engines worked magnificently, and higher results than trials were obtained, and I cannot speak too highly of the Medical Staff and arrangements on subsequent trip, the ship being nothing but a hospital of a most painful description.

PROCEEDINGS OF THE FLOTILLA OFF THE COAST OF BELGIUM, OCTOBER TO NOVEMBER 1914

From Rear-Admiral the Hon. Horace L.A. Hood, CB, MVO, DSO,
to the Admiralty
Office of Rear-Admiral, Dover Patrol, 11th November, 1914

Sir,

I have the honour to report the proceedings of the flotilla acting off the coast of Belgium, between October 17th and November 9th.

The flotilla was organised to prevent the movement of large bodies of German troops along the coast roads from Ostend to Nieuport, to support the left flank of the Belgian Army, and to prevent any movement by sea of the enemy's troops.

Operations commenced during the night of October 17th, when the *Attentive*, flying my flag, accompanied by the monitors *Severn, Humber*, and *Mersey*, the light cruiser *Foresight*, and several torpedo-boat destroyers, arrived and anchored off Nieuport Pier.

Early on the morning of the 18th October information was received that German infantry were advancing on Westende village, and that a battery was in action at Westende Bains. The flotilla at once proceeded up past Westende and Middlekirke to draw the fire and endeavour to silence the guns.

A brisk shrapnel fire was opened from the shore, which was immediately replied to, and this commenced the naval operations on the coast which continued for more than three weeks without intermission.

During the first week the enemy's troops were endeavouring to push forward along the coast roads, and a large accumulation of transport existed within reach of the naval guns.

On October 18th machine guns from the *Severn* were landed at Nieuport to assist in the defence, and Lieutenant E. S. Wise fell, gallantly leading his men. The *Amazon*, flying my flag, was badly holed on the waterline and was sent to England for repairs, and during these early days most of the vessels suffered casualties, chiefly from shrapnel shell from the field guns of the enemy.

The presence of the ships on the coast soon caused alterations in the enemy's plans, less and less of their troops were seen, while more and more heavy guns were gradually mounted among the sand dunes that fringe the coast.

It soon became evident that more and heavier guns were required in the flotilla. The Scouts therefore returned to England, while HMS *Venerable* and several older cruisers, sloops and gunboats arrived to carry on the operations.

Five French torpedo-boat destroyers were placed under my orders by Admiral Favereau, and on the 30th October I had the honour of hoisting my flag in the *Intrépide* and leading the French flotilla into action off Lombartzyde. The greatest harmony and enthusiasm existed between the allied flotillas.

As the heavier guns of the enemy came into play it was inevitable that the casualties of the flotilla increased, the most important being the disablement of the 6-inch turret and several shots on the waterline of the *Mersey*, the death of the Commanding Officer and eight men and the disablement of 16 others in the *Falcon*, which vessel came under a heavy fire when guarding the *Venerable* against submarine attack; the *Wildfire* and *Vestal* were badly holed, and a number of casualties caused in the *Brilliant* and *Rinaldo*.

Enemy submarines were seen and torpedoes were fired, and during the latter part of the operations the work of the torpedo craft was chiefly confined to the protection of the larger ships.

It gradually became apparent that the rush of the enemy along the coast had been checked, that the operations were developing into a trench warfare, and that the work of the flotilla had, for the moment, ceased.

Horace L.A. Hood
Rear-Admiral

AERIAL ATTACK ON FRIEDRICKSHAFEN, NOVEMBER 1914

Memorandum by the Director of the Air Department

Admiralty, 17th December, 1914

On 21st November, 1914, Squadron Commander E. F. Briggs, Flight Commander J. T. Babington, and Flight Lieutenant S. V. Sippe, Royal Navy, carried out an aerial attack on the Zeppelin airship sheds and factory at Friedrickshafen on Lake Constance.

Leaving French Territory shortly before 10 a.m., they arrived over their objective at about noon, and, although under a very heavy rifle, machine-gun and shrapnel fire from the moment they were sighted, they all three dived steeply to within a few hundred feet of the sheds, when they released their bombs—in all eleven.

Squadron Commander Briggs was wounded, brought down, and made a prisoner, but the other two officers regained their starting-point after a flight of more than four hours across hostile country under very bad weather conditions.

It is believed that the damage caused by this attack includes the destruction of one airship and serious damage to the larger shed, and also demolition of the hydrogen-producing plant, which had only lately been completed. Later reports stated that flames of considerable magnitude were seen issuing from the factory immediately after the raid.

Aerial attack, Friedrickshafen, November 1914

Legend:

- Important battle areas of interest
- Towns / Villages
- Cities
- Rivers/Lakes
- Country borders

FRANCE

Mulhouse

Freiburg

Kandern

Lorrach

Basle

Liestal

Langenthal

Aarau

Blasien

Neustadt

Stühlingen

Baden

Winterthur

Zürich

Horgen

Zürichsee

Zugersee

Wald

Einsiedeln

SWITZERLAND

Tuttlingen

Singen

Schaffhausen

GERMANY

Pfullendorf

Ravensburg

Friedrickshafen

Konstanz

Lake Constance (Bodensee)

Weinfelden

Gallen

Herisau

Bregen

AUSTRIA

OPERATIONS ON THE GALLIPOLI PENINSULA, APRIL 1915

The reader is advised to refer to the maps on pages 8, 33 and 134 when reading these despatches.

MILITARY DESPATCH DESCRIBING THE LANDING OF THE ARMY

From the General Commanding the Mediterranean Expeditionary Force to the Secretary of State for War

General Headquarters, Mediterranean Expeditionary Force

20th May, 1915

My Lord,

I have the honour to submit my report on the operations in the Gallipoli Peninsula up to and including the 5th May.

In accordance with your Lordship's instructions I left London on 13th March with my General Staff by special train to Marseilles, and thence in HMS *Phaeton* to the scene of the naval operations in the Eastern Mediterranean, reaching Tenedos on the 17th March shortly after noon.

Immediately on arrival I conferred with Vice-Admiral de Robeck, Commanding the Eastern Mediterranean Fleet; General d'Amade, Commanding the French Corps Expéditionnaire; and Contre Amiral Guepratté, in command of the French Squadron. At this conference past difficulties were explained to me, and the intention to make a fresh attack on the morrow was announced. The amphibious battle between warships and land fortresses took place next day, the 18th of March. I witnessed these stupendous events, and thereupon cabled your Lordship my reluctant deduction that the co-operation of the whole of the force under my command would be required to enable the Fleet effectively to force the Dardanelles.

By that time I had already carried out a preliminary reconnaissance of the north-western shore of the Gallipoli Peninsula, from its isthmus, where it is spanned by the Bulair fortified lines, to Cape Helles, at its extremest point. From Bulair this singular feature runs in a south-westerly direction for 52 miles, attaining near its centre a breadth of 12 miles. The northern coast of the northern half of the promontory slopes downwards steeply to the Gulf of Xeros, in a chain of hills, which extend as far as Cape Suvla. The precipitous fall of these hills precludes landing, except at a few narrow gullies, far too restricted for any serious military movements. The southern half of the peninsula is shaped like a badly worn boot. The ankle lies between Kaba Tepe and Kalkmaz Dagh; beneath the heel lie the cluster of forts at Kilid Bahr, whilst the toe is that promontory, five miles in width, stretching from Tekke Burnu to Sedd-el-Bahr.

The three dominating features in this southern section seemed to me to be:

(1) Saribair Mountain, running up in a succession of almost perpendicular escarpments to 970 feet. The whole mountain seemed to be a network of ravines and covered with thick jungle.
(2) Kilid Bahr plateau, which rises, a natural fortification artificially fortified, to a height of 700 feet to cover the forts of the Narrows from an attack from the Ægean.
(3) Achi Babi, a hill 600 feet in height, dominating at long field gun range what I have described as being the toe of the peninsula.

A peculiarity to be noted as regards this last southern sector is that from Achi Babi to Cape Helles the ground is hollowed out like a spoon, presenting only its outer edges to direct fire from the sea. The inside of the spoon appears to be open and undulating, but actually it is full of spurs, nullahs and confused under-features.

Generally speaking the coast is precipitous, and good landing-places are few. Just south of Tekke Burnu is a small sandy bay (W), and half a mile north of it is another small break in the cliffs (X). Two miles further up the coast the mouth of a stream indents these same cliffs (Y2), and yet another mile and a half up a scrub-covered gully looked as if active infantry might be able to scramble up it on to heights not altogether dissimilar to those of Abraham, by Quebec (Y). Inside Sedd-el-Bahr is a sandy beach (V), about 300 yards across, facing a semi-circle of steeply rising ground, as the flat bottom of a half-saucer faces the rim, a rim flanked on one side by an old castle, on the other by a modern fort. By Eski Hissarlik, on the east of Morto Bay (S) was another small beach, which was however dominated by the big guns from Asia. Turning northwards again, there are two good landing places on either side of Kaba Tepe. Farther to the north of that promontory the beach was supposed to be dangerous and difficult. In most of these landing-places the trenches and lines of wire entanglements were plainly visible from on board ship. What seemed to be gun emplacements and infantry redoubts could also be made out through a telescope, but of the full extent of these defences and of the forces available to man them there was no possibility of judging except by practical test.

Altogether the result of this and subsequent reconnaissances was to convince me that nothing but a thorough and systematic scheme for flinging the whole of the troops under my command very rapidly ashore could be expected to meet with success; whereas, on the other hand, a tentative or piecemeal programme was bound to lead to disaster. The landing of an army upon the theatre of operations I have described—a theatre strongly garrisoned throughout, and prepared for any such attempt—involved difficulties for which no precedent was forthcoming in military history except possibly in the sinister legends of Xerxes. The beaches were either so well defended by works and guns, or else so restricted by nature that it did not seem possible, even by two or three simultaneous landings, to pass the troops ashore quickly enough to enable them to maintain themselves against the rapid concentration and counter-attack which the enemy was bound in such case to attempt. It became necessary, therefore, not only to land simultaneously at as many points as possible, but to threaten to land at other points as well. The first of these necessities involved another unavoidable if awkward contingency, the separation by considerable intervals of the force.

The weather was also bound to play a vital part in my landing. Had it been British weather there would have been no alternative but instantly to give up the adventure. To land two or three thousand men, and then to have to break off and leave them exposed for a week to the attacks of 34,000 regular troops, with a hundred guns at their back, was not an eventuality to be lightly envisaged. Whatever happened the weather must always remain an incalculable factor, but at least by delay till the end of April we had a fair chance of several days of consecutive calm.

Before doing anything else I had to redistribute the troops on the transports to suit the order of their disembarkation. The bulk of the forces at my disposal had, perforce, been embarked without its having been possible to pay due attention to the operation upon which I now proposed that they should be launched.

Owing to lack of facilities at Mudros redistribution in that harbour was out of the question. With your Lordship's approval, therefore, I ordered all the transports, except those of the Australian Infantry Brigade and the details encamped at Lemnos Island, to the Egyptian ports. On the 24th March I myself, together with the General Staff, proceeded to Alexandria, where I remained until 7th April, working out the allocation of troops to transports in minutest detail as a prelude to the forthcoming disembarkation. General d'Amade did likewise.

On the 1st April the remainder of the General Headquarters, which had not been mobilised when I left England, arrived at Alexandria.

Apart from the re-arrangements of the troops, my visit to Egypt was not without profit, since it afforded me opportunities of conferring with the GOC Egypt and of making myself acquainted with the troops, drawn from all parts of the French Republic and of the British Empire, which it was to be my privilege to command.

By the 7th April my preparations were sufficiently advanced to enable me to return with my General Staff to Lemnos, so as to put the finishing touches to my plan in close co-ordination with the Vice-Admiral Commanding the Eastern Mediterranean Fleet.

The covering force of the 29th Division left Mudros harbour on the evening of 23rd April for the five beaches, S, V, W, X, and Y. Of these, V, W, and X were to be main landings, the landings at S and Y being made mainly to protect the flanks, to disseminate the forces of the enemy, and to interrupt the arrival of his reinforcements. The landings at S and Y were to take place at dawn, whilst it was planned that the first troops for V, W, and X beaches should reach the shore simultaneously at 5.30 a.m. after half an hour's bombardment from the fleet.

The transports conveying the covering force arrived off Tenedos on the morning of the 24th, and during the afternoon the troops were transferred to the warships and fleet-sweepers in which they were to approach the shore. About midnight these ships, each towing a number of cutters and other small boats, silently slipped their cables and, escorted by the 3rd Squadron of the Fleet, steamed slowly towards their final rendezvous at Cape Helles. The rendezvous was reached just before dawn on the 25th. The morning was absolutely still; there was no sign of life on the shore; a thin veil of mist hung motionless over the promontory; the surface of the sea was as smooth as glass. The four battleships and four cruisers which formed the 3rd Squadron at once took up the positions that had been allotted to them, and at 5 a.m., it being then light enough to fire, a violent bombardment of the enemy's defences was begun. Meanwhile the troops were being rapidly transferred to the small boats in which they were to be towed ashore. Not a move on the part of the enemy; except for shells thrown from the Asiatic side of the Straits the guns of the Fleet remained unanswered.

The detachment detailed for S beach (Eski Hissarlik Point) consisted of the 2nd South Wales Borderers (less one company) under Lieut.-Colonel Casson. Their landing was delayed by the current, but by 7.30 a.m. it had been successfully effected at the cost of some 50 casualties, and Lieut.-Col. Casson was able to establish his small force on the high ground near De Totts Battery. Here he maintained himself until the general advance on the 27th brought him into touch with the main body.

The landing on Y beach was entrusted to the King's Own Scottish Borderers and the Plymouth (Marine) Battalion, Royal Naval Division, specially attached to the 29th Division for this task, the whole under the command of Lieut.-Colonel Koe. The beach at this point consisted merely of a narrow strip of sand at the foot of a crumbling scrub-covered cliff some 200 feet high immediately to the west of Krithia.

A number of small gullies running down the face of the cliff facilitated the climb to the summit, and so impracticable had these precipices appeared to the Turks that no steps had been taken to defend them. Very different would it have been had we, as was at one time intended, taken Y2 for this landing. There a large force of infantry, entrenched up to their necks, and supported by machine and Hotchkiss guns, were awaiting an attempt which could hardly have made good its footing. But at Y both battalions were able in the first instance to establish themselves on the heights, reserves of food, water and ammunition were hauled up to the top of the cliff, and, in accordance with the plan of operations, an endeavour was immediately made to gain touch with the troops landing at X beach. Unfortunately, the enemy's strong detachment from Y2 interposed, our troops landing at X were fully occupied in attacking the Turks immediately to their front, and the attempt to join hands was not persevered with.

Later in the day a large force of Turks were seen to be advancing upon the cliffs above Y beach from the direction of Krithia, and Colonel Koe was obliged to entrench. From this time onward his small force was subjected to strong and repeated attacks, supported by field artillery, and owing to the configuration of the ground, which here drops inland from the edge of the cliff, the guns of the supporting ships could render him little assistance.

Throughout the afternoon and all through the night the Turks made assault after assault upon the British line. They threw bombs into the trenches, and, favoured by darkness, actually led a pony with a machine gun on its back over the defences and were proceeding to come into action in the middle of our position when they were bayonetted. The British repeatedly counter-charged with the bayonet, and always drove off the enemy for the moment, but the Turks were in a vast superiority and fresh troops took the place of those who temporarily fell back. Colonel Koe (since died of wounds) had become a casualty early in the day, and the number of officers and men killed and wounded during the incessant fighting was very heavy.

By 7 a.m. on the 26th only about half of the King's Own Scottish Borderers remained to man the entrenchment made for four times their number. These brave fellows were absolutely worn out with continuous fighting; it was doubtful if reinforcements could reach them in time, and orders were issued for them to be re-embarked. Thanks to HMS *Goliath*, *Dublin*, *Amethyst*, and *Sapphire*, thanks also to the devotion of a small rearguard of the King's Own Scottish Borderers, which kept off the enemy from lining the cliff, the re-embarkation of the whole of the troops, together with the wounded, stores and ammunition, was safely accomplished, and both battalions were brought round the southern end of the peninsula. Deplorable as the heavy losses had been, and unfortunate as was the tactical failure to make good so much ground at the outset, yet, taking the operation as it stood, there can be no doubt it has contributed greatly to the success of the main attack, seeing that the plucky stand made at Y beach had detained heavy columns of the enemy from arriving at the southern end of the peninsula during what it will be seen was a very touch-and-go struggle.

The landing-place known as X beach consists of a strip of sand some 200 yards long by 8 yards wide at the foot of a low cliff. The troops to be landed here were the 1st Royal Fusiliers, who were to be towed ashore from HMS *Implacable* in two parties, half a battalion at a time, together with a beach working party found by the Anson Battalion, Royal Naval Division. About 6 a.m. HMS *Implacable*, with a boldness much admired by the Army, stood quite close in to the beach, firing very rapidly with every gun she could bring to bear. Thus seconded, the Royal Fusiliers made good their landing with but little loss. The battalion then advanced to attack the Turkish trenches on the Hill 114, situated between V and W beaches, but were heavily counter-attacked and forced to give ground. Two more battalions of the 87th Brigade soon followed them, and by evening the troops had established themselves in an entrenched position extending from half a mile round the landing-place and as far south as Hill 114. Here they were in touch with the Lancashire Fusiliers, who had landed on W beach. Brigadier-General Marshall, commanding the 87th Brigade, had been wounded during the day's fighting, but continued in command of the brigade.

The landing on V beach was planned to take place on the following lines:

As soon as the enemy's defences had been heavily bombarded by the fleet, three companies of the Dublin Fusiliers were to be towed ashore. They were to be closely followed by the collier *River Clyde* (Commander Unwin, RN), carrying between decks the balance of the Dublin Fusiliers, the Munster Fusiliers, half a battalion of the Hampshire Regiment, the West Riding Field Company, and other details.

The *River Clyde* had been specially prepared for the rapid disembarkation of her complement, and large openings for the exit of the troops had been cut in her sides, giving on to a wide gang-plank by which the men could pass rapidly into lighters which she had in tow. As soon as the first tows had reached land the *River Clyde* was to be run straight ashore. Her lighters were to be placed in position to form a gangway between the ship and the beach, and by this means it was hoped that 2,000 men could be thrown ashore with the utmost rapidity. Further, to assist in covering the landing, a battery of machine guns, protected by sandbags, had been mounted in her bows.

The remainder of the covering force detailed for this beach was then to follow in tows from the attendant battleships.

V beach is situated immediately to the west of Sedd-el-Bahr. Between the bluff on which stands Sedd-el-Bahr village and that which is crowned by No. 1 Fort the ground forms a very regular amphitheatre of 300 or 400 yards radius. The slopes down to the beach are slightly concave, so that the whole area contained within the limits of this natural amphitheatre, whose grassy terraces rise gently to a height of a hundred feet above the shore, can be swept by the fire of a defender. The beach itself is a sandy strip some 10 yards wide and 350 yards long, backed along almost the whole of its length by a low sandy escarpment about 4 feet high, where the ground falls nearly sheer down to the beach. The slight shelter afforded by this escarpment played no small part in the operations of the succeeding 32 hours.

At the south-eastern extremity of the beach, between the shore and the village, stands the old fort of Sedd-el-Bahr, a battered ruin with wide breaches in its walls and mounds of fallen masonry within and around it. On the ridge to the north, overlooking the amphitheatre, stands a ruined barrack. Both of these buildings, as well as No. 1 Fort, had been long bombarded by the fleet, and the guns of the forts had been put out of action; but their crumbled walls and the ruined outskirts of the village afforded cover for riflemen, while from the terraced slopes already described the defenders were able to command the open beach, as a stage is overlooked from the balconies of a theatre. On the very margin of the beach a strong barbed-wire entanglement, made of heavier metal and longer barbs than I have ever seen elsewhere, ran right across from the old fort of Sedd-el-Bahr to the foot of the north-western headland. Two-thirds of the way up the ridge a second and even stronger entanglement crossed the amphitheatre, passing in front of the old barrack and ending in the outskirts of the village. A third transverse entanglement, joining these two, ran up the hill near the eastern end of the beach, and almost at right angles to it. Above the upper entanglement the ground was scored with the enemy's trenches, in one of which four pom-poms were emplaced; in others were dummy pom-poms to draw fire, while the débris of the shattered buildings on either flank afforded cover and concealment for a number of machine guns, which brought a cross-fire to bear on the ground already swept by rifle fire from the ridge.

Needless to say, the difficulties in the way of previous reconnaissance had rendered it impossible to obtain detailed information with regard either to the locality or to the enemy's preparations.

As often happens in war, the actual course of events did not quite correspond with the intentions of the Commander. The *River Clyde* came into position off Sedd-el-Bahr in advance of the tows, and, just as the latter reached the shore, Commander Unwin beached his ship also. Whilst the boats and the collier were approaching the landing place the Turks made no sign. Up to the very last moment it appeared as if the landing was to be unopposed. But the moment the first boat touched bottom the storm broke. A tornado of fire swept over the beach, the incoming boats, and the collier. The Dublin Fusiliers and the naval boats' crews suffered exceedingly heavy losses while still in the boats. Those who succeeded in landing and in crossing the strip of sand managed to gain some cover when they reached the low escarpment on the further side. None of the boats, however, were able to get off again, and they and their crews were destroyed upon the beach.

Now came the moment for the *River Clyde* to pour forth her living freight; but grievous delay was caused here by the difficulty of placing the lighters in position between the ship and the shore. A strong current hindered the work and the enemy's fire was so intense that almost every man engaged upon it was immediately shot. Owing, however, to the splendid gallantry of the naval working party, the lighters were eventually placed in position, and then the disembarkation began.

A company of the Munster Fusiliers led the way, but, short as was the distance, few of the men ever reached the farther side of the beach through the hail of bullets which poured down upon them from both flanks and the front. As the second company followed, the extemporised pier of lighters gave way in the current. The end nearest to the shore drifted into deep water, and many men who had escaped being shot were drowned by the weight of their equipment in trying to swim from the lighter to the beach. Undaunted workers were still forthcoming, the lighters were again brought into position, and the third company of the Munster Fusiliers rushed ashore, suffering heaviest loss this time from shrapnel as well as from rifle, pom-pom, and machine-gun fire.

For a space the attempt to land was discontinued. When it was resumed the lighters again drifted into deep water, with Brigadier-General Napier, Captain Costeker, his Brigade Major, and a number of men of the Hampshire Regiment on board. There was nothing for them all but to lie down on the lighters, and it was here that General Napier and Captain Costeker were killed. At this time, between 10 and 11 a.m., about 1,000 men had left the collier, and of these nearly half had been killed or wounded before they could reach the little cover afforded by the steep, sandy bank at the top of the beach. Further attempts to disembark were now given up. Had the troops all been in open boats but few of them would have lived to tell the tale. But, most fortunately, the collier was so constructed as to afford fairly efficient protection to the men who were still on board, and, so long as they made no attempt to land, they suffered comparatively little loss.

Throughout the remainder of the day there was practically no change in the position of affairs. The situation was probably saved by the machine-guns on the *River Clyde*, which did valuable service in keeping down the enemy's fire and in preventing any attempt on their part to launch a counter-attack. One half-company of the Dublin Fusiliers, which had been landed at a camber just east of Sedd-el-Bahr village, was unable to work its way across to V beach, and by mid-day had only twenty-five men left. It was proposed to divert to Y beach that part of the main body which had been intended to land on V beach; but this would have involved considerable delay owing to the distance, and the main body was diverted to W beach, where the Lancashire Fusiliers had already effected a landing.

Late in the afternoon part of the Worcestershire Regiment and the Lancashire Fusiliers worked across the high ground from W beach, and seemed likely to relieve the situation by taking the defenders of V beach in flank. The pressure on their own front, however, and the numerous barbed-wire entanglements which intervened, checked this advance, and at nightfall the Turkish garrison still held their ground. Just before dark some small parties of our men made their way along the shore to the outer walls of the Old Fort, and when night had fallen the remainder of the infantry from the collier were landed. A good force was now available for attack, but our troops were at such a cruel disadvantage as to position, and the fire of the enemy was still so accurate in the bright moonlight that all attempts to clear the fort and the outskirts of the village during the night failed one after the other. The wounded who were able to do so without support returned to the collier under cover of darkness; but otherwise the situation at daybreak on the 26th was the same as it had been on the previous day, except that the troops first landed were becoming very exhausted.

Twenty-four hours after the disembarkation began there were ashore on V beach the survivors of the Dublin and Munster Fusiliers and of two companies of the Hampshire Regiment. The Brigadier and his Brigade-Major had been killed; Lieutenant-Colonel Carrington Smith, commanding the Hampshire Regiment, had been killed and the adjutant had been wounded. The adjutant of the Munster Fusiliers was wounded, and the great majority of the senior officers were either wounded or killed. The remnant of the landing-party still crouched on the beach beneath the shelter of the sandy escarpment which had saved so many lives. With them were two officers of my General Staff—Lieutenant-Colonel Doughty-Wylie and Lieutenant-Colonel Williams. These two officers, who had landed from the *River Clyde*, had been striving, with conspicuous contempt for danger, to keep all their comrades in good heart during this day and night of ceaseless imminent peril.

Now that it was daylight once more, Lieutenant-Colonels Doughty-Wylie and Williams set to work to organise an attack on the hill above the beach. Any soldier who has endeavoured to pull scattered units together after they have been dominated for many consecutive hours by close and continuous fire will be able to take the measure of their difficulties. Fortunately, General Hunter Weston had arranged with Rear-Admiral Wemyss about this same time for a heavy bombardment to be opened by the ships upon the Old Fort, Sedd-el-Bahr Village, the Old Castle north of the village, and on the ground leading up from the beach. Under cover of this bombardment, and led by Lieutenant-Colonel Doughty-Wylie and Captain Walford, Brigade-Major R.A., the troops gained a footing in the village by 10 a.m. They encountered a most stubborn opposition and suffered heavy losses from the fire of well-concealed riflemen and machine-guns. Undeterred by the resistance, and supported by the naval gunfire, they pushed forward, and soon after midday they penetrated to the northern edge of the village, whence they were in a position to attack the Old Castle and Hill 141. During this advance Captain Walford was killed. Lieutenant-Colonel Doughty-Wylie had most gallantly led the attack all the way up from the beach through the west side of the village, under galling fire. And now, when, owing so largely to his own inspiring example and intrepid courage, the position had almost been gained, he was killed while leading the last assault. But the attack was pushed forward without wavering, and, fighting their way across the open with great dash, the troops gained the summit and occupied the Old Castle and Hill 141 before 2 p.m.

W beach consists of a strip of deep, powdery sand some 350 yards long and from 15 to 40 yards wide, situated immediately south of Tekke Burnu, where a small gully running down to the sea opens out a break in the cliffs. On either flank of the beach the ground rises precipitously but, in the centre, a number of sand dunes afford a more gradual access to the ridge overlooking the sea. Much time and ingenuity had been employed by the Turks in turning this landing place into a death trap. Close to the water's edge a broad wire entanglement extended the whole length of the shore, and a supplementary barbed network lay concealed under the surface of the sea in the shallows. Land mines and sea mines had been laid. The high ground overlooking the beach was strongly fortified with trenches to which the gully afforded a natural covered approach. A number of machine guns also were cunningly tucked away into holes in the cliff so as to be immune from a naval bombardment whilst they were converging their fire on the wire entanglements. The crest of the hill overlooking the beach was in its turn commanded by high ground to the north-west and south-east, and especially by two strong infantry redoubts near point 138. Both these redoubts were protected by wire entanglements about 20 feet broad, and could be approached only by a bare glacis-like slope leading up from the high ground above W beach or from the Cape Helles lighthouse. In addition, another separate entanglement ran down from these two redoubts to the edge of the cliff near the lighthouse, making intercommunication between V and W beaches impossible until these redoubts had been captured.

So strong, in fact, were the defences of W beach that the Turks may well have considered them impregnable, and it is my firm conviction that no finer feat of arms has ever been achieved by the British soldier—or any other soldier—than the storming of these trenches from open boats on the morning of 25th April.

The landing at W had been entrusted to the 1st Battalion Lancashire Fusiliers (Major Bishop) and it was to the complete lack of the senses of danger or of fear of this daring battalion that we owed our astonishing success. As in the case of the landing at X, the disembarkation had been delayed for half an hour, but at 6 a.m. the whole battalion approached the shore together, towed by eight picket boats in line abreast, each picket boat pulling four ship's cutters. As soon as shallow water was reached, the tows were cast off and the boats were at once rowed to the shore. Three companies headed for the beach and a company on the left of the line made for a small ledge of rock immediately under the cliff at Tekke Burnu. Brigadier-General Hare, commanding the 88th Brigade, accompanied this latter party, which escaped the cross fire brought to bear upon the beach, and was also in a better position than the rest of the battalion to turn the wire entanglements.

While the troops were approaching the shore no shot had been fired from the enemy's trenches, but as soon as the first boat touched the ground a hurricane of lead swept over the battalion. Gallantly led by their officers, the Fusiliers literally hurled themselves ashore and, fired at from right, left and centre, commenced hacking their way through the wire. A long line of men was at once mown down as by a scythe, but the remainder were not to be denied. Covered by the fire of the warships, which had now closed right in to the shore and helped by the flanking fire of the company on the extreme left, they broke through the entanglements and collected under the cliffs on either side of the beach. Here the companies were rapidly reformed, and set forth to storm the enemy's entrenchments wherever they could find them.

In making these attacks the bulk of the battalion moved up towards Hill 114 whilst a small party worked down towards the trenches on the Cape Helles side of the landing-place. Several land mines were exploded by Turks during the advance, but the determination of the troops was in no way affected. By 10 a.m. three lines of hostile trenches were in our hands, and our hold on the beach was assured.

About 9.30 a.m. more infantry had begun to disembark, and two hours later a junction was effected on Hill 114 with the troops who had landed on X beach.

On the right, owing to the strength of the redoubt on Hill 138, little progress could be made. The small party of Lancashire Fusiliers which had advanced in this direction succeeded in reaching the edge of the wire entanglements, but were not strong enough to do more, and it was here that Major Frankland, Brigade Major of the 86th Infantry Brigade, who had gone forward to make a personal reconnaissance, was unfortunately killed. Brigadier-General Hare had been wounded earlier in the day, and Colonel Woolly-Dod, General Staff 29th Division, was now sent ashore to take command at W beach and organise a further advance.

At 2 p.m., after the ground near Hill 138 had been subjected to a heavy bombardment, the Worcester Regiment advanced to the assault. Several men of this battalion rushed forward with great spirit to cut passages through the entanglement; some were killed, others persevered, and by 4 p.m. the hill and redoubt were captured.

An attempt was now made to join hands with the troops on V beach, who could make no headway at all against the dominating defences of the enemy. To help them out the 86th Brigade pushed forward in an easterly direction along the cliff. There is a limit, however, to the storming of barbed-wire entanglements. More of these barred the way. Again the heroic wire-cutters came out. Through glasses they could be seen quietly snipping away under a hellish fire from the enemy as if they were pruning a vineyard. Again some of them fell. The fire pouring out of No. 1 Fort grew hotter and hotter, until the troops, now thoroughly exhausted by a sleepless night and by the long day's fighting under a hot sun, had to rest on their laurels for a while.

When night fell, the British position in front of W beach extended from just east of Cape Helles lighthouse, through Hill 138, to Hill 114. Practically every man had to be thrown into the trenches to hold this line, and the only available reserves on this part of our front were the 2nd London Field Company R.E. and a platoon of the Anson Battalion, which had been landed as a beach working party.

During the night several strong and determined counter-attacks were made, all successfully repulsed without loss of ground. Meanwhile the disembarkation of the remainder of the division was proceeding on W and X beaches.

The Australian and New Zealand Army Corps sailed out of Mudros Bay on the afternoon of April 24th, escorted by the 2nd Squadron of the Fleet, under Rear-Admiral Thursby. The rendezvous was reached just after half-past one in the morning of the 25th, and there the 1,500 men who had been placed on board HM ships before leaving Mudros were transferred to their boats. This operation was carried out with remarkable expedition, and in absolute silence. Simultaneously the remaining 2,500 men of the covering force were transferred from their transports to six destroyers. At 2.30 a.m. HM ships, together with the tows and the destroyers, proceeded to within some four miles of the coast, HMS *Queen* (flying Rear-Admiral Thursby's flag) directing on a point about a mile north of Kaba Tepe. At 3.30 a.m. orders to go ahead and land were given to the tows, and at 4.10 a.m. the destroyers were ordered to follow.

All these arrangements worked without a hitch, and were carried out in complete orderliness and silence. No breath of wind ruffled the surface of the sea, and every condition was favourable save for the moon, which, sinking behind the ships, may have silhouetted them against its orb, betraying them thus to watchers on the shore.

A rugged and difficult part of the coast had been selected for the landing, so difficult and rugged that I considered the Turks were not at all likely to anticipate such a descent. Indeed, owing to the tows having failed to maintain their exact direction the actual point of disembarkation was rather more than a mile north of that which I had selected, and was more closely overhung by steeper cliffs. Although this accident increased the initial difficulty of driving the enemy off the heights inland, it has since proved itself to have been a blessing in disguise, inasmuch as the actual base of the force of occupation has been much better defiladed from shell fire.

The beach on which the landing was actually effected is a very narrow strip of sand, about 1,000 yards in length, bounded on the north and the south by two small promontories. At its southern extremity a deep ravine, with exceedingly steep, scrub-clad sides, runs inland in a north-easterly direction. Near the northern end of the beach a small but steep gully runs up into the hills at right angles to the shore. Between the ravine and the gully the whole of the beach is backed by the seaward face of the spur which forms the north-western side of the ravine. From the top of the spur the ground falls almost sheer, except near the southern limit of the beach, where gentler slopes give access to the mouth of the ravine behind. Further inland lie in a tangled knot the under features of Saribair, separated by deep ravines, which take a most confusing diversity of direction. Sharp spurs, covered with dense scrub, and falling away in many places in precipitous sandy cliffs, radiate from the principal mass of the mountain, from which they run north-west, west, south-west, and south to the coast.

The boats approached the land in the silence and the darkness, and they were close to the shore before the enemy stirred. Then about one battalion of Turks was seen running along the beach to intercept the lines of boats. At this so critical a moment the conduct of all ranks was most praiseworthy. Not a word was spoken—everyone remained perfectly orderly and quiet awaiting the enemy's fire, which sure enough opened, causing many casualties. The moment the boats touched land the Australians' turn had come. Like lightning they leapt ashore, and each man as he did so went straight as his bayonet at the enemy. So vigorous was the onslaught that the Turks made no attempt to withstand it and fled from ridge to ridge pursued by the Australian infantry.

This attack was carried out by the 3rd Australian Brigade, under Major (temporary Colonel) Sinclair Maclagan, DSO. The 1st and 2nd Brigades followed promptly, and were all disembarked by 2 p.m., by which time 12,000 men and two batteries of Indian Mountain Artillery had been landed. The disembarkation of further artillery was delayed owing to the fact that the enemy's heavy guns opened on the anchorage and forced the transports, which had been subjected to continuous shelling from his field guns, to stand further out to sea.

The broken ground, the thick scrub, the necessity for sending any formed detachments post haste as they landed to the critical point of the moment, the headlong valour of scattered groups of the men who had pressed far further into the peninsula than had been intended—all these led to confusion and mixing up of units. Eventually the mixed crowd of fighting men, some advancing from the beach, others falling back before the oncoming Turkish supports, solidified into a semi-circular position with its right about a mile north of Kaba Tepe and its left on the high ground over Fisherman's Hut. During this period parties of the 9th and 10th Battalions charged and put out of action three of the enemy's Krupp guns. During this period also the disembarkation of the Australian Division was followed by that of the New Zealand and Australian Division (two brigades only).

From 11 a.m. to 3 p.m. the enemy, now reinforced to a strength of 20,000 men, attacked the whole line, making a specially strong effort against the 3rd Brigade and the left of the 2nd Brigade. This counter-attack was, however, handsomely repulsed with the help of the guns of HM ships. Between 5 and 6.30 p.m. a third most determined counter-attack was made against the 3rd

Brigade, who held their ground with more than equivalent stubbornness. During the night again the Turks made constant attacks, and the 8th Battalion repelled a bayonet charge; but in spite of all the line held firm. The troops had had practically no rest on the night of the 24/25th; they had been fighting hard all day over most difficult country, and they had been subjected to heavy shrapnel fire in the open. Their casualties had been deplorably heavy. But, despite their losses and in spite of their fatigue, the morning of the 26th found them still in good heart and as full of fight as ever.

It is a consolation to know that the Turks suffered still more seriously. Several times our machine guns got on to them in close formation, and the whole surrounding country is still strewn with their dead of this date.

The reorganisation of units and formations was impossible during the 26th and 27th owing to persistent attacks. An advance was impossible until a reorganisation could be effected, and it only remained to entrench the position gained and to perfect the arrangements for bringing up ammunition, water, and supplies to the ridges—in itself a most difficult undertaking. Four battalions of the Royal Naval Division were sent up to reinforce the Army Corps on the 28th and 29th April.

On the night of May 2nd a bold effort was made to seize a commanding knoll in front of the centre of the line. The enemy's enfilading machine guns were too scientifically posted, and 800 men were lost without advantage beyond the infliction of a corresponding loss to the enemy. On May 4th an attempt to seize Kaba Tepe was also unsuccessful, the barbed-wire here being something beyond belief. But a number of minor operations have been carried out, such as the taking of a Turkish observing station; the strengthening of entrenchments; the reorganisation of units; and the perfecting of communication with the landing place. Also a constant strain has been placed upon some of the best troops of the enemy who, to the number of 24,000, are constantly kept fighting and being killed and wounded freely, as the Turkish sniper is no match for the Kangaroo shooter, even at his own game.

The assistance of the Royal Navy, here as elsewhere, has been invaluable. The whole of the arrangements have been in Admiral Thursby's hands, and I trust I may be permitted to say what a trusty and powerful friend he has proved himself to be to the Australian and New Zealand Army Corps.

Concurrently with the British landings a regiment of the French Corps was successfully disembarked at Kum Kale under the guns of the French fleet, and remained ashore till the morning of the 26th, when they were re-embarked. Five hundred prisoners were captured by the French on this day.

This operation drew the fire of the Asiatic guns from Morto Bay and V beach on to Kum Kale, and contributed largely to the success of the British landings.

On the evening of the 26th the main disembarkation of the French Corps was begun, V beach being allotted to our Allies for this purpose, and it was arranged that the French should hold the portion of the front between the telegraph wire and the sea.

The following day I ordered a general advance to a line stretching from Hill 236 near Eski Hissarlik Point to the mouth of the stream two miles north of Tekke Burnu. This advance, which was commenced at midday, was completed without opposition, and the troops at once consolidated their new line. The forward movement relieved the growing congestion on the beaches, and by giving us possession of several new wells afforded a temporary solution to the water problem, which had hitherto been causing me much anxiety.

By the evening of the 27th the Allied forces had established themselves on a line some three miles long, which stretched from the mouth of the nullah, 3,200 yards north-east of Tekke Burnu, to Eski Hissarlik Point, the three brigades of the 29th Division less two battalions on the left and in the centre, with four French battalions on the right, and beyond them again the South Wales Borderers on the extreme right.

Owing to casualties this line was somewhat thinly held. Still, it was so vital to make what headway we could before the enemy recovered himself and received fresh reinforcements that it was decided to push on as quickly as possible. Orders were therefore issued for a general advance to commence at 8 a.m. next day. The 29th Division were to march on Krithia, with their left brigade leading, the French were directed to extend their left in conformity with the British movements and to retain their right on the coast-line south of the Kereves Dere.

The advance commenced at 8 a.m. on the 28th, and was carried out with commendable vigour, despite the fact that from the moment of landing the troops had been unable to obtain any proper rest.

The 87th Brigade, with which had been incorporated the Drake Battalion, Royal Naval Division, in the place of the King's Own Scottish Borderers and South Wales Borderers, pushed on rapidly, and by 10 a.m. had advanced some two miles. Here the further progress of the Border regiment was barred by a strong work on the left flank. They halted to concentrate and make dispositions to attack it, and at that moment had to withstand a determined counter-attack by the Turks. Aided by heavy gun fire from HMS *Queen Elizabeth*, they succeeded in beating off the attack, but they made no further progress that day, and when night fell entrenched themselves on the ground they had gained in the morning.

The Inniskilling Fusiliers, who advanced with their right on the Krithia ravine, reached a point about three-quarters of a mile south-west of Krithia. This was, however, the farthest limit attained, and later on in the day they fell back into line with other corps.

The 88th Brigade on the right of the 87th progressed steadily until about 11.30 a.m., when the stubbornness of the opposition, coupled with a dearth of ammunition, brought their advance to a standstill. The 86th Brigade, under Lieutenant-Colonel Casson, which had been held in reserve, were thereupon ordered to push forward through the 88th Brigade in the direction of Krithia.

The movement commenced at about 1 p.m., but though small reconnoitring parties got to within a few hundred yards of Krithia, the main body of the brigade did not get beyond the line held by the 88th Brigade. Meanwhile, the French had also pushed on in the face of strong opposition along the spurs on the western bank of the Kereves Dere, and had got to within a mile of Krithia with their right thrown back and their left in touch with the 88th Brigade. Here they were unable to make further progress; gradually the strength of the resistance made itself felt, and our Allies were forced during the afternoon to give ground.

By 2 p.m. the whole of the troops with the exception of the Drake Battalion had been absorbed into the firing line. The men were exhausted, and the few guns landed at the time were unable to afford them adequate artillery support. The small amount of transport available did not suffice to maintain the supply of munitions, and cartridges were running short despite all efforts to push them up from the landing-places.

Hopes of getting a footing on Achi Babi had now perforce to be abandoned—at least for this occasion. The best that could be expected was that we should be able to maintain what we had won, and when at 3 p.m. the Turks made a determined counter-attack with the bayonet against the centre and right of our line, even this seemed exceedingly doubtful. Actually a partial retirement did take place. The French were also forced back, and at 6 p.m. orders were issued for our troops to entrench themselves as best they could in the positions they then held, with their right flank thrown back so as to maintain connection with our Allies. In this retirement the right flank of the 88th Brigade was temporarily uncovered, and the Worcester Regiment suffered severely.

Had it been possible to push in reinforcements in men, artillery and munitions during the day, Krithia should have fallen, and much subsequent fighting for its capture would have been avoided.

Two days later this would have been feasible, but I had to reckon with the certainty that the enemy would, in that same time, have received proportionately greater support. I was faced by the usual choice of evils, and although the result was not what I had hoped, I have no reason to believe that hesitation and delay would better have answered my purpose.

For, after all, we had pushed forward quite appreciably on the whole. The line eventually held by our troops on the night of the 28th ran from a point on the coast three miles north-west of Tekke Burnu to a point one mile north of Eski Hissarlik, whence it was continued by the French south-east to the coast.

Much inevitable mixing of units of the 86th and 88th Brigades had occurred during the day's fighting, and there was a dangerous re-entrant in the line at the junction of the 87th and 88th Brigades near the Krithia nullah. The French had lost heavily, especially in officers, and required time to re-organise.

The 29th April was consequently spent in straightening the line, and in consolidating and strengthening the positions gained. There was a certain amount of artillery and musketry fire, but nothing serious.

Similarly, on the 30th, no advance was made, nor was any attack delivered by the enemy. The landing of the bulk of the artillery was completed and a readjustment of the line took place, the portion held by the French being somewhat increased.

Two more battalions of the Royal Naval Division had been disembarked, and these, together with three battalions of the 88th Brigade withdrawn from the line, were formed into a reserve.

This reserve was increased on the 1st May by the addition of the 29th Indian Infantry Brigade, which released the three battalions of the 88th Brigade to return to the trenches. The Corps Expéditionnaire d'Orient had disembarked the whole of their infantry and all but two of their batteries by the same evening.

At 10 p.m. the Turks opened a hot shell fire upon our position, and half an hour later, just before the rise of the moon, they delivered a series of desperate attacks. Their formation was in three solid lines, the men in the front rank being deprived of ammunition to make them rely only upon the bayonet. The officers were served out with coloured Bengal lights to fire from their pistols, red indicating to the Turkish guns that they were to lengthen their range; white that our front trenches had been stormed; green that our main position had been carried. The Turkish attack was to crawl on hand and knees until the time came for the final rush to be made. An eloquent hortative was signed Von Zowenstern and addressed to the Turkish rank and file who were called upon, by one mighty effort, to fling us all back into the sea.

> Attack the enemy with the bayonet and utterly destroy him!
> We shall not retire one step; for, if we do, our religion, our country and our nation will perish!
> Soldiers! The world is looking at you! Your only hope of salvation is to bring this battle to a successful issue or gloriously to give up your life in the attempt!

The first momentum of this ponderous onslaught fell upon the right of the 86th Brigade, an unlucky spot, seeing all the officers thereabouts had already been killed or wounded. So when the Turks came right on without firing and charged into the trenches with the bayonet they made an ugly gap in the line. This gap was instantly filled by the 5th Royal Scots (Territorials), who faced to their flank and executed a brilliant bayonet charge against the enemy, and by the Essex Regiment detached for the purpose by the Officer Commanding 88th Brigade. The rest of the British line held its own with comparative ease, and it was not found necessary to employ any portion of the reserve. The storm next broke in fullest violence against the French left, which was held by the Senegalese. Behind them were two British-Field Artillery Brigades and a Howitzer Battery. After several charges and counter-charges the Senegalese began to give ground and a company of the Worcester Regiment and some gunners were sent forward to hold the gap. Later, a second company of the Worcester Regiment was also sent up, and the position was then maintained for the remainder of the night, although, about 2 a.m., it was found necessary to despatch one battalion Royal Naval Division to strengthen the extreme right of the French.

About 5 a.m. a counter-offensive was ordered, and the whole line began to advance. By 7.30 a.m. the British left had gained some 500 yards, and the centre had pushed the enemy back and inflicted heavy losses. The right also had gained some ground in conjunction with the French left, but the remainder of the French line was unable to progress. As the British centre and left were now subjected to heavy cross fire from concealed machine guns, it was found impossible to maintain the ground gained, and therefore, about 11 a.m., the whole line withdrew to its former trenches.

The net result of the operations was the repulse of the Turks and the infliction upon them of very heavy losses. At first we had them fairly on the run, and had it not been for those inventions of the devil—machine guns and barbed wire—which suit the Turkish character and tactics to perfection, we should not have stopped short of the crest of Achi Babi. As it was, all brigades reported great numbers of dead Turks in front of their lines, and 350 prisoners were left in our hands.

On the 2nd, during the day, the enemy remained quiet, burying his dead under a red crescent flag, a work with which we did not interfere. Shortly after 9 p.m., however, they made another attack against the whole allied line, their chief effort being made against the French front, where the ground favoured their approach. The attack was repulsed with loss.

During the night 3rd/4th the French front was again subjected to a heavy attack, which they were able to repulse without assistance from my general reserve.

The day of the 4th was spent in reorganisation, and a portion of the line held by the French, who had lost heavily during the previous night's fighting, was taken over by the 2nd Naval Brigade. The night passed quietly.

During the 5th the Lancashire Fusilier Brigade of the East Lancashire Division was disembarked and placed in reserve behind the British left.

Orders were issued for an advance to be carried out next day, and these and the three days' battle which ensued, will be dealt with in my next despatch.

The losses, exclusive of the French, during the period covered by this despatch were, I regret to say, very severe, numbering:

177 Officers and 1,990 other ranks killed,
412 Officers and 7,807 other ranks wounded,
13 Officers and 3,580 other ranks missing.

From a technical point of view it is interesting to note that my Administrative Staff had not reached Mudros by the time when the landings were finally arranged. All the highly elaborate work involved by these landings was put through by my General Staff working in collaboration with Commodore Roger Keyes, CB, MVO, and the Naval Transport Officers allotted for the purpose by Vice-Admiral de Robeck. Navy and Army carried out these combined duties with that perfect harmony which was indeed absolutely essential to success.

Throughout the events I have chronicled the Royal Navy has been father and mother to the Army. Not one of us but realises how much he owes to Vice-Admiral de Robeck; to the warships, French and British; to the destroyers, mine sweepers, picket boats, and to all their dauntless crews, who took no thought of themselves, but risked everything to give their soldier comrades a fair run in at the enemy.

Throughout these preparations and operations Monsieur le Général d'Amade has given me the benefit of his wide experiences of war, and has afforded me, always, the most loyal and energetic support. The landing of Kum Kale planned by me as a mere diversion to distract the attention of the enemy was transformed by the Commander of the Corps Expéditionnaire de l'Orient into a brilliant operation, which secured some substantial results. During the fighting which followed the landing of the French Division at Sedd-el-Bahr no troops could have acquitted themselves more creditably under very trying circumstances, and under very heavy losses, than those working under the orders of Monsieur le Général d'Amade.

Lieutenant-General Sir W. R. Birdwood, KCSI, CB, CIE, DSO, was in command of the detached landing of the Australian and New Zealand Army Corps above Kaba Tepe, as well as during the subsequent fighting. The fact of his having been responsible for the execution of these difficult and hazardous operations—operations which were crowned with a very remarkable success—speaks, I think, for itself.

Major-General A. G. Hunter-Weston, CB, DSO, was tried very highly, not only during the landings, but more especially in the day and night attacks and counter-attacks which ensued. Untiring, resourceful and ever more cheerful as the outlook (on occasion) grew darker, he possesses, in my opinion, very special qualifications as a Commander of troops in the field.

Major-General W. P. Braithwaite, CB, is the best Chief of the General Staff it has ever been my fortune to encounter in war. I will not pile epithets upon him. I can say no more than what I have said, and I can certainly say no less.

I have many other names to bring to notice for the period under review, and these will form the subject of a separate report at an early date.

IAN HAMILTON
General Commanding Mediterranean Expeditionary Force

NAVAL DESPATCH DESCRIBING THE LANDING OF THE ARMY

From Vice-Admiral John M. de Robeck, to the Admiralty

Triad, July 1, 1915

Sir,

I have the honour to forward herewith an account of the operations carried out on the 25th and 26th April, 1915, during which period the Mediterranean Expeditionary Force was landed and firmly established in the Gallipoli Peninsula.

The landing commenced at 4.20 a.m. on 25th. The general scheme was as follows:

Two main landings were to take place, the first at a point just north of Gaba Tepe, the second on the southern end of the peninsula. In addition, a landing was to be made at Kum Kale, and a demonstration in force to be carried out in the Gulf of Xeros near Bulair.

The night of the 24th–25th was calm and very clear, with a brilliant moon, which set at 3 a.m. The first landing, north of Gaba Tepe, was carried out under the orders of Rear-Admiral C. F. Thursby, CMG. His squadron consisted of the following ships:

Battleships: *Queen, London, Prince of Wales, Triumph, Majestic.*
Cruiser: *Bacchante.*
Destroyers: *Beagle, Bulldog, Foxhound, Scourge, Colne, Usk, Chelmer, Ribble.*
Seaplane Carrier: *Ark Royal.*
Balloon Ship: *Manica.*
Trawlers: 15.

To *Queen, London,* and *Prince of Wales* was delegated the duty of actually landing the troops. To *Triumph, Majestic,* and *Bacchante* the duty of covering the landing by gunfire.

In this landing a surprise was attempted. The first troops to be landed were embarked in the battleships *Queen, London,* and *Prince of Wales.* The squadron then approached the land at 2.58 a.m. at a speed of 5 knots. When within a short distance of the beach selected for landing the boats were sent ahead. At 4.20 a.m. the boats reached the beach and a landing was effected.

The remainder of the infantry of the covering force were embarked at 10 p.m., 24th.

The troops were landed in two trips, the operation occupying about half an hour, this in spite of the fact that the landing was vigorously opposed, the surprise being only partially effected.

The disembarkation of the main body was at once proceeded with. The operations were somewhat delayed owing to the transports having to remain a considerable distance from the shore in order to avoid the howitzer and field guns' fire brought to bear on them and also the fire from warships stationed in the Narrows, Chanak.

The beach here was very narrow and continuously under shell fire. The difficulties of disembarkation were accentuated by the necessity of evacuating the wounded; both operations proceeded simultaneously. The service was one which called for great determination and coolness under fire, and the success achieved indicates the spirit animating all concerned. In this respect I would specially mention the extraordinary gallantry and dash shown by the 3rd Australian Infantry Brigade (Colonel E. G. Sinclair Maclagan, DSO), who formed the covering force. Many individual acts of devotion to duty were performed by the personnel of the Navy; these are dealt with below. Here I should like to place on record the good service performed by the vessels employed in landing the second part of the covering force; the seamanship displayed and the rapidity with which so large a force was thrown on the beach is deserving of the highest praise.

On the 26th the landing of troops, guns and stores continued throughout the day; this was a most trying service, as the enemy kept up an incessant shrapnel fire, and it was extremely difficult to locate the well-concealed guns of the enemy. Occasional bursts of fire from the ships in the Narrows delayed operations somewhat but these bursts of fire did not last long, and the fire from our ships always drove the enemy's ships away.

The enemy heavily counter-attacked, and though supported by a very heavy shrapnel fire he could make no impression on our line, which was every minute becoming stronger. By nightfall on the 26th April our position north of Gaba Tepe was secure.

The landing at the southern extremity of the Gallipoli peninsula was carried out under the orders of Rear-Admiral R. E. Wemyss, CMG, MVO, his squadron consisting of the following ships:

Battleships: *Swiftsure, Implacable, Cornwallis, Albion, Vengeance, Lord Nelson, Prince George.*
Cruisers: *Euryalus, Talbot, Minerva, Dublin.*
Fleet Sweepers: 6. Trawlers: 14.

Landings in this area were to be attempted at five different places; the conditions at each landing varied considerably. The position of beaches is given below.

Position of beach
"Y" beach, a point about 7,000 yards north-east of Cape Tekeh. "X" beach, 1,000 yards north-east of Cape Tekeh. "W" beach, Cape Tekeh–Cape Helles. "V" beach, Cape Helles–Seddul Bahr. Camber, Seddul Bahr. "S" beach, Eski-Hissarlik Point.

Taking these landings in the above order:

Landing at "Y" beach

The troops to be first landed, the King's Own Scottish Borderers, embarked on the 24th in the *Amethyst* and *Sapphire* and proceeded with the transports *Southland* and *Braemar Castle* to a position off Cape Tekeh. At 4.00 a.m. the boats proceeded to "Y" beach, timing their arrival there at 5.00 a.m., and pulled ashore covered by fire from HMS *Goliath*. The landing was most successfully and expeditiously carried out, the troops gaining the top of the high cliffs overlooking this beach without being opposed; this result I consider due to the rapidity with which the disembarkation was carried out and the well-placed covering fire from ships.

The Scottish Borderers were landed in two trips, followed at once by the Plymouth Battalion Royal Marines. These troops met with severe opposition on the top of the cliffs, where fire from covering ships was of little assistance and, after heavy fighting, were forced to re-embark on the 26th. The re-embarkation was carried out by the following ships: *Goliath*, *Talbot*, *Dublin*, *Sapphire*, and *Amethyst*. It was most ably conducted by the beach personnel and covered by the fire of the warships, who prevented the enemy reaching the edge of the cliff, except for a few snipers.

Landing at "X" beach

The 2nd Battalion Royal Fusiliers (two companies and MG Section) embarked in *Implacable* on 24th, which ship proceeded to a position off the landing-place, where the disembarkation of the troops commenced at 4.30 a.m. and was completed at 5.15 a.m.

A heavy fire was opened on the cliffs on both sides. The *Implacable* approached the beach, and the troops were ordered to land, fire being continued until the boats were close into the beach. The troops on board the *Implacable* were all landed by 7 a.m. without any casualties. The nature of the beach was very favourable for the covering fire from ships, but the manner in which this landing was carried out might well serve as a model.

Landing at "W" beach

The 1st Battalion Lancashire Fusiliers embarked in *Euryalus* and *Implacable* on the 24th April, who proceeded to positions off the landing-place, where the troops embarked in the boats at about 4 a.m. Shortly after 5 a.m. *Euryalus* approached "W" beach and *Implacable* "X" beach. At 5 a.m. the covering ships opened a heavy fire on the beach, which was continued up to the last moment before landing. Unfortunately this fire did not have the effect on the extensive wire entanglements and trenches that had been hoped for, and the troops, on landing at 6 a.m., were met with a very heavy fire from rifles, machine guns, and pom-poms, and found the obstructions on the beach undamaged. The formation of this beach lends itself admirably to the defence, the landing-place being commanded by sloping cliffs offering ideal positions for trenches and giving a perfect field of fire. The only weakness in the enemy's position was on the flanks, where it was just possible to land on the rocks and thus enfilade the more important defences. This landing on the rocks was effected with great skill, and some maxims, cleverly concealed in the cliffs and which completely enfiladed the main beach, were rushed with the bayonet. This assisted to a great extent in the success of the landing, the troops, though losing very heavily, were not to be denied and the beach and the approaches to it were soon in our possession.

The importance of this success cannot be over-estimated; "W" and "V" beaches were the only two of any size in this area, on which troops, other than infantry, could be disembarked, and failure to capture this one might have had serious consequences as the landing at "V" was held up. The beach was being continuously sniped, and a fierce infantry battle was carried on round it throughout the entire day and the following night. It is impossible to exalt too highly the service rendered by the 1st Battalion Lancashire Fusiliers in the storming of the beach; the dash and gallantry displayed were superb. Not one whit behind in devotion to duty was the work of the beach personnel, who worked untiringly throughout the day and night, landing troops and stores under continual sniping. The losses due to rifle and machine-gun fire sustained by the boats' crews, to which they had not the satisfaction of being able to reply, bear testimony to the arduous nature of the service.

During the night of the 25th–26th enemy attacked continuously, and it was not till 1 p.m. on the 26th, when "V" beach was captured, that our position might be said to be secure.

The work of landing troops, guns, and stores continued throughout this period and the conduct of all concerned left nothing to be desired.

Landing at "V" beach

This beach, it was anticipated, would be the most difficult to capture; it possessed all the advantages for defence which "W" beach had, and in addition the flanks were strongly guarded by the old castle and village of Seddul Bahr on the east and perpendicular cliffs on the west; the whole foreshore was covered with barbed wire entanglements which extended in places under the sea. The position formed a natural amphitheatre with the beach as stage.

The first landing here, as at all other places, was made in boats, but the experiment was tried of landing the remainder of the covering force by means of a collier, the *River Clyde*. This steamer had been specially prepared for the occasion under the directions of Commander Edward Unwin; large ports had been cut in her sides and gangways built whereby the troops could reach the lighters which were to form a bridge on to the beach.

"V" beach was subjected to a heavy bombardment similarly to "W" beach, with the same result, i.e., when the first trip attempted to land they were met with a murderous fire from rifle, pom-pom and machine gun, which was not opened till the boats had cast off from the steamboats.

A landing on the flanks here was impossible and practically all the first trip were either killed or wounded, a few managing to find some slight shelter under a bank on the beach; in several boats all were either killed or wounded; one boat entirely disappeared, and in another there were only two survivors. Immediately after the boats had reached the beach the *River Clyde* was run ashore under a heavy fire rather towards the eastern end of the beach, where she could form a convenient breakwater during future landing of stores, etc.

As the *River Clyde* grounded, the lighters which were to form the bridge to the shore were run out ahead of the collier, but unfortunately they failed to reach their proper stations and a gap was left between two lighters over which it was impossible for men to cross; some attempted to land by jumping from the lighter which was in position into the sea and wading ashore; this method proved too costly, the lighter being soon heaped with dead and the disembarkation was ordered to cease.

The troops in the *River Clyde* were protected from rifle and machine-gun fire and were in comparative safety.

Commander Unwin, seeing how things were going, left the *River Clyde* and, standing up to his waist in water under a very heavy fire, got the lighters into position; he was assisted in this work by Midshipman G. L. Drewry, RNR, of HMS *Hussar*; Midshipman W. St A. Malleson, RN, of HMS *Cornwallis*; Able Seaman W. C. Williams, ON 186774 (RFRB 3766), and Seaman RNR George McKenzie Samson, ON 2408A, both of HMS *Hussar*.

The bridge to the shore, though now passable, could not be used by the troops, anyone appearing on it being instantly shot down, and the men in *River Clyde* remained in her till nightfall.

At 9.50 a.m. *Albion* sent in launch and pinnace manned by volunteer crews to assist in completing the bridge, which did not quite reach the beach; these boats, however, could not be got into position until dark owing to heavy fire.

It had already been decided not to continue to disembark on "V" beach, and all other troops intended for this beach were diverted to "W".

The position remained unchanged on "V" beach throughout the day, men of war and the maxims mounted in *River Clyde* doing their utmost to keep down the fire directed on the men under partial shelter on the beach. During this period many heroic deeds were performed in rescuing wounded men in the water.

During the night of the 25th–26th the troops in *River Clyde* were able to disembark under cover of darkness and obtain some shelter on the beach and in the village of Seddul Bahr, for possession of which now commenced a most stubborn fight.

The fight continued, supported ably by gunfire from HMS *Albion*, until 1.24 p.m., when our troops had gained a position from which they assaulted Hill 141, which dominated the situation. HMS *Albion* then ceased fire, and the hill, with the old fort on top, was most gallantly stormed by the troops, led by Lieutenant-Colonel C. H. H. Doughty-Wylie, General Staff, who fell as the position was won. The taking of this hill effectively cleared the enemy from the neighbourhood of the "V" Beach, which could now be used for the disembarkation of the allied armies. The capture of this beach called for a display of the utmost gallantry and perseverance from the officers and men of both services—that they successfully accomplished their task bordered on the miraculous.

Landing on the Camber, Seddul Bahr
One half company Royal Dublin Fusiliers landed here, without opposition, the Camber being "dead ground". The advance from the Camber, however, was only possible on a narrow front, and after several attempts to enter the village of Seddul Bahr this half company had to withdraw after suffering heavy losses.

Landing at "De Totts" "S" beach
The 2nd South Wales Borderers (less one company) and a detachment 2nd London Field Company RE were landed in boats, convoyed by *Cornwallis*, and covered by that ship and *Lord Nelson*.

Little opposition was encountered, and the hill was soon in the possession of the South Wales Borderers. The enemy attacked this position on the evening of the 25th and during the 26th, but our troops were firmly established, and with the assistance of the covering ships all attacks were easily beaten off.

Landing at Kum Kale
The landing here was undertaken by the French. It was most important to prevent the enemy occupying positions in this neighbourhood, whence he could bring gun fire to bear on the transports off Cape Helles. It was hoped that by holding this position it would be possible to deal effectively with the enemy's guns on the Asiatic shore immediately east of Kum Kale, which could fire into Seddul Bahr and De Totts.

The French, after a heavy preliminary bombardment, commenced to land at about 10 a.m., and by the afternoon the whole of their force had been landed at Kum Kale. When they attempted to advance to Yeni Shehr, their immediate objective, they were met by heavy fire from well-concealed trenches, and were held up just south of Kum Kale village.

During the night of the 25th–26th the enemy made several counter-attacks, all of which were easily driven off; during one of these 400 Turks were captured, their retreat being cut off by the fire from the battleships. On the 26th, when it became apparent that no advance was possible without entailing severe losses and the landing of large reinforcements, the order was given for the French to withdraw and re-embark, which operation was carried out without serious opposition.

I now propose to make the following more general remarks on the conduct of the operations:

From the very first the co-operation between army and navy was most happy; difficulties which arose were quickly surmounted, and nothing could have exceeded the tactfulness and forethought of Sir Ian Hamilton and his staff. The loyal support which I received from Contre-Amiral E. P.A. Guepratte simplified the task of landing the Allied armies simultaneously.

The Russian fleet was represented by HIRMS *Askold*, which ship was attached to the French squadron. Contre-Amiral Guepratte bears testimony to the value of the support he received from Captain Ivanoff, especially during the landing and re-embarkation of the French troops at Kum Kale.

The detailed organisation of the landing could not be commenced until the Army Headquarters returned from Egypt on the 10th April. The work to be done was very great, and the naval personnel and material available small.

Immediately on the arrival of the Army Staff at Mudros, committees, composed of officers of both services, commenced to work out the details of the landing operations, and it was due to these officers' indefatigable efforts that the expedition was ready to land on the 22nd April. The keenness displayed by the officers and men resulted in a good standard of efficiency, especially in the case of the Australian and New Zealand Corps, who appear to be natural boatmen. Such actions as the storming of the Seddul Bahr position by the 29th Division must live in history for ever; innumerable deeds of heroism and daring were performed; the gallantry and absolute contempt for death displayed alone made the operations possible.

At Gaba Tepe the landing and the dash of the Australian Brigade for the cliffs was magnificent—nothing could stop such men. The Australian and New Zealand Army Corps in this, their first battle, set a standard as high as that of any army in history, and one of which their countrymen have every reason to be proud.

In closing this despatch I beg to bring to their Lordships' notice the names of certain officers and men who have performed meritorious service. The great traditions of His Majesty's Navy were well maintained, and the list of names submitted of necessity lacks those of many officers and men who performed gallant deeds unobserved and therefore unnoted. This standard was high, and if I specially mention one particular action it is that of Commander Unwin and the two young officers and two seamen who assisted him in the work of establishing communication between *River Clyde* and the beach. Rear-Admirals R. E. Wemyss, CMG, MVO, C. F. Thursby, CMG, and Stuart Nicholson, MVO, have rendered invaluable service. Throughout they have been indefatigable in their efforts to further the success of the operations, and their loyal support has much lightened my duties and responsibilities.

I have at all times received the most loyal support from the Commanding Officers of His Majesty's ships during an operation which called for the display of great initiative and seamanship.

Captain R. F. Phillimore, CB, MVO, ADC, as principal Beach Master, and Captain D. L. Dent, as principal Naval Transport Officer, performed most valuable service.

JOHN M. DE ROBECK
Vice-Admiral

INDEX

The Dardanelles Commission, 1914–16

Notes

1) Entries beginning with a number are listed, Arabic and Roman interfiled, before the alphabetical sequence.

2) If a person's rank changed during the period covered by the text, only the higher rank is given in the index entry.

INDEX

British Battles of World War I, 1914–15

Notes

1) Entries beginning with a number are listed, Arabic and Roman interfiled, before the alphabetical sequence.

2) If a person's rank changed during the period covered by the text, only the higher rank is given in the index entry.